For Chloe

HELENIO HERRERA
FOOTBALL'S ORIGINAL MASTER OF THE DARK ARTS

Richard Fitzpatrick

BLOOMSBURY SPORT
LONDON · OXFORD · NEW YORK · NEW DELHI · SYDNEY

BLOOMSBURY SPORT
Bloomsbury Publishing Plc
50 Bedford Square, London, WC1B 3DP, UK
Bloomsbury Publishing Ireland Limited,
29 Earlsfort Terrace, Dublin 2, D02 AY28, Ireland

BLOOMSBURY, BLOOMSBURY SPORT and the Diana logo are trademarks of Bloomsbury Publishing Plc

First published in Great Britain, 2026

Copyright © Richard Fitzpatrick, 2026

Photographs © Getty Images, with the exception of p. 226 © Alamy

Richard Fitzpatrick has asserted his right under the Copyright, Designs and Patents Act, 1988,
to be identified as Author of this work.

For legal purposes the Acknowledgements on p. 270 constitute an extension of this copyright page.

All rights reserved. No part of this publication may be: i) reproduced or transmitted in any form, electronic or mechanical, including photocopying, recording or by means of any information storage or retrieval system without prior permission in writing from the publishers; or ii) used or reproduced in any way for the training, development or operation of artificial intelligence (AI) technologies, including generative AI technologies. The rights holders expressly reserve this publication from the text and data mining exception as per Article 4(3) of the Digital Single Market Directive (EU) 2019/790.

Bloomsbury Publishing Plc does not have any control over, or responsibility for, any third-party websites referred to or in this book. All internet addresses given in this book were correct at the time of going to press. The author and publisher regret any inconvenience caused if addresses have changed or sites have ceased to exist, but can accept no responsibility for any such changes.

A catalogue record for this book is available from the British Library.

Library of Congress Cataloguing-in-Publication data has been applied for

ISBN: HB: 978-1-3994-2510-0; ePDF: 978-1-3994-2508-7; eBook: 978-1-3994-2509-4

2 4 6 8 10 9 7 5 3 1

Typeset in Adobe Garamond Pro by D.R. INK
Printed and bound in Great Britain by Clays Ltd, Elcograf S.p.A.

To find out more about our authors and books visit www.bloomsbury.com and sign up for our newsletters
For product safety related questions contact productsafety@bloomsbury.com

CONTENTS

Author's Note	vi
Dramatis Personae	x
Prologue	xx

I RISE (1910–58)

1.	A Disease of the Bones	2
2.	Good Men Who Lost Their Way	8
3.	Scent of Cut Flowers	18

II BARÇA (1958–60)

4.	Thou Shalt Not Kill	26
5.	Crazy About Money	33
6.	People Should Talk About You Even If It Is Good	43
7.	The Face You Saw Everywhere	48
8.	Their Tongues Were 'Dirty'	57
9.	Sodom and Gomorrah	65
10.	A Cancer in the Team	74
11.	Barça of the Hungarians	80
12.	Speed	87
13.	Don Santiago	92
14.	'He Could Have Played with a Tuxedo On'	97
15.	A Murder of Crows	103

III INTER (1960–68)

16.	The Sweet Life	114
17.	Angel With a Dirty Face	123
18.	Great White Nights	132
19.	Team of a Million Stars	146
20.	When a Bad Man Behaves Well	157
21.	Il Mago	166
22.	Vienna	172
23.	'There Is a Small Annoyance'	178
24.	'Made it, Ma! Top of the World!'	184
25.	Voices in the Head	187
26.	Man in the Middle	193
27.	A Ninth Circle of Hell	198
28.	Szobel's Show Girls	205
29.	The Pits	213
30.	Cooked	220

IV ROMA (1968–70)

31.	The Red Lady	228
32.	'How Can an Athlete Die Like That?'	237
33.	Tuscany	248
34.	Inquest	254

Epilogue	262
Career and Honours	266
Acknowledgements	270
Notes	272
Select Bibliography	278

AUTHOR'S NOTE

I moved to Barcelona in early 2010. I spent my first year living in Spain devouring books on the country, trying to get a feel for its culture, and reading about football. As a sports journalist and a lifelong football fan, I knew a bit about the history of Spanish football, in particular stories about the stars of La Liga. I've been fascinated by Ferenc Puskás since reading as a 10-year-old about the Battle of Bern in the 1954 World Cup. A family friend was an au pair for Alfredo Di Stéfano while she lived in Madrid in the 1960s. And, to borrow an expression, I loved Diego Maradona more than my children.

I knew little, however, about Helenio Herrera – or 'HH', as he was known in the world of football – but you can't escape him if you live in Barcelona and follow football. His name keeps appearing in the pages of *Sport* and *El Mundo Deportivo*, Catalonia's two daily sports newspapers. His antics were legendary. He had no scruples. He was an outrageous character with an Olympic ability to blow his own trumpet. 'They say I know everything,' he said, before adding: 'It's not true – I don't know failure.' When I mention his name to friends or journalists in Barcelona, they can recite his famous utterances: 'We'll win without getting off the bus', 'We play better with 10 than 11.' His words are remembered in Spain, as they are in Italy, in the same way British football fans remember, say, Bill Shankly's quip: 'Some people think football is a matter of life and death. I assure you, it's much more serious than that.'

HH was a mysterious man. There was something enigmatic about him, an undealt card. During his life, no one knew if he was from Buenos Aires or Casablanca or what year he was born. The world was his country. He carried passports from France, Morocco, Italy and Spain, and spoke several languages. A trail of rumours followed him into the grave about doping and match-fixing. He was full of contradictions: a violent man who practised yoga for 50 years; a man with devastating charm but no friends. He was a football revolutionary. So much of the modern game is influenced by him. He was a mentor to Fabio Capello and Jock Stein, although his relationship with Celtic's immortal manager soured.

During my initial years in Barcelona, I lived on Tallers, a side street off La Rambla, in the Raval district – close to where HH had lived when he was Barça's manager. The longer I stayed in Barcelona, the more I found I couldn't shake off an image of him in my head. Every day, I used to walk our dog, Ismael, down La Rambla – the famously long avenue that stretches for more than a kilometre through central Barcelona. As the manager of Barça, HH had triumphed. Yet on a sunny day in May 1960, he was chased down La Rambla like a criminal by irate Barça fans. What could he possibly have done to so enrage those men?

He knew more than the devil: HH dressed in his iconic cloak.

HH with Sandro Mazzola, son of the legendary Valentino Mazzola and scorer of the two decisive goals that defeated Alfredo Di Stéfano's Real Madrid in the 1964 European Cup final.

DRAMATIS PERSONAE

Gianni Agnelli (1921–2003): The uncrowned king of Italy in the second half of the twentieth century. A business titan, head of Fiat, war veteran, bon-vivant, adrenaline junkie, art collector, fashion icon, womaniser known as the Rake of the Riviera, political power broker and one-time chairman of Juventus.

Umberto Agnelli (1934–2004): Younger brother of Gianni Agnelli; spent his life in his shadow until he finally ascended to the Fiat throne in 2003, only to die a year later. He was chairman of Juventus (as was his son, Andrea) for seven years, and a sworn enemy of HH.

Antonio Valentín Angelillo (1937–2018): As a teenager in 1957, he was immortalised as one of Argentina's 'Angels with Dirty Faces' forward line. Two years later, he set a record that stood for almost half a century, scoring 33 goals in 33 Serie A games for Inter. He fell foul of HH because of his love affair with a cabaret singer, Ilya López.

Santiago Bernabéu de Yeste (1895–1978): Held all the portfolios in Real Madrid – player, captain, coach, director, president. The stadium was named after him in 1955, a third of the way through his 35-year presidency. Helped create the European Cup. Served as a corporal in Franco's Army in the Spanish Civil War. Didn't much care for Catalans.

Fulvio Bernardini (1905–1984): One of Italy's great footballers before the Second World War, predominantly with AS Roma as a midfielder in the 1930s. As a coach, he etched his name into the record books, winning improbable Serie A titles with mid-ranking clubs, Fiorentina (1956) and Bologna (1964).

Gianni Brera (1919–1992): Italian football's greatest man of letters. During the Second World War, he enlisted as a paratrooper and later fought as a *partisan*. After the war, he returned to journalism and writing novels. When he wasn't holding court in A'Riccione, a Milanese restaurant, he published books prolifically. Once memorably summed up HH as 'clown and genius, vulgar and an aesthete, sultan and believer, boorish and competent, megalomaniac and health freak'.

Fabio Capello (1946–): Although troubled by knee injuries, he enjoyed a long career in Serie A, winning several *scudetti*. Came under HH's spell as a young player at AS Roma, and remained a devoted disciple, crediting HH as his greatest mentor in football. Coached Milan, Real Madrid, Roma and Juventus to league titles (although his two championship wins at Juve were revoked because of the *Calciopoli* scandal). Also led Milan to Champions League victory on a famous night in Athens in 1994, filleting Johan Cruyff's 'Dream Team' 4–0.

Franco Cordova (1944–): A swashbuckling character with an energetic love life. Played for almost a decade in Roma's midfield, and as club captain. HH was suspicious of him, a distrust that was mutual. In 1970, he married Roma president Alvaro Marchini's daughter Simona (the year HH was fired by Roma's president). His career ended in ignominy when he was banned for 14 months in 1980 as part of a match-fixing scandal.

Jim Craig (1943–): Immortalised as one of the Lisbon Lions who helped Celtic win the 1967 European Cup. Qualified as a dentist before committing himself to full-time professional football. A ball-playing right back. Nicknamed 'Cairney' (after a lead actor's surname in 1960s Scottish TV drama series *This Man Craig*). His son James Craig played international rugby for Scotland.

Zoltán Czibor (1929–1997): Member of the famous Mighty Magyars team that controversially lost the 1954 World Cup final to West Germany 3–2. Nicknamed 'Crazy Bird' due to his wavy, Woody Woodpecker-like hair and maverick personality. Hungarian State Security forced him to write espionage reports for them. Fled Hungary with his family after the 1956 Hungarian Rising. Joined Barça in 1958. Struggled with alcoholism. One of a handful of players to score in both World Cup and European Cup finals.

Renato Dall'Ara (1892–1964): Entrepreneur who made his fortune from knitwear. Bologna named its football stadium after him. As president, he led the club to four Serie A titles before and during the Second World War. According to some reports, he died in the arms of Inter president Angelo Moratti in June 1964, four days before an historic play-off between their clubs for the Serie A title.

Alfredo Di Stéfano (1926–2014): In the conversation for greatest footballer of all time. In HH's eyes, he was better than Pelé. He arrived at Real Madrid as a 27-year-old and immediately transformed the club's fortunes, winning five European Cups in a row and eight La Liga titles in 11 seasons. Notoriously grumpy. His insatiable appetite for winning is still evident in Real Madrid's DNA today.

Giacinto Facchetti (1942–2006): One of the finest full-backs to play the game, runner-up to Eusébio on the Ballon d'Or podium in 1965. Blond and built like a doorframe. Member of Italy's European Championship-winning team in 1968. A club legend at Inter: one-club man, captain, president. HH adored him and bequeathed his football notebooks to him.

Eddie Firmani (1933–): Grew up in Cape Town, South Africa. Made his mark as a footballer in England with Charlton Athletic, which earned him a move to 'the land of the lira' in 1955. Only player to score more than 100 league goals in both English and Italian football leagues. Had a picaresque coaching career with clubs in North America and the Middle East, where he was held captive (and later released) during the First Gulf War.

Francisco Franco Bahamonde (1892–1975): Youngest captain in Spanish Army at 22; youngest general in Europe since Napoleon. Made his name in Morocco with the Spanish Foreign Legion, whose mercenaries wreaked havoc in the Spanish Civil War. His fascist dictatorship was intent on killing 'those who do not think as we do', which included 200,000 executions between 1936 and 1945, with thousands more dying of disease and hunger while incarcerated. His favoured method for execution was strangulation. Died in his bed aged 82.

Fiora Gandolfi (1936–): A vivacious woman. Daughter of a wealthy aristocratic Treviso family. Made her mark in the 1960s as a journalist writing celebrity profiles; in 1964 she became the first female reporter to cover the Giro d'Italia. Married to HH from 1972 until his death in 1997; they had two children, one of whom was adopted. She is the keeper of his flame, having authored several books about him.

Aristide Guarneri (1938–): A wily central defender on HH's *La Grande Inter* team. Served a ban for doping in 1962. Scored his only goal for Italy against the Soviet Union in 1966, outfoxing Lev Yashin in goal. Played on Italy's 1968 European Championship-winning team.

Helenio Herrera Gavilán (1910–1997): Born in Buenos Aires; grew up in Morocco. Emigrated to France to pursue a career as a semi-professional footballer in the 1930s. His head coaching career began in France as the Second World War was ending. The following decade, in Spain, he found international fame. Notable triumphs include back-to-back league titles with Atlético Madrid (1949/50, 1950/51) and Barça (1958/59, 1959/60); and three *scudetti* (1962/63, 1964/65, 1965/66) as well as consecutive European Cup wins (1963/64, 1964/65) with Inter. He also managed the France, Spain and Italy national teams. He fathered seven children with three separate women; he also adopted a daughter and had two stepchildren.

Sándor Kocsis (1929–1979): One of the greatest goalscorers in history, scoring 75 goals in 68 internationals for the Hungary team that famously beat England 6–3 at Wembley in 1953. Joined Barça in 1958; played for seven seasons, but injuries badgered him. His prodigious ability to score headers earned him the nickname 'Head of Gold', the name of a bar he ran in Barcelona after retiring from football. An introvert. Died from suicide. Something about his artistic, doomed personality lives on in the melancholic soul of Barça.

László Kubala (1927–2002): There are only two statues outside the Camp Nou: László Kubala and Johan Cruyff. Kubala was so popular in the 1950s that often 5,000 fans would be shut out of Barça's stadium, which accelerated construction of the Camp Nou, Europe's largest stadium. Having defected from behind the Iron Curtain in 1949, he was used by General Franco as a propaganda tool in Spain's battle with Communism, notably in a fictionalised biopic of his escape from Hungary, starring Kubala, called *Aces in Search of Peace*. When HH took charge of Barça in 1958, he was controversially sidelined because his powers were waning due to injury and a carousing lifestyle.

Denis Law (1940–2025): Grew up in Aberdeen. A squint in his eye meant he played football with his right eye closed (and was called 'Cockeye' in the schoolyard). Played under Bill Shankly at Huddersfield Town in the late 1950s. An operation shortly after joining the club straightened his eye; he played all his career, however, with poor vision, but it didn't stop him scoring goals. Joined Torino in 1961. Returned homesick to Britain a year later, joining Manchester United as part its Holy Trinity along with Bobby Charlton and George Best. Ballon d'Or winner in 1964. Missed United's 1968 European Cup final victory because of a knee injury.

Alvaro Marchini (1916–1985): A resistance hero, fighting with partisans against the Nazis in Italy during the Second World War. Known in the press as 'the communist billionaire' because his construction company hoovered up money in the 1950s and '60s. In December 1968, he became president of AS Roma, where he inherited HH's contract as the best-paid football coach in the world. He fired HH in 1970, and stepped down himself shortly afterwards. He disliked the spotlight as Roma president, noting Italy's Tax Office conducted four audits on him during two years at the club's helm, which he described as 'harassment'.

Ferruccio Mazzola (1945–2013): Youngest son of Valentino Mazzola, one of Italy's greatest footballers. Always suffered from comparison with his father and his older brother Sandro. Midfielder. Made two Serie A appearances for Inter in 1967. Captained Lazio. His 2004 book *Il terzo incomodo* blew the whistle on Inter's doping culture in the 1960s, which led to Inter suing him for libel. Giacinto Facchetti, as Inter president, signed the defamation lawsuit. All the living Grande Inter greats were hauled into court to give testimony in the case. In 2008, the judge ruled against Inter.

Sandro Mazzola (1942–): Eldest son of the iconic Valentino Mazzola. Recognisable by his distinctive moustache. Linchpin of HH's Grande Inter team. Scored on his debut for Italy against Brazil in 1963. Scored twice in Inter's 1964 European Cup final victory over Real Madrid. Winner of the 1968 European Championship with Italy. Lost the World Cup final to Pelé's Brazil in 1970. One-club man; made Inter captain in 1970. TV co-commentator for both Italy's World Cup wins in 1982 and 2006.

Josef Mengele (1911–1979): SS camp physician at Auschwitz from 1943 until January 1945. In addition to overseeing the mass extermination of camp prisoners – which *The New York Times* estimates at 400,000 – he carried out gruesome medical experiments on children and other inmates, which earned him the nickname 'Angel of Death'. After the war, he escaped through ratlines to South America, eluding capture from Mossad agents using six aliases, until he drowned on a beach off the Brazilian coast.

Francesc Miró-Sans (1916–1989): Catalan textile entrepreneur (like several Barça presidents in the twentieth century). Famous as the president who built the Camp Nou stadium (sinking Barça in debt as a result), which opened in 1957. First Barça president in history to be re-elected the following year. The man who signed HH as manager in 1958 (and the man who sacked him in 1960).

Marzia Nannipieri (1945–): Fell in love and married footballer Giuliano Taccola when she was a teenager growing up in a Tuscan village. Her world caved in when he died following a Cagliari v Roma league match in March 1969, leaving her a 23-year-old widow with two small children to raise. In 1971, the inquest into his death was leaked. She has spent her life since looking for justice and closure, following his mysterious death – a quest that throws up more questions than answers.

Dramatis Personae

José María Ortiz de Mendíbil (1926–2015): A Basque-born referee who coincidentally refereed several of Inter's important international victories, including a play-off win against Independiente in the 1964 Intercontinental Cup final and their 3–0 comeback victory against Liverpool in the second leg semi-final of the 1965 European Cup. (Luisito Suárez once quipped that Ortiz de Mendíbil had more winners' medals with Inter than himself.) Also refereed the 1968 European Championship final and the 1969 European Cup final.

Joaquín Peiró (1936–2020): An idol at Atlético Madrid, helping the club win the 1962 Cup Winners' Cup (scoring in both legs of the final). Played under HH for Spain at the 1962 World Cup finals, as part of the Grande Inter team and as captain for his Roma team. Played with his socks conspicuously rolled down around his ankles, which was unusual for the 1960s. He pinched the ball from Liverpool goalkeeper Tommy Lawrence's hands, scoring Inter's crucial second goal in the 1965 European Cup semi-final at San Siro, which earned him the nickname '*Rapinatore*' ('Thief') in Milan for years afterwards.

Armando Picchi (1935–1971): Sweeper and captain of HH's Grande Inter team. The team's leader in the dressing room. Wasn't good in the air, but canny at reading the game. Scapegoated for Inter's loss to Celtic in the 1967 European Cup final, and transferred that summer, ending an often-fractious relationship with HH. Died aged only 35, having contracted cancer midseason while managing Juventus.

Ferenc Puskás (1927–2006): Captain of the Mighty Magyars team. His injury against West Germany in a group game possibly cost Hungary the 1954 World Cup. (He played not fully fit in the final.) An extrovert, unafraid to challenge authority in communist Hungary, once greeting Minister of Defence Mihály Farkas, who was wearing an all-white general's military uniform, with the quip: 'I thought you were the ice-cream boy, at last.' His left foot was kissed by God. Scored four goals in Real Madrid's famous 1960 European Cup final victory over Eintracht Frankfurt at Hampden Park, and a hat-trick aged 35 in their 1962 final defeat by Benfica. Struggled with weight issues in the second half of his career. Real Madrid teammates nicknamed him '*Pancho*' ('Belly').

Antoni Ramallets Simón (1924–2013): Dubbed the 'Cat of Maracaná' for his heroics at the 1950 World Cup in Brazil. Arguably Barça's greatest goalkeeper. He was even a rung up the ladder from Víctor Valdés and Andoni Zubizarreta, as a five-time winner of Spain's prestigious Zamora Trophy for best goalkeeper and winner of six La Liga titles. Revered in particular because of his dignified aura.

Adelardo Rodríguez (1939–): Iconic Atlético Madrid midfielder who played during a golden era at the club, winning three La Liga titles, several domestic and international cups and came within a whisker of European Cup glory in 1974. He played for Spain under HH in the 1962 World Cup finals.

Josep Samitier (1902–1972): Barça's first great idol, a darling of Barcelona's cabaret scene in the 1920s. Scored hundreds of goals in the interwar years. Twice he moved from Barça to Real Madrid – as a player in 1932, and as a sporting director in 1959, after being isolated by HH, part of the collateral damage in a political tussle between HH and László Kubala (his friend). A charismatic figure, he was one of the few sportsmen to win the affection of General Franco.

Joan Segarra (1927–2008): An immortal at Barça. Played 14 seasons for the club until he retired in 1964. Nicknamed '*El Gran Capitán*', notably captaining 'Barça of the Five Cups' in 1952. HH's most loyal servant and confidant during his first reign as coach, 1958–60. Served as HH's assistant coach when HH returned to the club during the 1979/80 season. Key figure in the evolution of La Masia, Barça's youth academy.

Bill Shankly (1913–1981): Although a Scot, who worked as a coal miner in his teens, he is synonymous with the (socialist) spirit of Liverpool. Played most of his career, which was interrupted by the Second World War, alongside Tom Finney at Preston North End. Arrived as manager at Liverpool in 1959 when it was in the old Second Division. He transformed the club, winning promotion, three league titles and several other cups, and is remembered for his wit: 'Me havin' no education, I had to use my brains.'

Dezső Solti (1911–1994): Born Dezső Steinberger, a Jew in Hungary. Rounded up during the Holocaust, but survived both Auschwitz (where he worked as a fixer for Josef Mengele) and Dachau concentration camps, unlike dozens of his family members. The mother of his ex-wife said he was like God in Auschwitz because of the power he wielded. Changed his name after the war to Dezső Solti, and defected to Italy, working as an international smuggler, pimp and probably a Cold War spy. He came into Inter's orbit by fixing up prostitutes for the club. Worked in the shadows for decades as a match fixer for clubs like Inter and Juventus until he was finally banned for life by UEFA in 1974.

Ian St John (1938–2021): His father, 36, died, leaving six children to be reared by his mother in a tenement house in Motherwell, Scotland. Known as 'The Saint'. He was Bill Shankly's first great acquisition when he joined Liverpool in 1961. Formed a lethal strike partnership with Roger Hunt. Scored one of the club's most famous goals, a glancing header deep into extra time against Leeds United at Wembley to secure Liverpool's first ever FA Cup in 1965. Enjoyed a famous second act as part of the popular broadcasting duo, Saint & Greavsie, with Jimmy Greaves.

Jock Stein (1922–1985): A giant of a man, in physique and personality, known as 'Big Jock'. Two things shaped his character: working for over a decade as a coal miner (he claimed that underground was where he met the finest men in his life); and the sectarian abuse he suffered as a Protestant, while captain and, later, manager of Celtic. As Celtic's coach, he led the club to nine league titles in a row (having ended a 12-year drought) and his Lisbon Lions became the first British club to win the European Cup. Collapsed in a Cardiff dugout during a Wales v Scotland World Cup-qualifying game in 1985 and died minutes later.

Luisito Suárez (1935–2023): Grew up in Galicia. Known as 'Luisito', HH transformed his career at Barça in 1958, betting on him as a youthful pillar for his team at the expense of the club's ageing idol, László Kubala. However, Luisito became a lightning rod for fan dissent in the club's civil war between *kubalistas* and *suaristas*. HH brought him to Inter in 1961, and he was the most important player in the Grande Inter team. The great Alfredo Di Stéfano christened him 'The Architect'. He won the Ballon d'Or award in 1960 and the European Championship with Spain in 1964.

Gonzalo Suárez Morilla (1934–): A gifted artist – a pioneer of New Journalism in the 1960s; a novelist; a ghostwriter for two HH books in the 1960s, written under the pen name Martín Girard; a filmmaker and close friend of Sam Peckinpah. His mother spent 20 years with HH, and gave birth to two of HH's children. He got to know HH as a teenager. A decade later, in the early 1960s, he spent a couple of years working for him as a spy, writing reports on rival teams when HH was manager of Inter.

Giuliano Taccola (1943–1969): Talented young striker. Came up through the ranks at Genoa. Played two seasons in the first team before transferring to AS Roma in 1967. During his second season in Rome, he scored seven goals in 12 Serie A games by Christmas but was debilitated by regular fevers. In March 1969, he collapsed in Cagliari's dressing room after a league game and died. At the inquest into his death, two people were charged for involuntary manslaughter: Roma's doctor and his coach, HH.

Justo Tejada (1933–2021): A winger. Once scored four goals for Spain against Northern Ireland in 1958. One of a few high-profile players to play for Barça and Real Madrid, winning two La Liga titles with both clubs. When he crossed the Great Divide in 1961, joining Real Madrid, he was forced to give Barça president Enric Llaudet and two directors 500,000 pesetas as a bribe ('enough to buy an apartment') to green light the transfer. He signed the release contract at Llaudet's apartment beside Barcelona's Arc de Triomf, which was full of rhinoceros heads and stuffed lions.

Enrique Vila-Matas (1948–): Spain's greatest living novelist, according to his contemporary Roberto Bolaño. His 'uncle' was Francesc Miró-Sans, the Barça president who built the Camp Nou; and he is also related to Francesc Mitjans Miró, the Camp Nou's architect. He has known Pep Guardiola since Guardiola was a player in the 1990s. Whenever they used to meet, Guardiola wanted to know about his books while Vila-Matas wanted to know about dressing room gossip. Guardiola once brought Luís Figo along to meet him; Vila-Matas noted that Figo had 'tremendous success with women'.

Franco Zaglio (1936–): Italian international midfielder at Inter for four seasons. Banned for doping in 1962. Part of HH's maiden Serie A title-winning team in 1963, but injury kept him out of the club's 1964 European Cup starting XI the following season. Sold to Mantova in 1964 at 28 years of age. Retired two years later.

Dramatis Personae

A favourite son: HH with Giacinto Facchetti, one of the greatest ever full-backs and the man to whom HH bequeathed his precious football notebooks.

PROLOGUE

The papal basilica of San Paolo fuori le Mura (St Paul Outside the Walls) in Rome is enormous and opulent. It's believed the apostle Paul was buried on the site after his martyrdom. Paintings by Raphael, Leonardo da Vinci and other Italian masters hang in its picture gallery. The dimensions inside the church are larger than a football pitch. It has a marble floor and is lined by majestic columns. A temple built to the glory of God. High above, 30 metres overhead, the ceiling is panelled in gold and stucco. The images of every pope in history look down on those below.

The church was full on 20 March 1969. There was a bright sun and a clear sky that morning. Mourners gathered for the funeral of AS Roma's star striker, Giuliano Taccola. He had died four days earlier on the island of Sardinia, on a massage table, in Roma's dressing room, half an hour after a game against Cagliari. He was 25 years old. Cagliari's team convened at the airport for a guard of honour as his corpse was flown back to Rome. Players from clubs around Italy converged on Rome for the funeral, including Jair, a World Cup winner with Brazil in 1962, and Helmut Haller, scorer of the opening goal in the 1966 World Cup final. Lazio's squad, the rival team in the city, came to pay their respects. Wreaths were sent by Real Madrid and several British clubs.

It seemed as though all of Rome stood outside the church. Some reports said 100,000 people congregated; others put the figure at 50,000. Mourners crowded along Via Ostiense, packed tightly. Traffic stood still on nearby streets. Apartment windows lay open, Rome's citizens standing to attention by them. Some threw flowers, which floated towards the coffin below. The pallbearers – Taccola's teammates, including Alberto Ginulfi, Paolo Sirena, Angelo Orazi, Franco Cordova – pushed through the crowds with the coffin. People wept openly. Women fainted and had to be carried away. Large Roma flags fluttered everywhere. A No. 9 jersey emerged from the crowd and was draped over the coffin.

Inside the church, the atmosphere was tense. Roma coach Helenio Herrera, the most famous football manager in the world, stood at the top flanked by some players and the club's president, Alvaro Marchini. HH, as he was known to everyone, was ignored by Marchini. The bereaved members of Taccola's family – including his widow – were on the other side of the aisle. Marchini and Roma's players, including Fabio Capello, took it in turns to offer their condolences to Taccola's family. But not HH. He stayed away. He looked gaunt, his face the colour of ashes. There was a slight trembling of his cheeks during the funeral service. Nobody was more alone in that church. Eyes bore into him.

HH's cold and cynical behaviour after Taccola's death had shocked people. He had seemed consumed with preparing Roma for a cup tie against Brescia three days later. HH could now sense the hostility towards him in the church, and at large. In the days after Taccola's death, the press quoted both players and Marchini voicing their revulsion at HH's authoritarian management style, at his insistence that Taccola train and play while clearly unwell, at his contempt for doctors. HH was in the crosshairs, under investigation by police and the judiciary. Taccola had suffered underlying health problems. Had these been aggravated by HH's treatment? Was Taccola, in fact, a victim of manslaughter?

When cornered by adversaries, HH was ruthless, believing: 'With the good be good, with the bad be three times bad, with the cunning be three and a half times cunning.'

Ready to eat the world: HH, pensive, in a packed stadium, at the foothills of his illustrious coaching career.

I
RISE
(1910–58)

1. A DISEASE OF THE BONES

1.

Death by diphtheria is a painful end. Swelling in the neck glands can make it impossible to breathe. In Spain, a diphtheria epidemic ripped through the country in 1613, which is forever remembered as *El Año de los Garrotillos* – the Year of the Strangulations. The disease is especially fatal for children and the elderly. It latched on to Helenio Herrera – or 'HH', as he was nicknamed in football – when he was three or four years old. This was on the eve of the First World War.

All three of HH's brothers had already died. Poverty chased his parents around the world. They fled from Andalusia, Spain to Buenos Aires. When they found no luck in Argentina, they got on a boat to Morocco. It was in the Moroccan city of Casablanca that HH was struck down with diphtheria, which, in the days before antibiotics, could be a death sentence. A military hospital took him in. There the medics cut a tracheostomy, effectively a hole, in his neck to create an airway for him to draw breath.

Despite hospital regulations, HH's mother refused to leave his side. She was a fierce woman, and no one was going to stop her keeping vigil. One night, HH's ventilator shuddered to a halt. He began choking. His mother went berserk. She started screaming, pacing through the corridors, opening and slamming doors. A nurse emerged, to be grabbed by her uniform and dragged to the ward, where she helped to save HH's life.

As an adult, HH would have killed for his mother. In the early 1950s, while managing Atlético Madrid, he received a telegram after a derby match against Real Madrid. His mother had died during the game. He returned to Casablanca to bury her in a small graveyard. Days later, an Atlético fan made the mistake of insulting his mother with too much persistence during a match: 'Herrera, you're a bastard! You son of a bitch! You fuck with your mother!'

After the game, HH enquired about the fan, and was told where he could be found on the club's premises. HH tracked him down. As soon as HH saw him, he attacked, kicking and punching, beating him like a rented mule. The fan stumbled backwards, retreating in terror, grabbing chairs to protect himself and hurling anything he could get his hands on at HH.

A strange thought dropped into HH's head: to embed a billiard ball into the fan's mouth. To shut him up. Luckily for the fan, Larbi Benbarek – Atlético's star forward – intervened. He managed to calm HH down enough to give the fan a chance to flee down a staircase. With his life and his teeth intact.

2.

HH was born in Buenos Aires, like his sister, Aurora, who was 17 months older. His family left the city around 1913, bound for Morocco. They spent a month travelling across the Atlantic Ocean in the hold of a ship. During the voyage, which seemed to go on forever, his parents tried to stave off the pangs of hunger by singing songs. On arrival in Casablanca, the port was undergoing construction, so they disembarked by rowing boats. HH's mother slipped into the water trying to pass from one boat to another. Instead of rushing to save her, the Moroccans working on the boats started haggling with his father, who was forced to cough up a fee to get her fished out of the water. HH came to understand that people in Casablanca would do anything to turn a buck. Life was a hustle.

The city, which was a French Protectorate, was exploding. Its population grew ninefold in the space of 15 years around the time of the First World War. French administrators sketched out its development from the air. It was probably the first city in history to be laid out by aeroplane. The best architects in France were enticed into making their mark. This was a chance for them to build a city from scratch, something to trumpet France's colonial might.

HH's family set up their home on the outskirts of the city. A wooden shack on stilts in the dunes. It was far from the boulevards in the centre that sold Parisian dreams in its stores. Far from the town houses with their tropical gardens and wispy trees that locals called *filles de l'air* (girls of the air). To visitors, Casablanca, 'the white house', seemed dazzling. It was a popular destination during the interwar years for French jet-setters, including Édith Piaf, who were keen on soaking up some winter sun.

But for anyone who only knew the toil of day-to-day life there, the city was misery. Even the camels roamed around with a despondent air. The scorching sun hurt HH's head. His family longed to live under a roof free from scorpions and snakes. There were no lights on the lanes around his shanty town. When his father left to go to work at night, it was already dark, and he carried a lantern so he wouldn't step on the people asleep on the ground. In the morning, a cart passed along picking up those who had died during the night.

HH's father was a carpenter by trade, and an anarchist by disposition. When he was a young man, coming of age in Spain at the turn of the twentieth century, anarchism was in the air. There's a biographical detail cited in stories about HH that his father had to escape to Argentina before the First World War because he tried to kill the King of Spain, Alfonso XIII. There was indeed an attempt to assassinate Spain's king on the day of his wedding in 1906. A Catalan anarchist, Mateo Morral, threw a bomb concealed in a bouquet of flowers out of the window of a Madrid hotel, as the newlyweds passed underneath. Twenty-four people were killed in the blast, but the monarchs escaped unharmed. The queen's wedding dress was splattered in horse blood. The king lived to reign for decades more, although he was bedevilled by plots to kill him. From what we know, it seems far-fetched that HH's father was a key player in any of those misadventures.

Although the city of Casablanca kept growing, the fortunes of HH and his father didn't. They lived almost like nomads, having to uproot their shack and move it further out into scrubland. Always on the outskirts. HH said one day that they'd have to use the boards of their shack for a raft if they kept being pushed back towards the sea. His father didn't find the joke funny.

If HH's father didn't work, the family went hungry. They lived on the edge, fretful about his father's health and what it meant for all their chances. More than hunger, what haunted HH's mother was the fear of disease. She knew how precarious life was for the poor: she had already buried three young sons. Money was something other people had. HH wore clothes made by his mother. When some soldiers gave him an old blanket, she fashioned a coat from it. HH learned to hate summer holidays from school, as it meant working his guts out doing two jobs – in a stationery store and a foundry. He never knew what it felt like to rest. Once primary school was done, he left his schooling behind.

HH discovered how to steal from the warehouses by the docks. He was a street urchin, but he was only doing what he saw respectable people around him do. He stuffed his face with bananas, chocolate, whatever food he could get his hands on; whatever he could fit under his shirt, he brought home. His father scolded him when he found out he'd been stealing, claiming that he didn't want a thief for a son – but with his big belly, he was the first person in their shack to eat the stolen goods.

Every day was a struggle, and the stress marked HH. 'Poverty is a disease that gets into a man's bones,' as the Irish playwright Seán O'Casey remarked. 'No matter what comes afterwards, it never leaves him.'

3.

Casablanca was flooded with colonial soldiers. It was one of Africa's most important ports during a time of epic jostling in international relations. However, the city portrayed in *Casablanca*, the famous 1942 film with Humphrey Bogart and Ingrid Bergman, was based more on Tangier, a city teeming with spies and intrigue. (Rick's Café was based on Charlie's Bar, a gambling den-cum-nightclub in Tangier run by a North African who spoke with a posh British accent.)

Some of the French soldiers in Casablanca fooled around with the kids on the streets. They taught HH a few boxing licks, and he got handy. He was tough, a born fighter, and when he was still only eight years old, roaming the lanes around Casablanca, a colonial soldier persuaded him to box another boy of his age in a proper bout. Inside a ring with a referee. With an audience. It would be a show. HH liked the sound of that song.

The experience led to a great discovery: the poison of popularity. For the rest of his life, he never forgot the feeling of intoxication. The rush of adrenaline. The faces of the spectators who encircled the boxing ring, which was parked in the middle of a circus tent. The names of the two boxers were called out before they entered the ring. When the crowd turned to see them, they howled in laughter, but all HH could hear were the cheers for an idol ringing in his ears. He felt like a god between those ropes. His heart raced. It told him he had to win. As soon as the bell rang, he tore into his opponent. He put the beats on him. The other poor boy thought he was surrounded.

After winning the fight, HH was given a trophy. The next day, he drank in the acclaim of neighbours in his shanty town. It was invigorating. He had tears in his eyes. People knew his name: Helenio Herrera. Something crystallised in his mind. Whatever happened in life, he was going to become someone. Whatever it took.

4.

Boxing didn't pull at HH's heartstrings, though. Football did. He was born kicking. The game dominated his thoughts. He couldn't fully explain it – this love for football. He felt like it was a benign demon that entered his body, which he never managed to expel. There was something about the bounce of the ball, something about the sound that was magical. From the moment he could hear, it called him. Like when a dog hears his master's whistle. He found it arousing, like 'the music of serpents'. He had to have football in his life.

When he went to school, he kicked a stone or a tin can along his path for company. Then he hid the tin can so he could kick it home again after school. He made his first football from an old stocking stolen from his mother. He organised games between different neighbourhoods. He watched every game he could. He played from morning to night on the beach, indifferent to the scalding sun. Building up his stamina. Running, running, running. He wasn't skilful with a ball, but he had one unbelievable strength: his endurance. He had an iron constitution. Life was a marathon, and nobody ran harder than HH. Nobody was tougher. Obstacles were kicked out of the way. Like a stray foot in the way of the ball. He had no interest in dribbling or shooting, or weaving magic. That wasn't what excited him. His only obsession was in winning, which drove him on. His team always, in those improvised matches that children play, won, or that's the way he remembered it.

Albert Camus, too, grew up football-mad in a slum in Algiers, kicking around balls made from rags. He was unable to play much, however, after contracting tuberculosis aged 16. Both HH and Camus were born just before the outbreak of the First World War. There's a striking similarity between them, and how they developed a philosophy of life through football. Camus believed that football and theatre were his two 'real universities'. Football is threaded throughout his novels.

Playing the game was where Camus felt most alive, free from distractions. The closest he got to feeling innocence as an adult was in the middle of a crowded terrace during football games on a Sunday. For Camus few things in life compared to the euphoria and shared communal feeling of a tight, tit-for-tat match. He worked with the French Resistance during the Second World War, but on hearing the Allies had landed in Normandy in June 1944 his reaction was to dwell on a cancelled championship match. There was something about the immediacy of football that enchanted him. He may have grown tired of the Parisian intelligentsia in the 1950s waffling in smoky cafés on the Left Bank, but he remained enchanted by football.

5.

HH began playing organised football at 12 years of age, mostly in defence. He made it on to the first team of his second club, Racing Casablanca, when he was only 16 years old. He made the grade so young because of his stamina, and he looked older than his age – he had a shock of wavy black hair on his head (which he kept dyed in later life), and his skin was already starting to shrivel from exposure to the sun. He never aged much during adulthood. He was a handsome man, in an old shoe kind of way.

HH got noticed. A Parisian football club, touring North Africa, offered him a trial if he could make his way to Paris. This was HH's ticket to heaven. He made his pitch to his parents. They threw it back in his face. The opportunity made his father dwell on his own failures. Immigrating had never worked for him. Why would it work for his son? Big cities made him anxious. He couldn't cope with their cut and thrust. He was no good at fighting for a knife in the mud. The only place he had felt at home was the Andalusian village of his childhood. Paris, which was damn near the world's capital, would chew up his son.

HH didn't worry about this opinion, from a man who hid from the world. His mother was the real obstacle. She ran the house. She fretted, too, though. He would go hungry. What if he got sick? Nobody would be there to help him. Besides, his father chipped in, how was he going to pay for the trip? With what money? Money! Always money. If only HH had some money.

Playing football was always his ambition in life. But it wasn't enough to play football. The game was only a means to an end. Money was the key that unlocked doors. With money, he could help his mother. He could kill that worm, that fear of disease, which gnawed at her brain. Without money, she was defenceless against the anxieties she carried around with her every day. Money was the elixir of life. Only with money could he go to Paris. Only with money could he get ahead.

So HH cadged a loan from a friend. It was enough to get him a place in the hold of an old sailboat to Bordeaux. He would figure the rest out later. He could travel on foot to Paris if necessary. His mother still didn't want him to go, but his decision was taken. She knew better than anyone that nobody stood in the way of her son. Better to let him take his chances in Paris than hang around in their spider hole in the desert, sulking, consumed by bitterness.

For the crossing to Europe, HH huddled together with a hundred other desperate, penniless men. They slept on bare boards in the open air, left to God's mercy as the boat was tossed around the Atlantic Ocean. HH couldn't give a fig about a few sore bones from his makeshift bed. He didn't care about a growling stomach, which he partly alleviated by getting a job washing plates in the boat's kitchen for extra rations. Not now. He was on his way, eager to devour the world.

2. GOOD MEN WHO LOST THEIR WAY

1.

HH hadn't the talent to make it as an elite player. His football career never caught fire. He was a journeyman, and juggled his career as a semi-pro, jumping from club to club while working regular jobs on the streets like selling coal from the back of a wagon and hawking brass polish door-to-door to housewives. Later, he worked gigs with an aeroplane engine factory, which went bust, and the car manufacturer Citroën. His existence was hand-to-mouth. He could never make enough money to put towards some savings.

While working with Citroën, he broke his collarbone in a match. He was so nervous about losing his car factory job that he continued working through the pain. HH had enormous reserves of strength. He worked hard to stay fit. The thief he lived with (who ended up in prison) couldn't understand why he did so many exercises early in the morning. As a footballer, HH sometimes played as a central defender, sometimes as a centre-forward. He was better in defence, having good weapons to stop players from scoring – his speed and his strength. He was missing one key quality, though: skittish on the ball, he lacked calm.

HH didn't, however, lack confidence. On arriving in Paris, he walked the streets like a *made man*, convinced he would carve a successful career in football. He got fixed up for a season with CASG Paris. After years of playing organised matches on Casablanca's dirt pitches, Paris's football fields were enchanting. He felt as if he was born to play on their lush grassy surfaces.

After a season with CASG Paris, he played two seasons with Stade Français, before moving on to Charleville, on the Belgian border, where he experienced a career high by captaining the club in the 1936 Coupe de France final. His team lost 1–0 to Racing Club, that season's league title winners. The winning goal came in the second half. (Towards the end of his playing career, while the Second World War was at its height, HH won a Coupe de France winner's medal with Red Star Olympique in 1942, although he wasn't wearing the captain's armband for his second cup final.)

HH enjoyed the bachelor's life in the 1930s. Parisian women – intrigued with his sexual prowess, or so HH claimed – nicknamed him 'The Argentinian'. HH saw female temptation everywhere but maintained that football always came first in his priorities. His philandering caught up with him in the spring of 1937. He was called to heel by his mother. She ordered him back to Morocco to marry Lucienne Léonard, a young woman he'd seduced in a dance hall. She was a dressmaker and had fallen pregnant.

In May 1937, HH's son, Francis, was born in Paris, the first child of HH's sprawling, complex family network. While HH continued to pursue a nomadic football career, which involved eight, if not nine football clubs in Paris and northern France (excluding wartime football in Vichy France), Lucienne gave birth to another three children, Hélène (born in 1938), Linda (1941) and Danièle (1942). HH fathered more children, with different women, after the war.

2.

In his memoirs, HH makes great mileage out of his selection for France's national football team. He was eligible because he took out French citizenship. He maintains he made his debut in a triangular tournament with England and Belgium while he was a player with Charleville. Apparently, he helped France win the tournament for the first time. Yet France never played England when HH played with Charleville, from 1935 to 1937.

Among other fables in his autobiography, HH was heroic in France's drawn game with Belgium at the Heysel Stadium. France drew 1–1 with Belgium away in 1935. However, the events of the match didn't unfold as he described. What's more, France played Belgium 12 times in the 1930s and there is no mention in any French Football Federation reports that HH took part in one of these games. He might have played twice, though, for France's Army team.

So much is mysterious about HH's life. Did he invent *catenaccio*, the defensive system he is synonymous with, while playing in France, as he claimed in his autobiography? In his telling, HH was playing a match during the 1942/43 season. His team, Stade Français, led by a goal. The opposition team was hunting furiously for an equaliser. HH was playing as one of three central defenders. He got a brainwave to pull a midfield teammate into his position so he could slip into a 'sweeper' role behind his team's line of defence, helping to preserve his team's lead. Or did HH latch on to the sweeper system, which was already popular in Italian football, decades later? (It's widely accepted that *catenaccio*, the 'door-bolt' defensive ploy of lining up with an extra defender as a sweeper, was first deployed by the Austrian coach Karl Rappan in the 1930s. There's no denying, though, that it suited HH's temperament: he craved control and his teams defended like soldiers.)

There are so many stories about HH that don't stack up – like the rumour he played for the Argentine club River Plate. (He left Buenos Aires aged three and played his professional football career in France.) There are other yarns

– preposterous, laugh-out-loud tales – and details that are difficult to verify. There is a story, for instance, about his time coaching in France in the mid-1940s. He had a good goalkeeper in his squad and one who was so-so. The good one was jilted by his wife and became so depressed he didn't want to play an important match on a Sunday. HH hatched a plan. He told the goalkeeper that he had spoken with his wife, and convinced her to come to the stadium for the game – and afterwards they could talk things through.

The goalkeeper agreed to play. He went out on to the pitch before kick-off, and in the VIP section of the stand saw a woman with dark sunglasses and a headscarf who shook her head enthusiastically and waved at him. HH's team won the match; the goalkeeper was outstanding. The woman wasn't his wife, though, but a double paid to act the part. Nobody knows what happened afterwards when the goalkeeper found out he had been duped. HH left France shortly afterwards, lured to the big leagues in Spain.

I asked Pere Escobar, HH's biographer, what he made of the story. 'Is that goalkeeper story true? I don't know. Is it possible that it's something Helenio would do? Yes. Is it something Zinedine Zidane or Pep Guardiola would do? No. Guys from the street have a spark about them. Footballers from Argentina who grew up playing on dirt patches are called *potreros*. Like Maradona scoring a goal with his hand. He did it without thinking. If you're hungry, you'll find bread wherever you can. If you don't have a football, you'll steal one.'

3.

The Nazis arrived on HH's doorstep in 1939. He had done 11 months of French military service in the 1930s. When the Second World War broke out, his regiment was mobilised. HH was sent to work on fortifications along the Maginot Line, France's defence line, which stretched from Switzerland to the Ardennes Forest. He organised football games in camp. He enjoyed the better food in military uniform, but mostly he spent his days toiling, digging trenches and putting up barbed wire, as the French Army naïvely got ready to fight the First World War all over again.

Before the war, when HH wasn't playing football, he got a job with Saint-Gobain, a titan of French industry. Saint-Gobain is a glass manufacturer, whose origins date back to the seventeenth century and the reign of Louis XIV. It is famous for having produced the glass in the Hall of Mirrors in the Palace of Versailles. HH was canny. He listened to the news. Conscious that the Nazis were gearing up to possibly invade France (and elsewhere), he clung on to his job at Saint-Gobain like a raft at sea. He tooled up. He did courses in England and Switzerland, landing a post as foreman in a fibreglass division specialising in thermal insulation, working on insulating oil tankers and battleships such as the *Normandie*.

While labouring on the Maginot Line, HH got lucky. He was 'overjoyed to get the long-awaited call from Saint-Gobain' to come back to work. It was just in the nick of time. The French Army's High Command was on the point of dispatching him to the Ardennes in May 1940, but HH preferred to play 'at the back' for this one. Being a factory foreman saved him. Deemed to be in a job crucial for France's war effort, he was exempted from military duty. It was therefore a get-out-of-jail-free card from the ravages of life on the front line, and almost certain death.

Adolf Hitler's Wehrmacht blitzed the French, outflanking the Maginot Line, and entering France through the Ardennes. According to HH, none of his army company survived the invasion. By the time the Nazis waltzed into Paris in June 1940, his factory had already joined the stampede south to what became known as Vichy France. HH went with them. He kept his head down, using a bicycle to get around. Neither a coward nor a hero, he had only one focus: survival.

4.

HH was never a fool. He always had his eye on the next move. He knew his time as a footballer would not go on forever, but he loved the game. He wanted to stay in it and so, while he was still playing football during the war years, he began laying foundations for the moment his playing career would end. He took football coaching courses. At this stage, he was back in France's northern, Nazi-occupied zone, playing with Stade Français, for a second stint, during the 1942/43 season. In the evenings, he coached amateur clubs in the suburbs of Paris. He was always tinkering, testing new methods to bamboozle other teams. He attended PE classes and began teaching. He also trained as a masseur in a hospital in Paris.

HH was insatiable. No other rival coach had an engine like him. Every spare second, he filled with ways that were going to make him a better coach. No one was as ambitious. He was still playing the game, too. He had experience as a veteran footballer. This was something significant. Once all the threads were pulled together, it led to his first professional coaching job. As the Second World War drew to a close, he obtained a gig as player/coach for Puteaux, a suburban club in Paris.

It didn't take long before HH began making a name for himself. Stade Français hired him as manager. He had two players who went on to become legends in the game in his team – Marcel Domingo and Larbi Benbarek, both of whom HH headhunted as players later in his management career. Domingo became a French international goalkeeper and is one of three Atlético Madrid icons, along with Luis Aragonés and Diego Simeone, to win league titles as both player and manager. Benbarek was born in Casablanca. He was the first international superstar – or *crack*, as they say in Spain – in La Liga, as the game began to explode in popularity during the post-war years.

In his first season in charge with Stade Français, HH won promotion in 1946. Off-season, he looked to beef up his attack. A young forward, István Nyers, had caught his eye during a match HH watched while in Prague. Nyers was born in a town in north-eastern France, which would be a key detail in his story with HH, but he moved to Budapest, Hungary as a 14-year-old. He won his first international cap for Hungary in 1945. He played for Ganz, a club in Budapest, towards the end of the war with László Kubala, someone who crossed HH's path later in a titanic clash of personalities.

After the war, Nyers was playing with a Czech club, Viktoria Žižkov, when HH made his move, travelling to Prague to persuade him to join Stade Français. When word got around that HH was looking to sign him, Viktoria Žižkov seized the player's passport. HH met with Nyers and assured him everything would be OK, but during their meeting, the police, tipped off by Viktoria Žižkov, arrived and detained Nyers. HH hatched a plan to spring the player, even though Nyers was languishing in a police station.

HH went to the French Embassy in Prague. He asked for their help, grandly introducing himself as a sports delegate for the French government, which was half-true – among the many hats HH wore, which still included his job at Saint-Gobain as well as coaching Stade Français, was a post working for the French Football Federation as Professor-Coach General, with a brief to run football clinics.

HH explained that he had been sent to Czechoslovakia by the French government to find exiled French athletes like Nyers, with the purpose of regenerating the French race, the young male population having been decimated during the war. HH was unsure how persuasive the logic of his argument was, but he won over his audience with his enthusiasm. The embassy issued Nyers and his wife a letter of safe conduct to France. HH rushed back to Nyers' apartment. He cajoled Nyers' wife into packing their bags. Then they stopped off at the police station where Nyers was released and 'returned' to France. HH had got his man.

Nyers never played for the country of his birth, France, but he scored plenty of goals for HH over two seasons with Stade Français before Inter lured him to Italy, where he remains a revered Inter player. HH made newly promoted Stade Français competitive in France's top flight. Dropping six points in their last five games of the 1946/47 season cost them a possible league title. For the first time, people started whispering that he was a magician. HH said there was nothing magical about what he did as a coach, merely that he surrendered completely to his trade. The French Football Federation took note. He was made national team coach, but his powers were limited – he had to answer to a selection committee led by Gaston Barreau.

5.

HH's fame was spreading beyond France. This was good news for Luis Guijarro, his friend and the man who became his agent. He had sold cars in Madrid with his brother before switching lanes to football – a world that has always attracted crooks and good men who have lost their way. This was where Guijarro felt at home. The two men met in France in the early 1940s, and it was the start of a business relationship that lasted longer than any of HH's marriages. They shared an understanding of how human nature worked.

Guijarro was dapper. His moustache was as slim as a toothpick (though it gathered some heft by the 1970s). At the end of the Second World War, after spending eight years in France, he moved back to Spain. No one had more contacts in the world of football. For decades, he was in the middle of big deals involving, for example, Larbi Benbarek, Marcel Domingo, Raymond Kopa and Joaquín Peiró. He negotiated the contract for Alfredo Di Stéfano's first foray into management. He was football's original superagent, the first to get a UEFA licence. (This was revoked in 1978 after a series of complaints that he'd swindled clubs, including Boca Juniors, Elche and Málaga. The investigation concluded that he had 'acted illegally throughout his career'.)

Guijarro was an innovator. He could visualise the future, and he changed the way agents did business. In the old system, football agents worked for a single club. In Spain, they were known as *patrones de pesca*, like the 'fishing skipper'. Agents recommended footballers to clubs. They were paid a commission for their scouting. Guijarro went a step further. He treated his role as an 'intermediary' more like an industry than a job. He bought the federation rights of emerging players and then hawked them around to big clubs (an odious practice that wasn't outlawed by FIFA until 2015).

Guijarro bought a big van for his trawling and trafficking. He visited the villages of Spain gathering up the best talents he could find, then loading them into the back of his van. He discovered Paco Gento early, and got him on the cheap. 'His father gave me the agreement for a very small amount,' Guijarro boasted. 'I remember that I signed the deal on the back of the player himself.' He sold Gento to Real Madrid in 1953 – and Gento became the first footballer to win six European Cups.

Nothing was ever enough for Guijarro. He spent his life on the road, often travelling more than 200 days a year. His best friend was money: the clubs he traded with had big operating budgets, but none bigger than his own. He branched out beyond agenting. He organised lucrative summer tournaments, often more than a dozen during the off-season. He lured South America's top clubs, the likes of Boca Juniors, Santos and Peñarol, to Europe. They'd rattle through eight to 12 games over a few weeks. The public in Spain loved it. Guijarro organised everything: travel, advertising, licences, fixtures. It was a big earner.

Bribing referees was another cash cow. It was easy money and a popular grift with his peers, too. Ángel Rodríguez was a rival football agent with the nickname '*El Feo*' ('The Ugly One'); he identified himself on the phone with the greeting: 'I'm The Ugly One'. Agents like Guijarro and The Ugly One would ring up a club and offer to bribe the referee for an upcoming match. The ref himself would never know that technically he had been 'bought'. If the match was won, as promised, the agent would pocket the bribe. If the match was lost, the bribe would be returned to the club. No harm done.

Guijarro was not a man to be crossed. He kept a pig farm and called his pigs after the names of football club executives who got on his wrong side. He preyed on football club presidents, and knew what buttons to press. A lot of Spanish football clubs were run by mayors of coastal towns – men with big egos, but small pockets. They weren't rich, but they liked to behave as if they were. Lavishing money on a football star was one way they could do that. Guijarro could help them fulfil their dreams.

6.

In 1948, Guijarro made a dream come true for HH. He was packing his bags again. Another country beckoned. He was going south of the border, returning to the land of his parents. Guijarro had hooked him up with Atlético Madrid, one of the giants of Spanish football. Atlético Madrid was founded in 1903 by Basque students. In 1911, it changed the colour of its jerseys to the distinctive red-and-white stripes known the world over today. It earned them the nickname '*Colchoneros*' (meaning 'Mattresses') due to the similarity with mattress covers of the era, a nickname that still holds over a century later. When the Spanish Civil War ended in 1939, the club merged with the sports section of Spain's air force. For eight seasons, including back-to-back title-winning campaigns in the early 1940s, it played under the name Atlético Aviación, becoming a de facto Franco regime team.

By 1947, having changed its name to Atlético Madrid, its football had come to captivate fans around Spain. Its five-man forward line – Adrián Escudero, Alfonso Silva, Juncosa, Antonio Vidal and Paco Campos – were known as 'the silky forwards', because their style and interpassing was elegant and smooth like silk stockings, but in title races they fell short, finishing third and fourth to champions Barça in both 1948 and 1949. On arrival in Spain, HH went out on loan to manage newly promoted Real Valladolid for a season, maintaining the club's premier division status, before returning to Atlético in the summer of 1949, where he doubled his salary. He had served his apprenticeship and he was now ready. His impact was immediate – and it was stunning.

Atlético hadn't won a La Liga title since 1941. The vaunted 'silky forwards' forward line was broken up – Vidal had to retire prematurely, owing to lung problems, and Campos, 32, was sold to Sporting Gijón. HH's five-man attack was rechristened 'the crystal forwards' a reference to the newfangled crystal-based women's tights that had become all the rage. Escudero, who had broken into Atlético's first team as a 17-year-old in 1945; Juncosa, the right winger; and Silva were still there. HH added the centre-forward Henry Carlsson, a gold medal winner with Sweden at the 1948 Olympics, and the gifted Benbarek, who HH enticed from Stade Français to La Liga, where he got the nickname 'The Foot of God', to complete the deck.

HH's 'crystal forwards' played attractive football, including a chaotic 6–6 draw with Athletic Bilbao at Atlético's Metropolitano stadium in January 1950, but mostly his team played 'practical football', doing what it took to put points on the board: a win here, a draw there. Crucially, in a four-team title race, Atlético put the burners on in the second half of the season, only losing twice in the final 13 games of the season, pipping Deportivo La Coruña by a point, with Valencia and Real Madrid another point behind. His top scorer was Escudero with 19 goals, half the tally that season of Telmo Zarra, Athletic Bilbao's legendary striker. This was a feature of HH's teams: he won seven league trophies during his career without ever having an outright Golden Boot winner for those title-winning campaigns.

During the summer, HH added Jose Luis Pérez-Payá, a young striker from Real Sociedad, to his attack, relegating Silva to a substitute's role. HH started the following season with a bullseye on his back. His needling of rival clubs drove fans demented. In October 1950, Atlético travelled west to Galicia to play against Celta Vigo in the league. Atlético were winning 2–0 when the game was suspended because Celta fans were throwing stones at Atlético's players taking corner kicks. They also threw everything they could get their hands on at HH, including umbrellas and false teeth. HH didn't let rival fans' antics go unpunished. During another Atlético match that season, a guy stuck his leg between the metal bars separating the terraces from the tunnel, trying to kick HH in the nose. HH grabbed his foot, and when the fan's shoe stayed in his hand, threw it as far as he could on to the pitch.

In November 1950, a month after the ruckus at Celta Vigo's ground, Atlético went to Real Madrid's stadium. Derby day. The city of Madrid came to a standstill. What happened that autumnal afternoon went down in history. It is a game remembered for its frenetic pace. A shoot-out. Nine goals and a missed penalty. The fans hardly had a moment to draw breath.

Early in the second half, one of Atlético's midfielders, Manuel Santana Farias, was struggling. Farias had been a fitness concern before kick-off, but HH threw him in. By the second half, he was spent. He came up to HH on the sideline and told him he couldn't continue. This was in the days before substitutions were allowed. He could barely stand from the dizziness. HH knew the player was worried he had a brain tumour, and shared his concern. But now – in the middle of a game for the ages – wasn't the time to go soft.

'Withdraw? Don't talk nonsense! Get back out there on the pitch!' yelled HH above the din. The player did as he was told, but returned shortly afterwards. He couldn't continue; he was too dizzy to function. HH was having none of it. 'Get back out there! You're fine! You're playing a blinder! Do you think if you had something seriously wrong with you, you could play like that?'

The scene replayed itself a few times, but HH wouldn't cede an inch. Each time, HH tried to convince Farias that he was fine, before sending him back over the top. Farias finished the match. With a few minutes to go, Atlético were leading 5–3. Real Madrid won a penalty. The game was again up for grabs. Farias was the player who conceded Atlético's penalty because of a handball. Marcel Domingo, who HH had brought with him to Spain, having coached him at Stade Français, saved the penalty kick.

Atlético scored the game's final goal from a counter-attack moments later. Larbi Benbarek famously celebrated scoring with an unprecedented dance. Fans were mesmerised by his impromptu jiving – a precursor of the samba-style goal celebrations that would become commonplace half a century later.

HH's ungodly methods were vindicated. Atlético won 6–3, and went on to retain their title, finishing two points clear of Sevilla in second place. A symphonic 7–0 win at the Metropolitano in January 1951 against Real Valladolid was HH's season highlight, an afternoon in which Juncosa scored a hat-trick and the ball circulated with mathematical precision among HH's 'crystal forwards'. (It is likely that a century will have passed before Atlético win consecutive league titles again. If they ever do.)

The thrilling 6–3 win against Real Madrid, in which HH strong-armed his midfielder Farias to stay on the pitch, wasn't the first time, nor the last, in which HH drove one of his players to the limit. HH knew it was a dangerous side effect of the power he wielded over his men. People spoke about the hypnotic influence he had over his players. It was said HH could coax a dog off a meat wagon. Most tended to blindly obey his orders, whether they were delivered with the carrot or the stick. He knew the confidence they had in him could be abused.

Back when he was managing Stade Français, a defender told HH he couldn't play because he was running a temperature. HH told him to wise up.

'Thirty-eight degrees? Brilliant! All the great athletes break records when they're running a temperature! This is fantastic, man! You're gonna play the game of your life!'

'But it's still going up,' the player pointed out.

HH was unconvinced: 'Nah, nah, with a temperature of thirty-nine, you'll play even better.'

And that, HH claimed, is how it went.

Only one day, HH – so cavalier when it came to the well-being of his players – would go too far.

A smiling HH receives a gift from the rival captain before the 1936 Coupe de France final at the historic Colombes Stadium in Paris.

3. SCENT OF CUT FLOWERS

1.

There was a change of president at Atlético Madrid in the summer of 1952. HH didn't see eye to eye with the new man in charge, the Marquis of Florida. 'He was so rich,' said HH, 'that he believed himself to be intelligent.' Their working relationship broke down within six months. Things came to a head in January 1953. Atlético were lying closer to the foot of the table than the top and facing Málaga, who were second from bottom. Atlético took an early lead in the match but lost 3–1. HH got the sack. Then immediately signed for Málaga.

His brief at Málaga was simple: keep them up. On the third-last weekend of league fixtures, Málaga got a priceless 1–0 win against Athletic, one of the lords of the league. On the same afternoon, Deportivo La Coruña, Málaga's direct rival in the relegation battle, got a 3–3 draw on the road against Real Oviedo. It left Málaga trailing Depor by two points. HH was livid. Something was fishy. He went on national radio and started ranting that the 'fix' was in at Oviedo – that the game was rigged. His words were like dynamite.

'Herrera's outburst caused a national scandal,' declared Alfredo Relaño, an author, long-time editor of sports newspaper *Diario AS* and a childhood friend of HH's son, Helenio Jr. 'For Herrera to say this kind of thing, to make an allegation like this on the radio, was unheard of at the time. It was like something José Mourinho would say, but this was a different era, a lot more reserved. People had better manners. They kept their counsel. Remember, this was in the middle of the Franco dictatorship. People were a lot more circumspect. For good reason.'

There was a shadow over Spain in the early 1950s. Franco's prolonged authoritarian rule had a profound impact on civil society. It created a docile population. The losers in Franco's Spain lived in perpetual fear. His bloodletting was relentless. He never let up on the state terror unleashed after the civil war. Hardly a day passed without arrests, police beatings and courts-martial. Union leaders who led strike actions were rounded up and brought to concentration camps. Men were shot while 'trying to escape'. Prisoners died from injuries received in custody. All told, during the first years of his dictatorship, he threw 260,000 people into prison camps. Even Heinrich Himmler, a key architect of the Holocaust, cautioned Franco against his mania for exacting revenge on the working class.

As well as wiping out dissidents, another feature of Franco's management style was procrastination. A British ambassador in the 1950s said there were two folders on Franco's desk: 'problems which time will solve' and 'problems which time solved'. Letting things drift suited him. It left him more time to indulge his hobbies. Unless hunting down his enemies – or harpooning whales in the ocean – Franco wasn't much interested.

Living in a police state was suffocating. People whispered to each other in their own homes. Several family members of Catalan writer Guillem Martínez fled to exile in France in the 1940s. They went on the run because of their involvement in anarchist cells, having been ratted out to the police. 'People who haven't lived under fascism can't understand what it's like. My father listened to BBC radio at night. When he did, he spoke in a very low voice to me and made me promise that I'd never repeat what he'd said at school. Because a lot of my family no longer had Spanish passports – they were exiled in France – the police kept a close eye on us. They came to the house every day just to touch your balls.'

Franco wouldn't let go of the past. In July 1953 – a couple of months after Deportivo La Coruña's 3–3 draw, the one that HH alleged was rigged – he gave a speech in Madrid on the anniversary of the start of the Spanish Civil War. 'It was not a civil war between Spaniards,' he bellowed. 'No. It was a fight between Spain and Anti-Spain. That of good against evil. We had to mutilate the body, prune the rotten and worm-eaten branches of the old Spanish trunk, eradicate the cancer that corroded us.'

Whenever Franco gave a public address, they were grand affairs. They provided him with a platform to rant about his insecurities: the civil war, which always remained an open sore; the threat of communism; and the dangers of liberalism. He was a prude. When he announced the entrance of US military bases in 1953 – the start of an alliance that ended Spain's international ostracism – Franco remarked that 'the best thing that the Americans did for us was empty the Madrid bars and cabarets of whores since they almost all marry American sergeants and GIs.'

In October 1953, 125,000 people were packed into Real Madrid's stadium for an event to mark the 20th anniversary of the Falange, the state's ruling political party. Franco wore black for his speech. Workers and peasants were bussed into Madrid and given lunch and a day's pay to cheer him on. His crowds always worked themselves into a frenzy, waving hankies deliriously at the sight of him. He had a surprisingly shrill voice. He was a peculiar figure: bloodthirsty yet timid when it came to things like sacking his ministers, who often found out their fate from a dispatch rider on a motorcycle.

Physically, Franco wasn't a fearsome warlord. He was no Genghis Khan (who once vowed to slaughter all Tartar males taller than a wagon wheel). Franco was almost feminine, with long eyelashes. A short, balding man with a big belly and small, sweaty hands. He kept his hand near his waist so visitors were obliged to bow to shake his hand. He was inscrutable. Franco was a stereotypical Galician: if you meet one on a staircase, it's impossible to tell if he or she is going up or down. Whether Franco liked football or not is debatable. He played the football pools, but he didn't display emotion when he was at a match. Was he bored? He was silent on many subjects, simply because he had no opinions. He lacked curiosity, but he was interested enough in the politics of football to keep an eye on developments at Real Madrid and Barça. He also appreciated the propaganda value of the sport. Attending the finals of the Copa del Generalísimo, and presenting the cup, gave him a mass stage to show himself off.

By 1953, HH started to rival Franco for showmanship. It didn't cost him a moment's thought to thunder scandalous accusations of match-fixing across the airwaves. He loved the attention, come what may. As luck would have it, HH's team, Málaga, travelled to La Coruña, the Galician city, to play Depor, the club HH had just slandered. Málaga had two league games left to save their skin. In La Coruña, they were ready to roast HH on a spit. Depor's president demanded that HH be banned from the sideline for the match – and succeeded. HH watched the game from a radio booth, which he accessed flanked by bodyguards. Málaga lost the match 1–0 and were condemned to relegation. The club wanted HH to stay and help with their promotion battle the following season, but the Second Division wasn't where HH liked to roll.

2.

Meanwhile, Depor entered play-offs in a mini league to survive: six teams, a collection of Premier Division and Second Division teams fighting it out for two places in the following season's top division. Depor got off to a bad start, losing one and drawing one in their opening two games. They sacked their coach, and turned to HH as a gun for hire. 'In the same month HH was *persona non grata* in the city of La Coruña, he returned to manage Deportivo La Coruña!' said Relaño in exasperation.

Depor hired HH on a short contract: 100,000 pesetas, a sizeable sum at the time, to oversee 10 games. The brief was simple: secure them Premier Division status for next season. HH didn't mind the abuse he received in La Coruña. He didn't take it personally; he only cared about business. Wary, though, about being shafted, he demanded the club pay him up front. So the first thing HH did when he got to La Coruña was to collect his money from the bank. Then he met up with his new squad of players.

HH embraced the local culture. During an early training session with his new squad, the players got him to crawl under a huge rock on a local beach with them, scuttling like crabs. The miraculous rock commemorates the Virgin of Pastoriza. They did it for good luck. People, mostly kids, still perform the custom to this day. HH got results (with or without the Virgin's help) – winning four and drawing one from nine matches, which set up a tantalising tiebreaker. Everything came down to the last match: a derby against local rivals Celta Vigo. A win would keep Depor up. All Vigo required was a draw. HH's men travelled to Balaídos, Vigo's stadium for the game. HH took no chances. He didn't trust Galicians – he brought his own stash of tea and coffee to Balaídos so his squad could avoid getting poisoned.

The crunch match was due to start at 5 p.m. It was the middle of July, but the rains poured down in Vigo that afternoon. Five minutes before kick-off, the ref rang the bell for the two teams to take the pitch. Celta came out under the deluge, but there was no sign of Depor. At 5 p.m., the ref rang the bell again. This time with more gusto. Still no sign of Depor. At five past, the ref grabbed the bell and started swinging it furiously, but the sound was muffled, as HH had wrapped cloth around the gong. The ref went to Depor's dressing room and threatened HH with a fine – which under regulations was an insignificant amount – if his players didn't get out on the pitch. Celta's players and their fans were growing increasingly restless. And wet. Eventually, the game kicked off at five-twenty. Depor won 3–1, winning the mini league on goal difference. Celta were relegated. Depor retained their Premier Division status. Another success for HH.

3.

For his next trick, HH joined Sevilla in the summer of 1953. Andalusia was his parents' heartland, and he was never happier than when coaching in Seville. The connection felt right. But what made it work – more than any sentimental reason – was the fact that HH connected with the club president, Ramón Sánchez Pizjuán. A man who understood him, who saw the possibilities in him. After only three months in the job, he renewed HH's contract for two more years, doubling his wages. He wanted him to stay in Seville forever. HH later admitted that Sánchez Pizjuán had identified his Achilles' heel: money. So long as Sánchez Pizjuán kept throwing money at him, their enterprise would be blessed.

Sánchez Pizjuán was obviously a wise man, reckoned HH. He was also a gentleman, an Atticus Finch-type lawyer, who often worked legal cases for free. During his career, HH worked with good presidents (those who bent to his will) and bad presidents and their directors (those who didn't). When HH worked with 'good' presidents, the winning of football matches, trophies and long-term relationships ensued. Gate receipts increased. The air smelled of freshly cut flowers. When HH worked with 'bad' boards of directors, it always ended abruptly, with blood on the boardroom floor.

Sevillians had an unquenchable thirst for life. They laughed at the world. The heat, though, got to people. It made them crave cold beer. They also liked to party at the drop of a hat. This was an explosive cocktail. More than at any other time in his career, HH spent much of his days trying to keep professional footballers on the straight and narrow.

HH never let up on his Sevilla players, whispering in their ears, trying to convince them they must look after themselves. Some were beyond saving. His legendary defender, Marcelino Campanal, was different. He was monk-like: whenever HH met him in a café, he was drinking milk. He was also one of the most notorious enforcers in the history of Spanish football. People talked about how violent he was on the pitch, often injuring teammates during training – an excess of enthusiasm, said HH, who loved him like a son.

When things got out of hand or there was a big game on the horizon, HH locked his team up for *ritiro*, a practice popular in continental football where teams closeted themselves in hotels or training camps for a few days. HH, more than any other coach, became famous for them. He loved control, and was never happier than when players were under his watchful gaze, removed from the temptations of booze and the witchery hidden in the eye of Spanish women. Even so, when Sevilla players were in *ritiro*, they sang and danced without rest. There was nothing HH could do.

When they were training at the club's stadium, local bullfighters trained with Sevilla's players. Before games, they sang and clapped to motivate themselves. Invariably, one of the players would start clapping slowly like a flamenco dancer to relieve the tension. HH could only throw his eyes up to heaven. Once, after beating Real Madrid 5–1 at their stadium in Seville, the players stayed out on the pitch afterwards dancing with the ball between their feet. The crowd were in ecstasy, chanting and clapping them on with their hands. This kind of spontaneity didn't sit well with HH, but he was powerless to intervene.

He could, however, exercise some control over their wilder superstitions. In Seville, people believed it was bad luck to meet the deceased. So if the Sevilla team passed a hearse before a match, it was a sign that they'd lose. This kind of thinking drove HH mad. To counter it, he invented his own superstitions. So the next time they passed a hearse on the road, HH got in a pre-emptive strike.

'Magnificent, *muchachos*! In France, they say that meeting a corpse brings good luck! We're going to win for sure! We'll definitely win. Wait till you see!'

Ramoní, a big, burly midfielder, was unsure: 'Don Helenio, here in Seville, it's bad luck to cross [paths with] a dead person.'

'Shut up with your foolishness!' roared HH. 'In France, they know what they're talking about! They're smart. It's why they know how to speak French.'

If HH found broken glass in a dressing room, he'd explode in delight, screaming so everyone could hear him: 'Broken glass! A sign that we're going to score more than three goals!' He took advantage of any opportunity to boost morale. To instil the mentality of winners. By hook or by crook.

4.

In October 1956, disaster struck. Sánchez Pizjuán died. He was only 55. When Sevilla's new stadium opened two years later, it bore his name, and still does. The city of Seville fell into mourning. HH was despondent. Sánchez Pizjuán had given him free rein. He had been the only man who spoke at the club – except, obviously, HH – when it came to football matters. Club directors, who previously had never opened their mouths, now couldn't shut up. They started meddling, getting in HH's way. HH had seen this before, at Atlético. The writing was on the wall.

On the pitch, Sevilla were motoring. They overachieved, finishing their league campaign in second place, pipping Barça on goal difference for a coveted place in the following season's European Cup. HH wanted out of the club, but he still had two years to run on his contract. He knew he was in demand. Sevilla's directors didn't want to lose him, even though he was insufferable, and felt he must honour his contract. They also knew Real Madrid were eyeing him as a replacement for their coach, José Villalonga, who got the sack in June 1957 (cruelly, as he'd just led them to a league and European Cup double).

HH tried an old trick. During the summer, he picked a fight with a club director in a public place. Making a fool out of him, spraying him with professional-grade insults. The row caused a scene – and HH was sure the fracas would be enough to get him kicked out of the club. He was wrong. Sevilla reported HH to the Royal Spanish Football Federation. Sevilla dropped him as their coach, but they made sure he couldn't work for anyone else.

Banned for two years from working in Spanish football, he was in limbo, left to bide his time. He ended up coaching at Os Belenenses in Portugal. The club wasn't quite at the end of the world, but he could see it from there. He picked up their 'Mayday' call in November 1957. The Lisbon club was in tenth position in the league, hovering dangerously close to relegation from Portugal's 14-team premier division. HH had hauled them up to fourth position in the table when, in the spring of 1958, another call came in over the airwaves. It was from Barcelona, a city still haunted by the Spanish Civil War and its aftermath.

Master of all he surveys: HH at Barça's recently opened the Camp Nou stadium, monitoring a training session during the 1958/59 season.

II

BARÇA
(1958-60)

4. THOU SHALT NOT KILL

1.

Barcelona faces the Mediterranean Sea. France is behind it. The city is shaped like a bowl – Montjuïc is one of several mountains surrounding it. Its rooftops are flat, which gives it a distinctive, Eastern feel. Viewed from the top of Montjuïc, the city looks as if it is carpeted in buildings – except for Antoni Gaudí's mad, magnificent church of the Sagrada Família, which bursts out of the skyline like Jack's beanstalk.

At the end of the Spanish Civil War in 1939, the bodies of those executed in Barcelona during General Franco's purges were dumped in a quarry on the southern flank of Montjuïc. In the late 1950s, if the soil on Montjuïc was damp from rain, a faint, persistent smell of decaying corpses could be smelled in the city below. There was no escaping the horrors of the civil war. It was still in people's nostrils.

Word reached Barcelona on 23 January 1939 that General Franco's Army was at the River Llobregat, south of the city. Panic spread. The Republican government, which was based in the Catalan capital, fled north to Girona. One of the biggest refugee crises of the twentieth century ensued: 450,000 desperate souls hiked on foot through sleet and snow across the eastern Pyrenees to France. Teresa Pàmies, a young communist who was evacuated from Barcelona, captured the sense of fear that seized the city, knowing Franco's troops were coming:

'The wounded who crawled out of Vallcarca hospital, mutilated and bandaged, almost naked, despite the cold, they went down to the street, shrieking and pleading with us not to leave them behind to the mercies of the victors … those with no legs dragged themselves along the ground … the youngest cried in their fear, the older ones went mad with rage. They grabbed the sides of lorries loaded with furniture, with bird cages, with mattresses, with silent women, with indifferent old people, with terrified children. They screamed, they ululated, they blasphemed and cursed those who were fleeing and were abandoning them.'

The roads to France were like scenes from Dante's *Inferno*. Children were trampled to death. Women gave birth in ditches. Babies died of the cold. 'At the side of the road,' recorded one witness in a radio interview, 'a man hung himself from a tree. One foot had a rope sandal, the other was bare. At the foot of the tree was an open suitcase in which lay a small child that had died of cold during the night.'

The lives of those left behind, who were on the losing side, were blighted. Franco invested in terror. Republicans who weren't executed were packed into concentration camps. Men ended their lives as slave labour, including 20,000 who spent the next two decades building the so-called *Valle de los Caídos* (Valley of the Fallen), Franco's gigantic mausoleum – or 'the other woman', as his obsession was known – in the mountains outside Madrid.

Those who went into exile were pursued. False confessions were extracted by torture. Rape was rife during police interrogation. Women were forced into prostitution to feed their children; they were thrown in prison on absurd charges like, for example, washing clothes for Republican soldiers or working as cleaners in Republican hospitals. Mothers were not allowed to take children over three years of age into prison with them. Often there was no one they could turn to, to care for their abandoned children, as other family members were dead, exiled or also imprisoned. It caused unspeakable anguish, as mothers feared for their children's chances at life on the streets.

Society was completely fractured, divided between winners and losers. Thousands of homeless, starving children of Republican prisoners were taken into religious orphanages, one estimate by the chaplain of Barcelona's prison, Fr Martín Torrent, claiming as many as 7,000. There, they were fed on a diet of *franquista* indoctrination. After one woman's husband was shot in front of both her and her young daughter, she was arrested, and her child was sent to a Catholic orphanage. The mother wrote regularly to her daughter until she received a cutting reply: 'Don't write to me any more about Papa. I know he was a criminal. I am taking the veil.' Livelihoods were destroyed. Once Catalonia had been occupied, out of 15,860 civil servants, 15,107 lost their jobs. Denunciations by neighbours were the cruellest blow.

'Fascism didn't just kill, and this is the awful thing, which makes it impossible even today to solve matters legally by means of "the memory laws",' said Guillem Martínez, a Catalan writer and journalist. In 2007, the Spanish government passed the Law of Historical Memory. This formally condemned the repression of the Franco regime, giving rights to the victims and descendants of victims of the Spanish Civil War and the subsequent dictatorship. Martínez continued: 'When Franco's regime killed Republicans, they kept their properties and their land. If you were, say, a socialist with a grocery shop, and your neighbour reported you, Franco's men would come and kill you. Your neighbour would be rewarded by getting to keep your shop because he reported you.'

'I'll tell you a story from here,' he said while we are chatting outside a café in a plaza in Sarrià, a neighbourhood in Barcelona. 'There was a woman who sold smuggled tobacco. It was very good. She came from L'Empordà, a province in northern Catalonia. She sold her tobacco in the middle of the street here in

Sarrià, where people came to smoke and chat. This woman had nothing. She sold cigars to the men who killed her husband. She was happy to make money for her children, but when her customers were out of earshot, she muttered "sons of bitches".

'That was the problem with *franquismo* – you couldn't choose. You had to swallow it. They stole from dead people. There are grandchildren of widows, people I know, that lost everything. In rural areas in particular, it was terrible. Even now, the consequences still linger: the family of your childhood friend took your grandparents' land.'

The Catholic Church besieged the factories of Barcelona in the 1950s with masses and homilies, as part of an expiation campaign. It was an exercise in atonement. For Franco's Spain, Catalonia had committed a great sin during the civil war. Now its factory workers were made to feel regret and remorse for even having flirted with communist and anarchist ideologies.

'The repression was spectacular,' said Martínez. 'It started with the Catalan language. It was banned, which was brutalising. Under Franco in the 1950s, children's school notebooks were full of political slogans: *¡Viva España!* Long Live Christ the King! The children were fed stories about Saint Augustine and Isidore of Seville. It was terrible, the mix of Catholicism and fascism. There was a terrible sadness in the air because people had known freedom and progressive thinking under the Republic. Under Franco, they sang fascist hymns with priests that hit them and buggered them.'

2.

The poverty across 1950s Spain was crushing. Per capita income was considerably lower in 1950 than it was in 1930. Meat consumption in 1950 was half what it was in 1926. Inflation was rampant, which put Spain on the edge of bankruptcy in 1957. Families were forced to buy food at twice the price on the black market. Immigrants from other, poorer areas in Spain flocked to Barcelona in the 1950s. There were jobs to be had, even though they were badly paid. One third of the city's population during the decade lived in slum conditions.

'The city was in ruins,' said Martínez. 'There wasn't any penicillin. It was only sold in Andorra. Here in Barcelona, it was sold by soldiers, by smugglers. Shanty towns sprang up around the city, with immigrants living in wooden shacks. There was one at Camp de la Bota. It's where the Forum is now, down by the beachfront. That was an execution area in the early 1950s. The executions were carried out at seven o'clock in the morning. I have met men that were children back then. Sometimes, they found eyes from executed men on the beach.

'You had two areas in Barcelona: Diagonal, where the rich lived, and the rest. It was incredibly cruel, the cruelty of the defeated. I'm from outside the city, but people have told me stories like the one about the only *franquista* in a building in Barceloneta, a neighbourhood by the port. He used to stomp upstairs making loud noises from the coins in his pockets. It drove his neighbours crazy because they were often dying from hunger.'

The austerity didn't trouble Franco. He believed himself to be an austere man. There were two life events that shaped him. One was the years he spent fighting in Morocco with the Spanish Foreign Legion. His experiences in the desert gave him a bloodlust that never left him. It fuelled the state terror he practised until his death in 1975. More than 50,000 executions were carried out after the Spanish Civil War ended. Needless murder in peacetime. A favoured method for executions was by strangulation, which shocked the international community.

The other formative incident in Franco's life happened the day his father walked out on the family. Franco was 14 years old. His mother took to wearing black clothes, like a widow. Franco never forgave him (although Franco's siblings did). Franco's adult life, as his biographer Paul Preston commented, was a repudiation of his father's feckless lifestyle: Franco never smoked. He drank wine in moderation at mealtimes. He didn't womanise. He said the rosary daily. He reckoned himself to be a good Catholic, although he struggled with the sixth commandment.

There is evidence Franco wasn't interested in sex, perhaps due to a war wound from 1916, which was described as an injury to his groin. It's rumoured that Franco's only child was fathered by his brother, Ramón, and that the baby's mother was a prostitute, and not Carmen, Franco's wife, who was never seen pregnant.

'One is happier living austerely,' Franco said without irony, while holidaying near San Sebastián in the mid-1950s on a deep-sea fishing expedition. It cost the gold reserves of a small nation to fund his hobbies. His yacht required year-round maintenance and a supply of naval escorts while he scurried around the Atlantic chasing tuna and whales. Large swathes of the ocean were baited over lengthy periods so there was a better chance fish would find their way on to the end of his hook. His hunting and freshwater fishing triumphs, which employed other travelling courts, involved similar stage management. Whenever he harpooned a whale, he'd dump it on the quays of fishing villages in Galicia and demand payment from the local municipality for any oil they extracted.

The women in his life had a weakness for life's comforts and glitter. His wife's nickname was 'Doña Necklaces'. Their daughter was notorious for her stinginess and sense of entitlement. *Me. Me. Me.* She put the fear of God in jewellers in Barcelona and Madrid. They took out insurance indemnifying themselves against her pillaging of their stores. When she married a minor aristocrat and playboy in 1950, the press was ordered not to report on the lavish wedding presents the bride accumulated. In exchange for their gifts, 800 guests were treated to a bacchanalian banquet at the Royal Palace of El Pardo.

In contrast, there was little glamour about life in Barcelona in the 1950s. The city, which was once an enchantress, lost its sparkle. It was no longer the exhilarating metropolis that had once beguiled Federico García Lorca. 'Barcelona is something else, isn't it?' he wrote to a friend in the 1920s. 'There you have the Mediterranean, the spirit, the adventure, the high dream of perfect love. There are palm trees, people from every country, surprising advertisements, Gothic towers and a rich urban tide… What a pleasure it has been for me to meet that air and that passion!'

Under Franco, passion dwindled on Barcelona's La Rambla. Life became grim. Dull, grey. 'The colour of a dog running away,' as Catalans say – something there, but without colour. 'It was terrible. There was nothing,' added Martínez. 'It was like life during the pandemic when the city was shut down because of Covid, when there were no lights on at night. Elderly people said to me: "Look, it's like the 1950s." Sundays back then were dreadful. Everything was closed. There was nothing to do, only go to the cinema or football. And movies were censored.'

3.

Barça, the city's biggest football club, wasn't bringing much relief or joy to its fans in the spring of 1958. Their team, which was stacked with international stars, was misfiring. László Kubala, who towered over the club like a giant, was a decadent presence. Injuries and a reckless, whoring lifestyle were catching up on him. When Barça lost 2–1 to Espanyol in the city derby in March 1958, it marked an end to any hopes of winning La Liga. Real Madrid were coasting to another league title, their fourth in five seasons. Barça's board of directors were furious. They fired off a stinging letter to Kubala, the team's leader, castigating him for his team's 'deplorable' performance against Espanyol and the troubling squad discord 'on and off the pitch'. They complained he was cheating the club with his pharoah's salary.

At the same time, the world of football was falling in love with a new tournament: the European Cup, which had been established in 1955. Just three years into its existence, Real Madrid already had it in a stranglehold. Barcelona could only look on in envy: its eternal rival stood on the cusp of winning a third consecutive title while it couldn't even qualify. Other clubs in Spain could: Athletic Bilbao in 1956, as winners of La Liga, and, Sevilla, as league runners-up in 1957. Barça's failure to join in the party was driving people in Catalonia mad. That Real Madrid were the toast of Europe made everything harder to stomach. The names of the club's attacking line-up will be forever remembered by football fans in Spain: Gento, Rial, Kopa, Puskás (who joined in summer 1958) and Di Stéfano, king of them all.

Barça had been the dominant force in football in Spain until Alfredo Di Stéfano's arrival at Real in 1953. With him in their ranks, Real Madrid immediately began plundering silverware and Barça began to cower. Twice Real Madrid beat them in La Liga during the 1957/58 season: 3–0 and 2–0. When Real Madrid scored the opening goal in their 2–0 victory at Barcelona's stadium in February 1958, Barça fans waved their hankies in disgust, a gesture borrowed from bullfighting.

Rival political factions within Barça created a poisonous atmosphere. The local media revelled in bad news: stoking enmities, disseminating propaganda, leaking stories, playing one side off the other, needling fans. Hysteria reigned. The club was rotting from the inside. Its president Francesc Miró-Sans had enemies around every corner, and they sensed blood, as the club was sinking in debt he'd saddled them with. In 1953, he campaigned and won a presidential campaign promising to build a new stadium. In September 1957, the Camp Nou was unveiled. The following month Franco visited the ground for a game, accompanied by his wife and a retinue of ministers. 'It was a source of joy for citizens' that El Caudillo took time for the visit, reported the *Barça* magazine deferentially.

The construction of the Camp Nou, a modernist marvel, left the club with an unsustainable level of debt. In April 1958 at an extraordinary general assembly, Josep Domènech, a rival of Barça's president Francesc Miró-Sans, uncovered holes in the club's accounts. Someone from the president's board had their fingers in the till. And the team's poor performances – which made a mockery of their grandiose stadium, the largest in Europe – were compounding the bleak financial outlook.

Barça's coach, Domènec Balmanya, dropped Kubala for the remaining five league games of the season. This did nothing to stop the bleeding. Nor did it save Balmanya's job. He was sacked five days after the extraordinary general assembly and with two league games to play. Barça had again failed to qualify for the European Cup; Atlético Madrid, as runners-up, qualified instead. Balmanya left the club through the back door. The board wouldn't even allow him – a man who had spent almost a decade at the club as a player – to formally say goodbye to his players after three years in charge.

Football can be a cruel business. The board had already hired the man to replace him, and he watched Balmanya's final game in charge against Real Zaragoza from the stands. It annoyed Balmanya that the club had been trying for months to hire this coach behind his back – a man ostracised from football in Spain, and banned from coaching in the country.

But Barça was desperate. They were gambling, but they sensed Balmanya's usurper could fix their problems. They leaned on the Royal Spanish Football

Federation to lift his two-year suspension and paid Sevilla a million pesetas to forget about their grievances with him. They then forked out another 200,000 pesetas to extract him from his job in Portugal. He was the bomb they needed to topple Real Madrid: *la bomba HH*. This was the atomic age. People said the H-bomb was 50 times more powerful than the A-bomb, but that the HH-bomb was a hundred times more powerful. His initials alone were enough to send a charge of electricity through the masses. HH – *Habla, Habla*, Talk, Talk. He had a lip that made some people think he might have invented the world. The rest thought he was destroying it. 'His Holiness,' as Gabriel García Márquez called him.

Yes, sir! HH was back. He knew he had work to do, but he couldn't help feeling giddy: 'I was in Barcelona! Again in Spain! And the sanction had gone to the devil!'

4.

HH knew all about the internal problems at Barça. They were always tearing each other asunder at that club. A poisonous need for intrigue festered within its walls. Rival factions. Constant arguing. Men with political ambitions. Men on the make. Excitable fans. A toxic local press, constantly looking to cause trouble. Bitching and betrayal. Vested interests and other filth. Envy was the order of the day in that city of Barcelona, one of the most beautiful cities in the world, but a cursed place. It forever had been so.

Legend has it that one sunny day, years beforehand, when Jesus Christ was in the middle of a 40-day fast in the desert, the devil took Jesus to the top of Tibidabo, one of the several mountains overlooking Barcelona. The devil showed Jesus all the kingdoms on earth, which were spread out below them. Playgrounds. Places of sin and pleasure. Magnificence. Pointing at Barcelona, he said: 'Tibidabo' – 'To thee I will give.' Jesus shook his head. He wasn't tempted. It wasn't for him. He went back to wandering in the desert. HH was made of sterner stuff. He would take Barcelona. He knew more.

Barça were a *big* club. They had a squad of players kissed by God, with a subs' bench overflowing with international players. Every team selection would be a news story. HH was ready for whatever battles were sent his way. He would take on all comers. He'd trample to death anybody who got in his way. They would come to know HH the fighter in Barcelona.

5. CRAZY ABOUT MONEY

1.

At one stage during contract negotiations with Barça in the spring of 1958, HH flew back to Lisbon, where he was still contracted to Os Belenenses. This was a few weeks after the Munich air disaster. Just as his plane was about to touch down in Lisbon Airport, it started to fly in an unusual manner. HH could see the runway below out of his window. The plane dipped. It passed over the runway, almost at ground level, tantalisingly close, as if about to land, and then suddenly, abruptly, it took flight again. HH asked a flight attendant what was happening. He was told there was 'too much traffic'.

The plane then started doing laps around the Tagus River. The pilot was dumping fuel into the sea. But best not to alarm the passengers. The plane's landing wheels wouldn't come out of their sockets. The pilot was going to have to land without them, but his plane was like a tinderbox, with so much fuel on board. It would take just a spark to turn the plane into a whoosh. The pilot was doing so many loops around the Tagus River that his passengers became dizzy. HH closed his eyes to fight the dizziness and fell asleep. He woke up with a bang. He looked out of his window and all he could see was a Red Cross ambulance on the runway while a fire brigade hosed down the plane.

That was a stroke of luck, thought HH. And a good omen – for the work ahead in Barcelona.

2.

The first thing HH did when he arrived in Barça was sort out the money. He had watched the last game with his predecessor Domènec Balmanya in charge from the stands, when Barça beat Real Zaragoza 5–1. Justo Tejada scored Barcelona's last goal. Tejada was a young Catalan winger with an eye for a goal. Several months later, he scored four goals for Spain in a 6–2 win against Northern Ireland, one of the unexpected sensations of that summer's World Cup finals. Tejada could land a ball on a sixpence – he was renowned for his ability to reach the byline and whip over precise crosses. He also followed orders. HH liked that in his soldiers.

Tejada always kept himself fit. (He would play tennis into his eighties.) He was pragmatic when it came to violence in the game, partly because he was often himself on the receiving end of a kicking during his career. 'A full-back who doesn't hit a winger might as well stay at home,' he said. He remembers once playing a game in Cairo when fans rained down glass Coca-Cola bottles on to the pitch. The police on the sidelines picked up the bottles and hurled them back into the terraces. After the Real Zaragoza game at the Camp Nou in April 1958, HH summoned Tejada to his apartment.

'Justo Tejada, are you happy in Barcelona?' asked HH.

'Yes,' said Tejada.

'You're an international footballer. How much do you earn?'

'One hundred and twenty-five thousand pesetas.'

'Listen, I've seen you play. You should be paid 200,000.'

'*Hostia*, I would die for you, *Míster*,' replied Tejada, using the title that players in Spain call their coaches, which comes from the time early in the twentieth century when most football coaches in Spain were British gentlemen. 'Do you know what that does to a footballer when your coach says something like that to you? He did this for me, and he did this for everyone. For Luisito Suárez. With Joan Segarra. With everyone. All the Catalan players. "*Míster*, whatever you want." We were bowing to him.'

The club lavished money on its foreign stars. The local press fawned over them. The homegrown players were often taken for granted. HH was gathering the Catalan players in close. He also made sure the physio Ángel Mur and the kitman Claudio Pellejero – as well as all the subs on the squad – were paid more money. They couldn't believe he was fighting their corner. It was unprecedented. HH was buying their loyalty.

In the 1957/58 season, Kubala, the team's franchise player, made seven times what Tejada earned. The following season, HH's first full season in charge, Kubala made a little over twice what Tejada earned. HH wanted to level the playing field. He didn't like the star system unless it was his name in lights. Typically, Kubala made four times as much as the coach; in his second full season in charge, HH surpassed Kubala in income. God help any club director who got in his way when it came to money. HH was obsessed with money.

'Herrera was like Salvador Dalí,' claimed Frederic Porta, a Catalan broadcaster and biographer of Kubala. 'Herrera was crazy about money. If you change the letters of Salvador Dalí you can read in Latin the words "Avida Dollars", which means passion for money. It's a famous saying in Catalonia. Herrera was all about money and more money.'

Arguably, Salvador Dalí is Catalonia's most famous artist. He was a mercenary, unlike his contemporary Pablo Picasso. 'Picasso is a communist, me not so much,' Dalí once said. Picasso moved to Barcelona as a teenager and wouldn't allow his painting *Guernica* to be displayed in Spain until Franco had died. Dalí would do anything for cash, including painting a portrait of Franco's daughter.

HH did whatever it took to obtain better payment for his players. At one stage, four of HH's Catalan players – Rodri, Martí Vergés, Ferran Olivella and Sígfrid Gràcia – were looking to renew their contracts. Gràcia was nominated to negotiate on their behalf. He trundled along to the boardroom to plead their case. All the club's directors – including HH, who said nothing – sat around, as Gràcia made his pitch. The players agreed their targets in advance. They were looking for a pay rise. They reckoned figures of 300,000, 350,000 and 400,000 pesetas for each of the following three seasons would be acceptable. They built in a cushion of 50,000 pesetas extra for each season so there was room for haggling.

The board, however, played hardball. They refused Gràcia's offer, and instead held out an olive branch. Gràcia could get the proposed salary, but the other three players would have to renew based on their existing salaries. Gràcia held his ground. He wasn't going to break ranks: 'We're either all Moors or all Christians.' There was an impasse. HH suddenly jumped out of his seat, exploding with rage.

'Gentlemen, look at the paperwork your players are doing for you! They have given this man a licence of conduct. An honest man. You're going to pay them what they're asking for. Right now! All four of them. No questions asked. You have no right to argue with them. Not over a single penny.' The president coughed up the money. HH had only disdain for the board of directors at Barça. He wasn't intimidated by their wealth. Posh types fed by silver spoons in childhood. Merchant princes whose self-confidence came from old money and expensive schooling.

According to Pere Escobar, HH's biographer, 'Herrera's ego was bigger than the Sagrada Família. He achieved his position in life despite everything. Let me explain. I'm from the Raval. It's a poor neighbourhood in the city of Barcelona. Very humble people live there, working-class people. My father worked long hours so I could be given an education. I am always proud to say that I'm from Raval. I never hide this fact when I'm meeting important people I know in life – people much more important than me. It's something to be proud of. It's the pride of having been able to come from such a low start, and to rise so high.

'Herrera had that self-pride – someone who had dragged himself up by the bootstraps. We can't begin to imagine his life circumstances as a child. He grew up in Morocco in incredible poverty – tormented by mosquitoes, hunger, the heat, just after a world war. It must have been horrifying. He always needed security. But everything Herrera earned in life, he did it on his own. He was the king of self-reliance.'

Escobar got to know him towards the end of his life, commissioned to write his biography for Barça's centenary. 'I remember I did a programme on TV3,

Catalonia's main television station. It was the last television interview Herrera carried out in Spain. He was known as a friend of mine. He always asked for money, always, always, always, but for me he didn't request payment. Afterwards he did a special programme for Barça's centenary. He refused to do it unless the club paid him to do it. They wouldn't pay him, so he didn't do it.'

In HH's eyes, the board of directors at Barça knew nothing about football. When he took charge, they gave him the names of players to put on the transfer list: the goalkeeper Antoni Ramallets; the team's Brazilian striker Evaristo; a defender Joan Segarra; and Luisito Suárez. HH tore up the list. Ramallets stayed in goal. Evaristo was his top scorer the following season.

HH made Segarra his captain. He told him he had a good wife, who took care of him, and that he could play until the age of 40 without fooling anyone. Segarra was his coach on the pitch. And his eyes and ears off it, his confidant. He kept HH informed about family news: like, for instance, what player had a baby or who was getting married, as well as the dirty stuff. Segarra was an animal on the field, who went down in club history as 'The Great Captain'.

'Segarra was an extraordinary character,' recalled Escobar. 'There was a Paraguayan player called Cayetano Ré in the 1960s. He was a very good striker. He was small. During a match, he was out on the wing when the opposing team's full-back battered him. As the game carried on, he fell back into his own half and wouldn't cross the halfway line. There were no TVs like today. He was terrified he'd get battered again.

'At half time in the dressing room, Segarra grabbed him by the lapels of his jersey, and he hung him up against the wall and told him, "If you don't get beyond the halfway line in the second half, I am the one that will be waiting for you." Cayetano Ré spent the rest of the match in the opposition's half. He preferred his chances there than incurring Segarra's wrath. Segarra had a savage personality. He was *grandísimo*.'

HH had known about Luis Suárez – another player on the list of those players the board wanted to axe – since his time in La Coruña in the summer of 1953 when HH helped Deportivo La Coruña avoid relegation. Suárez – or Luisito, as he was known by his teammates – was an academy player for Deportivo La Coruña at the time. HH tried signing him for Sevilla, but the player joined Barça instead. Suárez was an attacking midfielder, who played in a similar position to the one Xavi Hernández later occupied at the club, but Suárez was more of a goalscorer, knocking in 15 to 18 goals a season at Barça.

Like Xavi, Suárez always played with his head held high: scouting for his teammates' positions. Suárez said he doesn't remember ever heading the ball during his career; his head was for thinking. At Barça, they were suspicious of him. He never won the confidence of his coaches: Balmanya, or the two men beforehand, Franz Platko and Sandro Puppo. HH saw something in him they didn't and wanted to build his team around him. Nobody knew the geography of a pitch like Suárez. He became HH's organiser, the ideal man to launch swift counter-attacks. Di Stéfano called him 'The Architect'.

'When Herrera arrived at the club, they told him to get rid of Luisito because he was too "timid",' said Tejada. 'They were set in that judgement, but Herrera was smart. He couldn't believe it. He said he'd get rid of them all before Luisito. He was the greatest player in Spain of all time, better than Xavi or Andrés Iniesta. Herrera said: "If I have to sleep with him, I'll sleep with him, but this won't be necessary. Leave him to me."'

3.

HH was a stickler when it came to discipline. He knew his authority lay in establishing a reign of fear. The players must abide by his rules. Total subjugation. There was no other way. Josep Maria Fusté, an academy player – who played on the Spain team that won the 1964 European Championship – arrived late one day for training. HH berated him in front of his teammates, then fined him his bonus for the season: 40,000 pesetas. Said he'd have to find work elsewhere to put food on his table. Players vomited during his first training session. During preseason, he trained them three times a day.

HH ripped a cast off one player, Ferran Olivella, cracking it open with a stone himself. Told him he was malingering. He fired the club doctor for being soft. HH continued with the beatings until morale improved. He was harder, more aggressive and more direct than any of the players' previous coaches. Tejada said the players were onside, though. HH was welcomed with open arms (by most of them). They knew what he had achieved. He was a winner, who understood the game.

Tejada gave an example: 'Before Herrera arrived, I was a winger. I stayed in my position. I just tried to dribble with the ball and send in crosses for Kubala. With HH, everything changed. I played on the right wing. Paco Gento was on the left for Real Madrid. All his football was based on his speed. It gave him an edge. I trained with him in Madrid. We raced each other over 100 metres. I was quick, but he could beat me by 10 metres.

'I remember Herrera telling me: "Keep an eye on Gento. He's very fast. Try to intercept the ball from him in the middle of the pitch. Don't leave all the marking to Olivella. Or fall back into our half. It will make it difficult for him if you lie back. It will squeeze the space he has to run into. He won't be able to get up a head of speed. We don't want him going superfast."

'No coach ever gave me advice like that. Herrera was a deep thinker about the game. All he thought about was football. He was aware of every detail.

He studied the opposition like a general on the battlefield. He was great at taking the stress away. When he saw his players, he sat down beside them, advising them. He'd tell you where your opponent would run, whether to take your marker on his right side or the left, if he was tall or short, if he was good or bad in the air. He was 15 years ahead of his time. He was the first coach to say that the responsibility of a coach is much greater than it is for any player so he should be paid twice as much as the players. Other coaches around Spain should have been thanking him *rápido!*'

HH changed the profile of coaches in Spain – and in the world of football. Previously, there had been successful coaches in Spain like the British manager Fred Pentland, who was nicknamed '*El Bombín*' because he wore a bowler hat, but none who owned the stage like HH. As Tejada explained, HH argued his role as manager was more important than any individual player in Barça's squad. The buck stopped with him. Before HH, football coaches were in the background. No one knew their names. Fans fell in love with 'the team of Mazzola' at Torino in the 1940s and with 'the team of Di Stéfano' at Real Madrid in the 1950s. The trainer was the man who carried the bags. HH changed all that. He moved the coach from the margins to centre stage. He guaranteed his employers at Barça that his team would triumph. Gate receipts would increase as a result. All boats would rise.

In 1958, his counterpart at Liverpool – Phil Taylor, Bill Shankly's predecessor – was referred to as a Player Liaison Officer by the club's board of directors. He was there to take orders, a link man between the gentlemen in the boardroom and the working-class players in the dressing room. He had neither power nor standing at Liverpool. His status was only marginally higher than the club's physio, down the ranks in football's caste system. His salary was pitiful, on a par with a civil servant. By the time of HH's second full season in charge at Barça, he was earning more than any of his players (who themselves earned vastly more than British players).

HH led a revolution. Times were changing. He surfed a wave. The great films of the era were no longer star driven. Moviegoers primarily went to see the works of directors like Alfred Hitchcock and Ingmar Bergman, more than the actors in their films such as James Stewart and Max von Sydow. By the 1950s, football hadn't altered much in half a century. In some senses, a coach was restricted in what he could do. There were no substitutions allowed. There was inbuilt resistance to change and new ideas, especially in Britain, which was dismissive of the tactical ideas percolating in the coffee houses of Vienna before the war. It was an island where the spirit of amateurism pervaded. There was a feeling that football was born in the Victorian Age fully formed. It was a simple game. It didn't need changing or elaborate coaching.

There was resistance to the notion of having an England national team manager, for example. Walter Winterbottom was the first England manager to be appointed in 1946. The guardians of the game in Britain even felt it unnecessary to have prematch training sessions for international matches. It was enough to pick the players and let them get on with it, a belief that top players didn't need coaching. They were the best in the country. They could already tackle, shoot and dribble the ball. What more could they learn?

After England's embarrassing exit from the group stages of the 1950 World Cup finals, when the team of Billy Wright and Tom Finney lost 1–0 to a team of part-timers from the United States, the Football Association (FA) launched an enquiry. It examined other footballing nations, like the tournament's hosts, Brazil, to see what they did differently. It was telling that the FA's report concluded that England had nothing to learn from their peers, believing, for instance, that English players wouldn't bend to Brazilian training methods.

Walter Winterbottom was a former schoolmaster, who played a couple of seasons as a semi-professional for Manchester United before the Second World War. His powers as England manager were limited. He couldn't pick his own teams. He had to make do with the players chosen by a selection committee. It wasn't until 1962 that he convinced his masters, the FA, that the manager should have sole responsibility for team selection, which paved the way for the success of Alf Ramsay and his 'Wingless Wonders' at the 1966 World Cup.

At club level, it took Messianic figures like Matt Busby, Bill Shankly and Jock Stein to usher in a cult of the manager in the British game. At Manchester United, Busby redefined 'the role of the manager as Boss rather than servant,' to quote from Eamon Dunphy's biography, *A Strange Kind of Glory*. He was the greatest manager that Santiago Bernabéu knew. His players revered him. There was a wonderful romance about his European Cup triumph in 1968, with a team built from the ashes of the Munich air disaster a decade earlier, but Busby – and Shankly and Stein – were still deferential to their boards of directors. Nor did they ever match HH, football's first celebrity coach, in earnings. HH was the bridge between the days of working-class coaches under the thumb of selection committees and the millionaire managers of the modern era.

4.

HH coerced and cajoled. He was a master at lifting the morale of his players. David Salinas, a journalist with *Sport*, provided an example: 'Barça was in a Nordic country on a tour, and a local newspaper fell into Herrera's hands. He saw that the sports page was talking about Barça and some of its players. He picked up the newspaper and said to Rodri, the player beside him, a defender:

"Hey, they're talking about you here." Rodri enquired: "And what do they say about me?" Herrera replied: "Well, they say that you're one of the best players in the world in your position. In England, in Italy, in Scandinavia – you're known everywhere!" The player suddenly grew six inches taller. Herrera used these tactics to big up his players. He had a great team, but he made them better.'

HH had an extraordinary mind. He operated in an age before match recordings on digital media. HH didn't have a team of video analysts to call on to create three-minute packages on, say, the penalty techniques of a rival striker. He benefited from a photographic memory and remembered individual performances. He stored player details somewhere in the recesses of his brain and in his notebooks, which he compiled like a crazed natural scientist. His players got such detailed notes on rival players they could recognise them without seeing a photograph of them beforehand. He kept stats assiduously. He weighed players before and after games. The statistics didn't lie: if a player hadn't run enough during the game, he wouldn't have perspired much. A lack of weight loss ran the risk of a slaughtering from HH.

'When Herrera took over at Barça, he met the players one by one in the dressing room,' said Escobar. 'He weighed them. Afterwards he spoke to them. Sígfrid Gràcia, one of his defenders, told me: "After Herrera weighed me, he told me to sit down. He said: 'You're overweight.' I was angry. 'Hey, *Míster*, excuse me, you're insulting me. I'm a professional footballer with Barcelona. I'm not fat.'"

'Herrera said, "Yes, you are overweight. You're three kilos overweight. Three seasons ago, you had the best season of your career. Do you remember? Well, you were three kilos lighter that season." This was in the 1950s. There wasn't any internet. Data like that wasn't captured. How did Herrera know this information? Herrera had a computer in his brain. Gràcia said he left him speechless because he was right: "He knew me better than I knew myself." To that man, whatever Herrera told him, he believed it. Gràcia did whatever Herrera said.'

Tejada remembered HH the control freak. The man who tried to socially engineer every detail. 'He got angry with waitresses if they put water and wine on the table before our food arrived.' Escobar, HH's biographer, told me a story about an incident before a match in Madrid. The team was billeted at their regular hotel. Same hotel, same menu every time: pasta for starter; steak for the main course. The goalkeeper Antoni Ramallets and captain Joan Segarra were two of the team's senior figures and liked to enjoy a *carajillo*, a shot of brandy mixed in coffee, after their meal.

On the day of the match in Madrid, the waiter arrived with coffees at the end of the team's lunch. He served HH. 'No, not this one. I want this one,' said HH, pointing at one of the *carajillos* across the table from him. The dining room fell silent. The waiter started sweating and placed one of the *carajillos* in front of HH. HH drank it. Once he'd finished it, he stood up and announced: 'We're leaving the hotel.' The players looked at each other in disbelief. HH told them to go to their rooms and pack their bags. 'Everyone out of here!' he shouted. After packing, the players met in the lobby of the hotel.

The waiter was distraught, apologising every few seconds to HH. The *maître d'hôtel* and the hotel manager crowded around HH, pleading with him. HH put on a show: 'Just like that, you fill me with brandy without me knowing it. You're trying to poison my players!' In the end, it all came to nothing. HH told his players to return to their rooms and unpack. However, a *carajillo* was never served again. At least, not in Madrid. HH had eyes in the back of his head, which he supplemented by hiring detectives to spy on his errant players.

'The control that HH exercised was excessive – in the way he managed information and his relationships,' said Escobar. 'I've thought about this a lot. In 1960, it was not the norm. You'd want to be the police to know all the things that he knew. Nothing could escape him. He had an obsessive personality. That incident with the *carajillo* showed the players he was smarter than them. Footballers at the end of the day are like children: "He's smarter than us, we better be careful." A coach once told me, "A squad is made up of 25 sons of bitches. Each of them have huge egos. They must have huge egos to get to the top in professional football. And the biggest son of a bitch has to be the coach."'

HH was the biggest *hijo de puta* of them all. He was a lion tamer. He was maniacal when it came to diet, and terrorised Eulogio Martínez, one of his forwards, who had a weakness for putting on weight. HH was always telling him he was too fat. The day before a game, while Barça's other players were enjoying their dinner, instead Martínez would have an apple set on the table in front of him. HH told him that it would help him sleep better.

Martínez was a prodigy. He was capped at international level with Paraguay at the age of 16. His teammates gave him the nickname 'The Can Opener' because of his ability to unlock difficult defences with the game's first goal. He was Barça's top scorer three times during his six seasons at the club. He jostled with Evaristo to be Barça's centre-forward.

Barça signed Evaristo, the only Brazilian player to score five goals in an international match for his country, in 1957. He came to Barcelona to look for an apartment before joining up with the squad for the following season. While taking a break from house-hunting, he watched the team play in the quarter-final of the cup against Atlético Madrid. Martínez ran riot, scoring seven goals in an 8–1 victory. Evaristo was left scratching his head. After the game he commented to the press: 'With a forward like this, I don't know why they signed me. Maybe they want me to sweep the dressing room floor.'

When it came to goals, HH had an embarrassment of riches up front. He knew he was working with the best squad of players he'd ever had. They were underperforming. He just had to get them firing. Martínez and Evaristo were two of eight top-class attacking players in his ranks. They battled with each other for five positions. The others were Tejada; the Hungarian stars Sándor Kocsis and Zoltán Czibor, who joined in the summer of 1958; Luisito Suárez; Ramón Villaverde, a Uruguayan striker who played in the Colombian pirate league, as a teammate of Alfredo Di Stéfano, before signing for Barça; and Kubala, the club's franchise player.

Martínez was the bravest of them all, an incredibly gutsy player. The ideal target man. 'He was a man of iron, like an armoured tank,' according to HH. A footballer who was fearless, especially in hostile stadiums. He always did what was least expected. He excelled at dragging defenders out of position. He was street smart. Real Madrid's goalkeeper Rogelio Domínguez said he gave him nightmares because of his ability to block a goalkeeper's line of sight at the moment the ball entered the box, which allowed his teammates to score.

Martínez died prematurely. After retiring, he ran a bar in Calella, a seaside resort north of Barcelona. In 1984, he pulled over to the side of the motorway in between Barcelona and Lleida to fix a flat tyre on his car when he was mowed down in a hit-and-run incident. He fought for 23 days in a coma before slipping away. Barça's fans were devastated. 'Goodbye to the battering ram,' remarked Juan José Castillo, one of Spain's iconic broadcasters.

6. PEOPLE SHOULD TALK ABOUT YOU EVEN IF IT IS GOOD

1.

HH's first test as Barça coach came at the end of the 1957/58 season. Barça were representing the city of Barcelona in the final of the Fairs Cup, a tournament conceived under FIFA's auspices to promote international trade fairs. Some cities sent individual teams to represent them. Inter, for example, represented the city of Milan. Other cities sent representative teams, culled from several clubs. The competition became a consolation prize for teams – like Barça – who struggled to qualify for the European Cup in the late 1950s and 1960s. Real Madrid's president Santiago Bernabéu referred to it as 'the Villages Cup'.

Barça drew 2–2 with London in the first leg of the 1958 final, which was played at Stamford Bridge, a few weeks before HH's arrival. The tournament had kicked off way back in 1955. In the second leg of the final, which was played at the Camp Nou, London had a useful starting XI, a representative team selected from London's 11 Football League clubs' finest players, including Jimmy Greaves, Danny Blanchflower and England's best player at the time, Johnny Haynes. HH's Barça crushed them 6–0. Eulogio Martínez scored, and both Luisito Suárez and Evaristo scored a brace.

The rout was an indication of the raw material at HH's disposal. The Hungarian forwards, Sándor Kocsis and Zoltán Czibor, were also set to be incorporated into his squad in the summer. Everywhere he looked, HH had cannons to fire. Behind them, he had a solid base of Catalans, all internationals for Spain: in goal, Ramallets, a hero from the 1950 World Cup in Brazil; and Ferran Olivella, Joan Segarra, Enric Gensana, Sígfrid Gràcia, Rodri and Martí Vergés to choose from in defence and midfield for five positions.

In preseason, HH's Barça racked up 26 goals in five games during a tour of Switzerland, Belgium and the Netherlands. When their league campaign started, they continued to crush teams. In their first six games, they went unbeaten, scoring 22 goals. In week seven, they met Real Madrid at the Camp Nou, and smashed Di Stéfano's team 4–0. Their work seemed easy. The goals flew in. It was like shelling peas.

Another key test arrived in February 1959 when they visited San Mamés Stadium in Bilbao – killing fields. Athletic Bilbao had won the title in 1956, and they were known to be a team of hard bastards, especially in their own stadium. At this point, Barça were top of the table, and Athletic were lying in third. Tejada scored in the first half to put Barça in front. Ignacio Uribe equalised for Athletic. Then Eulogio Martínez got a red card, and Barça were down to 10 men. HH brushed it off.

'Herrera had so much personality,' said Tejada. 'He coined some famous phrases. One of them was that day in Bilbao after Martínez was sent off, [when] he said to us: "We play better with 10 than 11." It was a nightmare to win at San Mamés in those days. Athletic's nickname was the "Lions". It wasn't just any old team. Their fans used to go crazy in the terraces, but Herrera could convince you of anything.'

Herrera's 10 men beat Athletic that afternoon. Joan Segarra scored a late winner. Barça won 2–1.

2.

In March 1959, Barça travelled down to Seville to play Real Betis. There were five league games to go in the season and they were only two points ahead of Real Madrid. They couldn't afford a slip-up. Real Betis had lost only once at home that season – to Real Madrid, 3–2, back in October. HH decided to make some mischief, announcing before the match that it would be easy for Barça. 'We'll win without getting off the bus,' he said. It was an instant newspaper headline. They went buck-mad in Seville. Barça left Barcelona on Thursday night and arrived in Seville on Saturday, on the eve of the match. By this stage, the Andalusian city was baying for Catalan blood.

'Herrera's statement created a mess,' said Tejada. 'On the Saturday, we went to the cinema on Las Sierpes. We couldn't get in. We had to go back to the hotel. People were jumping on top of us. It was scary. The following day, the fans at the stadium were going crazy.'

There was bedlam inside the ground. Half an hour before kick-off, HH put on his beige trench coat and left the dressing room. He started circling the pitch, goading the home fans. They hurled missiles at him – coins, stones, shoes – and yelled abuse. He did about four or five laps of the pitch and then returned to the dressing room: 'Don't worry, *muchachos*, their fans are tired of screaming. They're hoarse – they won't bother you anymore!'

However, Barça's players still had to contend with the players. 'The Betis players murdered us with kicks,' recalled Tejada. 'They kept cursing us during the game over Herrera's phrase. You could tell that they were furious about it.' But they couldn't convert their rage into enough goals. Barça won 5–2.

After the game, Barça's president Francesc Miró-Sans went down to congratulate his triumphant players in their dressing room. As soon as HH saw him coming, he gathered his players around him and started shouting: 'Come on, boys! A big round of applause for the president. He has just doubled our match-winning bonus!' Miró-Sans froze. HH had him over a barrel.

The players couldn't get enough of their coach. Or most of them couldn't – the ones who followed his orders. He kept them winning football matches. And they kept earning bigger bonuses. 'Before games, Herrera would get everyone singing on the bus,' said Tejada. 'We'd sing songs like, "Nobody can beat, nobody can beat / Herrera's boys! / Forget all the failures with the other coaches / This is a new era, a new era / Always with Herrera, always with Herrera!"

'Herrera couldn't wipe the smile off his face.'

3.

Two weeks after the win against Real Betis, Barça were on the road again. They flew to the Canary Islands to play Las Palmas, who were in a relegation battle. Barça were still top of the table, still two points ahead of Real Madrid, with three rounds of games to go. Facing the press before the game, HH was in a buoyant mood. He told journalists in Las Palmas that if Barça lost, they wouldn't return to Barcelona; instead they would go straight to Madrid to train hard for their penultimate match – a tough fixture against Atlético Madrid in their stadium, the Metropolitano. Someone asked a follow-up question about where he saw himself the following week. 'Enjoying a vermut in the *Ciudad Condal*,' he quipped, referring to Barcelona's nickname, the 'City of Counts', which reflects its historical place as the seat of the Counts of Barcelona.

The local press in the Canaries hated his boasting, but HH backed it up with results: Barça defeated Las Palmas 2–0 and could return to Barcelona for some rest before their important tie against Atlético. HH was incorrigible. He used the press to turn himself into a star. He understood how show business worked, that all he had to do was keep talking and keep winning. He was a provocateur, a magnet for attention. He dressed smartly, in three-piece suits, but with a dash of colour: a splash of yellow in his tie or alligator shoes, like a gangster. Not loud, but a bit sudden, as the English used to say. Anything so he could stand out from the crowd.

HH always had to be the centre of the story. He knew that publicity helped him climb the ladder more quickly. Needling rival fans could be more profitable than charming them. People would pay money to see him beaten, defeated, quietened. The goading, the outrageous comments kept him in the public eye. It enabled him to become more famous than his players – so he could be better paid than them – and certainly more notorious than his club presidents.

'Herrera's ego was gigantic,' remarked Alfredo Relaño. 'He was funny. He wasn't arrogant. He was an absurd character. He said arrogant things, but he did it because he was playing a game with the media. He knew it was important to be famous to earn more money, which is partly why he would say shocking things.' Relaño recalled HH asserting: 'People should talk about you even if it is good' – meaning that if it is bad, so much the better. And further: 'Herrera was an ambitious guy to the point of being immoral, although I don't think he was a bad man. He did whatever it took to win football matches, to make money. He didn't have any scruples.'

Underpinning HH's bravura was insecurity. Somewhere buried within his soul, he needed to assert himself. 'Herrera was always saying, "I'm the best",' declared Pere Escobar. 'He kept repeating it throughout his career. It showed he wasn't sure he really was the best. If he had been so sure, he wouldn't have felt the need to reiterate it constantly. You'd need to speak to a psychologist about it, but his results validated his work.'

Barça drew 1–1 with Atlético Madrid. The draw was enough to clinch the league title with a game to spare. It was the club's first championship win in six years. Finally, Barça qualified for the European Cup. HH's team had smashed all kinds of records, including their points tally. They went undefeated all season at the Camp Nou: 15 games, 15 wins. They set a new goalscoring record: 96, averaging more than three goals a game. The club's board of directors organised a banquet to celebrate the title. A thousand guests were handpicked for the dinner. HH wasn't allowed to speak. The president, Francesc Miró-Sans, who dedicated the victory to Franco, was jealous of HH's growing popularity.

4.

HH didn't have time to dwell on slights. His sights were set on closing out the season by winning the double. To do so, Barça would have to overcome Real Madrid, who had just won their fourth European Cup, in the semi-final of the Copa del Generalísimo, Spain's cup competition, renamed in honour of General Franco. The tie was over two legs, the first in Madrid, four days after Real Madrid's European Cup final win over a Reims team featuring Just Fontaine.

And so the mind games began. Before the match, HH told the press that Barça could lose by two goals, and it wouldn't matter because his side would thrash Real Madrid back at the Camp Nou in the second leg. His players didn't know what to make of his comments. Barça went in at half time 2–0 down.

Segarra, Barça's captain, was disturbed by HH's attitude. 'You see what a fucking mess he's made of our heads? They're walking all over us. Don't ask him anything. It's all our fault,' he told a teammate on the way into the dressing room for the half-time break.

HH strolled into the dressing room. He closed the door, took off his coat and began shouting: 'Very good, lads, very good! We have them where we want them. They will wilt. Now, in the second half, we will win.'

Segarra, playing in defence, was unconvinced. He thought HH was a fool, but his words came to pass. Two of Real Madrid's players faded in the early summer heat. Substitutions weren't allowed at the time, and the team collapsed. Barça went to town with the extra space, scoring four goals in the second half to win 4–2. By full-time, Segarra was a converted disciple. 'I remember Martí Vergés [a midfield teammate], as if it was now, saying: "This guy is a magician."'

Barça then won the second leg 3–1 to advance to the final, which would be played at Real Madrid's stadium. Victory in enemy territory would leave a particularly sweet taste in the mouth for Barça's fans. All Barça had to do was overcome Granada.

HH used a different psychological approach this time. He gave no hostages to fortune to the press. He was low-key. He didn't feed them any sticks to beat his men. But his prematch team speech – behind closed doors – was a stirring call to arms.

'A man can lose a game,' he told his players. 'This is a game. It can happen. But he must have a clear conscience. He must know that he has tended to every detail. That he has not forgotten anything. That he knows everything he needs to know. His obligation is to have everything ready. Before you go out on the pitch, I want you to think about your children, your wives, your parents. Surely, they are listening to the match on the radio. They are suffering for you. I don't think it's too much to ask of you: to work for an hour and a half for them. For your pride. For your dignity. With an hour and a half of work well done, you will make them happy for a week. They will be able to go out on to the street happy. They will be congratulated. You have no choice but to give it your all.'

HH's men won 4–1.

7. THE FACE YOU SAW EVERYWHERE

1.

I often pass Enrique Vila-Matas. Spain's greatest living novelist, according to Roberto Bolaño, lives a block away in Barcelona's neighbourhood of Eixample. I see him shuffling around the streets in his black trench coat, looking like a character from a film noir. He has a pair of hooded eyes. He's reserved, like a lot of Catalans, the kind of person who smiles but never laughs. He says he has a sense of humour about everything except football.

Barça fans 'suffer' a lot during games. They will tell you in advance they are going to 'suffer'. After a good result against a difficult opponent, they announce proudly that they 'suffered'. It's almost as if they seek out the suffering.

I spot Vila-Matas most regularly in Bernat, a bookstore around the corner from his apartment building. The bookstore has been on Buenos Aires Street since the 1970s. The floor is panelled with wood. It has a café inside, and plays jazz music softly throughout the day. There's usually a copy of Vila-Matas's latest novel on display in the window. Pep Guardiola is a fan of his books, and has known the author since he was a Barça player in the 1990s.

Barcelona is peppered with bookstores. On the Festa de Sant Jordi, on 23 April, there's a tradition whereby couples exchange books and roses. (The day celebrates Catalonia's patron saint, Saint George, whose flag is stitched into Barça's crest.) The city's pavements are taken over with bookstalls and vendors of roses. It's charming. Barça, like the city of Barcelona, is enamoured with books.

There are libraries full of books on its football stars and the history and identity of Barça. What it means to be a *culé*, a Barça fan, and the club's position as a flagbearer for Catalonia's push for independence. The navel-gazing reflects a curiosity, and an insecurity about the club's history. Real Madrid feels more secure about their place in the world. You could hardly fill a bookshelf with the number of books written about Real Madrid. The club is concerned only with success, with looking ahead, not backwards or inwards.

The difference in approach to the Spanish Civil War in the cities of Barcelona and Madrid is curious. At a civic level, Barcelona remembers it; Catalonia has more civil war museums than any other region in Spain. Madrid – although enduring the worst of the fighting – has airbrushed it from memory. Madrid, for example, doesn't have any plaques at notable fortifications in the city like, say, the Parque del Oeste.

It's impossible to avoid the ghosts of Barça in the city. Josep Samitier, Barça's first great idol, from his days as a star in the 1920s – and a man who made the mistake of crossing HH – was born on the same street where Vila-Matas lives. If you head northwards from his apartment building towards Tibidabo, crossing Diagonal – the long avenue where Franco's troops marched into the city in January 1939 – you'll hit Casa Tejada, a tapas bar that Tejada opened in 1964 as his football career came to a close. One street over from the apartment building of Vila-Matas, Sándor Kocsis, the Hungarian striker on HH's Barça team, also ran a bar.

In between that bar, which trades under a different name these days, and the apartment building of Vila-Matas, is the site where Barça's old stadium stood. It was at its height just after the First World War. Known as the '*Camp del carrer Indústria*', it held around 6000 spectators. When it overflowed, passers-by outside were met with the sight of a line of backsides draped over the stadium wall. *Cul* means 'ass' in Catalan. Ever since then, Barça fans have been known as '*culers*' or '*culés*'.

2.

Vila-Matas is related to Francesc Miró-Sans, the man who signed HH for Barça in 1958. Miró-Sans is his 'second uncle'. The architect of the Camp Nou, Francesc Mitjans Miró, also married into the family, and Vila-Matas was at the Camp Nou the day it was opened in September 1957. As a kid, on the day of games at the Camp Nou, he went with several members of his family, all season ticket holders. They sat together behind the north-end goal and knew everyone sitting close to them. Barça is a family club in that sense. When Vila-Matas thinks about those games, he remembers the smell of cigars, an odour he associates with football and bullfighting.

'As you can imagine, being from Barça meant you were militating for a certain *catalanismo*,' he recalled, 'but nobody in the stadium was visibly political. There weren't any demonstrations against rival teams. There were no placards. You had police inside the stadium. You could end up in jail if you put a foot wrong. It was like living in an Eastern Bloc country.'

'I remember as a boy going to the Bernabéu with my father. I was about 10 years old. We were close to the directors' box where Franco was seated. It was a Real Madrid versus Barcelona match. My father all of a sudden told me: "If Barcelona scores a goal, keep your mouth shut and don't move. Don't say, 'Goal!' Don't say a word because we're beside Franco. We're in a totally different stadium to normal." It wasn't because of Franco's presence he gave me this warning; it was because of the atmosphere in the stadium. It was unthinkable that you would cheer a goal for Barcelona. It was a shock for a young boy because it was instinctive that I would celebrate a goal for Barcelona, but not on that day. It made an impact on me because I had no idea it was so dangerous.'

Vila-Matas was born in 1948. It's not surprising that the figure of Franco made an impression on him as a child growing up in the 1950s. 'We were conscious that he was a dictator. In theory, he banned Catalan. Catalan was the mother tongue of my family. With my sisters, my parents, everyone in my family – we spoke in Catalan,' he asserted, banging the table with his knuckles. 'We spoke Catalan all the time. I wrote in Spanish, but we knew that Franco had banned the Catalan language. We lived in a police state.'

When Vila-Matas was in his early twenties, he remembers having problems with the police. In 1970, he went to Montserrat for a meeting of intellectuals. Montserrat is a mystical place. If you were hunting for the soul of Catalonia, it would be a good place to start. Catalans get goose pimples when you ask them to describe Montserrat. It's about an hour's drive north-west of Barcelona, and the site of a monastery spectacularly chiselled into a mountainside. Pilgrims have gone there since the twelfth century. Heinrich Himmler visited in 1940, convinced that he would find the Holy Grail – the talisman that would win the war. Thirty years later, Vila-Matas and artists like Joan Miró met together at Montserrat for three days to protest against the Franco regime. As a result, they were persecuted.

'It damaged me a lot,' said Vila-Matas. 'I got fined. They sent me to Africa to do military service. I got a feeling of how dangerous the regime was and how easy it was to end up in prison. I did things before that could have got me imprisoned, like carrying communist propaganda in a car to another destination. If you were stopped by the Guardia Civil, and they found what you were carrying, you could end up in prison for six years.

'After military service, I went to Paris in 1974. Franco was about to die. It's surreal, but the thing that struck me most in the city was that there were *terrazas* with tables alongside each other, and people spoke and chatted out loud. In Barcelona, this wasn't possible. You couldn't speak critically about Franco out loud. Or you couldn't hail a taxi because all the taxi drivers were informers. People whispered because you were afraid you would be denounced by someone at the table beside you. It was unforgettable – this sense of freedom in Paris. It was intoxicating. I'll never forget it.'

3.

The memories of Vila-Matas, and the prohibition of the Catalan language, tally with those of Tejada. People spoke Spanish in public places. When Tejada joined Barça in 1950, he remembers his coach pulling him aside one day. Ramón Llorens asked him: 'Are you Catalan?' Tejada was born in Barcelona, although his parents were born outside Catalonia. When he told him he was Catalan, Llorens replied: 'Good, from tomorrow, here you speak Catalan.' But they had to be careful.

A brief history lesson. Catalan is more than a dialect. It's a language closer to French than the Spanish spoken across the rest of the country (Castilian Spanish). This was a surprise to me when I moved to Barcelona, hearing this strange sound on the streets. The people in Barcelona use it as their first language. Schooling is done through Catalan, as are Barça press conferences when the club has a Catalan coach.

Catalonia, this region in the north-east of Spain, with a population close to 8 million, has a tradition of independence stretching back a thousand years. Its parliament is older than Westminster. It has always fancied itself as a beacon for freedom and expression. For progress. It had its own bill of rights 150 years before the Magna Carta. It's always been prosperous, too. As a Mediterranean port, Barcelona jockeyed with Genoa and Venice during the Middle Ages for mastery of the spice trade, which brought its merchants vast wealth.

The region hit its golden age in the fourteenth century. Most of Barcelona's solid, austere buildings in the Gothic Quarter and the district known as El Born were built back then, including several of its giant churches, such as Santa María del Mar (which has a stained-glass window inside with the Barça crest). Once the Atlantic eclipsed the Mediterranean as the world's foremost trading route, though, Barcelona began to decline.

Politically, two key events copper-fastened Catalonia's demise (although as recently as the 1930s, Barcelona's population was greater than Madrid's). It lost its lands north of the Pyrenees to France in the seventeenth century after the War of the Reapers. And at the start of the eighteenth century, in 1714, following a 14-month siege, it fell under the rule of Madrid when it lost a succession race for the Spanish Crown. The day of its defeat, 11 September, is remembered as Catalonia's National Day of Independence. At the time of writing, Barça fans chant for 'independence' at the 17th minute of each half during games at the Camp Nou.

When the city surrendered in 1714, writing and teaching in Catalan were banned. Books were burned. The city's university was closed. A light went out. In the nineteenth century, the territory's national identity began to flourish again, experiencing a cultural revival. Catalan publishing houses sprung up. Barcelona's great opera house, the Liceu, opened its doors. Walking groups, as part of a movement known as *Excursionisme*, took to hiking around the mountains in the province of Tarragona and the Pyrenees in search of the spirit of Catalonia. Catalan painters decamped to the countryside to paint in the open air.

Modernisme, an artistic movement, left its mark all over Barcelona, most notably with the construction of Eixample, the fashionable neighbourhood where Vila-Matas lives, with its octagon-shaped blocks. Gaudí set to work on the Sagrada Família basilica and his unrivalled portfolio of buildings and parks. Separatist political parties began nourishing grievances and stoking resentment towards Madrid, the region's traditional oppressor. It was against this background – of renaissance and national identity – that Barça was founded in 1899. It had a patriotic agenda. Significantly, its city rival Espanyol – or 'The Spanish One' in English – made King Alfonso XIII its patron.

With time, Barça became a powerful symbol of the city's greatness and a flagbearer for the region: 'the unarmed army of Catalonia' in the evocative words of author Manuel Vázquez Montalbán. The club has always been a political project – though how militant it is depends on its president. In 1937, for example, at the height of the civil war, Barça went on a four-month fundraising tour to Mexico and the United States as a representative of Republican Catalonia. By contrast, when HH was coaching at Barça in the late 1950s, its role as ambassador was lying dormant. This was precisely at the moment Real Madrid – led by the brilliance of Di Stéfano – became Spain's ambassador on the international stage. At a time when he was an international pariah, Franco hijacked Real Madrid's success for propaganda purposes.

He had already taken the wind out of Barça's political sails. At the end of the Spanish Civil War in 1939, the club's name was changed from FC Barcelona – *el Futbol Club de Barcelona*, in Catalan – to CF Barcelona – *Club de Fútbol Barcelona*, in Spanish. Barça's club crest was also altered: the four red bars in the Catalan flag, *la Senyera*, were replaced with Spain's triband of red and double width of yellow in the centre. In 1949, Salvador Grau Mora, a club member, suggested to Barça's president that the *Senyera* be returned to the crest to coincide with the club's 50th anniversary celebrations. For this, he was tossed into jail.

Barça's files were pored over by secret police. The club became a focal point for anti-Franco feeling in Catalonia. Its fans, after centuries of oppression in their region, developed a tendency to wallow in misery. And at this time, they fixated on the loss of Di Stéfano. The Argentine maestro joined Real Madrid in 1953 – over Barcelona – in a transfer saga that is still disputed, and which has been unpicked in countless books and documentaries. The reason is that Di Stéfano was a colossus, a player who precipitated a shift in the balance of power in Spanish football. Before joining Real Madrid, the club hadn't won a league title in 20 years. With Di Stéfano, it won eight in 11 seasons and became unbeatable in Europe.

Barça were consumed with Real Madrid, who replaced Espanyol and the Basque clubs as its chief rival in the 1950s. Real Madrid were full of daring and defiance. Self-doubt never visited this club. By contrast, Barça shrunk in on itself and developed an inferiority complex. Di Stéfano led a team that conquered the world. Barça's *victimismo* caused it to revel in conspiracies, real and imagined. That Di Stéfano was robbed from them. That all refs were crooked. That Franco persecuted them. 'Losing league titles in the last game because of decisions by God and the Generalísimo,' as they say in Barcelona. Slights. Injustices. Setbacks. Looking for excuses why they couldn't win. It made losing – their political autonomy and football matches – easier to take. Barça became its own jailor. It was a choice that was made – this sickness developed. *Madriditis* – fear of Madrid. HH had to break that defeatist mindset.

'Barça has built itself a legend of victimhood,' said Alfredo Relaño, author and newspaper editor. 'Take, for example, the murder of Josep Sunyol. He was a deputy with the political party Esquerra Republicana de Catalunya (ERC). He resigned from the presidency of Barça in July 1936. He was killed in the mountains outside Madrid in August 1936. It was a disgraceful crime, but it had nothing to do with Barça or football.'

Yet politics and football are always mixed, although the lines are often blurred. It couldn't be otherwise. To borrow a phrase from *The New Yorker*'s film critic Anthony Lane, to separate them would be like taking the sweat out of sex. '¡*Visca el Barça!* ¡*Visca Catalunya!*' is the rallying cry of Barcelona's players to fans whenever their club captain holds aloft a trophy. During HH's time as Barça coach in the late 1950s, though, politics could only be hinted at among his players, beyond the political act of speaking Catalan.

'Because there were so many foreigners in the squad – Czibor, Kocsis, Kubala, Villaverde, Eulogio, Evaristo and Herrera – we spoke mainly in Spanish. But the Catalans – eight, nine of us were Catalan – we spoke Catalan amongst ourselves. Kubala and the other players, we never talked about politics. Today, footballers talk about politics all the time. Today 90 per cent of football is politics. In my era, one per cent of football was about politics. You couldn't talk about it. If you spoke badly about Franco, you were finished. As footballers, more than anyone, we couldn't speak out,' Tejada told me, laughing ridiculously at the notion.

Meddling with politics raises the stakes. 'It's the problem with this slogan *més que un club*,' said Vila-Matas, referencing the motto that Barça adopted in the 1960s. '"More than a club." Why can't it just be "a club"? All that I want as a fan is a football club that wins its matches. *Més que un club* only complicates matters.'

'Barça is a patriotic cause, the idea of dying for your country,' added Relaño. 'In Madrid, it's not a matter of patriotism. We're very proud of Real Madrid's success in the city. In Madrid, the Prado Museum is more important than any other institution. In Barcelona, what is most important is Barça. More than the Sagrada Família. It has a symbolism for reasons of local pride, and also for nationalist reasons. In Barcelona, if you're not a Barça fan it would be impossible to get a job as a newspaper editor. I have friends from Barcelona who are Espanyol fans. But they can't triumph as journalists in Barcelona. Here in Madrid, you can be from Atlético; there are a lot of Atleti fans in the press. In Barcelona, if you are not a fan of Barça, you are against Catalonia. It would be seen as disloyal, treacherous – to be against your country.'

4.

Francesc Miró-Sans, the 'second uncle' of Vila-Matas, made his money from textiles like several of Barça's presidents in the twentieth century. Franco was good for business; the textile industry thrived under his protectionist regime. It was only after Franco's death – and the transition to a democratic regime – that competition from cheap foreign clothing imports killed profits. Once Franco began bedding in his dictatorship in 1939, artists and intellectuals fled the country or went to ground. Businesspeople, though, found ways to prosper.

Miró-Sans had a framed portrait of Franco behind his office desk at the club. Nothing unusual there: the most powerful man in the history of Spain was omnipresent. His was the face that you saw everywhere: in newspapers and magazines; on the walls of shops; on street names (Barcelona's Diagonal was called Avenida del Generalísimo Francisco Franco); on coins; on stamps; on propaganda newsreels at the cinema; towering above you on horseback in imposing statues in Barcelona and Madrid; in official classroom portraits (to the right of the crucifix); and he was prayed for in churches on Sunday mornings, compared with the Archangel Gabriel. *Homo missus à Deo cui nomen erat Franciscus* – the man sent by God whose name is Francisco. Franco didn't have to answer to anyone. He was responsible only to God and to history.

One of the features of living in Spain today is the disappearance of Franco from public discourse. He died in 1975 – a protracted, painful death. He had three heart attacks in October 1975, only days after executing five political prisoners. He was operated on several times the following month in a makeshift operating theatre in his palace, El Pardo. He was kept alive by blood transfusions but in great agony. 'Dear God,' he complained, 'how long it takes to die.'

Since his death, a veil of silence has descended. Once he was everywhere in the country. Now he has vanished. As if scrubbed out by washing detergent. My four-year-old son, Liam, came home one day from school singing a rhyme in

Spanish from the days of *franquismo* (sung to the tune of the Spanish national anthem): 'Franco, Franco / He has a white ass / Because his wife / She washes it with Ariel / Franco, Franco...'

Miró-Sans, the president of Barça, was careful to pay his respects to Franco. He was a businessman and he couldn't afford idealism, especially *catalanismo*. He was careful to conduct Barça's board meetings in Spanish, not Catalan, the language his Catalan players used on the training ground.

'He was a Franquista,' remarked Escobar. 'In every walk of life there are degrees. He was on the side of Franco for pragmatic reasons. As we say here: "Cash is cash" – let's sort out the cash first and then we can talk about rights and principles. There's a lot of people like that in life. It's a question of priorities – in a club like Barça, in the country, in how a match might unfold, in politics, with people in general.'

David Salinas, a writer with *Sport*, concurred: 'In that era you couldn't be an *independentista*. Miró-Sans had business interests. He kept onside with the regime. It wouldn't have served his interests to be critical of Franco. A rebel would never be president of Barça in the 1950s. A lot of people thought one thing and said the other. It was a hard decade under *franquismo*. You couldn't go against the regime. If you did, you were asking for problems for your wife, your children, your siblings, the rest of your family. For your livelihood.'

The unspoken intimidation was evident in the terraces at the Camp Nou, too, added Salinas: 'You couldn't openly criticise Franco in 1959 or you'd be tossed in prison. Fans at the Camp Nou shouted and whistled by instinct, but little else. They were cowed. They were afraid. When Real Madrid ran out on to the pitch, Barça fans applauded them. They didn't know who was beside them, watching them. They put on a front that they didn't feel in their hearts.'

The upper middle-class family of Vila-Matas were an interesting, and not unusual, mix for Catalans in the 1950s. His immediate family were left wing. They voted for Esquerra Republicana de Catalunya, the region's separatist party on the political left. Barça's president at the start of the Spanish Civil War, Josep Sunyol, was a member of parliament for Esquerra Republicana de Catalunya. The grandfather of Vila-Matas was a friend of Lluís Companys, a Republican, who was president of Catalonia from 1934 until he was executed by a firing squad on Montjuïc in 1940. Miró-Sans, however, was on the other side of the political divide.

'My uncle Miró-Sans and his family were all bourgeois,' said Vila-Matas. 'They were from the right wing, like all the bourgeoisie. They were *franquista* but they didn't call themselves *franquista*. They toed the line. They abided by the rules of *franquismo* because the civil war was so horrible. They preferred the tranquillity of an "ordered" life. I wouldn't describe Miró-Sans as a pragmatist.

He was sympathetic to Franco, but he wasn't like the far-right parties today in Europe. He wasn't an extreme right-wing person. He was only thinking about how to do business, and how to get things done under *franquismo*.'

Barça were at a crossroads. They had a Franco-supporting president, yet the majority of their working-class fanbase were anti-Franco. Their fans were getting testy. With Fidel Castro's storming of Havana in January 1959, revolution was in the air. In the early months of 1959, Josep Benet, a Catalan nationalist, came up with the idea for a 'P' campaign. 'P' stood for *protesta*. People began scrawling 'P' on walls all over the city of Barcelona.

In June 1959, Luis de Galinsoga, director of *La Vanguardia*, Barcelona's leading newspaper, became irritated because the homily in his church was in Catalan. In a fit of pique, he pronounced a phrase that no Franco regime stooge had uttered in public before, despite wanting to: 'All Catalans are pieces of shit.' Catalans boycotted his newspaper. Sales dropped by 10,000. Several months later, in February 1960, there were protests against De Galinsoga outside the Camp Nou after a Barça v Real Oviedo game. Franco's government was obliged to sack him. It was a small victory for *catalanismo*.

8. THEIR TONGUES WERE 'DIRTY'

1.

When I moved to Barcelona in 2010, I chaired an English conversation class for an hour each week, in exchange for free Spanish classes at a language institute. There were about 15 students in the class. The majority were middle-aged, and I picked a different topic each week for debate – Spanish cuisine, say, or overtourism. We discussed the ban on bullfighting one week, as Catalonia became the first mainland region in Spain to ban it that year. There was skin and hair flying. Two fellas had to be almost pulled off each other.

One week, I announced we'd chat about the Spanish Civil War. There was silence. When they talked, it was only hesitatingly. I couldn't believe it. I'm Irish. We had a civil war in the 1920s. I remember my granny had a 'Republican room' in her house where gunmen on the run slept. I grew up during a civil war in Northern Ireland, Britain's 'dirty war', which went on for decades. Endless no-warning terrorist bombs. Children maimed and killed. Irish people of my age and my parents' generation can discuss relatively freely either civil war. In Spain, it's a different story. It's too raw.

There is a sense, according to the writer Colm Tóibín, in which there was two civil wars in Spain: one for outsiders like Ernest Hemingway and W.H. Auden (who wrote about 'the necessary murder'), which has been romanticised; the other one for Spanish people living in a country that tore itself apart, and who suffered the consequences for the rest of their lives, compounded by the investment of terror during Franco's long-running dictatorship.

There is also the unresolved issue of the dead – more than 100,000, including the poet and playwright Federico García Lorca – who lie in unmarked graves. Only Cambodia has more mass graves than Spain. There was nothing heroic or romantic about the war for Spaniards. It was different to the 'cause' that led foreign intellectuals like the poet Auden, who volunteered as an ambulance driver, and religious crusaders to get involved. Spaniards' memories of it – which evoke pain and fear – have been repressed.

'We never spoke about the Spanish Civil War in our homes in the 1950s,' said Vila-Matas. 'I was born only nine years after the war ended. People simply didn't speak about it. It was only mentioned during mealtimes if, as a child, you weren't eating your food: "Eat up because during the war people were very hungry." It was the only reference. The hunger during the war was appalling.

'I got more information from books than my family. I remember there was a book in English by the historian Hugh Thomas entitled *The Spanish Civil War*, which came out in the 1960s. It was the first time I was able to read something about it. That book wasn't censored. It's like the Covid pandemic. People don't want to talk about what happened because it reminds them of something horrible. It pains us to talk about these things.'

The blood spilled by both sides in the Spanish Civil War was horrific. In the Republican zone, anarchist death squads went on vicious killing sprees. Law and order collapsed. Thousands of common criminals were released from prison. Old scores were settled. Landowners, merchants, Army officers who sided with Franco and the clergy – in particular – were hunted down and killed. Churches and convents were sacked. Republicans, as heirs of the French Revolution, were intent on breaking the power of the Catholic Church. The clergy were singled out as a class enemy, reviled because they ingratiated themselves with property owners and factory bosses, and for using the confessional to seduce their congregation. 'The Church must disappear forever,' insisted an editorial in an anarchist trade union periodical in the summer of 1936. 'Churches will no longer be used for filthy pimping.' Spaniards have always followed their priests either with a candle or a club.

In the last week of July 1936, 160 priests and nuns were shot in Catalonia. Groups of priests hid in the dressing rooms of Barça while awaiting safe passage out of Catalonia. In October 1936, a Carmelite priest, recovering from wounds, was grabbed from a hospital in Barcelona and thrown into the sea down the coast at Garraf. Lurid newspaper headlines by the foreign press in Catalonia, such as 'PRIESTS DIE PRAYING' and propaganda stories of naked nuns forced to dance in public and gang-raped by Republican militiamen, caused consternation overseas. The hysteria prompted a flood of international brigades into volunteering for a religious crusade.

An Irish brigade, for example, set sail for Spain in December 1936 to fight on Franco's side. They were absorbed into the Spanish Foreign Legion, and performed adequately on a quiet stretch of the front until ordered to attack. Their unit leader, Eoin O'Duffy, didn't fancy their chances, sensing too much danger afoot (even with God on their side), so Franco sent the brigade home in disgrace. The Irish writer Brendan Behan said they were the only army that went to war and came home with more men.

According to Paul Preston, one of the world's foremost historians of twentieth-century Spain, Franco's forces carried out three times more repression than the Republican side. The atrocities carried out behind Republican lines weren't as systematic as Franco's purges, nor as perverse. Antonio Vallejo-Nájera, Franco's notorious head of psychiatric services, experimented on Republican prisoners to locate 'the red gene'. More than anything, what petrified people across Spain was the violence unleashed by Franco's Army of Africa.

2.

Franco's so-called Column of Death were the shock troops of Spain's colonial army. Volunteer infantrymen. Mercenaries brutalised by their time in North Africa, as Franco had been. The bloodthirsty soldier in Franco was forged by his tours of duty in Morocco. He spent a decade in the desert. The violence there dehumanised him. In his war diaries, published in 1922, he writes matter-of-factly about sacking Moroccan villages. Prisoners were decapitated. In one passage, he remembers a captain ordering his men to stop firing because their targets were women. When a legionnaire protested ('but they are factories for baby Moors'), Franco records they all burst out laughing.

As Franco's legionnaires laid waste to Republican Spain, they applied techniques learned in Morocco. Franco likened Spain's proletariat to Moroccans – they were an inferior race who must be subjugated by torture and killing. The violence served a double purpose. It laid the foundations for the authoritarian regime that was to come, cowing the population, eliminating 'without scruple or hesitation those who do not think as we do,' as Emilio Mola, one of his generals, remarked.

Franco's legionnaires were recruited with promises of pillage. When a town or village was captured, they were given free rein for two hours. Shops were looted. Casualties were mutilated: ears, noses, sexual organs, heads were cut off. Sick people were buried alive. Hand grenades were tossed into hospital wards. Left-wing women who weren't shot or raped were humiliated. Their heads were shaved, and they were forced to swallow castor oil because their tongues were 'dirty'.

Executions were held in public, with the entire village forced to watch. Often the local priest recommended who was to be shot. To be a Republican signified to be condemned to death. There was nowhere to hide. Franco wouldn't consider an armistice, only unconditional surrender. He was bent on a slow war of annihilation. He preferred a total purge of conquered territory to a swift victory. As they marched up through Spain from Seville, word of the Spanish Foreign Legion's slaughter spread like rolling thunder. They generated paralysing terror, which is why the roads from Catalonia to France in January 1939 became clogged with refugees fleeing the Legion's imminent arrival.

3.

There are a hundred reasons why Spain imploded in July 1936. In the decades before, the country had been torn by a perpetual civil war. Between 1814 and 1923, there were 43 coups d'état. Surely a record. Conflicting ideologies left people cockeyed: Left v Right; church v anti-clericalism; democracy v despotism; republicanism v monarchism; regionalism v centralism; unions v the landed classes. Even the Left couldn't agree with each other, as Barcelona exploded in fighting between communists and anarchists in 1937.

When Franco's troops reached Catalonia, however, the focus was narrowed. It was about bringing a region to heel. Other ideological quarrels took a back seat. The rampaging became tribal. Racist in some people's minds. None of Franco's conquering generals referred to eliminating communism or anarchism in the region. In *The Spanish Holocaust*, the historian Paul Preston notes that their mission was to conquer Catalonia. One of Franco's officers told a Portuguese journalist the only solution to the 'Catalan problem' was to 'kill the Catalans. It's just a question of time.' Franco's brother-in-law Ramón Serrano Suñer, who later became his Minister of Foreign Affairs, believed the Catalans to be 'morally and politically sick'.

Once a village in Catalonia was captured, the Catalan language was banned, even though many villagers spoke no other tongue. There's evidence that peasants were shot for speaking Catalan. In El Pallars Sobirà, an area in the Pyrenees, 'suspect inhabitants' were rounded up. A 17-year-old girl asked to go along as an interpreter for her mother, who didn't speak Spanish. She was forced to watch her mother being executed, then the girl was gang-raped and killed herself.

Maials is another small Catalan village close to the foothills of the Pyrenees. It's about half an hour's drive from Lleida, the city where Enric Gensana – the towering defender on HH's Barça team – grew up. On Christmas Eve 1938, two years after Gensana was born, at least four women were raped by Franco's soldiers in Maials. One of the women was raped while her husband and seven-year-old son were forced to watch at gunpoint. In Marganell, a tiny nearby village, two women were raped, and killed afterwards by hand grenades placed between their legs. Atrocities that live on in folk memory. That same year Rodri, Gensana's partner in HH's defence, also lost his father, who died on a hill in Aragón fighting Franco's Army, aged 24. The son he left behind, who would go on to become an international footballer, was only two years old.

The Spanish Foreign Legion's carnage in Catalonia got so out of control that even Franco baulked, issuing an order that troops try to avoid 'errors' that might cause regret in the future. Yet when Juan Yagüe, who was known as the 'Butcher of Badajoz', reached the city of Barcelona in January 1939, he gave his Moors several days' leave to collect their 'war tax'. Italian officers in the city –

who were fighting as an ally of Franco – were taken aback by the massacre that was unleashed. Within five days, 10,000 people had been killed.

It wasn't as if Italian forces always practised restraint themselves. Italy's dictator, Benito Mussolini, believed aircraft could win a war with terror – by unleashing panic, killing civilians and destroying morale. In the middle of March 1938, his bombers left the island of Mallorca and descended on Barcelona. For three days, at three-hour intervals, the bombers glided in at high altitude to avoid detection by radar. As part of a 'silent approach' method, they restarted their engines only once their bombs were dropped, catching people below unawares.

Large tracts of Barcelona's city centre were turned into rubble. More than a thousand civilians were killed, and at least 2,000 more were maimed. The Gran Vía, one of the avenues that cuts across the city, was littered with body parts, which also hung from trees. International photojournalists captured images of the city's bombing. Newsreaders around the world witnessed the destruction wrought by aerial bombing – of children massacred and homes left in ruins – for the first time, a forerunner of the demonic fires unleashed over London, Dresden and other cities during the Second World War.

The goalkeeper on HH's Barça team was Antoni Ramallets. He dressed in black gear while playing, and never wore gloves. It's said that no rival player ever sledged him. Nor was even he mocked if he made a mistake. He radiated dignity, as if he was protected by an aura. Ramallets grew up in Gràcia, a low-rise neighbourhood of narrow streets and plazas in the upper part of Barcelona, known today for its village feel and bohemian character. He was 13 years old when the firebombing of Barcelona took place. It traumatised him for the rest of his days. In old age, he was interviewed on Catalan television and described how he made a conscious effort to block out the horrors of the war. They were too painful.

'One day, I decided to turn the page. I didn't want to remember anything anymore. They killed a few relatives on the front. At first, I used to ask, "Why? Why? Why?" But then you realise that it's out of your control. You start forgetting and forgetting until one day, like today, you're asked to talk about it. I wouldn't wish what happened on anyone, to go through it, because I was terrified. I was cold. I had so much fear. It was criminal – what they did,' he said, welling up in tears. 'I will never forgive what they did to us. I was in Mallorca, and somebody who lived through the war, explained to me that pilots before their bombing missions joked with each other: "How long were you there for? An hour? I'll drop my bombs in less time. I'll only take 25 minutes." They were all betting, drunk. That was told to me by somebody who was there.'

When HH wanted to motivate his Barça players, he talked money to his international stars. To his Catalan players, he spoke of patriotism. By waving the Catalan flag in front of their faces – especially before playing against Real Madrid, from the city that was the seat of Franco's power – the temperature in the dressing room immediately rose.

4.

Enrique Vila-Matas read HH's 1962 memoir when he was a boy. He still has the book in his apartment. HH's memoirs were ghostwritten by Martín Girard, the pen name of his stepson, Gonzalo Suárez Morilla, a famous film director and writer, who is a friend of Vila-Matas. The book is a marvel. A slim read. A classic of the genre. It perfectly captures HH's impish spirit and sense of bombast. The book's title alone says it all, his ego screaming from the front cover: *I: Helenio Herrera's Memoirs*, which evokes the title of Robert Graves' classic 1934 novel *I, Claudius*.

'Inside the book, there is a cartoon of a young boy,' said Vila-Matas. 'His father has brought him to a psychiatrist. "Look, Doctor, I've brought my son to see you because he doesn't know who Helenio Herrera is." It explains everything.

'I have absolute admiration for Herrera. He invented the role of the modern coach in football. He created the idea that it is the coach that makes the team win. He sold the idea any team could win if they hired him. He was a winner. He knew with a good team he would triumph. His way of thinking, a picaresque philosophy, is evident in the book. He knew his way around in a difficult world, moving from Argentina, to Morocco, to France, later arriving in Spain. His phrases are still known today: "We'll win without getting off the bus" became famous because in his time he attracted a lot of attention.

'When he arrived in Barcelona, Herrera changed things. Above all, he changed attitudes, persuading his players that it wasn't possible that Barcelona could have an inferiority complex in the face of Real Madrid. In its day, Real Madrid had state machinery behind it. It had the help of the Franco regime. In no time, the idea seeped in that Barça could never win. The refs were in the pockets of Real Madrid. It was a team of the state. But Herrera was defiant. He told his players: "You're as good as any team. You're great." He helped the team greatly in this aspect, in removing their fatalism. If he didn't, he knew the team would never win anything. He lifted the team's morale.'

I ask Vila-Matas about HH's obsession with money. His stepson Gonzalo Suárez said that HH was only interested in one thing more than football: money. 'Yes,' said Vila-Matas. 'Money always interested him. Is this a surprise for you? You should know, being Irish, that there is a lot of hypocrisy about money. In theory, people aren't interested in money. They say, "Oh you're a writer. You're not interested in money. You're only interested in working." When I changed publishers, few people congratulated me. Except Paul Auster. He said, "Ah, you changed publishers for better money. Well done." In the United States, there is a different mentality. The idea that people should work for free is *loco*.'

I also ask Vila-Matas what he made of HH's violent streak. There was always a sense of danger about him. He frightened people. His street-fighting instincts never deserted him. One afternoon in the 1950s, HH was walking through Seville with his 'second wife' at the time. He was in his mid-forties. A passer-by paid tribute to HH's wife, which set off a fuse. HH headbutted him, breaking the man's nose. 'It was a feature of Herrera's character,' said Vila-Matas. 'Like Zinedine Zidane. Everybody thinks that Zidane is very elegant. Zidane is elegant until he headbutts someone.'

5.

Vila-Matas remembers one of HH's foot soldiers fondly. Often, when HH's Barça played Real Madrid, HH got Isidre Flotats to do a man-marking job – most famously on Alfredo Di Stéfano or Paco Gento. Flotats, an uncapped utility player, would be like a shadow on the Real Madrid stars.

'Herrera's most interesting aspect was how he tricked or deceived his footballers,' explained Vila-Matas. 'How he motivated Flotats, for example. Flotats was a mediocre player. He wasn't a starter. He was a squad player. Before playing against Real Madrid, Herrera would tell him: "Today, you're going to play the game of your life. You're going to be the best player in the world."

'He convinced him psychologically that he would play a great game. Flotats was short. Really unattractive. His only task was to mark Gento, to follow him everywhere. It's why Herrera was famous as a motivator. He could lift the spirits of his players. It was why he was called "The Magician". He could get inside the minds of his players.'

When he retired as a footballer, Flotats worked in real estate in the city. Vila-Matas met him on La Rambla one day.

'I recognised him,' recalled Vila-Matas. 'I was carried away with emotion. I said to him: "Flotats. You're Flotats. Right?"

'"Yes," he said. "Yes, I am. So what? Given your age, it amazes me you know who I am."'

Flushed with enthusiasm, Vila-Matas followed up with more questions: 'And where are you going? What are you doing?'

'I'm going whoring. Is anything wrong with that?' he replied, before going on his way.

The encounter with Flotats still pleases Vila-Matas. 'It was *buenísimo*. Epic. It's why I love football stars of old. Today they don't live normal lives. They don't stop and talk to people on the street. This is all lost. Flotats was from another era. Now to meet one of them and chat is complicated. You can't bump into them while they're going down the street to find a whore.'

They will talk about him in a thousand years: Alfredo Di Stéfano, whom HH believed was a better player than Pelé.

9. SODOM AND GOMORRAH

1.

Kubala loved women. Women loved Kubala. The kids on the street knew it. They serenaded his philandering in the 1950s, adapting the lyrics of a popular *mariachi* tune: 'Silence in the room / Kubala's coming … with a hot babe.' Di Stéfano envied his prowess with women. 'Because of his prestige and his fame, there were a lot of men who would have been happy if their wives slept with him. He was a god,' said Gonzalo Suárez, the film director.

Barcelona is a licentious city. It has an open mind when it comes to sex. In the 1950s, there was a brothel in Eixample that played to the imagination. It aspired to grandeur, in a seedy kind of way. It had rooms of illusion: dungeons, fairy grottos and the like. One room was mocked up as a sleeping carriage on an imagined Orient Express. Its bed shook and a crudely painted diorama of the Alps unrolled past its window, which got stuck now and again.

Kubala – and in particular his Hungarian teammate Zoltán Czibor – revelled in the thrills the city offered, despite living under a dictatorship. As football stars, along with bullfighters, singers and visiting Hollywood actors, they were given licence. There were no tabloid newspapers to expose their misbehaviour, though journalists did gossip. Stories circulated about their carrying-on as was the case with Ava Gardner's cheating on Frank Sinatra with a Catalan *matador* while filming up the coast at Tossa de Mar. (Spain became poisoned in Sinatra's mind, as the love of his life couldn't resist taking bullfighting lovers: 'I'll never go back to that damn country.')

'Apart from the Catalans, the other players on the Barça squad loved the city's nightlife – bars, cabaret, whores,' said Frederic Porta, Kubala's biographer. 'The story of Barça in the late 1950s was like Sodom and Gomorrah. Everybody has a story about their antics. They were wild – Kubala and Czibor partied with transvestites and whores in Barcelona. Under Franco, in the 1950s. Can you imagine? Czibor had a bar called Kék Duna, which is Hungarian for the Blue Danube. It was on Capità Arenas Street, close to Diagonal. They locked the doors and had orgies inside it.'

It was a different world. 'Often Kubala was picked up on the morning of a Barça match in a pub by the club's physio,' said Zoltán Czibor Jr, Czibor's son. 'He'd be thrown in a shower and given a *carajillo*. He'd play the match, but he wouldn't know where he was in the first half. My father – and other players – did the same. Nowadays, it's totally the opposite. Discretion and humility are valued. Back then, the public tolerated wild behaviour. Players were asked to be excessive. To live like Clark Gable. People loved to see Kubala show up in a restaurant with his entourage. To have the life that others did not.'

2.

Kubala was fast. According to former teammate Gustavo Biosca, no one at Barça was quicker. He had the stamina of a broken-field runner. Although his boozing was legendary, he had a ferocious training ethic: practising his skills alone and with teammates outside regular team sessions; playing tennis; working out in the gym; swimming like a trout. A fitness frenzy that never left him. In his sixties, he was cycling 80km twice a week as well as playing football and tennis. He had the strength of a rugby prop forward. Di Stéfano said you couldn't knock him over with a cannonball. There's a statue of him outside the Camp Nou stadium. The rippling muscles on his legs are like those of a Greek god.

'He was a physical marvel,' agreed Sándor Kocsis Jr, son of Kubala's former Barça teammate. 'I played in a commemorative match for Barça's veterans' team against Bratislava. Kubala was sitting beside me in the dressing room before the game. He pulled down his pants. *¡Hostia!* I couldn't change beside him. It was too embarrassing. One of his legs was equal to both mine, and he was 30 years older than me. He was a phenomenon. The proportions in the statue at the Camp Nou are right. Once he wrapped his two legs around the ball it was impossible to get it off him. He was born to play sports.'

Kubala's birthplace was Budapest in 1927. He was an only child. His parents worked round the clock, leaving his grandmother to raise him, which is why he only spoke her language, Polish, until he was six years old. Life happened fast to him: at 15, he started playing professional football; at 17, he was an international footballer; at 19, he married the sister of Ferdinand Daučík, the famous Czech football coach (they had three sons); at 21, he defected from communist Hungary.

It was a brave move. It was 14 years before Kubala saw his own mother again. He escaped Hungary in a truck, disguised in a Soviet Army uniform, along with other political refugees, including three professional footballers. He got across the border without his passport, washing up in Italy, where he spent a year in a refugee camp. He had skipped military service, so a warrant was issued for his extradition. The Hungarian Football Federation came down hard, persuading FIFA to ban him. Inter tried to sign him on. So did Torino, who persuaded Palmiro Togliatti, head of the Communist Party in Italy, to intervene. But both clubs failed in their pursuits, dead-ending in FIFA's bureaucratic corridors.

During the summer of 1950, Kubala toured Spain with a refugee team called Hungaria. It was put together with other footballers who had defected to the West and coached by his brother-in-law Ferdinand Daučík. They played a series of friendlies, including one against Spain's national team, who were preparing for the World Cup finals in Brazil. Kubala wowed his Spanish hosts. Real Madrid, who sponsored the tour, Espanyol and Barça all swooped for him, despite the FIFA ban.

Josep Samitier, negotiating on behalf of Barcelona, persuaded Kubala to sign for Barça, and later smoothed the way so he could play for Spain after he became a citizen and the ban was revoked. The pair became intimate friends. Samitier was the first star player to cross 'the Great Divide' when he joined Real Madrid from Barça in 1932. After the civil war, he rejoined Barça as a coach, won a league title, and subsequently worked upstairs as the club's sporting director. He was good at his job: a canny networker responsible for some of the landmark signings in the club's history. He enjoyed a remarkable friendship with Franco, who personally signed the decree granting Kubala immediate Spanish nationality.

There was one sticking point in the deal that Samitier brokered with the player. Kubala insisted Barça appoint his brother-in-law Ferdinand Daučík as coach. It was a measure of the power he could wield. Daučík was an interesting guy. As a player, he was part of the Czechoslovakia squad that got to the final of the 1934 World Cup. 'He kept telling the coach what to do,' said his son Javier Daučík. He was a thinker, from a family of scientists, and a chess grandmaster. He had a Freudian approach to football. 'My father believed his involvement in the lives of his players should be as deep as possible. He liked to analyse their dreams. Like Sigmund Freud. He would bring them all in individually and question them: "Are you dreaming how you play, how you train? Tell me." A player's dreams were very important to him.'

It took until April 1951 for Kubala to fulfil his dream of playing again officially. After lengthy negotiations in Zurich, London and Brussels, the Royal Spanish Football Federation finally got FIFA to lift his ban. God had kissed him with good fortune. A month before Kubala was freed to play football again, one of his teammates on the Hungarian national team, Sándor Szücs, failed in an attempt to defect to the West. He was stitched up: the smuggler spiriting him out of the Eastern Bloc was an informant for ÁVH, Hungary's secret police. The ÁVH arrested him as he was about to cross the border into Austria. He was brought back to Budapest. In June 1951, Szücs was taken from his cell in the middle of the night and hanged.

3.

Franco's role in the Kubala saga was interesting. He wasn't an interventionist dictator, but he could be petitioned. Kubala became an important political pawn for Spain. In 1955, he starred in a biographical film about his defection to the West. The film's balmy title, *Aces in Search of Peace*, hints at the plot: star footballer escapes Red Terror; finds sanctuary in Franco's paradise. As sports films go, it holds up. Kubala was an actor to his fingertips. It features cameos for Samitier and several of Kubala's Barça teammates. The light it throws on Kubala's social life is telling: his wife is stoical; the love interest, a young dancer who flees with him into exile, spends her scenes staring at him longingly.

Why did Franco allow Kubala to sign for Barça over Real Madrid? Franco despised non-Spanish nationalism. This put Barça, as a bastion of *catalanismo*, in the firing line. Franco didn't, however, persecute the club. It wasn't his style. Franco never closed Barça's stadium, unlike Miguel Primo de Rivera, the pre-war Spanish dictator who shut it for six months (reduced to three months on appeal) after Barça fans whistled the national anthem before a game in 1925. Barça toed the line in the 1950s. Its presidents were subservient to Franco. As a social institution, Barça was useful to Franco. Its international profile reflected well on him. He also appreciated that the club was an escape valve for frustration and discontent in Catalonia. It was in his interests to keep it ticking over.

Franco was bored by the day-to-day machinery of government. His mandarins intuited the policies that would please him. By the 1950s, he was dialling it in as leader of the country. It was why the Spanish economy was run into the ground. It was why he let sides, including football clubs, play off each other. Corruption went unchecked. In a broken state, it was the only way to compete. When an informer came to Franco flagging something corrupt, Franco's habit was not to prosecute the guilty party, but to let them know who'd ratted them out.

Franco had a warping influence on Barça and Real Madrid. Their rivalry, *El Clásico*, and the politics that underpin it are complex. It's not a black-and-white story. Real Madrid has forever had establishment ties. It obtained its royal appendage in 1921. But its membership has also always been pluralist. It has fans from the Left and the Right. When the Spanish Civil War started in 1936, its president was Rafael Sánchez-Guerra. As a Republican politician, he tried to negotiate a surrender with Franco. In April 1939, he was put on trial for ties with 'the reds' and given life imprisonment. Released conditionally in 1944, he went into hiding for a couple of years before escaping to exile in France. After his wife died, he joined a monastery and returned to Spain.

Colonel Antonio Ortega, another Real Madrid president, was a communist. He was a secret police chief during the Spanish Civil War, executed by strangulation in July 1939. Even now his name is missing from the list of presidents on Real Madrid's own website. During the 1940s, Atlético Madrid was more closely identified with Franco's regime. It was known as Atlético Aviación because it was the team of the *franquista* pilots who had bombed the city for three long years. Real Madrid represented more the constituency of the bombarded city.

Barça fared better, financially, during the civil war than Real Madrid. It played about a hundred official games. Real Madrid didn't play any. The terraces at Real Madrid's stadium were used for firewood. Its pitch was turned into a vegetable patch. Barça went on a lucrative fundraising tour to the Americas in 1937. By the end of the civil war, Barça were one of La Liga's richest clubs. Real Madrid were one of its poorest.

Real Madrid didn't win a league title during the worst years of the Franco dictatorship, at a time when Barça were champions five times. It wasn't until the late 1950s that Real Madrid became inextricably linked with Franco. The club's triumphs in Europe conferred prestige on his regime, at a time when Spain was trying to come in from the cold. Franco's regime latched on to Real Madrid's successes – not the other way around. But a reciprocal relationship developed.

Real Madrid's president Santiago Bernabéu – who fought in Franco's Army – had a natural affinity with the regime. He commandeered cement from Franco's mausoleum Valle de los Caídos to help build the club's stadium, which opened in 1947. The men who ran the country enjoyed idling away their Sunday afternoons in Real Madrid's VIP box, which created a power structure that allowed the club to prosper.

4.

Kubala spent almost two-and-a-half years in the wilderness. His first game back was in Seville. At the time, Spain's cup competition was run off at the end of the season. Kubala scored on his debut in the competition against Sevilla, and five more in six games as Barça lifted the 1951 Copa del Generalísimo. The following season, he was unstoppable. It was insulting what he did to teams: in a game against Sporting Gijón, he scored seven goals, which is still a La Liga record. On the morning of a league game against Celta Vigo in November 1951, Kubala was AWOL. It was 11 a.m. The game was due to kick off at 3.30 p.m. The team's masseur, Ángel Mur, phoned a journalist who he thought might know of Kubala's whereabouts. The hack said they'd gone for dinner the previous night and afterwards for a drink. Then he went home to his wife, but Kubala kept going.

Mur and the journalist met at Les Corts, Barça's stadium. They headed for the Barceloneta, a *barrio* down by the port. It's an old fishing village. They found

Kubala asleep on a sofa in a *bodega*. They bundled him into a taxi and took him back to the stadium. Then Mur set to work: he poured two coffees down his throat, threw him into a sauna and chopped at his body with a vigorous massage before putting him under a cold shower. Kubala made it on to the pitch for the game. With less than an hour gone, Barça led 5–0. Kubala scored all five goals. The game finished 6–1. He could do no wrong.

The 1951/52 season became immortalised in the club's history. Its first great team, *Barça de les Cinc Copes*, did a quintuple, winning every competition it entered. The crowning piece of silverware was the Copa Latina. The tournament was a precursor of the Champions League, played among the continent's top clubs in south-western Europe. Barça beat Juventus in the semi-final and Nice in the final, which was held in Paris in June 1952. The team's journey home through Catalonia was like Palm Sunday.

'From the border in France until Barcelona, the team's coach was obliged to stop in every town,' said Frederic Porta, Kubala's biographer. 'People left their homes to acclaim the team, lining the streets. Nothing had been celebrated in Catalonia since the defeat by Franco in 1939. It's calculated that a million people came out on to the streets in Barcelona to receive their heroes.

'Because of censorship, the press were banned from publishing the figure. Why? To publicise having so many euphoric Catalans out on the streets like that because of football was unthinkable. This outpouring raised alarm bells in Madrid: "Hey, we can't have this showboating in Catalonia with their football team." It started a debate in Madrid about the need to make a strong team representative of the state, to build a national stadium, to come up with a response from Spain to Catalonia. It's an eternal dialectic in Spain. Spain v Catalonia. Catalonia v Spain.'

At the time, Manuel Vázquez Montalbán, the laureate of Spanish football writing, was a kid growing up on the streets of Raval, close to Barcelona's red-light district. He noted you couldn't sing Republican songs or *Els Segadors*, the Catalan national anthem, but you could belt out terrace football chants in the city celebrating Barça's achievements: 'There are six things on earth that shine brighter than the sun / The five cups of Barcelona and the shit of Espanyol.'

5.

Disaster struck the following season. Kubala got tuberculosis, a killer disease in the early 1950s. The public in Catalonia panicked. It caused the kind of anguish, according to one contemporary writer, comparable only to an increase in the price of bread.

'When Kubala got TB, it was a daily news story for several months in the NO-DO [the official newsreels shown at the cinema], in magazines and in newspapers,' said Alfredo Relaño. 'It was as if Franco or the Pope had fallen sick. Kubala appeared in a photo in the gardens in Castelldefels with a long-neck sweater. It went around the country. All the media were talking about it. Nobody thought he would play football again because of the damage to his lungs.'

Kubala had 'a hole in his lungs the size of a silver coin'. His lung capacity was reduced from 7kg to 5kg. The weight fell off him. Medical reports despaired of his chances of playing again, concluding he was 'unfit for sports'. Yet he recovered, miraculously, convalescing in a small village close to Montserrat, Catalonia's most sacred mountain. He missed five months of football, returning in February to help Barça climb up the table and finish the season with another 'double'.

Kubala was a brawler as well as being indestructible. He was sledged for being a foreigner in Spain. He fought his corner. Defenders complained about his use of elbows on the pitch. The stories about the boxer Kubala are legendary. As a kid, Kubala trained with a Hungarian boxing champion, but he gave up competitive boxing aged 11 – to concentrate on football – because of a short reach.

At the end of the season in the 1950s, Barça had a tradition of playing a friendly against a visiting South American team. It was a good money-spinner. The match was always held on 23 June, the night of Sant Joan, Barcelona's great summer celebration when the city explodes in drumbeating, bonfires and dancing, particularly down by the beachfront.

In 1956, Barça's visitors were Botafogo, Garrincha's club from Brazil. On the hour mark, a brawl broke out between both sides. One of Barça's players, Andreu Bosch, was knocked unconscious by Botafogo's goalkeeper. Barça's masseur, Ángel Mur, was also knocked out. Kubala stationed himself with his back to a goalpost and started picking off anyone who came near him. The number of casualties he took out has increased with the retelling of the story. 'To be honest, he knocked out two or three of their players, at least, while I took shelter,' said Tejada, who sprang up on his hindlegs to imitate Kubala's boxing stance and then illustrated how a windmill functions. 'He kept hitting them until he got fed up.' The game was suspended. Police intervened. Kubala and several other players spent the night in a cell.

Kubala lived in people's imaginations. His legend flowered in a pre-television age. The first *clásico* wasn't televised until February 1959. Either people saw him play in a stadium, or they imagined him through newspaper reports or radio commentaries. He was a face on chewing gum cards that schoolchildren traded. It made him a remote figure, for most people. This added to his mystique, to the epic nature of his feats, the goals, the womanizing, the punches.

The 1950s was a golden age of radio. The radio itself was a piece of furniture in homes, wooden and varnished, the size of a microwave. It had buttons and wheels and knobs. On the front pulsed a small light, which indicated the quality of the tuning. It had a fantastic name, the 'magic eye', remembers the Catalan writer, Ramón Solsona: 'You had to move the dial wheel ... with surgical precision, almost holding your breath, especially when tuning to foreign short-wave and long-wave stations such as the BBC, the Communist Pyrenees and many others from Paris, Berlin and Amsterdam ... which gave news about Spain that Franco censored.'

Sports fans gathered around the radio to listen out for Kubala's exploits. Joan Viñas i Bona was the iconic voice of Spanish radio commentary in the 1950s, a pioneer of live radio broadcasts. At Barça's stadium, Les Corts, he broadcast from the roof of a house adjoining the pitch. One of the goals was beyond his view, so he commentated parts of the match from intuition, channelling the reaction of the crowd.

6.

Kubala revolutionised football in Spain. Di Stéfano was a better, more effective footballer, but Kubala had a greater impact. Kubala conjured things with the ball that hadn't been seen before. He brought with him new-fangled ideas: shooting with his instep, curling the ball over the wall with free kicks. He used both feet. Players imitated the way he protected the ball with his body. With penalties, he was infallible. He invented the *paradinha*: the practice of stopping suddenly before hitting a penalty kick, letting the goalkeeper dive one way, then hitting it into the opposite corner. He opened his teammates' eyes to all the colours of football – so said César, a former teammate and a Barça top scorer second only to Messi.

His magic mesmerised Barça's fans. In the club's history, there is before and after Kubala. After the horrors of the civil war, his footballing heroics helped Catalans recover their self-esteem. The legend that he outgrew the club's stadium, Les Corts, is true: often 5000 fans would be left outside the gates for games. Although, technically, the club's decision to build a bigger, modern stadium predated his arrival: Barça bought the land the Camp Nou was built on in September 1950.

It was easy to love Kubala. He had charm. He was a social animal. He preferred to room with a teammate. He hated being on his own. He was affectionate, possessed of the innocence of a child, and famously generous. Teammates said he didn't know if money was measured in kilos or in kilometres. The masseur, Ángel Mur, took his watch and wallet off him on nights out because he kept giving them away. He was forever followed by seven or eight Hungarian refugees whom he fed and clothed. Even his rivals, like Di Stéfano, warmed to him.

His fame knew no bounds. He received a few hundred fan letters a day. Whenever he walked down the street in Barcelona, parades of people traipsed after him in wonderment. Market fruit sellers profited by using his name: 'Kubala oranges! Buy them, gorgeous, they're Kubala oranges! The best!' He was a hero. This created a problem for HH. There's only ever room for one cockerel in the henhouse.

The Hungarian László Kubala, arguably Barça's most revered player in the twentieth century. When HH became coach at the club, Kubala's fame was a problem for him.

10. A CANCER IN THE TEAM

1.

The toll that football took on László Kubala's body was savage. Some calculate he suffered 19 serious injuries – leading to 15 operations – during his career. The man could eat pain. In his youth, he played a season in Czechoslovakia with a fractured toe. In a league game against Racing Santander, he played the near full 90 minutes with a broken collar bone.

'Kubala was incredibly strong. Strong like a rock,' said Tejada, making a grunting noise. 'He took hit after hit after hit. Players just bounced off him. If you keep hitting a rock, though, it will eventually break into little pieces.' Tejada played alongside Kubala in San Mamés against Athletic Bilbao one afternoon in May 1954. Kubala got it in the ear from kick-off: 'Go fucking home, foreigner!' In the 12th minute of the game, Kubala ruptured knee ligaments. Ángel Mur, the team's masseur, patched him up with a splint and he played on for the rest of the match. He was never the same player again.

'It was an awful tackle,' said Tejada, making a snapping sound. 'Was he a different player after this injury? It was inevitable. It was a horrific injury. It didn't help that he led a disordered life off the pitch. The boozing. He didn't look after himself. He was weakened. It's impossible to say the opposite, but people wanted to hide the truth. Thing is, he was so good he could overcome this injury. Like if Messi dropped from 100 per cent to 70 per cent, he's still Messi. Kubala was still Kubala, but he lost something. He lost speed.'

In the snatches of film that remain of Kubala's playing days, you can see him slowing down play. Hoarding the ball. Taking an extra touch. Turning back on himself. Breaking up momentum. Doing flicks and circus tricks. The kind of play that fans in the 1950s enjoyed but that infuriated HH. The cornerstone of HH's football philosophy was speed. Doing things fast. Swift counter-attacks. It resonated with his own hyper personality.

HH's life was a race. He had overcome extreme poverty in childhood and once he escaped Morocco, he started running – and he didn't stop. He woke at sunrise. He was the first passenger on a plane and the first person off. When caught in a traffic jam, he drove on the hard shoulder. When entering a restaurant, he asked for the bill before sitting down at a table. While marching up the stairs to bed, he unbuttoned his shirt. Everything was done in a rush. No time to pause. No resting between laps. He was a man of conviction. He didn't recognise barriers. He bulldozed people out of his way. His last wife, Fiora Gandolfi, said HH didn't talk, he threw arrows. HH's strident way of communicating transmitted strength and speed into his players. It was contagious, although it provoked panic in club executives when he went banging on their doors demanding more money.

HH was always alert, suspicious, on edge, like a forest animal. He could never allow a moment's rest. He demanded focus. Distractions, especially in football matches, terrified him. He was an obsessive note-taker. He kept meticulous, museum-quality notebooks. On 30 June 1941, he etched into one of his diaries the observation that a moment's distraction decides the result of a match. He couldn't abide chaos, an inescapable feature of football matches, and of life. At the time, he was at the foothills of his coaching career. It was a week after Hitler's Nazi Army invaded the Soviet Union. The world was at war, but HH's mind was elsewhere. His lifelong battle to control the arbitrary roll of a ball was a kind of madness, like a man bent on wrestling waves in the sea.

HH always admired and feared Kubala. When he arrived at Barcelona in the spring of 1958, Kubala was still an immense player. He scored nine goals in 10 games for Spain during its failed bid to qualify for the 1958 World Cup finals. But HH didn't like the smell of *kubalismo,* the veneration of Kubala, around the Camp Nou. Kubala's powers were waning. HH knew all about his decadent lifestyle. A bad knee. The wrong side of 30. Celebrity status that threatened to eat the club, and overshadow him. Kubala was a marked man.

2.

HH didn't wait long to sideline Kubala. He couldn't stomach his carousing, which the club indulged for too long. He hit him with fines, told him he was a 'cancer' in the team – and said it in front of his teammates. Then HH went a step further. Towards the climax of the 1958/59 season, as Barça and Real Madrid gunned it out for the title, HH institutionalised a practice of dropping Kubala for away games.

Barça's 1–0 defeat to Real Madrid in the *clásico* in February 1959 was the last away game that Kubala played that season. He had already been sentenced. HH now picked a 25-year-old workhorse from the Catalan provinces to replace Kubala. A footballer called Enrique Ribelles, a utility player who was never capped internationally. Ribelles had none of Kubala's talent, but he defended better and he ran like a fallow deer.

'Nobody knew who Enrique Ribelles was, not even his dad,' said Tejada. 'The press saw blood. You know how they are. There were 20 or 30 of them with the same questions: "Why isn't Kubala in the team?" "Is it because you hate Kubala?" The fuss didn't bother Herrera. "Hey, *señores*," he said. "I don't feel that way at all. If my father scored goals, my father would be playing."

Herrera was too smart. He was pragmatic. He wouldn't throw a rock on his own roof. Ribelles was a fast runner, a young guy. Herrera saw something others didn't want to see. Kubala was over the hill. Kubala was just one more player for him.'

'In training,' added Relaño, 'Kubala would do tricks and a journalist would say to Herrera, "Would you look at this guy Kubala and what he can do? Isn't he amazing?" Herrera would reply: "Yeah, but he has to win the ball first to do those tricks. It's not the same in a game in the mud in Santander, as it is at a training session here under the sun in Barcelona." Herrera was ruthless. Football was about winning matches to him.'

Kubala was sore. He had never wanted HH as coach. Barça's president, Francesc Miró-Sans, promised Kubala that he would return Ferdinand Daučík, his brother-in-law, to Barça's dugout as coach in exchange for his support during the presidential election race in January 1958. Miró-Sans was re-elected president – and three months later, he appointed HH as coach.

Because he was dropped from the starting XI, Kubala became a cause célèbre. In March 1959, Barça travelled to Seville to play Real Betis – the game immortalised by HH's provocative 'We'll win without getting off the bus' prematch sledge. The week before, Barça's Brazilian striker, Evaristo, who was La Liga's top scorer, tore his knee ligaments. The injury put him out for the rest of the season. Kubala was the obvious player to replace him. But still HH looked elsewhere in his squad to plug the gap.

'When Evaristo got injured, we were missing a centre-forward,' said Tejada. 'The campaign to put Kubala into the team by the press intensified. There were 50,000 *socios* (Barça members) demanding Kubala be reinstated in the team.' Division lines were drawn in the dressing room. Kubala played the nationalist card with his Hungarian compatriots, Sándor Kocsis and Zoltán Czibor. Told them they should stick together in his fight with HH. Kocsis decided to confer with his wife, who explained to him how the world worked.

'My father in the beginning got caught up in it. He sided with Kubala,' said Kocsis's son. 'Herrera dropped my father for a game. My mother said to my father: "What are you doing? Are you a fool? Are you going to be a martyr over some row Kubala has with the coach? You have to look after yourself." Three weeks later, my father was back in the team for a friendly in Figueres and he scored three goals. When a player has a dispute with the coach, there's only one winner.'

A curious thing happened. The debate about Kubala's ostracism became framed in the minds of Barça's fans as a choice made between Kubala and Luisito Suárez. Many Barça fans never warmed to Suárez partly because, as a callow youth, he had a habit of shirking tackles. The division among Barça's fanbase solidified into two camps: *kubalistas* and *suaristas*. The civil war contained ironies: both players were good friends (Suárez signed for Barça on the recommendation of Kubala); and they didn't play in the same position.

There was, however, a truth in the idea that HH was betting on the future (Suárez, a future winner of the Ballon d'Or) over the past (Kubala). Suárez was an unfortunate casualty in a conflict between HH and Kubala. He was mystified to be blamed for Kubala being left in the dugout. He couldn't understand why he became a hate figure among his own fans, who jeered him during games at the Camp Nou.

'Fans whistled me whenever I made a mistake,' said Suárez. 'I remember in Barcelona on the street, people would stop me and say: "I'm not one of those who whistles you, OK." I said, "If no one is whistling me, how come the Camp Nou is whistling me?" My supporters were silent and those who weren't yelled at me … everyone was *kubalista*; only five per cent were *suarista* … it seemed like I was playing for the other team.'

Suárez was made out to be an interloper. An intruder in their house. Kubala was the idol of the masses, and the masses are invariably conservative and sentimental. In their eyes, Suárez usurped the throne. Barça's fans couldn't forgive him. It was a sickness in them, felt HH: this fatal attraction towards nostalgia, this self-destructive urge. Being led by the heart instead of the head. A sickness that manifested itself in fratricidal tendencies. Fighting among themselves instead of pulling together for a common cause.

'The problem was that football-wise, one was a thinker, Suárez, while Kubala was a stylist – he liked to do his own thing,' said Tejada. 'They weren't compatible. As our captain Joan Segarra said: "Kubala and Suarez couldn't fit in the same forward line. The same way that the two big actresses, Gina Lollobrigida and Sophia Loren, couldn't ever appear in the same film together – ever!"'

The media stoked the fires. They were playing an eternal game, goading indignation – Spain's great national pastime – among Barcelona's fanbase. 'They're always looking for motives to cause a split at Barça,' said Relaño. 'Here in Madrid, it's different. We're more united. They overanalyse in Barcelona. When I was a boy, it surprised me. At Real Madrid, there was only one magazine on sale at the stadium. I bought it when I started going to games in 1962.

'At Barça, there were two: *Barça* and *RB*. One spoke well about Barça and the other spoke badly, saying some directors were stealing, that these players were bad, acting as a magazine for the opposition of the board. I don't know why this is. I suppose it comes from the tension in the region between *catalanistas* and *non-catalanistas*, which is why, today, a person like Pep Guardiola, a *catalanista*, isn't universally admired within the club. It's why Luisito Suárez suffered, getting whistled whenever he touched the ball.'

The campaigns conducted by the magazine *Barça* angered HH. It was, he felt, acting as a mouthpiece for rival groups and critics who insisted on pissing inside his tent.

Things came to a head towards the end of the season. The club became engulfed in open war. After wrapping up the league title, Barça hosted Inter in May 1959 in the Fairs Cup. HH didn't play Kubala, even though the game was at the Camp Nou. Barça won 4–0, but the team's fans were irate. They wanted to know why their hero was missing. Forced to grasp the nettle, the board summoned HH for a brief about 'the Kubala case'. Josep Samitier – always a staunch ally of Kubala – joined the hearings as counsel for the defence. After hearing their conflicting accounts, a director conferred with the club's medical team about the injuries and ailments that Kubala had apparently suffered during the season. Then a bombshell: the board issued a press release, summarising the findings of its investigation.

The communiqué, whose phrasing had HH's fingerprints on it, opened with a heavy heart, explaining that the board was compelled to break its silence. It maintained Kubala had repeatedly made himself unavailable for matches during the season. The absences went back to a game against Real Oviedo in December 1958, but his injuries and illnesses were impossible to verify, although he seemed in good nick now. Seven times, the team's coach, HH, had fined him for missing training sessions. Allusion was made to his 'off-field' behaviour. The indiscretions resulted in Kubala being dropped for the Inter game and a further threat was built in: if Kubala didn't mend his ways, he would be transferred. The board said it realised Kubala's actions provoked 'jitteriness' among fans, which was badly affecting the rest of the squad.

Kubala countered by publishing an open letter two days later in *El Mundo Deportivo*. He denied feigning injury, something unthinkable for him to do during his nine seasons at the club. His words tugged at the heart strings, reminding Barça's fans that he had spent the happiest years of his life among them. Sadly, he said, sinister forces were at work: 'certain people' were trying to break his 'intimate ties to the club'.

Barça fans were incensed. The board got spooked. It had played its hand badly. Sensing the way the wind was blowing, seven board directors, including two future presidents, resigned in solidarity with Kubala. Battle lines were drawn. Amid the skirmishes, HH got Josep Samitier demoted, fed up with his meddling. Samitier's working title changed from sporting director to 'technical advisor' – reduced to a scout, basically.

Samitier, a club icon, was convinced he was the victim of jealousy. HH wouldn't brook any competitors in his workplace. In June 1959, he left the club, joining Real Madrid as its sporting director. This was a coup for Real

Madrid's president, Santiago Bernabéu: landing Samitier, a man who had the ear of Franco, filched from a rival. The move caused distress back in Barcelona, but it was still a notable political victory for HH, another scalp to fasten to his belt.

The problem of Kubala was left to fester over the summer. HH was annoyed by the board's indecision and told them to sell Kubala. They baulked, fearing a backlash from the fans. HH was disgusted at their lack of backbone. In September 1959, the board issued a press statement rejecting Kubala's request to be transfer listed. It was the end of the story. For now.

HH's feud with Kubala remained an open sore for the season ahead. A club divided between bickering factions: *kubalistas* and *suaristas/herreristas*. Kubala was such an enormous personality that he loomed larger when marginalised. He became a lightning rod for dissent in the club. HH was unfazed. He got on with his job. Besides, a bit of scandal was good for show business. People should talk about you even if it is good.

11. BARÇA OF THE HUNGARIANS

1.

HH's team is remembered as the 'Barça of the Hungarians'. In the summer of 1958, Sándor Kocsis and Zoltán Czibor joined Kubala at the club. Kocsis, Czibor and Ferenc Puskás were the three biggest stars of the 'Mighty Magyars', football's first great international team. The trio defected after the 1956 Uprising in Hungary, and spent over a year in no man's land until FIFA lifted their bans. Barça pounced for Kocsis and Czibor. Puskás joined Real Madrid.

Football has seen many outstanding goalscorers. Men with a nose for a goal. Romário. Cristiano Ronaldo. The bomber Gerd Müller. Assassins in the area. When Jimmy Greaves slipped the ball into the net 'it was like someone closing the door of a Rolls-Royce'. None of them could match Kocsis at international level. Kocsis got 11 goals in five games at the 1954 World Cup finals. In total, he scored 75 in 68 games for Hungary before defecting, which ended his international career aged 27.

Kocsis scored wondrous goals. In preparation for the 1952 Olympics, the Hungary team played a warm-up game against a club side, Austria Vienna. After scoring an overhead kick, Kocsis was swarmed by the Viennese players and their goalkeeper as well as his Hungarian teammates. None of them had seen a 'bicycle kick' before.

Arguably, Kocsis is the best header in football history. When he jumped in the air, he could hit the sun. He had a freakish ability to hold himself airborne, levitating for a moment, until he snapped at the ball with his head. His trademark headed goal was arrowed into the bottom corner of the net, the ball bouncing on the ground before crossing the line, which made it impossible for goalkeepers to stop. He once scored from outside the box with a header. *L'Équipe* christened him '*Tête d'Or*', 'Head of Gold'. The name stuck.

2.

In July 1979, Kocsis threw himself out a window from the fourth floor of a hospital in Barcelona and died. He was 49 years old. 'People think of a famous footballer – what a happy life, but if you scratch under the surface a little, and take a peek at their lives, you go, "*Hostia*, how terrible life can be",' said his son, Sándor Kocsis Jr.

Nothing went right for Kocsis after he finished playing football for Barça in 1965. Life as a professional footballer was stressful, especially for an introvert – playing for a demanding public, enduring political exile from his homeland, Hungary, and several bad injuries – but what the sport did do was gift him 20 seasons of certainty. A single focus. Life outside football was messy and complicated, depending more on emotional intelligence than spatial awareness and coordination.

After retiring, he tried coaching for a while, with Barça's youth academy and later with Hércules in Alicante, but he didn't have the temperament. Running a bar – called 'Head of Gold' – didn't suit him either. Then his health started to collapse. A small cupboard fell on his foot at home. The wound festered and got gangrenous. His foot was amputated. 'The amputation was brutal,' said Sándor Kocsis Jr. 'It was as if you cut off a painter's hand. It was very hard for him. He was really down in the dumps. He got very depressed.'

Misfortune pursued him. Cancer invaded his body. His son explained: 'He returned to Hungary for a spell around 1974 when he was sick. He thought it might lift him, more psychologically than physically, but it didn't. He never recovered – neither physically nor his morale. Above all his mood.' Kocsis was prone to melancholy and introspection. Fame as a footballer never sat easily with him. He preferred the shadows to the limelight.

'Czibor always said, "Your father when he went out on to the pitch, he became transformed. He lit up. He changed into another person." I know what he meant. Everything he played, he played to win. He hated losing, at chess, everything. He was a winner. But if you knew him outside the pitch, you wouldn't recognise him. It was a strange thing. He never liked it when people stopped him on the street for an autograph. He didn't like appearing on television or in the newspapers. He wasn't that type of person. He liked to stay out of the public eye. His personality was like Iniesta's. Kubala was different. Kubala said: "In life, people must talk about you, whether it is good or bad, but you should appear in the papers."

'My father wanted a quiet life. He was an introvert, which didn't allow him to socialise with people. He was always the last to arrive at training, but never late – he was a maniac about punctuality – and the first to leave after training finished. He was the opposite to Kubala, who would hang around, talking to everyone. My father's home was like a refuge for him. There nobody could annoy him. He never wanted to leave Hungary. It affected him a lot trying to adapt to life in Spain, especially the language. He felt like a fish out of water. He was a simple man. Once he was taken out of his *modus vivendi* in Hungary, he wasn't comfortable.'

3.

In Hungary, Kocsis took part in one of football's most beautiful adventures. Playing for the 'Golden Team', as they were known, in a communist country didn't make him rich. He drove a battered Mercedes car with broken indicator lights, and had to wave his arm outside the car's window when taking a turn, but he got to play in a football experiment that enchanted the world. The Ajax coach Rinus Michels, who later coached Johan Cruyff at Barça in the 1970s, said his understanding of 'total football' came from watching the Hungarian team in the 1950s: players exchanging positions effortlessly; playing football without the ball, hunting for space; always looking for an overlap, sowing confusion in opposition defences.

Hungary went six years without losing a match except for the 1954 World Cup final to West Germany, 'the surprise of the century'. Their 6–3 defeat of England at Wembley in November 1953 is a defining moment in the history of football. The result shook the world. It was the first time England had been beaten on home ground by a foreign enemy since 1066, as one commentator put it. The insularity of English football couldn't survive the lesson it was given by the dazzling Hungarians. Czibor said it was his greatest feat in football. 'For those who know football, there is only one match that fits the billing "match of the century",' said Alfredo Relaño. 'The 6–3 game explained to the world that football is for everyone and the inventors' patent had expired.'

People crowded the footpaths in Budapest listening to outside radio broadcasts of the game. The result was a balm for Hungarian refugees. Wherever Kocsis and Czibor travelled in Europe with Barça in the years that followed, Hungarian exiles would shout 'Six–three' in their ears. The Hungarians had done their homework before getting to London. Their coach got his hands on three English footballs for practice. His players couldn't believe how heavy the 'wooden' ball was. They trained on a pitch measured with the same dimensions as Wembley in practice matches against an XI organised with England's old-fashioned W-M formation. A machine on the sidelines pumped out vapour to replicate London fog.

The England team – which featured Alf Ramsey and Stanley Matthews – walked on to the pitch drunk with complacency. When their captain, Billy Wright, noticed the Hungarians were wearing lightweight boots that were cut away at the ankles like 'slippers', he turned to his teammate Stan Mortensen and said: 'We should be alright here, Stan. They haven't got the proper kit.' Hungary – who went 1–0 up after 45 seconds – taught them respect.

Mortensen had scored a hat-trick for Blackpool in the FA Cup final six months earlier in the vaunted 'Matthews Final'. Watching both games is instructive. Blackpool's players spent a lot of time charging around the Wembley pitch, crashing into Bolton's players. The ball arrived at most players' feet, like an alien, something to be hastily hoofed away – 'the English pass', as they say in Spain. The Hungarians gently circulated the ball to each other as if without thinking. They put on a recital of clever, short passing, full of verve and daring.

'I've watched that 1953 game at Wembley a million times,' said Sándor Kocsis Jr, laughing. 'I have the videotape of it at home. Hungary were playing a different type of football. England's players were all about running and strength. I always say Barça play their type of football thanks to that Hungary team. It wasn't Cruyff who revolutionised football. Kubala, my father and Czibor started playing one-touch football at Barça. The kind of football that was on display in that game at Wembley.

'Hungary had players who could play football in every position. England's players were running for the sake of running. My father said the ball should run, not the footballer. The luck the ball has is that it never tires. He said they went to England not knowing what would happen, but were clear about one thing: that their style had nothing in common with the way the English played football. Nothing. The English said the result was a fluke, so they went to Budapest the following year for a rematch. They lost that one 7–1.'

4.

Zoltán Czibor had a knack for scoring important goals. He's one of a handful of players, including Gerd Müller and Zinedine Zidane, who scored in both World Cup and European Cup finals. People in Barcelona remember him for his 'Olympic' goals – scoring directly from corner kicks. For its beauty, and its political significance, his greatest goal was scored in Moscow – an astonishing winner with the outside of his right foot in the dying minutes of the game. Hungary's 1–0 win against the USSR in September 1956 was the Soviet's first defeat on home soil. The victory also came a month before the Hungarian Uprising.

Czibor was a maverick. His nickname was 'Crazy Bird'. 'My father had a wave in his hair,' explained his son, Zoltán Czibor Jr. 'When he ran, his hair flew back like Woody Woodpecker. The American cartoon character was called "*El Pájaro Loco*" ("Crazy Bird") in Spain. Apart from the fact that he was half-crazy, which was something else.'

Czibor got to see the outside world with the golden team, a taste of freedom denied to his compatriots. He took advantage, like some of his teammates, by smuggling goods from the West back into Hungary. Prized items, both practical and glamorous, like radios, watches, razor blades, nylon stockings, sewing-machine needles. Czibor liked to speak his mind, and his rebellious spirit endeared him to the public in Hungary. 'Czibor was an iconic figure in

Hungary because he was an outsider,' said historian György Majtényi. 'People knew he was not a fan of the socialist system.'

Czibor played a dangerous game. Hungary in the 1950s was a prison state. Torture, show trials and political executions were commonplace. Dissidents were sent in droves to forced labour camps where death awaited them. In a two-year stretch, the ÁVH, Hungary's secret police, arrested 650,000 people. They used grisly methods of interrogation, coercing confessions for crimes both real and imagined.

Secret police files were compiled on nearly every citizen. People lived in a state of paranoia, never knowing if a neighbour was going to throw them to the wolves. Betrayal could come from anywhere – from families, from friends, from teammates. In 1954, Gyula Grosics, the national team's goalkeeper at Wembley, was arrested on suspicion of treason minutes before kick-off for a league game. Grosics reckoned it was a teammate who 'shopped' him. He was rattled by the experience, and his football career came to a halt. He spent 15 months under house arrest, and friends cut their ties out of fear. His family had to leave Budapest. He eventually resurrected his career by moving to another city where he transferred to a miners' club.

The ÁVH had informants under every rock. The radio commentator György Szepesi was a folk hero in Hungary. He was the voice that relayed the golden team's international exploits back to Hungary. He travelled everywhere with the team, standing pitch-side during games with his microphone, excitedly calling out the action like a horse-racing commentator. He was famous for his intimate, folksy broadcasting style; a friend of the team who could chastise the likes of Kocsis: 'Sanyi! Sanyi!' How on earth could you miss from there??'

Football fans nicknamed him the 'Twelfth Man' because of his exuberant commentaries. The ÁVH had their own name for him: '*Galambos*' ('Pigeon'), as he worked as an informant. According to historian György Majtényi: 'He was the most popular broadcaster of the era. Nobody had televisions in Hungary until 1957. People only had the radio. He worked as a spy for state security. We know this from the state files about him, which are preserved.'

The ÁVH also turned the screw on Czibor. Czibor's combative personality aroused attention. His background, too, made him stand out. He was a Ferencváros player, traditionally a right-wing club in Hungary, before being conscripted by Honvéd, the Hungarian Army's team. He was a rebel, and they had dirt on him. So they got him to sing.

'Football was a national issue in Hungary during the Cold War,' said Majtényi. 'We know that players of the golden team were subverted by Communist Party leaders. The State Security forced Czibor to sign a document saying that he would work for the ÁVH and write reports for them. All his reports were lost or destroyed around the time of the 1956 revolution. From the fragments we have left, it seems he spoke only about players' private lives. He did not give "useful" information about the team.'

5.

On 23 October 1956, students in Budapest took to the streets to protest against Soviet rule. Their ranks swelled to 200,000, as people finishing work joined them on their march, dreaming of political reforms. Traffic shuddered to a halt. Demonstrators levelled a 9-metre statue of Stalin. Men cried openly on the streets. On the balcony of a building, a nurse waving a Hungarian flag with the Communist hammer-and-sickle emblem ripped out launched a trend that was repeated by flag-waving protestors across the city.

The demonstrators marched until they reached the city's Radio Building, chanting: 'Death to the ÁVH!' The secret police responded by opening fire on protestors, killing many. Enraged Hungarian soldiers, who joined the protest, returned fire. The city became engulfed in street fights and riots. Fighting broke out across the country. The government collapsed. Some 200,000 refugees fled across the border into Austria.

Resistance fighters combed buildings, carrying out reprisals against the secret police and informants. A lynch mob raided the ÁVH headquarters. The dead bodies of ÁVH officers were taken outside and hung upside down on trees and lamp posts or thrown in the gutters. Their Communist Party paybooks were fixed to their lapels so people could see that they were earning about 10 times a manual worker's wage.

Hungary's football team was in Tata, about an hour from Budapest, the day the uprising started. They were preparing for a match against Sweden. The match was called off, but they stayed in the training camp, listening to reports of the chaos on Radio Free Europe. Five days into the revolution, they were allowed to return to their families. They got a train to the suburbs of Budapest and walked the remaining miles home. The streets were eerie. There was no traffic. There were people cheering. There were people scattered around, wounded and dying. The BBC mistakenly reported that Puskás had been killed. Honvéd gathered their players together, including Czibor and Kocsis, for their upcoming European Cup match against Athletic Bilbao. They left by coach for Vienna, and travelled from there to Bilbao.

The Hungarian Revolution was a defining moment in the Cold War. For 12 days, the Hungarians tasted freedom. The Soviets paused, observing, afraid of blundering like the British and French's handling of the Suez Crisis, which unfolded around the same time. The United States stood by. The Soviet leader

Nikita Khrushchev mocked the notion that the insurgents might benefit from an American ally, likening it to 'the support that the rope gives to a hanged man.' The Soviets weren't going to give up their European empire, though. On 3 November 1956, the Soviet Army encircled Budapest. At 3 a.m. the following morning, their tanks rolled into the city, and the rebellion was crushed within five hours.

Honvéd's players split up. Most chose to return to their families in Budapest. Czibor and Kocsis decided to make a break for it. They sent for their wives and children, paying with cash raised by Honvéd playing exhibition matches. Kocsis's Jewish wife – who had miraculously escaped a train taking her to a Nazi extermination camp in 1944 – made it across the Austrian border with her three-year-old daughter, hiking the last 21km on foot. They were reunited in Vienna with Kocsis, who subsequently sat out his FIFA ban in Switzerland. Czibor's wife fled to the border with her father, her baby son Zoltán Czibor Jr, and two daughters.

Zoltán Czibor Jr also recalled: 'We were refugees. We took nothing with us. The Soviets at the border were shooting those trying to flee. Walking across the border, we came to a fork in the road. We took one road, but because I started crying – I was only a one-year-old baby – the smugglers, who were guiding us across the border, took us back. The next day, we went again but took a different road. All those who took the road we took the day before were killed. It was pure luck. We spent two days walking until we arrived in Austria. I was in the arms of my grandfather. We then went to Italy, where we stayed until Kubala came knocking on my father's door and he signed for Barcelona in 1958.'

12. SPEED

1.

A childhood accident left Zoltán Czibor's son, who was named after him, with a dead leg, so he never followed his father into the trade. However, he did the next best thing: he spent his working life as a photographer for *Sport*. A lot of his beat was at the Camp Nou, covering the Barça circus. Kubala was best man at his wedding. He is lively company, laughing easily in anticipation at the telling of one of his anecdotes. His father was a nuisance for HH, and wouldn't obey orders.

'It was my father who had more problems with Herrera than Kubala,' Czibor Jr. recalled before further declaring: 'My father didn't like Herrera. There was a conflict between the two of them. They didn't talk to each other. Herrera was a son of a bitch. Nobody knew where he was born. It was weird how he suddenly appeared here in Barcelona. He was like one of those characters from the Wild West – those guys you see in Western movies – that sell you something for your hair to grow. He was a liar, a great talker, blah, blah blah,' he blurted, quacking like a duck. 'A big mouth, little else. A gangster.'

HH and Czibor fell out over drugs. Czibor wouldn't take the amphetamines HH doled out to the squad. By the 1950s, amphetamines had become popular in sport, especially professional cycling, where it was nicknamed '*la bomba*'. On the streets, it was known as 'speed', a word that sent HH into reverie. According to Enric Gensana, HH's gigantic Catalan central defender, HH crushed up amphetamine tablets into powder, which his players swallowed down by mixing it with liquids, usually tea or coffee. He told them they were vitamins. According to Kubala's biographer, Frederic Porta, HH got the team's physio, Ángel Mur, to administer the medicine: 'Take this. It's good for you. It'll help you run more. Trust me.'

Players had a problem coming down afterwards: they couldn't sleep. So HH adjusted the practice of gathering his footballers together in the camp before matches, now adding an extra night's stay *after* matches so players weren't strung out returning to their families. Then came an incident with Gensana. After a match one evening, Gensana was sitting at home. His mother was talking to him, but he couldn't respond. He could only babble, too spaced out. Gensana asked a doctor friend to lab-test the tablets. He confirmed they were amphetamines.

There have always been drugs in sport, going back to the Olympic Games in Ancient Greece. Sport has taken its cue from combat zones, from the Berserkers in the Viking Age taking psychoactive mushrooms so neither steel nor fire could harm them, to the drugging of soldiers in the twentieth century. In the Second World War, all the major warring sides were horsing amphetamines into their armed forces. The British Royal Air Force, for example, issued pilots with 'escape boxes' in case they were shot down in enemy territory that included Benzedrine tablets, a brand name for amphetamines, for stamina. Speed helped to counteract fatigue and increase endurance, although the comedown, especially in a warzone, was horrendous. It became the high command's drug of choice for their combatants, replacing cocaine because it could be taken orally in tablet form and its effects lasted longer.

In football, players were encouraged to take speed to give themselves a pep. In 1925, Arsenal's coach Leslie Knighton marvelled at the effect the drug had on his players, helping them to run like Olympic sprinters and jump 'like rockets'. After the Second World War, drug use became more systemic in the game. During the 1954/55 season, Bill Shankly gave his players at Workington speed before games. He didn't look kindly on those who abstained.

In a documentary, the Scottish winger Hughie Cameron recalled: 'Before you played, he put 11 wee tablets down there on the table. And he watched to see, and if you didn't take one of the tablets, you wouldn't be playing next week. It gave you a buzz. After the game, you couldn't eat or nothin'. You were on a high until eight or nine o'clock. After the game, you felt you could go again.'

In the 1954 World Cup final, according to research by Berlin's Humboldt University, some of West Germany's players were injected with the methamphetamine Pervitin, used by German soldiers in the Second World War. The reason this became known was because the players likely contracted jaundice from using dirty syringes, including Helmut Rahn, who scored the game's winning goal in the 84th minute. In the 'Miracle of Bern', West Germany – who lost 8–3 to Hungary in the pool games – came back from 2–0 down on a soggy pitch in the final to win 3–2.

'Hungary lost the final because of doping,' asserted Czibor Jr. 'It wasn't banned at the time. I was working at the Camp Nou around 1980 for a European match. I was one of the photographers on the pitch. We each had a cushion to sit down on, with our names on them. A French journalist from *L'Équipe* said to me: "Are you Czibor? I was at the World Cup final in Bern. The West Germans when they came out for the second half were flying around the pitch, more than in the first half. When the match finished, [Captain] Fritz Walter's eyes were bulging. He was frothing at the mouth like a dog with rabies."'

2.

Speed didn't suit Czibor. He had a nervous disposition. The drug increased the nervous tension in his body and in his head, leaving him with the jitters. Taking amphetamines was counterproductive for a highly strung person, and did nothing for his performance. That was the thing with speed: it agreed with some players, didn't with others, and was fatal for athletes with underlying medical conditions or those who were pushed to the limit.

By the early 1960s, speed had become a popular drug across society, even in Franco's Spain. The film director and stepson of HH, Gonzalo Suárez, declared: 'In those times, amphetamines were a very common stimulant. People had it in a flask when they were out and about. Students took it to stay up all night studying. You couldn't give amphetamines to everybody indiscriminately. For some people, it had terrible effects. Others felt stimulated by taking it.'

Czibor told HH to go to hell with his speed. When HH insisted that Kubala take the drug before a game, Kubala fobbed him off:

Kubala: Míster, do you love me?
HH: Yes, Laszi, of course I love you.
Kubala: But do you love me a lot?
HH: Yes, a lot.
Kubala: Well, if that's true that you love me a lot … take this yourself.

Other players were more docile. It was easier to follow orders.

'Herrera assured the players it was aspirin he was giving them at half time with a coffee,' recalled Sándor Kocsis Jr, laughing. 'He didn't care what it was, what it did to them: "Take this and shut up." My father didn't resist. He was told to take it. He took it, and that was it. My father wasn't into conflict. "What? Do I need to take this? OK." He did what he was told. He didn't question much. He was an introvert and liked a quiet life. If you told him "2 + 2 = 5", he'd say, "No problem. I won't quarrel with you." He wasn't an adversarial person.'

Czibor was the opposite; he loved to fight. The dressing room was split, and things got ugly. Someone in the club leaked the feud to the press. Czibor stood by his guns, denouncing HH for giving the players drugs. Fans turned on him. They started jeering him during games. During a match at the Camp Nou while he was out on the left wing, as a gesture of protest, he lay down and feigned being asleep on the pitch for a few seconds.

Czibor's supporters admired his courage in calling out HH's dirty tricks. Fliers were distributed at the Camp Nou, drawing the battle lines. The text laid everything out in black and white. It carried the warning: 'The friends of HH want to sow confusion in our ranks.' The dissidents called on the club to get rid of team captain Joan Segarra and forwards Evaristo and Eulogio Martínez for calling Czibor a liar. They also wanted to throw other players on to the street for taking drugs: goalkeeper Antoni Ramallets, Enric Gensana, Luisito Suárez and Kocsis. They praised Czibor because he had 'unmasked HH'.

The evidence suggests that HH introduced speed to La Liga. Alfredo Relaño claimed: 'Helenio Herrera was the first coach in Spain to give his players drugs. Real Madrid's players, who were friendly with Barça's players, said so. Later, there were other coaches.' Real Madrid gave its players speed in the European Cup in the 1960s. A lot of teams in Europe took drugs. In Italy, it was rampant. The Ajax team doctor John Rolink – who laid on a menu of nameless pills for the club's players – liked to use amphetamines himself. 'Real Madrid's players told me they couldn't sleep for two days after taking them,' said Relaño. 'When they took drugs, they weren't tired or they didn't feel pain. Herrera was very "forward-thinking". He did it without any sense of guilt. It was a very primitive thing at the time. People didn't fully understand the consequences.'

3.

The code of *omertà* in sport can be hard to crack. Justo Tejada stumbled when I asked him about the drugs HH gave them. 'Doping. Yes, yes, sometimes,' he said. 'Like students when they were studying for exams to keep awake and alert, they would take something … but some of the players didn't want it.' Then, regaining his composure, he remembered the party line from more than half a century ago: how HH discredited Czibor by suggesting it wasn't the place for a boozer like Czibor to pontificate about drug-taking.

'In Barcelona, there was no specific case. Czibor said Herrera gave drugs to the players. Herrera replied, "Who cares what 'Pepe Botella' has to say?"' HH's put-down was a reference to Napoleon Bonaparte's brother who ascended the Spanish throne in the early nineteenth century. He was known as 'Pepe Botella' ('José the Bottle') because he did nothing except get drunk while king.

HH believed that Czibor lacked moral authority. He was unapologetic, doing what he had to do to win. Nothing else mattered. He was prepared to do whatever it took to give his players an edge, to distract them from the pain in their lungs and their legs. Irrespective of the side effects. When Enric Gensana, who was playing at the heart of Barça's defence, damaged a retina in his eye during a game and was seeing double, HH rejoiced: 'Brilliant! Get back on your feet. You'll be able to clear twice as many balls!'

Throughout his coaching career, HH flogged his players like workhorses. This wasn't surprising for a person who had survived his hardscrabble childhood growing up in a Moroccan slum. Neither was it an approach that made him different from his peers in other dugouts in the post-war years. Men who were equally cavalier about how they treated their livestock.

The division in his ranks at Barça was unprecedented, though. The secret to HH's success was his ability to get inside footballers' heads so they would follow his lead. He told Enric Llaudet, Barça's president in the 1960s: 'To triumph in football is simple. All you must do is get the players in your pocket and the rest is done without any effort.'

At Barcelona, he had to deal with insurgents in his dressing room, but he crushed the rebellion. His methods worked. He had the luxury of a big squad overflowing with international stars. Czibor was marginalised. And though Kubala scored 20 goals in 25 games during the 1959/60 season – HH's second full season in charge – HH was vindicated in dropping him for big games. Barça retained their league title in 1960, edging Real Madrid on goal difference.

Still, it wasn't enough for Barça's fans. When Barcelona's players did a lap of honour to celebrate their La Liga triumph in April 1960, parading around the Camp Nou with HH on their shoulders, fans booed. They wanted their idol, Kubala, who was seated in the stands. It caused a scene. The Camp Nou wouldn't forgive HH for robbing them of the presence of their hero for so many matches during the season.

Kubala was cajoled into going down to the dressing room so he could switch into a tracksuit and join his teammates in their celebrations on the pitch. But this still didn't quell the discontent. Opposition groups knew that by destroying HH they would destroy Miró-Sans, the president, who could be replaced with their man and a new board of directors. HH was caught up in a toxic political game. Something was going to have to give.

'The cards are on the table. It's pointless fooling around with these charades. If Herrera stays, Kubala will have to leave. There is no other option,' warned a *Barça* magazine editorial in April 1960. The house wasn't big enough for the two of them. Nothing, it seemed, would satisfy these fickle Catalans. HH had Real Madrid's number – in the league, in the cup. But the real test awaited in Europe, where Santiago Bernabéu had built his kingdom.

13. DON SANTIAGO

1.

Franco said he could only explain himself to himself through his experiences in Africa. His tours of duty with Spain's Foreign Legion in Morocco forged his character. Morocco turned his heart to stone. It gave him a lust for bloodletting. His master in the desert was José Millán-Astray, founder of the Spanish Foreign Legion. Franco served as his second-in-command from 1920. Both men were Galician. Both shared a belief in blood sacrifice. Millán-Astray referred to their legionnaires as 'bridegrooms of death' and sent them storming into villages with the battle-cry: 'Long live death!'

In 1936, their roles reversed: Franco became his boss. As head of the Nationalist revolt in the Spanish Civil War, he gave Millán-Astray the job of managing propaganda. Millán-Astray ran his press office like a barracks, summoning journalists with a whistle and encouraging staff to threaten foreign reporters with execution. His body was tattooed with bullet wounds; he had lost his left arm and his right eye, which was covered with an eyepatch, in battle. He was now unhinged, and an addiction to cocaine didn't help.

One Sunday afternoon in the early 1950s, Millán-Astray showed up at Real Madrid's stadium for a game with two legionnaires and some friends, unannounced. First mistake. Santiago Bernabéu, the club's president, hated improvisations. He was a fussy man, who liked order. Di Stéfano said his abiding memory of Bernabéu was of him obsessively turning off the lights in the stadium. Guests had to abide by his house rules.

The unwelcome guests ran amok in the VIP area. Millán-Astray started groping the wife of a diplomat. A fight broke out. Bernabéu, appalled by the melee, banned Millán-Astray from the club's presidential box. For this, he was challenged to a duel by pistol. Bernabéu complained to General José Moscardó, head of sport in Spain, who did not take his side and instead ordered Bernabéu to apologise to a man 'who had done so much for the country'.

Bernabéu took a different tack: he went to his old army boss, General Agustín Muñoz Grandes. Bernabéu had been a soldier in his division in the civil war. During the Second World War, Muñoz Grandes led the Blue Division – Spanish volunteers who fought alongside the Nazis on the Eastern Front. Now passing his time as a minister in Franco's government, Muñoz Grandes pulled rank. He overruled Moscardó and upheld the ban on Millán-Astray, who was never allowed to return to Real Madrid's presidential box. Order was restored to the house that Bernabéu built.

2.

In 1955, Real Madrid's stadium, Chamartín, was renamed after Santiago Bernabéu. Having a stadium named in your honour in middle age – during a military dictatorship – must do curious things to a man's head. There was no one he bowed to in Spain, including Franco, whom he treated like a mate. When he heard one day that Franco drew a blank after a deep-sea tuna fishing expedition, he couldn't help himself: 'I heard, Excellency, that you were fishing for tuna. How did it go?' Caught off guard, Franco replied meekly: 'I just went for the air.'

Bernabéu was a peculiar mix. He had a sharp intellect. He read German philosophers – Kant, Nietzsche and Schopenhauer, the miserabilist – in German. Yet he left behind the life of the mind – or a career in the legal profession like his father, who was a judge – for work in the lawless world of football. Real Madrid was everything to him: as player, captain, coach, and president until his death in 1978, aged 82.

He never had children. He married at the age of 45, which he kept in-house: his wife was the widow of Real Madrid's treasurer, who had been killed in the civil war. He mastered the art of remote working, living in a beach house on the Mediterranean, close to Alicante. He received journalists in his pyjamas, sitting in an armchair. He managed the club's affairs by barking instructions to his lieutenant, Raimundo Saporta, from a telephone that rested on a coffee table beside him.

His genius was foreseeing that football would become the great entertainment vehicle for the working classes in the post-war world. He got a jump on his rivals in Europe, betting on his vision by opening a gigantic stadium in 1947 when a sports ground like, say, Barça's had a capacity of only 48,000. He sold fans tickets at cut-down prices. He signed the world's biggest stars to fill the stadium: Di Stéfano, Kopa, Puskás, Didí. When he took over as president in 1943, the average crowd for a Real Madrid game was 16,000. Fifteen years later, 120,000 fans were packing the stadium for big games.

Bernabéu instinctively understood how globalisation worked. As one of its architects, he bet on the European Cup, knowing that football was hitting new frontiers. People were curious about the exhilarating teams that came from other countries, such as Real Madrid, Honvéd, Manchester United. The European Cup, which grew out of the ashes of the Second World War and centuries of European conflict, was a noble enterprise, as Alfredo Relaño has remarked, drawing together capitalists and communists, dictatorships and democracies at the height of the Cold War. Sadly, England's Football League wouldn't permit Chelsea to play in the inaugural tournament in 1955.

Real Madrid immediately dominated the competition, but not without a helping hand: according to Julián García Candau, a former *El País* sports editor and historian, Saporta, Real Madrid's vice president, fixed the draw using hot and cold balls to ensure an easy passage. Out of Real Madrid's successes, the club's legend grew. In Spain, newsreel images of its glamorous continental triumphs transfixed cinemagoers during grey days. Abroad, clubs like Leeds United, who adopted Real Madrid's iconic white strip, tried to emulate them.

Bernabéu had an iron grip on his club. Players were petrified of him. When he entered a room, they stood to attention. He gave bonuses for good behaviour in hotels. As a result, Real Madrid could stay in hotels that other teams were banned from because of broken beds and debauched behaviour. He advised players on what to do with their savings. He scolded them if their hair got too long or they grew moustaches. If they underperformed on the pitch, they risked a lashing of his tongue, which was a terrifying experience.

Real Madrid failed to win the league title in 1956, but as holders of the first edition of the European Cup, they were given an exemption into the tournament. In the first round, first leg, they defeated Rapid Vienna 4–2 at the Bernabéu. In the return leg, they went 3–0 down at half time. They were on the rack: their defender, Joaquín Oliva, broke a leg and was taken by ambulance to hospital; their goalkeeper broke his hand, but continued playing with one hand, as there were no substitutes allowed.

At the break, Real Madrid's players were in the dressing room reeling when the door crashed open. Bernabéu entered, took off his hat with his right hand and flung it at the wall. Then he started screaming: 'Sluts! What are you doing here, whimpering? It makes me sick with shame to look at you, but I'm more embarrassed for the people out there! Do you know how many Spanish workers there are out there? Do you know how far some of them have come to get here? Do you know that tomorrow they will be made fun of? Do you know the sacrifices these people make to send foreign currency back to Spain? You're unworthy! Sluts!'

There was silence. Zárraga, who finished his career a multiple European Cup winner, protested. Bernabéu shot him down. Then resumed his bawling: 'If you've any shame left, get out there and behave like men. Don't embarrass me anymore!' When he left, he slammed the door, nearly lifting it off its hinges. Revitalised, Real Madrid grabbed on to a lifeline: Di Stéfano scored 15 minutes into the second half and they clung on to tie the game 5–5 on aggregate. In a play-off, Real Madrid won 2–0 and went through to the next round.

Bernabéu sucked up all the air at the club. Nobody remembers the names of the coaches who won Real Madrid's six European Cups during his presidency. Bernabéu set the standards at the club. He bought the best players. He had leaders in the dressing room, like Di Stéfano, who embodied his culture of excellence, men with an indomitable will to win.

Bernabéu's board of directors were stocked with the men who ran the country, including Francisco Gómez de Llano, a finance minister in Franco's government, and Fernando de Cárcer Disdier, who fought as a colonel in the Blue Division, sent by Franco in 1941 to lend support to the German Army on the Eastern Front. This created an intimidating environment. Bernabéu was a thoughtful man: he sent referees gifts for their birthdays. He set aside 2 million pesetas a year in the club's budget to pay journalists so they would report favourably on Real Madrid.

Bernabéu created a culture where coaches became expendable at the club, a policy that the autocratic Florentino Pérez, his greatest successor, carried on in the twenty-first century. At Barcelona, there is a cult of personality around the coach, which HH established with his Messianic behaviour. Later coaches such as Johan Cruyff and Pep Guardiola also became lionised, but they operated against a background of political infighting and rival factions at an institutional level – a world of perpetual civil war – which created a lethally unstable working environment that lives on today. At Real Madrid, under Bernabéu, there was stability, clarity; one leader, one voice.

3.

Bernabéu thought that HH was uncouth. He hated his vulgar tongue. HH lacked culture and breeding. Bernabéu was at ease circulating in aristocratic social circles. HH was *nouveau riche*, and carried huge wads of cash around with him rolled up in a ball like a cattle dealer. (The rest he kept in a Swiss bank account.) Spain's upper classes sniggered at his sense of taste. He lacked their appreciation for the finer things in life. When *ABC*, one of Spain's daily newspapers, did a soft-focus profile interview with him, HH revealed excitedly that he decorated his sitting room with 16 metres of fake book spines. No actual bookshelves and books, just smoke and mirrors.

Bernabéu also didn't much care for Catalans, and their dreams of secession, once notoriously remarking: 'Those who say that I do not love Catalonia are mistaken. I love Catalonia and admire the place, despite the Catalans.' Bernabéu didn't hate all Catalans, but *catalanistas* – those Catalans who wanted to separate from Spain. His political sympathies were far to the right. He was a monarchist. (Interestingly, this put him at odds politically with Franco, whose dread after the civil war was a possible return of the exiled Bourbons to the Spanish throne.)

Before the start of the Spanish Civil War, Bernabéu was a prominent activist for CEDA, a Catholic conservative political party. His brother, who shared his right-wing politics, was a member of the Spanish parliament. When the civil war started in July 1936, Bernabéu feared for his life. He hid in a Madrid hospital, afraid he'd be conscripted by the 'red' militiamen rampaging around the city. When someone recognised him, he took refuge in the French Embassy until he managed an escape to France.

As soon as he could, he returned to a Nationalist zone in Spain and enlisted in Franco's Army. He was 42 years old. He fought in several battles as a corporal, including the 're-conquest' of Catalonia. 'When we went through [the Catalan provinces], liberating the mountain villages, they did not come out to greet us,' he recalled. 'The streets were empty. Only old men dared to look out from the second floor, and they cried with hatred. And when old people cry with hatred, a town has no future.'

Bernabéu was wary of the bright future that HH was carving out for Barça. He couldn't stand the Catalan club. His only two friends at the club were Josep Samitier, who he poached as sporting director in 1959, and Francesc Miró-Sans, its right-leaning president. Bernabéu side-stepped pregame lunches with Barça's board of directors before *clásicos*. He made excuses and sent Raimundo Saporta, his right-hand man, or another director in his place.

Santiago Bernabéu in the trophy room at Real Madrid's stadium, which was renamed in his honour in 1955, a third of the way through his reign as president of the club.

14. 'HE COULD HAVE PLAYED WITH A TUXEDO ON'

1.

Barça's European Cup adventure began in September 1959. They drew CDNA Sofia in the preliminary round, Bulgaria's army team. They had just won six consecutive league titles. The first leg was fixed for Sofia. There was no love lost between Bulgaria and Spain; the countries – who were on opposing sides of the divide in the Cold War – didn't retain any diplomatic relations. Barça's three Hungarian players – Kubala, Kocsis and Czibor, all of them political exiles – stayed in Barcelona. None of them risked travelling behind the Iron Curtain, for fear of being detained by the Communist authorities.

Barça chartered a private plane for their journey. Flying in the 1950s was a slow, potentially treacherous endeavour. It was in the days before jet aircrafts, so people joked: 'Time to spare, go by air.' Unlike flying today, where hitting turbulence is a normal occurrence, a mild scare back then was terrifying: with inferior seat belts and low cabin ceilings, passengers who suddenly dropped 150 metres could snap their necks from the jolt. There were looser regulations governing pilots. Mid-air collisions were not uncommon. Kiosks at airports sold life assurance policies. It wasn't safe to land in fog, so there were unfortunate crashes.

Barça's flight into Sofia hit fog, at night-time. The plane started doing concentric circles about 1,500 metres above the runway. The passengers got jittery and asked their travel rep, who was sitting at the back of the plane, to make enquiries. He consulted with the pilots in the cabin, then returned and told HH and his players that there was a delay because the air-traffic controller in Sofia spoke Bulgarian and Russian, while the pilots spoke English. Both sides were deaf to each other. The impasse seemed to go on forever, until the pilots finally chanced a landing, with success.

Back on firm ground, Barça's prematch training session generated excitement in the Bulgarian capital. News of HH's sorcery had breached the Iron Curtain. More than a thousand people showed up to see him at work, including the Soviet Union's national team coach, Mikhail Yakushin. In the match, Luisito Suárez missed a penalty. The game ended in a tie, 2–2. Barça were satisfied with the result, confident they would win the return leg at the Camp Nou.

Everything was going fine on the flight home until they hit Rome. The weather broke. The plane started chugging. Seatbelts were fastened. Then it got worse. The plane hit the tail end of a tempest over the eastern Mediterranean. Rain and hailstones lashed the roof and sides of the plane, which was tossed around violently. The plane repeatedly sank into a void before rising again irresistibly, almost vertically, and then swung from right to left. The pilots, who were wrestling to maintain the plane's course, were in danger of losing their way and ending up over the Pyrenees.

The players on board were silent except for a few who were reciting the *Ave Maria* and acts of contrition. Shaken and terrified, they snapped out of it when HH let out a roar: 'Tomorrow, training at half past 10! On the dot!'

A few moments later, the pilot let his passengers know – after losing communication with air-traffic towers in Barcelona, Perpignan, Marseille, Nice and Corsica's capital, Ajaccio – that the plane was making an emergency landing on the island of Mallorca. Within a few minutes, the plane landed on a flooded runway. The water was up to their ankles when Barça's squad got off the plane. Getting them back on it 90 minutes later was a chore. Several players refused to board, insisting they preferred to return to Barcelona by boat. Eventually, they were coaxed on board. On landing in Barcelona, they were met by anxious family members, as it had been announced during the storm that communication with the plane had been lost.

A few weeks later, Barça advanced in the European Cup. They beat CDNA Sofia 6–2 in the second leg at the Camp Nou, with hat-tricks by Kubala and Evaristo.

2.

After crushing Milan – who were beaten finalists the previous year – Barça faced Wolves in the quarter-final. Wolverhampton Wanderers were the dominant force in England at the time. They'd just won back-to-back league titles, cracking in more than a hundred goals both seasons. In the spring of 1960, apart from their European Cup aspirations, they were chasing the century's first domestic 'double'. (They eventually fell short by a point in the league title race, but won the FA Cup.) Mighty Wolves travelled to Barcelona for the first leg and were humbled. They lost 4–0, even though Barça effectively played most of the game with 10 players, as Isidre Flotats was badly injured.

The night before the second leg in Wolverhampton, HH did his usual bedtime check on the players in their hotel rooms. Whenever Barça's players were in training camp before and after games at the Camp Nou or on a sleepover for an away match, they were ordered not to lock their hotel rooms. HH liked an open-door policy. On this occasion, HH found a locked room. He knocked on the door. One of the players inside the room opened the door. HH asked why the door was closed and then stayed for a chat with the two players, one of whom, Evaristo, was in bed. After drawing the conversation to a close,

HH said good night to the players and, just as he was about to leave, dramatically knocked on the closet door: 'Miss, do us a favour. We have to go.' A naked woman climbed out of the closet. Mortified, she grabbed her clothes and walked silently out of the door.

HH was obsessed by sex – or rather sex and what it meant for his players. The pursuit of it, the want of it could leave them frazzled. It sapped their energy, a fact that preyed on HH's mind. He tried to regulate the sex lives of the married players on his squad by giving gifts to their wives if they restricted their husbands to sex only twice a week. It drove him crazy when he heard bantering about sex. Players learned not to blurt out loose comments – like, say, 'Did you get a shag last night, eh?' – within his earshot during training sessions. When HH took the team to the cinema the afternoon before a game, he had strict criteria for choosing the type of film to watch. No naked women. He thought they were inappropriate. Just soldiers, Indians, macho men. He loved John Wayne's *The Alamo*, a film famous for failing to have a single scene that corresponded to the battle's reality.

The bachelors on Barça's squad were edgy around him. According to the defender Sígfrid Gràcia, HH once visited his bedroom. HH idled in the room, chatting to Gràcia and his teammate, who was lying in bed. Suddenly, HH whipped the bedsheets off, mistakenly believing that the player was masturbating. The player was horrified.

It wasn't that HH was prudish. He had an insatiable appetite for sex himself. The issue is that there was something untameable about sex, something almost impossible to control. HH hated lack of control.

'I like a clean, united dressing room and, if possible, a happy one,' he said. His players' happiness wasn't a prerequisite for success in football; it was a bonus. His total domination of them, though, was non-negotiable.

3.

Evaristo was dropped for the game against Wolves at Molineux because of his philandering the night before. Kocsis took his place. He had missed the first half of the season because of a brutal knee injury administered by José Santamaría – Real Madrid's hardman Uruguayan central defender – during a preseason tournament match in Andalusia.

Back in the team, Kocsis took his chance, despite playing with a dislocated shoulder, which caused him to faint in the dressing room at half time. He was given a pain-killing injection to get through the second half. He finished his shift with four goals. It was cruel what Barça did: massacre night at Molineux. Luisito Suárez 'could have played with a tuxedo on'.

In the first half, Eulogio Martínez left Wolves defender George Showell stranded with a pull-back that later became known as a 'Cruyff turn'. In the second half, Martínez picked up the ball on the right-hand side of the pitch close to the halfway line. He dribbled into the box, stopping by the end-line. The Wolves left-back Gerry Harris, who was tracking him, stood to attention, waiting to see what was going to transpire.

Next, an extraordinary piece of skill: on a muddy pitch, Martínez, with his back to the end-line, scooped the ball over the head of Harris in a single touch. He ran around him and, retrieving the ball, lobbed the goalkeeper. Only the crossbar prevented him from scoring. His artistry left the British Pathé news reporter breathless: 'Is there any reason why top stars can't play soccer with some comic touches? Martínez thinks why not. Poor Harris. Happily for Wolves no goal this time.'

The game ended 5–2 (and 9–2 on aggregate). The Wolves players gathered for an impromptu guard of honour, clapping Barça's players off the pitch. Barça – who had already secured a Fairs Cup final slot and were close to wrapping up the defence of their league title – were reaching nirvana. The BBC radio commentator John Camkin was in awe: 'In my memory, they will stand above Honvéd, Real Madrid and any other outstanding club team of the post-war years.'

British football had some catching up to do. HH couldn't resist a dig before leaving the UK. A clutch of reporters gathered around him at Birmingham airport to hear his verdict about the inventors of the game: 'You in England are playing now in the style we continentals used so many years ago, with much physical strength, but no method, no technique.'

4.

The European Cup's rules dictated that Spain's two teams couldn't meet in the final. This meant HH would get to test his techniques on Real Madrid in the semi-final. Real Madrid had sailed through the earlier stages, getting a bye in the preliminary round as reigning champions, and then defeating the Luxembourg entrants and Nice.

Barça would be their biggest examination yet in the European Cup since their ownership of it had begun, in 1956. Four days before the semi-final, Barça were again crowned winners of La Liga. Even Alfredo Di Stéfano admitted that Barça's players were better individually than Real Madrid's (but he told Bernabéu that Real Madrid had enough smarts to beat them over a two-legged tie in Europe).

Real Madrid were vulnerable. They had sacked their manager, the Paraguayan Manuel Fleitas Solich, before the semi-final. He was replaced by Miguel Muñoz, a former player who was coaching the reserve team. Didí, Real Madrid's *galáctico* signing in the summer of 1959, created a toxic environment in the club.

Didí arrived in Madrid to great fanfare. He had been the star of Brazil's World Cup win in 1958, as player of the tournament, and would be pivotal again in

1962. He was a master of the long pass, boasting that he treated the ball with as much affection as he showed to his wife. He had a statuesque, regal bearing. He never drifted far from the centre circle, from where, according to Eduardo Galeano, 'he would shoot his poison arrows'.

His languid style infuriated Di Stéfano, who saw him as a threat. The pair clashed immediately. A ship can't have two captains. Puskás, who had joined Real Madrid a year before Didí, understood this instinctively. He knew better than to challenge Di Stéfano's status, which helped him prosper at the club for eight seasons. Didí failed to integrate. On top of that, the Madrid winter depressed him. He lathered his hands in Vaseline in an attempt to stave off the freezing cold.

As the season wore on, Didí became more withdrawn while his second wife – the singer Guiomar Batista – became shriller. She was a firecracker, who once, allegedly, welcomed Didí home from international duty at the front door wielding a pistol. She regularly briefed the Brazilian press on life in Spain, denouncing Franco for being 'an elitist dictator' and Madrid's media for taking payments from Real Madrid's players to wage slanderous war on her husband. Her volatile behaviour unsettled Bernabéu, who wrote: 'We know for sure that she has been sending back articles to Río newspapers saying certain Madrid players are paying journalists here. Our players know about all this, and it's created a bad atmosphere around Didí. Di Stéfano does not like him.'

5.

The in-fighting at Real Madrid strengthened HH's hand. The first leg was fixed for Madrid towards the end of April 1960. Real Madrid held no fears for HH. He was sure his team would lick them. Even Puskás admitted privately that Barça had their number. In the lead-up to the game, HH trash-talked, maintaining the semi-final would be the death knell of Real Madrid's ageing team. The club was an elephant's graveyard. Its key players – Di Stéfano, Puskás and central defender José Santamaría – were all in their thirties.

HH's squad stayed in the Berzosa hotel for the match. This was the hotel where Spain's national team stayed. It was also where the matador Antonio Bienvenida retreated following an afternoon's bullfighting. He was Madrid's most famous bullfighter of the era. His fights sold out immediately once advertised. Exultant fans carried him on their shoulders through the streets of Madrid from the *plaza de toros*. He had started bullfighting competitively aged 10, joining his father – who was known as the 'Black Pope' – and his five brothers in the trade. People marvelled at his grace in the bullring, his ability to kill six bulls in an afternoon, and his courage in coming back from several gorings.

On the morning of Barça's match with Real Madrid, there was blood left on the floor of the Berzosa hotel. Hours before kick-off, Barça's players asked to meet with the club's CEO. HH urged them to look for an increase in their win-match bonus. Their stock was high. They had a strong bargaining position. Now was the time to strike. The players liked his thinking. Evaristo led the players' delegation. HH joined them for the negotiations.

The CEO wouldn't budge. He summoned the club's president, Francesc Miró-Sans, to help break the deadlock. Miró-Sans refused to yield. The club was drowning in debt because of the Camp Nou construction. According to Miró-Sans, the players threatened to down tools. Things got heated. HH got angrier and angrier. Miró-Sans stuck to his guns. The players and HH were forced to leave empty-handed. A fight between Zoltán Czibor – who was left out of the team – and his teammate, Eulogio Martínez, further dampened the mood. The Santiago Bernabéu Stadium, its terraces crackling with 120,000 screaming *madridistas*, was waiting to devour them.

15. A MURDER OF CROWS

1.

Real Madrid started the match cagily, but Di Stéfano settled nerves with a goal after 17 minutes, scoring with a header from a cross by Paco Gento. Di Stéfano always said the first goal is worth three. Puskás added one to make it 2–0. Barça got one back, but Di Stéfano scored again, a late goal, to give Real Madrid a two-goal cushion, 3–1, heading back to Barcelona. Real Madrid's inclusion of Luis del Sol – signed a couple of weeks before the match – was a surprise. The gamble paid off. He brought running and bite to their attack, but it was Di Stéfano's goals that proved decisive.

They will talk about Di Stéfano in a thousand years' time. In the minds of Barça fans, no other player has been more terrifying. Not even Cristiano Ronaldo. Di Stéfano terrorised La Liga's defences, finishing top scorer in 1954, 1956, 1957, 1958 and 1959. During his time at Barça, Lionel Messi scored incredible goals, hundreds of them. His small physique added a miraculous feel to his feats. Di Stéfano, however, had a greater impact in Spain, and in the history of club football. Messi stood on the shoulders of greats at Barça – Cruyff's breakthrough Dream Team, Ronaldinho, and others – when he broke into its starting XI.

The legend of Real Madrid was built by Di Stéfano. Before he joined in 1953, Real Madrid fans joked they had a First Division stadium and a Second Division team. Di Stéfano changed everything. After a barren spell of 20 years in La Liga, Di Stéfano won Real Madrid eight league titles in 11 seasons. He conquered Europe year in, year out. On arrival in Spain, he was 27 years old – and had already dominated football in South America for nearly a decade – which makes his achievements at Real Madrid the more remarkable.

Di Stéfano changed the culture at Real Madrid. There is a natural hierarchy in clubs: president, coach, players. At Real Madrid, Bernabéu, as president, was the boss. Underneath him, Di Stéfano was such a towering figure that he overpowered whoever happened to be coach of the team, helping to create a political structure at the club that still prevails today. Real Madrid is a players' club, not a coaches' club, overseen by an omnipotent president.

Justo Tejada, who joined Real Madrid a year later, in 1961, explained that Di Stéfano ordered the team around, not Miguel Muñoz, Real Madrid's most decorated coach in history: 'Di Stéfano was in charge of Real Madrid. Before matches, Muñoz limited himself to naming the starting XI. He gave four instructions. He always ended his team speeches with the same message, "... and what can I tell you that you don't already know?" Afterwards, we'd trot on to the pitch and only listen to Di Stéfano.'

(There is a pointless but entertaining debate about who is the greatest footballer of all time. 'Maradona was Maradona sometimes. Messi is Maradona every day,' remarked Jorge Valdano, but those who trust their eyes believe Maradona was the best. Pelé, the only player in history to win three World Cups, made football the 'beautiful game' with his artistry. Di Stéfano turned Real Madrid into the greatest club in the world. It is impossible to single one out. They are the Mount Rushmore of football.)

HH admitted there was no greater footballer in the world in the early 1960s than Di Stéfano. Forget Eusébio. Forget Pelé, 'a violinist'. Di Stéfano was, in his words, 'the entire orchestra'. (Pelé himself also said the best player ever was Di Stéfano.) He is the great exemplar of the 'false nine' forward. He never waited for the ball to come to him; he went hunting for it. He defended when he had to defend. He was a ferocious competitor, which was embodied in his all-terrain style of play.

No one was grumpier, no one more demanding: he instilled a winning, fight-until-the-death mentality that has become enshrined in Real Madrid's DNA. It's thanks to Di Stéfano that Real Madrid don't fluster. The club's famous *remontada* culture, their ability to mount epic comebacks, stems from Di Stéfano's team – in 1956, 1958 and 1960, they fell behind in the European Cup final, but each time they prevailed. The club has no truck with football ideologies. It's never been a slave to the chalkboard. It's not vain in that way. It never anchored itself to *catenaccio* or possession-based schools of football. This is due to Di Stéfano and his haughtiness. His legacy is a football philosophy that could not be more clear: sweat the jersey; get the job done. We're Real Madrid, the white knights of football.

A particular game featuring Di Stéfano left its mark on the language. In the opening game of the 1954/55 season, Real Madrid played Valencia. A curly-haired footballer called José Mangriñán did a crack man-marking job. He shut Di Stéfano out of the game, keeping him scoreless in a 2–1 victory for Valencia. Word spread around the country in disbelief. Who was this man Mangriñán who had policed the great Di Stéfano? A verb entered the Spanish lexicon to help explain the mystery of what happened in Valencia that afternoon: *mangriñánear* – to mark closely, to neutralise an opposition striker or playmaker. Soon Mangriñán became a metaphor at large: a possessive wife could *mangriñánear* her husband, a jealous boyfriend might *mangriñánear* his girlfriend.

Before Barça's quarter-final tie with Wolves in 1960, the English magazine *People* interviewed Di Stéfano. He was quizzed about Barcelona. In praising

Barça, Di Stéfano cited four of their key players: the man dressed in black, goalkeeper Antoni Ramallets; the huge Enric Gensana in defence; their playmaker Luisito Suárez; and Kocsis up front. This was a time before teams did scouting reports on their rivals, and Barça fans felt Di Stéfano was giving away trade secrets. Anything to nurture a slight.

So, when Di Stéfano ran out on to the pitch at the Camp Nou for the return leg of the 1960 European Cup semi-final, he couldn't hear himself think for all the blaring horns and shrieking Catalans. Real Madrid's players said they'd never encountered a sound like it before during a *clásico*. Fans unfurled a 50-metre banner: 'We don't want snitches in the stadium.' Every time Di Stéfano touched the ball, fans started spitting and yelling uncontrollably.

Barça fans had been jerky since the 3–1 first-leg defeat. Rumours abounded. There were doubts that HH would continue as coach. Word spread that he had signed a pre-contract with Real Madrid to become their coach the following season. There was talk about a mutiny in the hotel before the game at the Bernabéu: it was said Barça's players didn't win because they were sore about failing to negotiate a bigger bonus. *Peseteros* more interested in money than fighting for the colours of Catalonia.

HH had no time for the doubters. He was bullish. 'We'll beat them there [Camp Nou] and we'll win the final,' he said. All week, he repeated the message. It seemed to work. Barça started brightly – for 20 minutes – but then wilted. Puskás sentenced them, scoring midway through the first half, which killed the tie. There were tears in Barça's dressing room at half time. A dream destroyed. Recriminations around the corner. Real Madrid played as if in a state of grace, circulating the ball with ease. Were it not for several saves by Ramallets in goal, Barça would already have been thrashed.

Puskás scored again in the second half. The man was a freak of nature. He had arrived at Real Madrid in 1958, when he was 31 years old and hadn't played in almost two years. He was also a couple of stone overweight. Yet he went on to win four consecutive *Pichichi* titles, as La Liga's top scorer, in the 1960s. He scored 35 goals in 37 European Cup games for Real Madrid (and 84 in 85 internationals for Hungary). His teammates nicknamed him '*Pancho*', Spanish for 'belly', but it didn't matter that he looked like a darts player. His left foot was made from gold.

Paco Gento roomed with him. He used to throw a bar of soap into the shower, and watch Puskás trap it with his left foot and juggle it. The people of Madrid adored him. Nearly 80,000 *madridistas* went to the Bernabéu for his testimonial match against Rapid Vienna on a Monday night in 1969. Two days later, at the same stadium, only 31,000 showed up to see Cruyff's Ajax against Milan in the European Cup final.

The game at the Camp Nou finished 3–1. Kocsis scored a late consolation goal for Barça. Real Madrid advanced 6–2 on aggregate. Di Stéfano enjoyed himself. With three minutes to go in the match, he ran over to the touchline by Real Madrid's dugout to take a throw. 'Don't this lot ever tire of whistling? And who's blowing these damned trumpets?' he said to Miguel Muñoz. His coach replied: 'The ones who are losing.' HH was enduring his first defeat at the Camp Nou as Barcelona coach. Barça's fans showed no mercy, whistling him in the dugout.

The pain in Barcelona was unbearable. People couldn't read newspapers or listen to the radio for a week afterwards for fear of being reminded of what had befallen their team. The city became engulfed in hysteria. Scapegoats were sought. Someone to take the blame. Barça's board of directors drew in together closely, mindful of the angry hordes outside the castle gates. They knew where they would have to stick the knife.

2.

The day after the defeat at the Camp Nou, HH took some air with a French journalist. A magazine from France was doing a feature. HH had arranged the interview in advance, expecting a victory in the semi-final. He now took the journalist and the magazine's photographer around Barcelona for a drive to soak up the city's ambience. When they arrived at the top of La Rambla, the journalist asked him how far his popularity spread in Barcelona. HH said to him: 'Do you want to see?' They stopped the car and HH started walking down La Rambla, towards the port, by Canaletas, a stone's throw from where George Orwell manned a roof during street fighting in the civil war.

Canaletas is a landmark in the city: a black, regular-sized water fountain, about head high. It flowers into a lamp post. It has a discreet Barça crest above one of its taps. In modern times, on the night of a big Barça win, hundreds of fans will cavort around Canaletas celebrating. Back in 1960, on the day HH went for his walkabout, it was like the agora in Ancient Athens, except people congregated there to talk football instead of political philosophy. The talk that morning was that HH had cut a deal with Real Madrid to lose. When the throng there noticed HH walking in their midst, they were agog. They surged towards him like a murder of crows.

'It's Herrera! It's Herrera!'

They peppered him with questions.

'Is it true you sold the match to Madrid?'

'Not at all!'

'Why did you lose then?'

'Because in the first match we played badly and in the second match the goal by Puskás demoralised us and they played extraordinarily well. It's logical that we lost.'

'Why didn't Kubala play?'

'Because he lacks mobility. Madrid's team is old but very technical. We couldn't beat them with technique, but with energy.'

'If Kubala had been…'

'How long is it since you saw Kubala do the things that Puskás did yesterday?'

'Suárez had an injury in his foot. Why did you play him?'

'Because Suárez with one leg is better than another guy with two.'

The rebukes kept coming.

'Could it be that you have already signed a contract with Madrid?'

'No, sir. Madrid is my enemy. I have worked hard these past two years to beat them.'

'But, hey, you lost. Who's to blame?'

'Puskás.'

The French photographer had a brainwave and encouraged some fans to shoulder HH. It would make for a good photo. Some were encouraged and hoisted him on to their shoulders. Others – appalled by the idea – began protesting. The mood turned nasty. HH tried to discreetly depart the scene with his French entourage. They scurried down La Rambla, but a mob followed them, hurling abuse. The insults became more vicious.

HH ducked into the nearest hotel he could find, Hotel Oriente. The hotel was a favourite watering hole of Errol Flynn's, who spent a spell on the front line during the Spanish Civil War. Legend has it in Catalonia that he could play the piano with 11 fingers, when he wasn't chasing his life's dream, 'old whisky and young women'. He stayed at the hotel while shooting the 1955 film *King's Rhapsody*. HH's selection of the Oriente as a refuge was unfortunate: this was Real Madrid's hotel, which confirmed the mob's suspicions.

'Go collect your bribe!'

'Sell-out!'

'You're already hired by them!'

Police disbanded the rioters. HH stayed inside for a drink – congratulating Real Madrid's players on their marvellous performance the day before – until the coast was clear. He left the hotel with a police escort. The incident made the newspapers the next day: 'Helenio Herrera attacked by the public. Police force had to intervene.' People said HH was nothing but a charlatan – that he'd bribed four men to hoist him on their shoulders. Anything for a bit of publicity.

3.

Miró-Sans and Barça's board of directors met the day after the incident on La Rambla for a postmortem of the defeat to Real Madrid. They picked over the corpse with grim determination, alighting on a huge cancerous growth: HH and his lust for money. HH had erred – they maintained – in playing Luisito Suárez for the game at the Camp Nou because he was injured. They also suspected he was negotiating with Real Madrid and other foreign clubs, because he was evasive about renewing his contract for another season.

Private conversations between a director and HH led them to conclude he would not be staying. They were at the end of their tether with his persistent demands for more money at every turn. The club's physio, Ángel Mur, admitted to a director, Joaquim Viola, that HH had pressured senior players into demanding a 50,000 peseta win bonus for the match in Madrid. It was a minor betrayal by Mur, who had been close to HH, but Mur knew which side his bread was buttered. He was a company man. Coaches come and go.

The board felt they had no alternative but to sack HH. A press release was issued to the media. It announced his dismissal, and refuted allegations – 'the malicious lies circulated' – that the board reneged on their win-bonus obligations to HH and the squad before the semi-final against Real Madrid. HH's 'growing obsession with [money] before sporting interests' poisoned the team. He was only concerned with filling his pockets and negotiating 'his transition to other sporting entities'. The triumphant but polarising 'HH era' was over. The rupture was bloody and total.

The fools! HH couldn't believe their stupidity. He had long ago prepared his escape route. Inter's oil tycoon president Angelo Moratti had already seduced him with a lucrative contract to go to Italy. They met secretly at a toll booth on an Italian motorway to cut a deal. HH was tired of living in Barcelona with a knife to his neck and had hit a ceiling in La Liga. He spent half the previous year studying Italian, gorging on Italian newspapers and books. He took a language course with vinyl records, which he listened to each day in his apartment after training. HH was like a chess player, always three moves ahead.

HH guarded this secret closely. He was moonlighting as Spain's national team coach and didn't want to jeopardise the gig, feeling that if he announced midseason he was leaving for a foreign posting it wouldn't be looked on kindly by the Royal Spanish Football Federation. Days before the European Cup semi-final, some emissaries from Barça visited him in his apartment. It was close to midnight. They laid a contract out on the table for him to sign. A renewal for the following season. HH was non-committal.

With their clumsy political manoeuvres, Barça's board scored an own goal. They should have kept their cool and waited until the end of the season when

HH's contract finished. Barça were due to play Birmingham City in four days' time in the second leg of the Fairs Cup final (which they won 4–1 on aggregate, with Kubala restored to the starting XI). They were still involved in the Copa del Generalísimo.

The board just had to bide their time: tell the fans at the end of the season that HH wouldn't renew, that he preferred Inter over Barça. But they couldn't help themselves. They had to be the ones who threw HH out on to the street instead of admitting that HH was the one jilting them. The sin of pride. These were the same weak, indecisive men who couldn't get rid of Kubala. A bunch of cowards, muttered HH to himself. Now Miró-Sans was trying to be the hard man by making him walk the plank. HH knew that Barça's fans – or a large proportion of them – would turn on Miró-Sans for his short-sightedness and treachery. They were welcome to each other.

4.

Something solidified with Barça's defeat to Real Madrid in the semi-final of the 1960 European Cup. Something about their identities.

It was inevitable that Real Madrid would be victorious in the final at Hampden Park. They don't play finals; they win them. They defeated Eintracht Frankfurt 7–3, with four goals by Puskás and a hat-trick by Di Stéfano, who scored in his fifth consecutive European Cup final. It was the greatest day in the club's history, but it wasn't just the goals, or the marksmanship of Di Stéfano and Puskás.

It was one of those rare afternoons of near sporting perfection. All 11 Real Madrid players seemed to reach a celestial pitch simultaneously. There was a moment, for example, when Real Madrid's defender Marquitos – who was only 1 metre from his goalkeeper – cleared a dangerous corner with a back heel. Real Madrid played with such joy and abandon that none of the people at the stadium that afternoon – including Alex Ferguson – could forget their performance.

The following day, Real Madrid's players were paraded through Glasgow on an open-top bus and cheered home from the airport by hundreds of Scots. All of Europe was transfixed by the flag they had planted on the mountaintop. They were the undisputed kings of European football. A template was established, which was cemented by eight La Liga titles in the 1960s. Real Madrid became a byword for success, the epitome of haughtiness and heroics.

By contrast, Barça declined once HH left. Years of drift and infighting ensued. It only won two league titles over the next three decades. The club did reach the 1961 European Cup final, but it was the last kick of a dying horse. Barça were mired in so much debt they sold Luisito Suárez, their reigning Ballon d'Or winner, to Inter. HH picked him up in Bern, after Barça's lamentable 1961 European Cup final defeat to Benfica, and drove him back to Milan, over the Alps. Chatting, scheming.

All the old ghosts resurfaced in that 1960 European Cup semi-final defeat to Real Madrid: the *victimismo*, the self-destruction, the fear of triumph. It was the first of several great 'funerals' that haunt the club. These include the 3–2 defeat to Benfica in the 1961 European Cup final because of freakish bad luck, hitting the woodwork four times; the loss on penalties in Seville to Steaua Bucharest in the 1986 final; the capitulation of Messi's Barça to Liverpool at Anfield on the night of an electrifying four-goal comeback in the 2019 semi-final. Real Madrid are regal on big European nights; Barça remain notoriously fragile. Something about the soul of Kocsis, as the Spanish novelist Javier Marías remarked, lives on in the spirit of Barça decades later: artistic, indecisive, tortured. Barça the diva.

It wasn't an identity that fit with HH. Leave melancholy to the Catalans. Besides, he knew Barça would be back at his door, swirling fabulous contracts under his nose, begging him to return so he could fix their problems. (And they did, practically every other year for the next 20 years.) But HH didn't own a rear-view mirror. His default position faced forwards. HH was on his way again, galloping into the distance. New horizons beckoned. He was off to the land of the lira. Bigger, glorious chapters had yet to be written. More success awaited him. And more money, and more scandal.

'The Architect': Luisito Suárez, the playmaker of HH's two greatest teams, Barça (1958–60) and Internazionale in the 1960s.

HH with his captain Armando Picchi (centre) and defender Aristide Guarneri (left) as they return to the changing rooms for half time at the San Siro Stadium in the mid-1960s, a time when Inter were almost invincible.

III

INTER
(1960-68)

16. THE SWEET LIFE

1.

Football reached a point of perfection in terms of work-life balance at the New York Cosmos in the 1970s. It was a time before AIDS. Casual sex was easy to come by. On the flight to play in the Soccer Bowl Final in 1977, some of the Cosmos travelling party engaged in sexual acts to pass the time. It was enough to utter the four magic words 'I'm with the Cosmos' to access all the pleasures known to man. New York City. Limos everywhere. Disco beats. The legendary nightclub Studio 54 operated as the team's clubhouse. Mick Jagger was a team groupie. A grinning Franz Beckenbauer said joining the Cosmos was one of the best decisions he made in his life.

The Cosmos were the flagship team of a wild experiment that briefly captured the sporting public's imagination. The North American Soccer League had novel innovations like getting players to dribble from the halfway line towards an onrushing goalkeeper for a more dynamic penalty kick. The game's biggest stars – including Johan Cruyff, George Best and Eusébio – rushed to take the dollars on offer. The Cosmos played in front of a packed New York Giants Stadium. Its roster included Pelé, Beckenbauer, Carlos Alberto and the ungovernable Giorgio Chinaglia, who was regularly the league's top scorer.

Steve Ross – owner of Warner Bros, the biggest media company in the world – was the godfather of the league. He ran the Cosmos. He had a helmet of silver-coloured hair and liked to wear jackass chequered flared pants. He nurtured that childlike need – a weakness of many sports franchise-owning men – to be close to the locker room, so he overindulged his players. Chinaglia, who knew Ross was a soft touch, paraded around New York City flashing a Cosmos credit card to cover the expenses for his bacchanalian lifestyle. At games, Ross never sat in the president's box. Instead, he took up a seat upstairs in the second tier of the stadium with other, regular Cosmos fans. He loved nothing better than bollocking a referee. Because he got so worked up during games, an assistant strapped him in with a seatbelt to stop him from toppling over the railing to the ground below.

The ringmaster of the Cosmos travelling circus was Eddie Firmani, the team's coach. Sometimes, he felt like he was in charge of an asylum. Chinaglia was a particular headache. When Firmani once substituted the Italian striker during a game against Memphis, Chinaglia walked off the pitch cocking his fingers at him in a pistol gesture. Before he was a coach, Firmani was a player for HH at

Inter – and he is still the only man to score more than a hundred league goals in both England and Italy.

2.

Firmani grew up in Cape Town, South Africa. In 1950, Jimmy Seed, the former England international and Charlton Athletic manager, invited him to join his team at The Valley, having watched Firmani score five goals in a club game in Cape Town. Firmani was only 16 years old, but his parents allowed him to make the move 8000 miles north to London.

Firmani thrived at Charlton. By 1955, he had been headhunted by Sampdoria. Firmani grabbed his chance, leaving English football without a moment's hesitation, tired of the 'slavedom'. At the time, Italian football was opening its doors, and changed its rules to allow for three foreigners on each squad. Firmani left Charlton for a record transfer fee involving a British club – £35,000, which was £5000 more than Real Madrid paid for Alfredo Di Stéfano two years earlier – to join Sampdoria. Several other British stars, including John Charles, Jimmy Greaves and Denis Law, followed in his footsteps. They went for the money.

The year Firmani left Charlton, a professional footballer in England earned about £8 a week, which was less than an average factory worker, who could expect to earn £11 a week. There was a cap on wages at £20 a week – which wasn't broken until 1961. Bonuses were laughable. For the 1960 Fairs Cup final, Birmingham City's players were on a win bonus of £4; Barça's players got £218 each for lifting the trophy. When Firmani joined Sampdoria, he walked away with a signing-on fee of £5000, which brought him unimaginable wealth. He made another killing when he moved to Inter in 1958.

'I was very happy to go to Italy,' said Firmani. 'Financially, it was very good. It was my ancestry's homeplace as well. Also, I heard nice things about how Italians treated their players. If you did well for them, you were a God. In Italy, you're noted as a player whereas in England footballers led a very private life. Half the people didn't even know who I was.

'In Italy, they're football fanatics. I was more or less the leading goal scorer in the country, so everyone knew who I was. Simply because I was fortunate to score a lot of goals I was idolized by the people. I used to walk down the main street in the city and people would stop me and say nice things to me. People would call me into their shops, and they would give me, say, a shirt or a pair of shoes. A lot of things about Italy appealed to me.'

Firmani was embraced unconditionally on arrival in Italy. As soon as he showed his nose at the dressing room door, he was given a big hand. He got the nickname 'The Turkey' because he played with his head held high and was all arms and elbows. He needed to look after himself. He noticed defenders in Italy weren't as physical as British defenders, and they didn't snap into the tackle as aggressively. Neither were they as fit as footballers in England or as good in the air.

Italian defenders excelled, however, at intercepting the ball. They were cannier, more cynical. They double-marked centre-forwards. They used an arsenal of the dark arts whenever the ref was unsighted: spitting, standing on toes, clipping ankles, pulling hair, tugging a forward's jersey when he was jumping for a header, giving him a kick when the ball was in the other half. Anything to unsettle a striker. Despite their skulduggery, Firmani – who had a brilliant volley – prospered. As he remarked: 'I learned to move away from Italian defenders at strategic times – so I didn't get a whack.'

The game was played at a slower pace in Italy, on dreadful, bone-hard surfaces except for the stadiums in Italy's bigger cities like Milan, Rome, Turin and Naples. In Italy, the short pass was cherished. It was seen as a more artistic expression of how to play the game. Firmani noticed that football fans in Italy felt a result more than their British counterparts. He was surprised to see grown Italian men cry if their team lost a match, and women on the street told him – after a defeat – that he was the cause of their husbands failing to eat for a day or two. Italians still like to quote Winston Churchill, who is credited with saying: 'Italians lose wars as if they were football matches, and football matches as if they were wars.'

Professional footballers in Italy, though, were able to keep the game at arm's length. They didn't let football dominate their thoughts. They trained hard. They put everything into matches, but once the final whistle blew, they could detach themselves. They didn't inhale the game as much as British footballers. Their girlfriends were more important to them than a round ball. They thought British footballers were a bit mad, in fact, for prioritising football above sex. Pride in the club wasn't as important to Italian footballers. There was never an inquest after a defeat. That was somebody else's concern. British footballers were quicker to dissect games; they wanted to talk about what transpired, what could be done differently. Italians were more cavalier. Once the game was over, they preferred to let their thoughts drift towards the sweeter things in life.

3.

Life was sweet – as the title of the 1960 film *La Dolce Vita* implied – in Italy. The country had undergone a radical transformation. When the Second World War ended in 1945, Italy was cratered; the country was broken. After turning on its former ally, Germany, it was occupied by the Nazis. Terror reigned. The bodies of dead partisans were sent floating down rivers, held afloat by signs around their necks calling each out as *partigiano*. A warning to others.

This was the moment when Italy was ripped apart by civil war, the war within a war, as fascists fought it out with the partisans. After the Second World War, there was no reckoning, apart from Mussolini. Il Duce, his mistress and 16 other suspected fascists – many of them members of his cabinet – were executed in April 1945. Their bloodied corpses were hung upside down from metal hooks in a Milan square. Like carcasses in a meat-packing plant, with their eyelids left open.

War crimes went unpunished. Fascists were quietly assimilated back into society and powerful positions. Enmities inevitably festered. In the post-war years, there was intense poverty. Calorie intake was three-quarters what it had been 20 years earlier. A third of Italy's national wealth evaporated in a few years of war. Displaced, homeless people all over the country sought shelter in shacks, cellars, empty schools and caves on the outskirts of cities. Black markets thrived. Pawn shops were full of bed linen and socks.

In the 1950s, however, a page was turned. The economy took off, in a rise that became known as *Il Boom*. By 1960, Italy was the fastest-growing economy in the world. Milan was the engine of its economic miracle. The country industrialised, and people flooded into Italy's cities – especially to the industrial north – where there was full employment, providing cheap labour for factory owners. The country's peasantry seemed to disappear overnight, but instead of emigrating to, say, Toronto, they went to Turin. In 1962, for example, 100,000 migrants landed in Milan from the south. 'Bread was no longer made, it was purchased.' There was a rush to modernity. Social change occurred with unexpected haste.

Italians fell in love with the car. Italians fell in love *in* the car. It became the place where many of them lost their virginity. The Italian car industry created a car a minute, and soon they were clogging up city streets, bumper to bumper, honking and hooting. Taking citizens on summer holidays to Rimini and other seaside resorts. Cars were known by their numbers, as cheap models rolled off Fiat's production lines: the 600 (1955), the 500 (1957), the 850 (1964). Others were identified by their brand names: the Spider, the Punto, the Uno. At the top end of the market, Italy developed an unrivalled ability to create luxury cars. Lamborghini, Ferrari, Maserati, Alfa Romeo – names that echoed around the world.

Rome's film studio, Cinecittà, known also as 'Hollywood on the Tiber', was a magnet for the stars of the day, including Charlton Heston, Ava Gardner and Frank Sinatra. Richard Burton and Elizabeth Taylor began their love affair while filming there on the set of *Cleopatra*. When Federico Fellini's masterpiece *La Dolce Vita* was screened in Milan in February 1960, it was attended by the film's stars Anita Ekberg and Marcello Mastroianni as well as Inter's football team.

The reaction in the audience was mixed. Within the ovation, there were screams of protest: 'Coward!' 'Communist!' 'Shame on you!' Fellini was led by bodyguards through a mob of protestors, and spat on, leaving the theatre. The film was denounced by the Catholic Church leaders for corrupting morals. Despite the extraordinary social change that Italy was experiencing, it was still – and largely remains – a conservative country, with pockets of progressives and radicals. It didn't have a post-war, left-wing government until 1996.

The Catholic Church kept a firm grip on the thinking of Italian people, but it was impossible to keep liberalising ideas from creeping into people's living rooms. Television cast a spell over Italians. It became like a second father to children, but one that 'could only deliver tenderness'. In a telling passage in the 1963 film *I Mostri*, a cuckolded husband is so entranced by what he's watching on the TV that he neglects to notice his wife is carrying on an affair in the bedroom next door.

There were so many new glittering devices to distract the eye, designed by the finest Italian minds. Cheap consumer goods and home appliances made the lives of housewives easier. The washing machines of Candy and Zanussi found their way into homes around the world. In every facet of life, Italian brand names seemed to rise to the top: Olivetti typewriters, Pirelli tyres, Ducati motorbikes. The scooter – made famous by Gregory Peck and Audrey Hepburn zipping around Rome in the 1953 film *Roman Holiday* – was synonymous with Italian vitality and idealised romance.

The scooter was an upgrade on the bicycle; it had a similar 'leaping' effect in social behaviour. The Vespa, or the 'wasp' because of the buzzing sound of its motor, was cheap and affordable. It was easy to repair and maintain. Its design was ingenious. Its saddle sat above an enclosed engine. Its front shield offered protection for men in suits and women in skirts. Two could squeeze together on its tiny seat, the discomfort offset by the hint of sex. It epitomised an Italian sense of resourcefulness, of fun and flair, as did its competitor brand, the Lambretta, manufactured in Milan.

Italians have always had great self-regard. Now it felt like the world looked to Italy for leadership in design and invention. Italy had come into its kingdom, now a watchword for fashion and *élan*, an arbiter of taste, the capital of cool. The streets of bohemian New York, Paris and London were full of *modernists*, or 'mods' (so-called because they listened to modern jazz music). Working-class kids dressed in inexpensive but hip clothing designed in Italy. They mightn't have much money, but they made do. Their motto was 'elegant living in difficult circumstances'. They rode around on Vespas and Lambrettas imported from Italy, and they drank Italian espresso rather than beer. They took amphetamine pills so they could dance all night in jazz clubs and stay alert, and stay cool, unlike the fall-down drunks who spilled out of pubs. A reason why Italians don't drink alcohol to excess is they consider losing control to be ugly. Mods were down with Italian culture. They came to love the Spaghetti Westerns of Sergio Leone, which had a comedic strain lifted from *opera buffa*.

A curious chain of events contributed to the rise of London's post-war coffee house craze, and the counterculture revolution underpinning it. In 1951, Italy reintroduced conscription. The Cold War was at its height, the threat of Soviet expansion in Europe hung in the air. Italy needed a large standing army to maintain its colonies, and, as a NATO member, Italy had obligations in the Korean War. Post-Mussolini, it was easier to control an army of regular, part-time youngsters than a professional army who might fall under the spell of generals bent on a *coup d'état*, which was a threat: many high-ranking officers who had been in active service during the fascist years were still in charge. One way to sidestep being called up was to leave the country. A loophole allowed young Italian men to defer military service until the age of 36 if they found work abroad, which is why floods of them drifted to the UK in the 1950s, many settling in Soho, the neighbourhood that was Swinging London's ground zero.

The first Gaggia coffee machine – which was smuggled without an import licence through Ireland and the Isle of Man – arrived in Soho in 1953. It was sold to Maurice Ross, a Scotsman, who opened the famous Moka coffee bar on Soho's Frith Street in the same year. The Italian actress Gina Lollobrigida was hired for the opening. A trend began. Italian-style espresso bars began surfacing all over London and further afield, a thousand of them in England by 1957, their names writ large in vivid neon lights, including La Roca; Heaven & Hell Coffee Lounge; Las Vegas Coffee Bar; and Le Macabre, a horror-themed café with coffins for tables, replica skulls for ashtrays and a jukebox that groaned with funereal music.

Coffee houses were a refuge for hipsters. Teenagers too young to be served alcohol in bars could loiter there; they also stayed open till late whereas most pubs shut at 11 p.m. Art college students, poets and eggheads, admen and waitresses waiting for the next acting gig all mingled together, smoking and fomenting their ideas about fashion and politics, or just trying to look cool while playing chess in sunglasses. Bands played live music on the premises of 2i's Coffee Bar, the birthplace of British rock 'n' roll, which had a stage made from milk crates and planks, just 45cm wide. Tommy Steele, Cliff Richard and Screaming Lord Sutch performed there in front of jive cats twisting the night away. Fluffy-headed coffee became the quintessence of Italian sophistication, or pretentiousness. The hip and the fashionable youngsters in coffee bars looked down their noses at boozers, considering them boorish and uncool when it came to music; and pub drinkers despised them with equal disdain. As Max Bygraves sang in *Fings Ain't Wot They Used T'Be*, his 1960 hit: 'There's teds wiv drainpipe trousers and debs in coffee houses ... Once our beer was froffy, but now it's froffy coffee.'

Brylcreemed Teddy boys, who were inspired by the dandies of the Edwardian era, wore long and slim jackets with the so-called 'Italian cut'. Italian sportswear and knitwear was coveted. Brioni suits define the images of fictional characters like James Bond, Don Draper and early-era Beatles. Whenever Hollywood stars like, say, Henry Fonda were in Rome shooting a film, they'd stop by Brioni's atelier to pick up a custom-made suit. Italy had a way of seeing the world. Italy had attitude, an appreciation of elegance – whether it was in designing clothes or fridges, films and football. It was a thrilling place to visit and to live. Italians were connoisseurs of the good life. They understood pleasure, *la bellissima*, something that was captured in *La Dolce Vita*. It was no surprise that Serie A became the most glamorous, the richest league in the world with stars like Luisito Suárez, Omar Sívori and Gianni Rivera.

4.

Being a football star in Italy was like living in a fishbowl. There were eyes everywhere. One day when Firmani was at Sampdoria, he received a message telling him to immediately report to the club's secretary in his office. He was a married man with two young children, but the club had received information that he had been seen out late the night before with a woman. When presented with the charge, Firmani laughed. He had been with his mother-in-law. Someone had anonymously reported the 'facts' to the club.

The pressure from fans was relentless. During the week of a derby match, the phone calls for Firmani would begin on a Monday night at 1.30 a.m. They would continue through the night. There was never a word spoken from the caller on the other end of the line. Firmani couldn't take the phone off the hook because he shared a phone line in the same block of flats with a doctor. The only solution was to sleep in his children's bedroom with cotton wool in his ears.

When Firmani left Sampdoria for Inter, he noticed the public's focus – and expectations – went up a notch. He and his teammates were mobbed in the street like film stars. As a married man, he didn't much care for the attention of screaming girls, which he spelt out in his memoir: 'There are times when these young ladies become a nuisance and ought to be spanked and sent home to bed.' There was a downside to celebrity.

Footballers were hounded by a new phenomenon – the paparazzi. Italy developed a vibrant tabloid press. There were two branches: 'the pink press', which fed women's interest magazines, and a sister category, 'the black press', which focused on true crime stories. The public were mad for them. The most popular magazines sold more than half a million copies a week. Pictures made the magazines. They brought stories to life. It fed a frenzy for the work of street photographers, who began to haunt Italy's night spots. Mainly freelancers, they hunted for a big score, a sensational image, something outrageous, someone with star appeal caught in a compromising position.

A particular kind of photojournalist excelled: the hungry, the unscrupulous, the cunning. They didn't scare easily. They prowled the streets looking for action, letting the air out of celebrities' car tyres so they could snap them milling about, waiting for a mechanic to arrive. They drove scooters, some graduated to small Fiat cars. They dressed smartly – in sports jackets, ties, polished shoes – so they could get into swanky joints. They bribed doormen, chambermaids and taxi drivers. Anything to get a scoop. A shot that was scandalous enough could buy a man a new car. The best of them had nicknames: 'The Human Machine Gun', 'The Liar', 'The Hairy One', 'The Pastry Eater'. One fellow was called 'Buster Keaton' because he never smiled.

5.

'The Italian press were very busy into the world of football. They had their noses everywhere,' said Denis Law. 'Back then, Italy was the home of world cinema and stuff. There was so much glamour. The paparazzi fed on it. It was a different media culture to what I was used to, a totally different experience. Back in England, you wouldn't have to think about media intrusion. When we were in England, we went on a regular city bus with fans to the game. The manager would say, "You've got to be at the stadium for two o'clock." It was a different world.

'But in Italy in those days, the paparazzi were everywhere. They were always out, patrolling, looking for something out of the ordinary. You had to be careful what you said or what you did and whatnot. It's a bit like today where everyone has a camera in their phone. It makes it very difficult to go out being a footballer now, with everyone taking pictures all the time. Back in Italy, playing at Torino with Joe Baker, we had a couple of incidents. One in Venice. One in Rome, which was like a sting job. We were young. We didn't know better. I guess we were a bit naïve.'

The Superga air disaster in 1949 had wiped out *Grande Torino*, arguably the greatest Italian club side in history. Since then, Torino had been in the shadow of their city rivals, Juventus. In the summer of 1961, the Turin club made a splash, signing the 21-year-old Denis Law – who would become a Ballon d'Or winner within a few years – and the England international centre-forward Joe Baker, also 21 years of age. Twice in one season, Law and Baker were done over by the paparazzi.

In November 1961, Torino travelled to Rome for a game against Roma. Law was at the centre of the action, scoring once and missing a penalty in a 2–2 draw. After the game, Law and Baker, who were visiting the capital for the first time, were given a couple of days' leave for sightseeing while the rest of the team returned to Turin. The pair met an Italian girl who spoke English. They arranged to go out for dinner with her and her friend, who only spoke Italian.

After the meal, the girls invited them to wander along Via Veneto, where visiting film stars hung out. During the course of the night, the footballers switched partners because of the difficulty of one of the girls not speaking English. At the time, there didn't appear to be any significance to the switch. The following morning Baker was pictured all over the Italian newspapers: bleary-eyed drunk coming out of a nightclub, swinging off a tree, his tie round the back of his neck, sprawled over the bonnet of a car. The headline in one of the papers read 'LA DOLCE VITA'.

'We discovered sometime later that one of the girls was planted by a photographer,' said Law. 'The real target had been me, but because we switched girls during the night, they settled on Joe. We never saw the photographer. He must have been slick at his job. We both got in a lot of trouble with Torino. The club whacked us with fines. We were disgraced.'

A couple of months later, they were hit again by the paparazzi in Venice. The day before a game against Venezia, the pair were strolling around the city, taking in some sights. They noticed they were being tailed by a photographer, who kept materialising around every corner, snapping with his camera. Baker lost his patience and punched him. The photographer hit the deck, blood spurting from his face after striking the pavement. His glasses flew into the Grand Canal. A crowd gathered. The footballers fled the scene, but were picked up by cops later and taken to a police station for questioning.

The story made for juicy headlines the next morning, especially when it emerged that the photographer – who was taken to hospital, only to re-emerge in a photo spread covered in head bandages – had a club foot. Baker had to pay the photographer £1000 in compensation. 'There was no way he could play in the match against Venezia either,' said Law. 'He would have been lynched. Can you imagine? A foreigner coming to town and boxing a crippled photographer.'

There was no escaping the paparazzi. In Milan, their favourite prey was a celebrity couple: a footballer and a blonde cabaret singer with a pair of breasts that Italians like to call *prosperose*. The footballer was the great Antonio Valentín Angelillo, the proclaimed successor of Alfredo Di Stéfano, the angel with a dirty face, Inter's star striker. His chaotic love life gave his boss, HH, a pain in the head.

17. ANGEL WITH A DIRTY FACE

1.

HH's reputation preceded him in Italy. Football men formed an opinion about him before he arrived in Milan to manage Internazionale in the summer of 1960. HH had to deny he was a scoundrel and a vagabond.

'I'm not a charlatan,' he told an Italian reporter. 'I am a man who came to success by suffering and suffering. Success goes to those who deserve it. I deserve it. I have the courage of my convictions, and I never hold back. If the Inter players listen to me, we will be together for a very long time. If they don't listen to me, it will be the worse for them.'

HH's warning to his new players – about where authority lay – was directed at one man in particular: Antonio Valentín Angelillo. His striker's card was marked.

2.

Angelillo was adored in Milan. He was an idol for the masses, up there in their affections with a statue covered in gold on top of the city's cathedral: 'In Milan, there was *La Madonnina* and then came Angelillo,' he said of himself. At the San Siro Stadium, fans created a song in his honour: 'Valentín, who makes all the terraces tremble…' He had been a child prodigy. As a kid playing on the dirt patches around Buenos Aires, he came to the attention of Arsenal, one of the city's many professional football clubs. The then president of Argentina, Juan Domingo Perón and his wife Evita, watched him perform one day while he was a team mascot. Perón was so impressed he slipped him a hundred peso note for his display, a staggering sum for a kid from the *barrios* in 1940s Argentina.

While still a teenager, Angelillo scored 11 goals in 11 internationals for Argentina. He was part of a historic attacking line-up known as 'Angels with Dirty Faces', a moniker taken from the 1938 Jimmy Cagney gangster movie. Their goals helped to crush the Brazil of Didí and Evaristo 3–0 en route to winning the 1957 Copa América with a game to spare. Money men from Italy swooped that summer in 1957, carving up a great team, one immortalised for its *joie de vivre*. The three best dirty faces, known also as the 'Trio of Death', were taken back to the old continent: Angelillo joined Inter; Omar Sívori went to Milan and Humberto Maschio was signed by Bologna. All three got life bans from the Argentinian FA for defecting to Italy so, once in exile, they ended up playing for the Italy national team; Humberto Maschio captained Italy at the 1962 World Cup finals in Chile.

Angelillo found it hard to settle in Italy. He struggled with his new language. There was racism in Inter's squad – players who looked down on South American immigrants, resenting them for taking bread from the Italians' table. Benito Lorenzi's goals won Inter back-to-back league titles in 1953/54, their last *scudetti*. Angelillo was a threat, a rival, someone who was edging Lorenzi towards the exit door. He gave Angelillo the cold shoulder, wouldn't pass him the ball, made dismissive faces at him, deriding Angelillo as if he was a foolish child, undermining him in the eyes of other teammates. Angelillo went into himself. Luckily, he had an important ally – the club's president, Angelo Moratti.

Moratti had heavy eyelids. He was lazy when it came to smiling. He was born in 1909, the son of a pharmacist. His mother died young and Moratti left home early and began building, rig by rig, a vast empire, one of the biggest petrol-refining companies in the world, which included Europe's largest refinery (in Sardinia) and several in the Middle East. He profited greatly during the Second World War, becoming a millionaire by buying and selling oil. He acquired a chain of castles and country estates, at prices reduced in wartime. People in Italy knew him as 'the Great Oil Man', a tycoon as rich as Aristotle Onassis, the Greek shipping magnate.

Moratti took over Inter in 1955. The fans warmed to him. Italians love a Strong Man. Mussolini, Gianni Agnelli, Silvio Berlusconi. Men – and monolithic institutions like the Catholic Church – who can protect them from a competitive world. Inter fans saw him as their saviour. He was mad about football. He could talk about the game for several hours a day. He pampered his players. Eddie Firmani gushed when I asked him about Moratti: 'The president of Inter, Moratti, was fantastic. He was a great man, a lovely man. He was class. After every victory, he invited the whole squad to his house in the countryside to have dinner with him. He gave us expensive coins – we'd get our bonus, but then with each player he'd also give us a gold or a silver coin if we won. We kept them. Later on, you could sell them or whatever you wanted to do with them. I kept mine until I went back to England. He had impeccable manners. He was one of the nicest and classiest men I ever met in my life.'

Moratti was temperamental by nature. Football didn't always calm his nerves. His way of dealing with stress was to give it to other people, especially his coaches at Inter. He discarded them on a whim. He went through 10 managers in five seasons before hitting on HH in 1960. He cared not for reputation. Giuseppe Meazza was an iconic striker with the club and twice a World Cup winner, captaining Italy to their 1938 triumph. He is arguably Italy's greatest ever footballer. San Siro was renamed *Stadio Giuseppe Meazza* in his honour, a year after his death, in 1980. Moratti hired, fired, rehired and fired Meazza again in a two-year spell. Meazza was dizzy leaving the club gates.

Angelillo was Moratti's star signing. Moratti saw his potential and nurtured him. Angelillo became like a son. The oil baron took him on holidays as his guest to one of his holiday properties in San Remo on the Italian Riviera. He tasked two senior, bachelor players in the squad, Livio Fongaro and Enea Masiero, to buddy up with Angelillo. Their brief was to lift Angelillo out of his torpor and get him settled in Milan. The club knew that Angelillo was thinking about packing it in and returning to Argentina.

Fongaro and Masiero took Angelillo out on the town socialising. They helped rouse him from his melancholy. It was then that the goals started to come. In Angelillo's second season with Inter, he scored 33 goals in 33 league games. It was an incredible tally, which earned him the nickname '*Signor Record*'. It took almost half a century for another player to break the 30-goal barrier in Serie A – Luca Toni in 2006.

In October 1958, in the middle of his celestial goalscoring feats, Angelillo fell in love with Ilya López. At the time, he was engaged to Inés Olga Valle, an Argentine immigrant like himself, of Italian descent. She was studying in college and was his girl-next-door fiancée. He dumped her after meeting Ilya López in a nightclub in Milan, La Porta d'Oro, where she was performing. It was *the* nightspot in town, frequented by film stars like Ava Gardner and rich, horny middle-aged businessmen and mobsters. It had a dress code: suit and tie only. Inside, strippers did their work. Angelillo became a regular.

Ilya López was a dancer and a singer. She looked like Doris Day, but with dark, sultry eyes. Ilya López was her stage name. She grew up as Attilia Tironi in Brescia. Several years older than Angelillo, she was already married, and divorce was then illegal in Italy. Once she hooked up with Angelillo, the paparazzi made her life hell. Even overseas. Their holidays in Mallorca became a media event. Fans insulted her. They made abusive phone calls and threatened her. The club tried to end her relationship with Angelillo. She was followed by detectives. She had a miscarriage, apparently from the stress of being hunted and castigated on the streets. Everyone gossiped about their relationship, a scandalous romance that replaced the love affair between Fausto Coppi and the so-called White Lady in people's lurid obsessions.

3.

Fausto Coppi was Italy's finest ever cyclist. In June 1940, on the day before Mussolini declared war on Britain and France, Coppi won the first of five Giro d'Italia crowns. He enlisted and fought with the Italian Army in the deserts of Africa, where he was taken prisoner by the British. In 1945, he returned to

Italy, a free man, landing ashore in Naples. Someone put a notice in a local newspaper appealing to get him a bike, which he used to cycle hundreds of miles back home to his village in northern Italy. His mother was shocked to see him alive.

Coppi became a symbol of the industrialised north. He was an atheist, left wing and outspoken. He admitted in a TV interview that he took amphetamines – which weren't illegal in the 1950s – during cycling races 'practically all the time'. He acquired the nickname 'Fausto the Sinner'. His great rival Gino Bartali – who was venerated in the rural, conservative south – was a God-fearing man known as 'Gino the Pious'. Coppi was pilloried because of his private life, which turned into a national scandal.

Coppi began an affair with Giulia Occhini. Both left their spouses to be with each other. The press labelled her *La Dama Bianca* – the White Lady, because of a distinctive white Montgomery duffle coat she wore, and rarely referred to her by her name. Pope Pius XII asked Coppi to return to his wife. Coppi didn't listen. In 1954, the pope refused to bless the Giro d'Italia, as was tradition, because Coppi was cycling.

A couple of months after the 1954 Giro d'Italia, the police raided Coppi's Italian villa at 3 a.m. Their mission was to establish if Coppi and the White Lady were sleeping together in the same bed. The White Lady's doctor husband waited outside the villa while the police carried out their search. The cops were thorough, gathering evidence, checking the mattress in the spare bedroom to see if it was still warm. The White Lady was arrested for the crime of adultery, and spent four days in prison. She was pictured by the paparazzi leaving prison with her belongings in a pillowcase.

Several months later, their case came to court. Coppi's eight-year-old daughter was called to testify. The trial hinged on a bizarre line of questioning. The judge established that police found two pillows in the spare bedroom, but none in Coppi's bedroom. Coppi's maid told the court it took an hour for her master to let the police in the front door because he was sleeping soundly. The judge was sceptical: 'Without pillows?' The court case captivated the nation. 'By supporting Fausto and her [Giulia Occhini] it felt like we were part of a battle against centuries of traditionalism in our stupid and listless country,' concluded Gianni Brera, the great Italian sportswriter.

In summing up, the prosecutor argued the White Lady was only using Coppi as a meal ticket: 'The beautiful Giulia waited for her man at the crossroads – not only because he was a star of world cycling but also because he was an ace of diamonds'. They were both convicted for adultery and given suspended jail sentences. The White Lady was barred from seeing her two children. In 1957, she won the legal right to see both children again, but only every two months. Their visits with each other had to be inside a religious institution in the presence of a senior religious figure such as a Mother Superior.

The Catholic Church ruled the roost in Italy. Angelillo's lover, Ilya López, was also portrayed as a sinner and a man-eater. That she was an older woman from a broken marriage caused a sensation. People sneered, scoffing that she was leading Angelillo by the nose. She was vilified. In the prim eyes of the Italian public, she was a *femme fatale*, an interloper, bent on gold-digging and destruction like the White Lady. 'They say the crisis in Milan [is] your fault, Miss López,' growled the press. She had to defend herself from lies and 'malicious reporting', and her portrayal as a she-cat, which was utterly humiliating.

4.

Ironically, Ilya López was a maternal influence on Angelillo. He was only 21 years old when he fell in love with her. She persuaded him to shave off his silly, out-of-fashion moustache. She confided in Gianni Brera, the sportswriter, about their relationship. She told him that Angelillo was assessed by a psychologist whose verdict was that 'the greatest centre-forward in the world' had the emotional intelligence of a 14-year-old boy. Angelillo completed his emotional development with her. Brera said she practically 'breastfed' Angelillo, and that they had a tender love affair. She made him happy, broadened his horizons.

The tabloid press didn't do nuance, however. Italy was a *macho* society under the thumb of the Vatican. The country's scandalmongers couldn't help themselves from feasting on their love affair. Angelillo and Ilya López were the symbol of a vibrant and thrusting – and illicit – Milan.

Gianni Brera, Ilya López's confidant, was a shrewd observer of human behaviour. He was the great chronicler of Italian football in the twentieth century. He experienced a busy war, joining a parachute regiment and, when Italy signed an armistice with the Allies, fighting the Nazis with a partisan brigade. He took up sports journalism again after the war. He wrote widely about his interests, including travel and food, as well as authoring novels and plays. By 30, he was editor of the prestigious *La Gazzetta dello Sport*.

Brera was a pipe-smoking, heavy-drinking bon-vivant. He held court at a restaurant, A Riccione, in the centre of Milan, which he referred to as his 'office'. In looks, he was a short, stocky man with a shock of greying hair, a less gaunt-looking version of Charles Bukowski. Both men held ferocious opinions. Sandro Mazzola, a linchpin in HH's Inter team, dreaded reading Brera's match reports. Like a man given to self-flagellation, though, Mazzola couldn't avoid poring over the 'words that cut'.

Brera educated Italian football fans, instructing them on how to observe the game. He coined new terms, such as *libero* for a sweeper, and had a majestic power for imagery: 'Although generous in his efforts to recover the ball, Giorgio Chinaglia can't sing and carry the cross.' He gave players playful and often disparaging nicknames such as 'the Little Abbot' for Gianni Rivera. Brera thought that wispy No. 10s – like Rivera, winner of the Ballon d'Or in 1969 – were an extravagance.

Brera liked defensive football. He famously believed 'the perfect match would end 0–0' and that *catenaccio* – combined with opportunism and counter-attacking football – was a 'holy' practice. He had an odd anthropological theory about why *catenaccio* took hold in Italy. After the Second World War, Italy was in ruins. Its people were malnourished, its confidence at a low ebb. It had to be pragmatic. It couldn't think big. Italian football clubs must focus on the art of defending because of diet and genetics and circumstance; Italians were inferior physically to footballers in northern Europe. So, better to get men behind the ball.

HH, though, was surprised by how big his players at Inter were compared to the teams he had managed in Spain in the 1950s. Although HH claimed to have invented *catenaccio* while coaching in France in the 1940s, Brera maintained HH was 'forced' to adopt the philosophy when he came to manage in Serie A. His team at Barça – with the free-scoring Sándor Kocsis, Evaristo and Eulogio Martínez up front – was famous for its relentless attacking play. HH was part of a wave in Italy, one of many *difensivista* coaches, but eventually he became the poster boy for *catenaccio* because no one did it better.

HH grew to hate Brera, dismissing him as a 'drunken sclerotic'. Brera – who wrote a book about him – was ambivalent about the football coach. He thought HH was vulgar, a clown and a megalomaniac, but conceded that he was also 'a genius'.

5.

HH was exasperated when told about the Angelillo saga on his arrival in Italy. He'd just arrived, and they landed him with a 'Kubala case'. The goals had dried up for Angelillo. He scored only a third as many league goals in the 1959/60 season, compared with his record-breaking 1958/59 season. 'Angelillo's decline would be something of a mystery if we did not know that he is preoccupied with non-sporting passions,' concluded Brera.

Firmani confirmed Brera's assessment: 'The problem was his girlfriend. Every opportunity he got he took us to see her performing on stage. She was a singer in a group of three or four singers. They were often working in France. Angelillo would take off every weekend to see her. Sometimes driving from Milan over the border to France, as far away as Paris, just to see her and then driving back again the next day. I tell you it sapped him at the same time because he went off his game.'

HH was a pragmatist. He was ready to cut Angelillo a break. But being infatuated with a voluptuous showgirl wasn't Angelillo's only problem. HH felt he wasn't fit enough. He wanted to get him in shape, see if he responded to some tough love. Angelillo was still only 23 years old. His wayward lifestyle wasn't set in stone like Kubala's. HH had enough faith that under his command, Angelillo's panorama would change. He made the player his personal project. He gave him his undivided attention and the player responded to his methods. Angelillo started to warm to HH; he began to respect him. And began to deliver the goals.

Inter raced out of the blocks at the start of the season. They put 14 goals past Hannover over two legs in the first round of the Fairs Cup. In the league, they racked up 18 goals in their first four games. Angelillo was on fire, scoring seven goals in nine league games. The press fawned over HH's early season success: 'Herrera the Hurricane'. They compared him to Attila the Hun, the man who plundered Italy in the fifth century. Now here was HH, another foreigner conquering Italy. Inter's ultras chanted his name: 'Herrera! Herrera! You're the best!'

The plaudits, the adulation made HH edgy. He felt they were premature. What would happen when Inter suffered their first defeat? HH knew it took only one defeat at a big club like Inter for the coach's bench to tremble. A second defeat, and he mightn't be eating his Christmas cake in Milan. Sure enough, his team got a lesson from mid-table Padova on the road in mid-November. Inter lost 2–1, but the scoreboard didn't reflect how easy the game was for Padova. They were like granite, and Inter couldn't penetrate their defence. The press started beating the war drums, calling HH a 'fraud', accusing him of pushing his players too hard, that the pace and rhythm of their play was unsustainable over a long season. Rival coaches concurred: HH was a bluffer.

HH was fuming. His star striker Angelillo didn't perform during the Padova game. Then he ducked off the train home to Milan midway. Like a thief in the night. Getting off at the stop for Brescia, to see his lover in her hometown. A month later, a week before Christmas Day, HH dropped a bomb. He left Angelillo out of the starting line-up for Inter's game against Juventus; the *Derby d'Italia*, a phrase coined by Gianni Brera. It was a tie that invariably had a bearing on the title race. Juve, the biggest club in Italy, was owned by Fiat, the biggest company in Italy, and the Agnelli family. The club drew fans from all over the country. Since the 1930s, it has been known as '*La Fidanzata d'Italia*' ('The Girlfriend of Italy'). Inter were their ancient rivals.

HH was fed up with Angelillo. He wanted to play a fast, dynamic game. Speed was his greatest weapon. A soloist like Angelillo – who had no strength left in him from his trysts – was useless to him. HH hated footballers like Kubala and Angelillo who danced on the pitch with the ball. He preferred competitiveness to spectacle. The decision to axe Angelillo caused uproar. But HH had seen it all before. The public in thrall to an idol, devoting itself to false gods. It was a difficult moment for HH. He was risking all his hard work and prestige on one match, one roll of the dice. The media in Milan shuddered. Inter – who were 15 points adrift of defending champions Juventus the previous season – would have to nullify John Charles and Omar Sívori, who were scoring 50 league goals a campaign. 'How will Inter defend against Juve?' asked the press. HH replied that Juve would be doing the defending. So it was. Charles and Sívori were kept scoreless. Inter won 3–1, with Firmani scoring Inter's third goal. HH – once again – was vindicated.

HH stripped the captaincy from Angelillo and gave the armband to the team's *libero*, Armando Picchi. He couldn't stomach it when his players fell into the arms of desirable women. Only hard work and monk-like application could possibly save Angelillo now. HH gave him an ultimatum: stay away from your lover over Christmas, 'far away from temptation'. Angelillo ignored the warning. He was a possessive lover – he couldn't handle the thought of Ilya López being seduced in the nightclub where she worked. He rarely left her side. The paparazzi snapped the lovers dining together in a Milan restaurant over the Christmas period, and Angelillo's days were numbered. He played only a handful of games for the remainder of the season, scoring one more league goal for Inter. He was no longer a god of the ball. He was again a mere mortal.

Angelillo denied that he was destroyed by sex. He claimed HH was jealous of his fame and his vigorous love life. Brera shared this opinion, believing that HH was envious of Angelillo's success with women and his affair with the beautiful Ilya López. HH wasn't bothered by their speculation. He cared only about football results. Angelillo's performances had taken a nosedive. He was no good to him any more. He decided to get rid of him.

Firmani wasn't surprised: 'Helenio Herrera was a tough guy. He didn't take crap from anybody. Therefore, if you didn't do what Herrera wanted you to do, you were out of the team. There was no messing around.' Firmani himself was dropped by HH towards the end of his time as a player at Inter (and sold to Genoa). I asked him if he spoke to HH about being left out of the team. 'No. I didn't speak to Herrera about being dropped. You couldn't speak to Herrera. He'd talk you out of what you were thinking anyway. He was his own man 100 per cent.'

Before the season finished, HH persuaded Moratti to sell Angelillo, his surrogate son, to Roma. Moratti had to choose between HH and Angelillo, and he chose HH. He also paid HH a king's ransom for salary – 45 million lira per season, equal to the combined salaries of Nereo Rocco and Giuseppe Viani,

Milan's vaunted coach and sporting director duo, excluding a double rate for HH's win bonuses. Moratti also paid the fines HH accrued from the Italian Football Federation for misconduct. His wealth was a blessing for HH. 'We all pray for him,' said HH.

Moratti stepped with soft feet around HH. 'When Moratti wanted to suggest something to Herrera – like, say, selling a player or organising a friendly match in Germany – he went through Herrera's wife,' said Alfredo Relaño, referring to the mother of HH's fifth and sixth children. Around 1950, while coaching Atlético Madrid, HH deserted his first wife, Lucienne Léonard, and their four children, and began an affair with María Morilla Pérez, a married woman with her own children, who had left her husband. HH and María Morilla Pérez couldn't marry because divorce was illegal in Spain and Italy at the time. Nevertheless, they lived together and had two children, Helenio Jr, born in 1952, and Rocío, born in 1957.

Relaño continued: 'Moratti never made petitions directly to Herrera. Herrera always said, "No." So, instead, Moratti started using Herrera's wife as an intermediary. He actually paid a little money for that service. Herrera was very tight with money. He kept all his money for himself. He only gave his wife a pittance to run the house. I was friendly with his son, Helenio Jr. We did military service together. He told me these kinds of things. The only thing Herrera paid for himself while he was manager at Inter was a ticket to the cinema on the day of his daughter Rocío's birthday. Herrera loved his daughter Rocío. Herrera almost got "divorced" when he discovered that Moratti was giving money to his wife. He thought his wife and Moratti were lovers.'

HH used the money from the Angelillo sale to buy Luisito Suárez – or Luis Suárez as he became known in Italy – from Barça. Angelillo's career went south. He played in a more withdrawn role for several Serie A clubs during the 1960s, but he never again scaled the goalscoring heights of that glorious 1958/59 season. His relationship with Ilya López fizzled out after about a decade together. She carved out a minor career as an actress. Angelillo settled down in Tuscany, with his wife, Bianca, and two children.

Angelillo never forgave HH, even after being taken back into the bosom of Inter. Decades after leaving the club as a player, he worked as a scout for Inter. When HH died in 1997, Angelillo didn't go to his funeral. 'Why would I go to the funeral? To show what? After so many years of fighting what could I say?'

18. GREAT WHITE NIGHTS

1.

In the early hours of an August morning in 1962, the actress Marilyn Monroe died, in mysterious circumstances. Before dying, she was caught up in a love triangle with US Attorney General Robert F. Kennedy and his brother John F. Kennedy, the American president. The world was on edge, as JFK and Nikita Khrushchev hurtled towards a nuclear face-off over Cuba. Schoolchildren lived in fear of the dropping of the bomb.

A few days after Marilyn Monroe's death, JFK's wife, Jacqueline Kennedy, decamped to Italy for three weeks. Her entourage included her two children – toddler John Jr. and four-year-old Caroline – her sister and brother-in-law, a nurse, a personal assistant and Secret Service men. Everyone loved Jackie. She was young, beautiful and graceful – and she was married to the most powerful man in the world. Based on a recommendation by Gore Vidal, she chose Ravello, a seaside town on the Amalfi Coast, to holiday. There are few better places to forget your worries. The president's family stayed at the Palazzo Episcopio, a former residence of King Vittorio Emmanuele III.

In the mornings, Jackie Kennedy jumped into a convertible Fiat 600 and went waterskiing, her favourite sport. The Fiat magnate Gianni Agnelli put himself at her disposal, becoming her escort on vacation. The paparazzi pictured them lolling around in his yacht, sitting outside a bar in a plaza. The 41-year-old Agnelli, who was a magnet for gorgeous, glamorous women, looked like the cat that got the cream. He was nicknamed 'The Rake of the Riviera'. His lovers included Pamela Harriman (Winston Churchill's daughter-in-law), Rita Hayworth and Anita Ekberg, the star of *La Dolce Vita*. He married a Neapolitan princess, Marella Caracciolo, who was rumoured in royal circles to have the longest neck in Europe.

Marriage never got in the way of Agnelli's womanising. He reckoned that only maids fell in love. He had several *garçonnières* – lavish villas in which to cavort with mistresses, each one decorated with paintings and sculptures from one of the world's finest private art collections. During Jackie Kennedy's stay on the Amalfi Coast, Agnelli had his own room in her palatial villa. Tongues wagged. Gossip about their affair echoed around the world. The *New York Daily News* ran a headline: 'FIRST LADY IN PIRATE'S DEN'. JFK got spooked, firing off a telegram to his wife: 'More Caroline, less Agnelli.' She was ordered home.

Agnelli was the uncrowned king of Italy, one of the most powerful men in the world. He turned Fiat into a global conglomerate. As head of the corporation, he sat at the top of a feudal network of power. His influence went beyond industry into politics, the media, society and culture. Fiat workers had a slogan: 'Agnelli is Fiat, Fiat is Turin, and Turin is Italy.' Monarchs and governments came and went but, according to Henry Kissinger, Gianni Agnelli remained Italy's permanent establishment. He embodied the thrilling aspects of Italian character. His dashing, debonair style and sense of dress made him a fashion icon. Whatever he did was copied. His habit of wearing his wristwatch over his cuff became a trend, conveying the spirit of *sprezzatura*, the Italian art of making the difficult look easy.

Boredom was his enemy in life. He fought on the Eastern Front in the Second World War, and when Italy switched sides, he fought against the Nazis. After the war, he snorted a lot of cocaine. The great white nights. He loved bobsleighing. Anything to do with speed. His physical courage bordered on the suicidal. He careered around the streets of Turin in a Ferrari car as if he were in a Formula 1 race, oblivious to policemen, red lights and one-way streets. A near-death car crash left one of his legs badly crushed (although it never stopped him skiing). He liked to start his weekend by jumping out of a helicopter into the Mediterranean Sea and swimming ashore to meet his friends or a lover.

People were in awe. It felt like every woman wanted to sleep with him. And that every man envied him – none more than his youngest brother, Umberto, who lived in his shadow. Several times Umberto was passed over for the top job at Fiat. It's rumoured that he was illegitimate, the bastard son of Curzio Malaparte, a controversial writer. (Umberto's mother was killed in a car accident in 1945, shortly after his 11th birthday. She was seated beside a trouser-less driver – who escaped with minor injuries – when her neck broke.) Carlo De Benedetti, one-time CEO of Fiat, dismissed Umberto as weak. He continued playing second fiddle to his illustrious brother until Gianni died in 2003, enabling Umberto to belatedly ascend to the throne, if only for 18 months until he, too, died, leaving behind a personal fortune of $5.5 billion.

In the early 1960s, football was an arena where Umberto Agnelli could flex his muscles, a place he could assert himself, away from his brother. In 1956, while still only 21 years old and a law student at the University of Turin, he was given the chairmanship of Juventus. (A plaything that his son, Andrea Agnelli, inherited in 2010 until he stepped down as president in 2022.) In 1959, Umberto Agnelli was made president of the Italian Football Federation. Holding the two biggest jobs in Italian football made him a dangerous enemy for HH. His power was great, and he knew how to use it. He also despised

HH. The venom was real, though. HH never recalled saying or doing anything personal to provoke him. HH suspected the problem was that Inter were winning. If Inter had been losing, he would have been ignored. That's how it works.

2.

As the spring of 1961 kicked in, Inter were locked in a race against Juventus for the title. Midseason, HH discarded Angelillo, the club's ace striker, but his team was motoring. They were a compact unit. The players believed in him. They had no choice. The players knew the rules: they were under a dictatorship. Training with HH was like life in a military barracks. He didn't spare the rod. Some prospered, others fell by the wayside.

'He was tough on us, especially in training sessions,' said Firmani. 'He would be shouting, pushing you all the time. Push, push, push, push. He would speak with players openly. All the other players would hear what he was saying. So, whatever you did wrong, you wouldn't do it wrong again. Players would get upset, but you couldn't show you were upset with Herrera because he would take it out on you more. He would attack a player at every training session. There was no holding back with him.

'Herrera's notoriety came from him being tough, really tough. He was loud. He was tougher than any manager I played under. He demanded a lot from you – to do with stamina, your work rate, your application – and if you didn't give it in training, you weren't in the team. Other managers I worked with in football were nicer to the players. Some of them were strong men, but he was tough, an unbelievably rough guy. I suppose he had a tough upbringing where he had to fight for things whereas in Europe, it was much easier.'

HH batted off criticism that he was a tyrant. 'I like discipline. It's true,' he said. 'Players are the first to demand it because they are aware of being authentic professionals. They know they are in good hands. Without discipline, no club is sustainable ... we all have to sacrifice to get success.' He set the tone, demanding standards of excellence. Football was a competitive, contact sport. It was about bullying or being bullied. He wanted to create an unbreakable spirit in his teams. Discipline was the bedrock of that template. There was no room for mavericks in his camp.

For training sessions, HH didn't want assistants around. He did everything himself, all the drills. He showed them how it was done, even though he was in his fifties. He had unbelievable stamina, and he minded himself. He had an ascetic diet (chiefly plain pasta with olive oil and parmesan cheese). For half a century, he practised yoga naked every morning. He was blessed with a positive attitude, which he topped up with self-help mantras. 'I feel strong, serene, calm.

I am not afraid of anything … and I am good-looking,' he repeated to himself every morning after his yoga session. He studied Buddhism. He was a curious mix of influences and tensions – aspects of Zen, violence and skulduggery all thrown in together.

HH kept his players in *ritiro* from Friday to Monday. Add lengthy European trips to their working week, and the players were totally under his control. I asked Firmani how HH treated Firmani's wife. Did he know her? Did he build up a relationship with her? 'Your wives didn't come into it when you were under Herrera,' he said. 'The wives didn't come into it at all. In fact, you didn't even see your wife.'

Players had to be in bed at 10 p.m. every night (except Mondays). They were fined if late for training. In *ritiro*, players were obliged to play chess and to learn English. They weren't allowed to drink alcohol except for watered-down wine and weak beer at mealtimes. The smokers on the team – HH despised players who smoked – were allowed two cigarettes a day. He was fastidious about his players' diet. He decided what they ate. He always got his kitmen to cook for the squad. He was paranoid, didn't want any strangers around his kitchen.

HH found a house close to the club's training ground. He was always first to arrive, last to leave. He was a workaholic. He rose at 6 a.m. unless something was bothering him and he was already awake. Before training started, he wrote correspondence or articles for the press on a typewriter. He rarely took a *siesta* (although his players always took one at 2.30 p.m. for 90 minutes). When he got home from training, he spoke football with his wife. Or he might play a little football in the hallway with his young children, Helenito and Rocío.

Invariably, he'd lock himself away in his home office, reading press reports, preparing for matches, making notes or organising travel, food, hotels. The odd evening, he went to the cinema. He loved crime films. They were the only thing that could take his mind off football. On leaving the cinema, he'd drop by the club to take care of business, maybe do some press interviews. While waiting for dinner, he'd watch football reports on TV. He ate and drank the sport. 'I'm married to a ball,' said María Morilla Pérez, his second partner.

Dinner was at 9 p.m., but he continued to field questions from journalists if they phoned. He frequently disconnected the phone to get some peace. After dinner, he retreated to his study until late. Around his desk, he had the machinery of war: the fixtures list; tactical notes; a list with players' defects he had to fix. Or notes to himself written in large letters: 'HAVE CONFIDENCE IN YOURSELF … WHEN YOU'RE EATING, EAT; WHEN YOU'RE SLEEPING, SLEEP'.

Sleep was a stranger to him. His mind raced once his head hit the pillow. He'd run over events and errors in a game. Sometimes in the middle of the night, he'd shake his wife awake to discuss a tactical problem that was troubling him or to determine if one player was performing better than another. He tried all kinds of tricks to find sleep: sleeping pills, counting sheep, but none of them worked. He always ended up selecting, say, Italy's starting XI for the upcoming World Cup finals in Chile. (Coaching Italy's national team was another portfolio he held, along with his jobs as coach of Inter's first team and youths.) The only thing that might work was to think about the last film he'd seen. To try and think about nothing was fatal.

'Am I happy?' HH asked himself, in a moment of reflection. 'I don't have time to think about it. I suppose this is a form of happiness in the eastern sense. I've more things in common with a steam train that devours kilometres than a Buddhist in a monastery. I don't curse the vertigo of modern life. On the contrary, I find it is made for me. I congratulate myself for the luck I've had, but sometimes I would love to relax! Every time I leave a club, I believe that the next one will be less turbulent. It always ends up the same: mess, triumphs, defeats, more mess. And also, more money. Of course.'

3.

By the spring of 1961, the press in Italy – and HH's players at Inter – took to calling him '*Il Mago*' ('The Magician'). HH began working the *catenaccio* system effectively. He had a come-to-Jesus moment away to Padova in the league's seventh round of fixtures, earlier in the season, the day his relationship with Angelillo began to break down irrevocably. In a game that is famous in the annals of Serie A tactics history, Inter lost 2–1 to Padova. HH's team couldn't break down Padova's blanket defence. It came on the back of draws for Inter against two other struggling Serie A clubs, who also flooded their defences.

Briefly confounded, HH resolved to beat the Italians at their own game, adopting the in vogue *catenaccio* system. He installed an extra defender, a *libero*, in his line-up, and encouraged his full-backs not to stay fixed in position, but to join in the team's swift counter-attacks. HH's gift was in copying ideas and making them better. No crime in that, and because of his knack for self-publicity, they became polished to such perfection that it seemed as if they – as with *catenaccio* – had always been his ideas in the first place.

HH drove his men remorselessly. Every match was life or death. Speed, the essential ingredient of counter-attacking football, was his best weapon. His players did everything fast. (God help any player who was lazy on the pitch.) 'Modern football is speed,' he kept repeating to his players: move with speed; pass the ball with speed; think with speed. His players had to be aware of their position on the pitch and those around them, as well as the puddles. Full-backs doubled as auxiliary wingers. Rival clubs came to spy on HH's training sessions. They imitated his tactical innovations, even the food he fed the team.

In early March 1961, Inter trounced Lazio 7–0 to open a three-point gap over Juventus. Then there was a wobble. Inter lost three games on the bounce. Their lead in the title race disappeared like mist on a sunny morning. Critics warned that the relentless pace HH's Inter played was unsustainable over a long season. They criticised his gruelling training methods. Fatigue set in. Injuries piled up. Inter's international midfielder Franco Zaglio was recovering from a knee operation. HH was anxious to rush him back into the starting line-up against Sampdoria for their next league game. He was desperate to stop the losing streak. Zaglio didn't feel he was ready to play. HH banished his fears. 'Don't worry about your fitness. I'll take care of it.' Zaglio scored in a 4–2 defeat.

'To my surprise, I survived the 90 minutes easily,' said Zaglio. 'The problems began in the evening. We were still in *ritiro* because Herrera wanted us to stay in camp, and there was no way I could fall asleep. I complained to Mauro Bicicli, my roommate, but he just grinned: "Did he give you 'the coffee'?" I understood immediately.' Zaglio wasn't a complete fool. When he played with Spal during the 1957/58 season, the club's older players had their 'box of tricks'. At Roma – where he played from 1958 until joining Inter in 1960 – the team was given 'vitamins', which Zaglio claimed were systematically flushed down the toilet.

HH didn't invent doping in Italy, but he practised it with such gusto that it cast a shadow over his work. I asked Firmani about this. He denied taking drugs, said he was never offered 'vitamins' or pep drugs before a game, but that he heard rumours about drug-taking. 'I remember Dr Angiolino Quarenghi, the club doctor at Inter. He was very nice, very open with the players. I wouldn't think that he would get involved in that, but he may have done, I don't know. The [medics, the coaching staff] can also kid you, give you, say, a cold medicine injection which could be something else. If you had a cold or flu, you'd get injections. The doctor would give you a shot. That's the only thing that I can remember. I had those shots.'

4.

The defeat to Sampdoria left Inter trailing Juve by four points by the time they met each other in April 1961. With seven games to play in the league campaign, it was a last chance saloon for Inter in the title race. They had to win. The game was played a few days after Yuri Gagarin became the first human to travel in outer space and a day before the Bay of Pigs Invasion. The match was the biggest game in town. Juventus got greedy and sold more tickets than they should have. There was chaos at the turnstiles at their stadium in Turin.

Thousands of fans streamed into the ground without tickets. The stadium was so full that fans trickled on to the athletics track surrounding the pitch. Some crowded around HH's dugout. A few ended up sitting beside HH on the bench.

In the first quarter, Inter charged into Juve with a fury, pushing them backwards into their own half. The ref kept half an eye on the overcrowding, and at one stage he stopped the game to remove fans from the side of the pitch. The stadium shook on the half-hour mark when Inter's midfielder Egidio Morbello crashed a shot against the post. The excitement sparked a pitch invasion. The ref had had enough, and suspended the match.

Ten days later, Serie A's administrators awarded Inter the win, with a 2–0 scoreline, based on similar precedents. The law was clear. It was the shot in the arm that HH needed. It meant Inter closed the gap at the top of the table to two points. Going into the final day of the season, the two clubs were level on points. Juventus looked cooked, having lost their penultimate league game 1–0 to Padova.

Then Umberto Agnelli – as president of the Italian Football Federation – stepped in and played God. Juventus appealed the ruling to award Inter the points for the game in Turin, suspended because of a pitch invasion. Agnelli put pressure on the appeals committee to rule in Juve's favour, which it did. The game at Turin would have to be replayed a week later. Inter had their points for the win taken from them, and now trailed Juve by two points. News arrived in Inter's hotel on the eve of their final league game. HH and his players felt cheated. Their morale was left on the floor.

It didn't help that Inter faced Catania the following day in their small, noisy stadium on the island of Sicily. Earlier in the season, HH had shot his mouth off, mocking Catania after Inter thrashed them 5–0 in San Siro; four of Inter's scores came from own goals. 'We beat a team of telegraph workers,' said HH. The Sicilians put a hex on Inter. Before kick-off, a fan evaded security and threw a kilo of salt over HH in the dugout, a superstition that promised to bring the home side good luck. It worked. Inter couldn't raise a gallop. They lost 2–0. The title race was over. Juventus – who drew 1–1 with Bari – were declared champions with a game to spare.

Firmani reckons HH pushed his players too hard. They were spent by spring: 'Herrera wanted 110 per cent – not just 100 per cent – from you, every day in training, in matches. He was very, very intense. He did more mileage on the sidelines than the players did on the pitch. That's why he could win matches. He was very successful as a coach at Barcelona and all these teams in Spain, but he worked us so hard that season. It was punishing. We were top of the league, but when it came towards the end of the season, we had nothing left in the tank. It backfired. We lost the league because some of the players were too tired.'

HH didn't have an 'off' button. It wasn't in his make-up. This man of furious ambition. He was on it seven days a week. He never took his foot off the gas, never let his guard down. He could be exhausting to be around. As Inter's team bus headed to the airport the morning after an away game, HH would be standing in the aisleway roaring at his players: '*Pensa alla partita! Pensa alla partita!*' ('Think about the [next] game!')

Six days after the loss to Catania, HH sent Inter's youth team to Turin for the replayed match with Juventus, which was now a dead rubber tie. He did it in spite so Juve couldn't enjoy their coronation, demeaning the fixture by sending out a team of kids. Juventus won 9–1, in what became known as 'the ghost match'. One footnote from the encounter was that an 18-year-old Sandro Mazzola, Inter's iconic player from the 1960s (and son of the great Valentino Mazzola who died in the 1949 Superga air disaster), made his debut. HH had pulled some strings to get his accountancy exams deferred so he could play the match – and Mazzola scored Inter's consolation goal.

As the youth academy's pearl, Sandro Mazzola trained all season with the first team. He remembers the team's older players were sceptical of HH when he first landed on their doorstep. 'Training always started with laps around the pitch,' he said. 'I remember the veterans running around the pitch a few days after Herrera was appointed, and they said: "This coach won't last long. Two weeks and he'll be gone." I was a young player and wondered why they said that. Then, we started winning games one after another, so there were some players joking with that lot: "You're the ones that will be kicked out now!" He was a great coach. He was Il Mago!'

A few weeks later, Inter's youth team returned to Turin for a decisive game in their under-age national championship. Inter's president Angelo Moratti ordered HH not to travel for the match because of the bad blood between the two clubs. HH couldn't resist the *morbo*, though, and went to Turin. Juve's fans were climbing the fences in the stadium. They wanted to kill him. Inter's youths won 2–0, which clinched the title. Their bus was attacked leaving the stadium, and they returned to Milan without a pane of window glass. HH and his young players huddled on the bus's floor until they got out of Turin. HH grinned all the way.

5.

The following season, 1961/62, began with two novelties. The season started early, so it could be finished by mid-April, which would give Italy's national team time to prepare for the World Cup finals in Chile in the summer of 1962. Doping controls were also introduced by the Italian Football Federation to try and combat a rampant problem in Italian football. A study in 1961 by the federation, entitled *Doping and Professional Football*, revealed that 22 per cent of Italian footballers in Serie A and Serie B took stimulants, or 'joy pills', predominately amphetamines.

During preseason, HH did a clear-out, shipping out 16 players, including Angelillo and Firmani. He brought in six players, among them Luisito Suárez and Gerry Hitchens, a striker from Aston Villa. The 26-year-old Hitchens, who had worked down the pits as a miner in his teens, hit pay dirt. He was coming off the back of a stellar season in which he had scored 42 goals for Villa, and got called up to the England national team, scoring two goals in a 3–2 win against Italy in Rome in May 1961. The rich form earned him a big money move to Italy. Joining Inter came with a £10,000 signing-on fee and a salary greater than that of the British prime minister, Harold Macmillan.

Hitchens was joined on his Italian adventure by Jimmy Greaves, who signed for AC Milan the same summer. During the season, the pair occasionally met up covertly, in the back room of a crowded bar at Milan's central station, for a few beers. The paparazzi hounded Greaves in particular, claiming he drank rivers of whisky. They coined the expression *jimmyfollie* (jimmymadness) for his drinking benders. He fled Italy midseason, retreating to London, joining Spurs. He couldn't handle the persecution by the press, the intrusion into his private life, being treated like a kid by the club. He was spied on. His letters were opened. His shopping habits were checked. His wife complained she was molested on the streets of Milan.

Hitchens adapted quickly on the pitch. He scored five goals in his first five Serie A games. Fans took to calling him '*Il Cannone*' because of his thunderous shot. His goals helped Inter race into a lead at the top of the table. By Christmas time, they were four points clear of the chasing pack. But again, it was the same story: in the second half of the season they began to wilt. On 25 February 1962, they faced Juventus at San Siro. Inter were lying in second place in the table, a point behind Fiorentina. They went 2–0 ahead, with goals by Mauro Bicicli and Hitchens, but two late goals by Juve tied the match.

After the game, three Inter players – Bicicli, who opened the scoring against Juve; Franco Zaglio; and the team's central defender, Aristide Guarneri, who was on Italy's European Championship-winning team in 1968 – were called for doping controls. All of them failed their tests, part of a cohort of eight players in Serie A that weekend who were busted. This was Serie A's first doping case. The levels of amphetamines found in Inter's players were through the roof, compared with other players from Bologna and Mantova who also tested positive. Each of the three convicted Inter players got a two-game suspension and a fine.

The weekend after, Gerry Hitchens also failed a drugs test after Inter lost 1–0 away at Palermo. (Omar Sívori, AC Milan's Ballon d'Or player, was also hooked in a raid that weekend.) When the results of Hitchens' failed drug test were made public a month later, the English press made hay. The story was front-page news. The *Daily Express* ran with a headline: 'BOMBSHELL ON EASTER'S BIG DAY OF SPORT: SOCCER DOPE ROW: ACCUSED: ENGLAND STAR HITCHENS.'

Interviewed by the English press, Hitchens denied taking dope. 'It's ridiculous. It must have been a Mickey Finn. If a doctor says traces of drugs were found I cannot argue, but I don't know how I got it. It must have been slipped into my food or drink. I have never knowingly taken any pep drugs.' Inter's medical officer, Dr Quarenghi, claimed the only stimulant Hitchens took was sugar: 'I think the medical experts have mistaken the symptoms and erroneously diagnosed the after-effects of sugar.' The club's president Angelo Moratti – who temporarily resigned from his post in March 1962 because of health problems – was forced to come out and defend the club from the scandal.

Hitchens was ultimately acquitted, but the quantity of drugs floating around the campus at Inter in the early 1960s meant the club was equipped like 'a small hospital', to borrow an expression used about the doping culture at Juventus in the 1990s. HH used the players on the youth team as 'guinea pigs' for his drug experiments, according to Ferruccio Mazzola, who was on the books at Inter's youth academy at the time (and a younger brother of Sandro Mazzola).

'I can describe the effects of those white tablets,' he wrote in a confessional memoir. He said he couldn't sleep after taking HH's pills. The hallucinations left him like a fish thrown up on the bank of a river. 'I was shaking all over. I looked like an epileptic. I was scared. Also, the effect lasted for days and was followed by a sudden, tremendous tiredness.' He said a lot of players were reluctant to take them. Taking advice from senior players, they hid them under their tongues and spat them out later in the toilet. But it was hard to dupe HH. 'Herrera didn't let himself be played so easily: he dissolved them into coffee, checking as much as possible in person that we took the medicine before the game.'

It was almost impossible for a youth team player to refuse the juice. (It's a bind for a young pro in the dressing room of any elite, dog-eat-dog sports team, unsure of themselves, trying to get ahead, not knowing the norms.) It wasn't the done thing to question HH's authority. 'Il Mago encouraged us to take [amphetamines], to use sugar,' said Egidio Morbello, a first team player. HH was the boss. It would have been fatal for a young player's career prospects to go against him. 'They were like bombs. They gave you a real kick,' said Pierluigi Gambogi, a youth team player at the time. 'We knocked them back. We wanted to get noticed – to get into the big leagues.'

The side effects from amphetamines can be brutal. Marcello Giusti was Pierluigi Gambogi's best friend. He was small in stature, a joker, who played as a centre-forward. Giusti was called up to the squad for a midweek reserve game in 1962 away to Como. He travelled with the team but didn't play. Perhaps as a joke or by coercion, he took one of the white pills that was going around. After the final whistle, he freaked out, climbing the walls in the dressing room and drooling at the mouth like a rabid dog. He was so out of it that his teammates thought he was kidding around. When the players got on the team bus, Giusti was missing. HH didn't care and nodded at the driver to leave: 'He can catch up with us at the toll bridge.' It was 2km to the highway. Giusti took off running. Luckily, the bus was held up in traffic, so he caught up.

6.

HH's Inter got off with a slap on the wrist for their doping convictions in April 1962 – a few fines, a few short player suspensions. The scare didn't knock HH off his stride. He carried on his regime, resolving not to be as sloppy in future. The doping controls were easily overcome. 'There were a thousand ways to get away with it,' said Zaglio. For European competition, there were no doping controls. It was the Wild West. 'Things changed in the international cups,' said Zaglio, 'because you know when a game is worth 3 million in prize money, anyone can decide to take a risk.'

For doping controls in Italy, vials of urine from a 'clean' player – often a substitute – were given to a doped player going in for a test. Or HH would put forward a player like Egidio Morbello because he knew he was clean, and his urine would always pass muster. Teams in Serie A went to elaborate lengths to hoodwink the testers. Carlo Petrini was a striker for Genoa and AC Milan in the 1960s. He gave some insight in his autobiography about one of the ploys used at Genoa: 'Before the game, the "clean" urine of some Genoa players who were on the bench was put inside five vials: the masseur then hid those vials in a double pocket inside our bathrobes, with a tip coming out of a slot protruding from inside the garment: it was enough to exert a slight pressure and the "clean" urine came out of the spout, filling the anti-doping bottle. An easy, easy operation, also because there was no type of control in the anti-doping room.'

It seems most Serie A clubs did it. 'It's naïve to think [Inter] was the only culprit, the only "white fly" in the ointment, amongst the great teams of

Italy, Europe and the world,' said Ferruccio Mazzola, who died in 2013. He published a football memoir in 2004, which detailed HH's doping practices. This caused a feud with his brother Sandro Mazzola, the great Inter star, and the club sued Ferruccio Mazzola for libel in 2005, claiming it was 'desecration' to suggest HH's team resorted to doping to achieve its glorious results.

The case was a sensation, as details filtered out about the concoctions HH got his players to ingest, including altered coffee, sugar mixed with strange powders, and vitamins that weren't vitamins. All the living greats from HH's Grande Inter were hauled into court, one by one, to give testimony. In 2008, the judge ruled against Inter. The club couldn't prove that the facts in Ferruccio Mazzola's book were not true, and incurred the costs for the lawsuit. Mazzola's old Inter teammates said he was a bitter man. That he bore a grudge because his time at the club was a failure. 'If I wanted to hurt Inter in the book, I would have talked about match-fixing and the referees who were bribed, especially in the cups,' he said.

When I asked his brother, Sandro Mazzola, about HH's doping programme, I discovered that his stance has softened since he first refused to accept his brother's whistle-blowing campaign almost two decades earlier. He explained HH's process, how his amphetamine pills were doled out.

'There was a massage therapist in Herrera's staff who was a close friend of mine. We grew up together in football. He told me everything. He recommended to me not to take those "tablets", but I couldn't be seen to be avoiding them by Herrera, so I would put the tablet under my tongue, faking it. The massage therapist was the one who gave you the tablets, but Herrera was also there to check everyone swallowed them down. I stood there, the tablet under my tongue, without doing anything – then, as soon as he went out of sight, I would put the tablet inside one of my boots. I always brought four pairs of boots with me, for every kind of pitch, rainy conditions, hard surface, and so on.

'I remember taking those tablets home. I used to see another massage therapist in Como – he was called Ferrario – because one year earlier I had had a muscle problem that was difficult to heal, but Ferrario fixed it. So, I kept seeing him for massages, and once, I took the tablets with me and asked: 'Can you check what's inside them so that I know? Maybe it's nothing.' After a week, Ferrario wanted to speak to me: "Thank God, you didn't take them – it's Simpamina [the product name for amphetamines sold by a pharmaceutical company in Italy in the 1960s]," he said. "You could've collapsed while running! It has very strong side effects. It's dangerous." Since then, I didn't take anything else.'

7.

Inter's club president Angelo Moratti didn't like the bad press that was engulfing his institution in the spring of 1962. He suspected his players were given energy drinks, 'pick-ups', and he wanted to stop the practice. He tasked Dr Manlio Cipolla, a former professional footballer now on the medical staff at the club, to do some checks. This put Dr Cipolla on a collision course with HH. The pair remained at each other's throats for several years. HH couldn't abide interference by a doctor in how he ran his dressing room. He believed he was in sole charge of the players' nutrition and 'therapy'. Besides, he drew on advice from his own medical experts, who included a mysterious man in Paris, Émile Wanono.

Wanono was born in Casablanca in 1920. He trained as a doctor in osteopathy in England, and made a name for himself in France in the 1950s, becoming one of the first famous sports osteopaths, using massage to treat injuries. He had notable names on his client roster, including the grumpy three-time Tour de France winner Louison Bobet and French football stars Just Fontaine (who also grew up in Casablanca) and Raymond Kopa. People began calling him 'The Sorcerer'. He could apparently cure all kinds of ailments, from sciatica and sexual dysfunctions to sinusitis and a stiff neck. HH began sending Inter players over the Alps to Wanono's clinic in Paris so they could benefit from his sorcery. Dr Cipolla was sceptical. He said there was more to the magic in Wanono's miraculous hands than met the eye, claiming that Wanono 'tried to make amphetamine traces disappear with cherry-flavoured herbal tea'.

HH's second tilt at the Serie A title with Inter fizzled out. His team ended the season in second place, five points behind city rivals AC Milan. Valencia dumped them out of the Fairs Cup in March 1962 at the quarter-final stage. His players were burnt out. The press questioned HH's 'magic'. They criticised him for so many gruelling training sessions. There was a sense of diminishing returns to his doping methods, according to his midfielder Franco Zaglio. 'All the "vitamins" they made us take … for months, they were effective,' said Zaglio. 'Then the body gets used to it and it becomes like taking fresh water. So it went – those two seasons at Inter.'

The Italian Football Federation got fed up with HH and his big mouth, particularly the game's powerbrokers who supported Juventus. They were upset when HH made fun of Juve for being ousted from the European Cup quarter-finals by Real Madrid in February 1962. They also feared all the bad press around the Inter doping scandal. The animosity flowed both ways. HH had begun to find the scene suffocating. He was sick of his overlords.

HH was part of the technical committee in charge of selecting and managing Italy's upcoming World Cup team. He lacked full authority.

It was not long before things came to a head. With only a few months to go until the World Cup finals in Chile, HH resigned as coach of Italy's national team. He could see how things were unfolding. He wasn't going to miss out on the biggest show on earth that summer. He'd catch another ticket to South America, an upgrade even, to first class, as head coach of the team of all talents.

The sweetest feeling: Brazilian winger Jair da Costa celebrates scoring the winner for Inter v Juventus in the *Derby d'Italia*.

19. TEAM OF A MILLION STARS

1.

There's a bronze bust of Pedro Escartín on a little patch of grass outside the Santiago Bernabéu Stadium in Madrid. On New Year's Eve 1961, Escartín resigned from his post as head coach of Spain's national football team. He was keeping his word. He had said he would step down once the team qualified for the 1962 World Cup finals, which it did, having overcome Wales and Morocco in its qualification matches.

Escartín spent almost 20 years as an international football referee before coaching Spain. Like a lot of refs, he was meticulous. As part of his handover to the new coaching regime, Escartín summarised the strengths and weaknesses of Spain's international footballers. He devoted six to eight lines to each player, and focused mainly on their defects. On 3 January 1962, *Marca* published his report. The sports newspaper claimed it had found the report in a Madrid taxi – and that a *Marca* editor had the huge fortune to stumble upon it. Escartín was raging. He blamed a lawyer attached to the Royal Spanish Football Federation for the leak. Santiago Bernabéu criticised Escartín for his carelessness: 'You have done wrong in writing it. If you wanted to inform, you should have done it orally. The words are carried away by the wind. You should be less naïve.'

The Escartín Report landed like a bomb. It made for dramatic reading. Escartín dismissed Real Madrid's José Araquistáin as 'nervous', a withering put-down for a goalkeeper. Carmelo Cedrún, his rival for the goalkeeper's jersey, was apparently less brave than Araquistáin. Luis Suárez got depressed easily. Eulogio Martínez was fat. Real Madrid's central defender José Santamaría was so slow he should never leave his box. Santamaría's clubmate Paco Gento was 'not leading a good life'. Alfredo Di Stéfano was a sullen, watchful character: 'He knows everything that's going on and you have to be careful of his mood.'

Spain's star players were furious, which caused tension around the camp. Heading into the World Cup, the team was at a crossroads. Spain were perennial underachievers – they'd failed to qualify for the last two World Cups. At club level, Spanish teams devoured opponents in European competition. Atlético Madrid won the 1962 Cup Winners' Cup; Valencia won that season's Fairs Cup, beating Barça in the final. Real Madrid, who did a domestic league and cup double, lost the European Cup final 5–3 to Benfica a few weeks before the World Cup finals were due to kick off in Chile. Spain had several nationalised stars to call on, including Di Stéfano, Puskás, the Uruguayan Santamaría and

Eulogio Martínez, as well as Ballon d'Or winner Luisito Suárez. The wellspring of talent at Spain's disposal created enormous anticipation around the country.

The Royal Spanish Football Federation chose Pablo Hernández Coronado as its team selector for the finals in Chile. This was a surprise appointment. Hernández Coronado announced he'd select the squad to travel to Chile but would leave the selection of his coach until the last minute. With several months of the club season to run, the press had a field day speculating about who he would pick from La Liga's battalion of head coaches.

Hernández Coronado was a strange cat. He was born in 1897 and died a month before he reached a hundred years of age. It was enough in Spanish football circles to mention 'Don Pablo' for people to know who was being talked about. He was a champion boxer, secretary of the Spanish Chess Federation and a goalkeeper for Real Madrid. He had a restless mind. He had studied medicine, engineering and business, but always dropped out of his courses halfway.

In the world of football, after retiring from the game as a player, Hernández Coronado turned his hand to every role imaginable. He was a referee, a journalist, a treasurer for the Royal Spanish Football Federation. As sporting director at Real Madrid, he signed the pre-war greats Ricardo Zamora and Pepe Samitier. He loved tinkering. He was the first person in Spain to use numbers on players' jerseys and tried – and failed – with an experiment to play different starting XIs at home and away. He eventually left Real Madrid after falling out with Santiago Bernabéu. He was one of the most famous refs in Spanish football history yet as a player he was unscrupulous, admitting he would happily win with an unfair penalty in the last minute. He thought girlfriends were one of the most frequent and grave injuries that could befall a footballer. He found a kindred spirit in HH.

On 7 March 1962, Inter played Real Madrid in a fundraising match for people in need of social housing. Hernández Coronado met secretly with HH at an Italian restaurant on Avenida del Generalísimo, the wonderful avenue known today as Paseo de la Castellana, which cuts a swathe through the heart of Madrid. Ostensibly, they met to talk about the form of Inter's player Luis Suárez. But Hernández Coronado made an offer to HH to go to Chile with him as coach of Spain. HH knew that his head was on the block. This was only three days after HH's Inter player Gerry Hitchens failed a drug test, and 10 days after Zaglio, Bicicli and Guarneri were busted. The Italian press was hounding him. He was in the mood to hear Hernández Coronado out.

Hernández Coronado made his case. HH said he wouldn't brook any interference as coach – i.e. the kind of selection committee structure that existed in Italian and English football – and that he wasn't cheap. They struck a deal in principle, which Hernández Coronado had to get signed off by Spain's football federation. A news agency leaked the story that HH was going to be Spain's new coach. Hernández Coronado said it wasn't true. A lot of Spanish media and most of La Liga's coaches despised HH. The Royal Spanish Football Federation didn't like the smell of him either. Moreover, HH had a contract with Inter; at this stage, he was still an assistant manager with Italy.

On 14 March 1962, the Spanish press published the news that HH had resigned from Italy's national team technical committee. The Italian Football Federation were vague in public about why he quit, but behind closed doors was a different story: the amphetamines scandal had damaged HH's standing with Italy's football authorities. HH spun his own tale, claiming he stepped down because of intolerable media pressure, a laughable claim given HH loved jousting in the press. Hernández Coronado got the Royal Spanish Football Federation to yield to his demands, and on 26 March 1962, the federation approved HH's appointment as his coach. He'd got his man. Two days later, HH resigned as coach of Inter, a decision prompted by the ill health of Inter's president Angelo Moratti, who also stepped aside. HH left the door open, however, for a return to Inter should Moratti be reinstated as president.

HH and Hernández Coronado – whom the press dubbed 'the HHHC formula' – made for a rum pair. There was outcry across Spain at the appointment. 'If you wanted to find the most discredited man to coach the Spanish team, you have succeeded spectacularly,' wrote *Marca*. Spain's La Liga coaches formed a line to take a pot at HH. 'It amounts to a total disregard for us. I think there are many other coaches in Spain who offer enough guarantees to go to Chile with the national team,' said Real Madrid's coach Miguel Muñoz. Kubala, who was in the dugout at Barça (the first of three unsuccessful stints in that seat), shared his disgust: 'The appointment of Herrera constitutes a contempt for Spanish coaches.'

The fallout made HH laugh. Small, petty minds. Jealousies. He knew he was the best man for the job.

2.

HH had been down this road before. Back in 1959, when he was waging war against Real Madrid as Barça's manager, HH was given the job as Spain coach. The day he was unveiled as coach, Real Madrid's stars – Alfredo Di Stéfano, Paco Gento and Enrique Mateos – refused to shake his hand. He was toxic. HH didn't take the slight personally. He won them round, proving he was a top-class coach – and not a charlatan. Di Stéfano later conceded: 'I understand now that Herrera's fame as a coach is justified.'

As part of the qualifying process for the inaugural European Championship in 1960, Spain were drawn against Poland. Two legs: a game in June 1959 in Poland, and one a few months later in Madrid. HH picked a team top-heavy with Barça players who knocked over the Poles 7–2 on aggregate. Di Stéfano scored in both ties. Spain drew the Soviet Union, Franco's great bogeyman, in the quarter-finals. Again, the tie was to be decided over two legs.

In mid-May 1960, 10 days before the first leg, HH travelled to Moscow to spy on the Soviets. Their team – with Lev Yashin, 'the Black Spider', in goal – were playing Poland in a friendly. HH used his French passport for the scouting expedition. His Spanish passport wouldn't have got him far, as it was branded with the words: 'This passport is valid for countries of the world except Russia and satellite countries.'

Franco's government kept an eye on HH's movements. When he came back from the Soviet Union, there was a gagging order put on him by the Ministry of Information. The Spanish football press was banned from quoting him about his reconnaissance trip to Moscow. Tensions between East and West were particularly fraught. On 1 May 1960, four weeks before the first leg kick-off, an American U-2 spy plane had been shot down by the Soviets over their territory. The incident led to the collapse of a summit meeting between President Dwight D. Eisenhower and Soviet leader Nikita Khrushchev, planned for Paris in the middle of May.

Franco was like a cat on a hot tin roof. Communists brought out the worst in him. It enraged him that soldiers from his Blue Division, which fought on the Eastern Front during the Second World War, were still rotting in Soviet gulags. Secret police reports piled up on his desk predicting popular demonstrations in Madrid in support of the Soviet team when they were set to visit, as an expression of hostility towards Franco. His life's work was a struggle to repel the infiltration of Marxism into Spain. Now the Soviets' communist football team – which was guaranteed to have spies embedded in their travelling party – was landing on his doorstep. The thought of the Soviet anthem echoing around the Santiago Bernabéu Stadium, and the hammer and sickle fluttering in the wind at full mast, left him nauseous.

Franco backed himself into a corner. He insisted that both legs be suspended. UEFA tried to get the games replayed at neutral stadiums. The Soviet Union refused to comply. Spain withdrew from the tournament. The Soviets got a bye into the semi-final (and went on to win the competition). Spain's football fans – in the month that Real Madrid won its fifth European Cup in a row at Hampden Park – knew that a chance had been missed. HH knew it too. The players were powerless. Justo Tejada, who played both legs against Poland, shrugged his shoulders. 'We had our bags packed ready to go. We were due to fly to Brussels first, before going to Moscow, but Franco interceded. He put his foot down. Said we couldn't play. Were we sad? No. We went where we were told. If Franco said we couldn't play against the Soviet Union, that was that.'

3.

Two years later, as the 1962 World Cup dawned, Adelardo was one of the bolters selected for HH's squad travelling to South America. The midfielder was coming off the back of a terrific season with Atlético Madrid. He went on to become an iconic figure in the club, spending 16 seasons in its first team: 'A is for Adelardo, A for is Atlético…' He grew up in Badajoz, at the foot of Spain, a few hundred metres from the border with Portugal. He remembers sleeping in his first pair of football boots he owned.

Ferdinand Daučík, Kubala's brother-in-law, spotted him in 1959 when he was Atlético's coach, and whisked him up to the capital. Even though Adelardo was still a teenager, he broke into the first team, alongside international stars like the steel-chested Vavá (one of only five players to score in two World Cup finals). Adelardo was enamoured of Daučík's attacking football philosophy. 'It was the beautiful game. *La salsa*. It was all about scoring goals to win, about playing in the opposition team's half of the pitch.'

By contrast, Adelardo found HH to be a different kettle of fish. He was intense, hot-headed, but, as a coach, exceptional: 'In training sessions with Herrera, you always had to be alert. Training was like a match. All the exercises had a purpose, whether they were with the ball or without it. Everything was done with speed. Rapid. He didn't like players who were slow. Everything was boom, boom, boom! He had so much energy, this nervous tension. He was such an intense guy, which was surprising because he was also a studious man. He was ahead of his time. He lived for football.

'I remember Herrera was in Madrid for a semi-final of the European Cup. This was a few years after the World Cup in Chile. Joaquín Peiró was playing with Herrera at Inter. Myself and Peiró were close friends. I was talking with Peiró at the end of a training session. Peiró came to say hello. Then we saw Herrera, who was with Moratti, the president of Inter. They were talking about the match. Herrera asked Moratti for an increase in the win bonuses if they won the match the next day. That was typical Herrera. He was a coach who always looked out for his players.'

In June 1960, at the end of his first season, Adelardo won the Copa del Generalísimo, as part of an Atlético team that beat Real Madrid 3–1 in the final at the Bernabéu. Atlético repeated the trick the following season: same rival in the final, same stadium, another sweet victory. In 1962, Atlético defeated Fiorentina to win the Cup Winners' Cup; the following season they lost in the final to Tottenham Hotspur. Jimmy Greaves scored two of Spurs' goals, but Adelardo remembers the match because of some bad medicine administered by Maurice Norman, England's international centre-half.

'Maurice Norman broke my nose with his elbow. I played most of the game breathing through my mouth. I was protecting the ball when he came in and clattered me. He was enormous. It was no accident. I remember he played in the 1962 World Cup. He didn't get a red card. In those days, there were no subs, so I played the whole match. There were very few stoppages in games, no yellow cards. You didn't get any protection from referees. Nothing.'

Adelardo also had enforcers minding his back: 'The toughest player I played with or against was Jorge Griffa, our central defender. He came from Newell's Old Boys, the same year as me, in 1959. He was an international with Argentina. He was so tough. If he had had to kick his father in the head to win, he would, whatever was needed. He was an animal, but an impressive footballer too. I'm glad I never had to play against him. What a guy to have on your team.'

Adelardo was chuffed to make the Spain squad for Chile, but he found the journey down to South America an ordeal. 'A year before the trip to Chile, we went on a tour to Argentina. We went by propeller plane, which had four engines. The noise was horrendous. We stopped on an island in the Atlantic Ocean to refuel. It was horrific. I was petrified. We went by jet plane to Chile. We left from Barajas Airport in Madrid. Then we stopped in Lisbon, Dakar, Rio de Janeiro, Buenos Aires, before flying on to Santiago.

'I remember that Di Stéfano was terrified of flying. For the flight to Chile, he spent the whole night in a seat beside the pilot, looking out of the window, holding on to the arms of his seat. I've no idea how he survived flying all over the world during his career. It must have been awful for him. The plane was big. There was a lot of space on board. I was only a kid. My clubmate Joaquín Peiró was older than me, so he pulled rank – he stretched out across three comfy armchairs. I had to sleep on the floor with a blanket covering me.'

Di Stéfano had another reason for not wanting to be on the plane. Before heading to Chile, HH had gathered his Spain squad in May for a training camp in Bilbao. His thinking was that the inclement weather in the Basque Country would most closely resemble the damp weather of winter in Chile. Di Stéfano and Spain's other Real Madrid players were late joining up, as they had to play Benfica in the European Cup final in early May.

HH lined up several club sides for training matches. On 13 May 1962, Di Stéfano played in the fifth one at Real Sociedad's ground, scoring twice in a 5–0 win – but picking up a bad muscle injury. He was crestfallen. He knew that the finals in Chile would be his last dance, his only chance at World Cup glory, a month before his 36th birthday. (In 1947, Di Stéfano had scored six goals in six matches for Argentina before going into exile by joining a pirate league in Colombia. In 1957, his international career was resurrected with Spain, but Spain failed to qualify for the 1958 World Cup finals.)

Di Stéfano went to great lengths to fix his injury, including contorting his body under a table lamp in his hotel room in the belief that heat would speed up the healing process. HH wanted him to lose weight. This caused a clash, as Di Stéfano reckoned the loss of musculature exacerbated the injury. Di Stéfano wanted to stay in Spain to give his leg more time to heal, suggesting he follow the squad out on a later flight to Chile. HH wouldn't hear of it; he wanted him mixing with the other players. Di Stéfano caved in to HH's demands and boarded the plane in a pig of a mood.

The public in Chile were warm hosts during the three-week carnival. On landing in Chile, people surrounded each team bus as they set off for their hotels, urging them onwards. Adelardo remembers constantly being invited back to people's homes for something to eat. But the press in Chile got hostile and tenacious. First they turned on the Italy squad because of some nasty reporting by two Italian journalists: Corrado Pizzinelli, who later covered the Vietnam War, and Antonio Ghirelli. The pair filed derogatory reports, writing that Chile was a backward country except for the art of prostitution, a land chafed with 'malnutrition, illiteracy, alcoholism and poverty', its capital Santiago a city where taxis were 'as rare as faithful husbands'.

Chilean media countered with headlines like 'DOPED ITALIANS'. Its journalists set on HH, the disgraced Inter coach, and his Spain squad, like dogs with a bone. Spain's players were peppered with questions about doping. Luis Suárez, Eulogio Martínez and Puskás all denied the presence of drugs in football. Di Stéfano, perhaps tired of the accusations, or maybe he was being playful, didn't swerve when quizzed: 'Yes, Italians and all the other footballers in the world take stimulants. They are like racehorses that get a jab. It is good that it is exposed once and for all, the same way it should be known about fake amateurism in the Olympics and in many other competitive sports ... a lot of players take jabs.'

HH made sure his racehorses had plenty of stimulants for the running on Chile's muddy tracks. He wasn't leaving anything to chance. 'When Herrera was coach of the Spain national team at the 1962 World Cup finals in Chile, his players used drugs,' said Alfredo Relaño. 'An Atlético Madrid player told me. He said Herrera gave the players a pill squashed up, saying it was a vitamin. Puskás, who was at the World Cup playing for Spain, didn't want to take it. The Atleti player took it. He was only a kid. He wasn't brave enough not to take it.'

4.

What struck the Czech players about their Spanish rivals, as both teams lined up in the tunnel before their opening World Cup game, was their smell. The Spaniards' aftershave was intoxicating. Puskás, Suárez, Gento and 'the team of a million stars' were a fragrant bunch. They had gel in their hair. They looked like film stars. Alongside them, the Czechs looked pitiful in their shabby gear designed for the 1960 Czechoslovakia Olympics squad (which were returned after the World Cup finished).

The Czechs, as ambassadors for communism, weren't in the game for money. Most of them played with Dukla Prague, the Army team. The Czech football federation sent only 18 players to Chile to save cash; all the other countries sent squads of 21, even the Soviets. Their overlords did, however, dispatch two secret policemen, as cultural attachés, to spy on their players. While Spain stayed in the glamorous Miramar hotel, and Brazil, another rival team in their group, relaxed in the Hilton, the Czechs were stuck in a fleapit three hours outside Santiago that had no running hot water. Its only luxuries were a billiards table and a gramophone player that played Bill Haley records on repeat.

A week before the game against Czechoslovakia, HH forced Di Stéfano to train for an hour. When the match came around, Di Stéfano refused to play. He wasn't fit. Czechoslovakia – who finished third at the 1960 European Championship – were no soft touch and provided a difficult test for HH's men. Without Di Stéfano – who scored 23 goals in 31 Spanish internationals – they struggled to breach the Czech defence.

When Spain's striker Eulogio Martínez lashed out, kicking Czech goalkeeper Viliam Schrojf in the stomach in frustration, the game got ratty. Two of Spain's defenders, Severino Reija and Feliciano Rivilla, got badly injured in the crossfire. Reija – who stayed on the pitch because substitutions weren't allowed – was at fault for Czechoslovakia's goal with 10 minutes to go when he misplaced a pass across his backline. The Czechs intercepted and swept forward, with Josef Štibrányi, a 22-year-old trainee teacher, delicately lobbing Spain's goalkeeper to score. Most of the photographers in the stadium missed the game's decisive action because they were stationed behind Czechoslovakia's goal.

As the Czech players left the pitch after their 1–0 win, they saw a man unravelling on the sidelines – HH grabbed his stool and smashed it into pieces. It was a sorrowful scene. A man at war with himself, plagued by a visceral need to win – what Bertolt Brecht called 'the black addiction of the brain'. His mind was a haunted house, full of deranged competitive fantasies.

The Chilean press castigated Spain for their dirty play, one headline anointing them, 'CHAMPION OF THE KICKING TOURNAMENT'. Other games played on the opening two days of the tournament also unleashed violent flurries, resulting in three broken legs, a fractured ankle and several cracked ribs. Punches were thrown during Uruguay's game against Yugoslavia. The Chilean newspaper *Clarín* concluded that the tournament was 'less a World Cup and more a World War'. So many players picked up injuries that local newspapers took to publishing lists of casualties.

There was one game in particular that encapsulated the violence of the bloodiest World Cup in history: Chile's game against Italy. This was no surprise. The slanderous comments by Italy's football press about Chilean society before the match left Chile's players consumed with murderous thoughts. Once the game kicked off, they began spitting at Italy's players. Chaos reigned. Football spectators had never seen such sustained levels of lawlessness on their TV screens before.

The World Cup matches were broadcast on the streets of Santiago, where crowds gathered around makeshift TV stands. Fans in Europe could only listen to live games on radio. After a game ended, though, the film for it was spirited back to Europe on the first flight out of Chile and broadcast the following day. David Coleman's immortal introduction for the BBC's delayed screening of 'the Battle of Santiago' was a mouth-watering piece of theatre. He was filmed high up inside Chile's national stadium as behind him, fans streamed out of the ground. Coleman, dressed in a suit and tie, with a handkerchief tucked neatly into his breast pocket, spoke straight to camera with the indignant tone of a schoolmaster.

'Good evening,' he said. 'The game you are about to see is the most stupid, appalling, disgusting and disgraceful exhibition of football in the history of the game. This is the first time these countries have met; we hope it will be the last. The national motto of Chile reads, By Reason or By Force. Today, the Chileans weren't prepared to be reasonable, the Italians only used force, and the result was a disaster for the World Cup. If the World Cup is going to survive in its present form something has got to be done about teams that play like this. Indeed, after seeing the film tonight, you at home may well think that teams that play in this manner ought to be expelled immediately from the competition. Just see what you think.'

The game was a flurry of wild kicks and rugby tackles. Often the English ref, Ken Aston, waded into a melee to separate players like boxers caught in a clinch. Italy's Giorgio Ferrini was red carded after eight minutes. When the Italian player refused to leave the pitch, he was escorted off by armed police. Leonel Sánchez, Chile's star player and the son of a professional boxer, broke the nose of Italy's captain Humberto Maschio with a left hook. Sánchez also boxed Mario David, who was sent off for retaliating with a spectacular kung fu kick to the head. The Italian football sage Gianni Brera was critical of David's sending off, wondering if he was 'clinically mad, or was driven so by chemicals?'

The match prefigured a series of filthy Intercontinental Cup finals in the 1960s between Europe's top clubs and their South American counterparts. Football took a nosedive during the decade. Pelé was kicked out of the 1966 World Cup finals in England. There were half as many goals scored per game in the 1962 World Cup as there were in the tournament finals in Switzerland eight years earlier, a move towards defensive football that was reflected in declining goal tallies in Europe's great leagues in the 1960s. Negative tactics, and a fear of losing, colonised the minds of coaches. HH, as the high priest of *catenaccio*, was in the vanguard of this shift towards anti-football. The clouds didn't lift again until Brazil's *jogo bonito* in the 1970 World Cup finals.

5.

After Spain eked out a 1–0 win over Mexico, Brazil was the problem facing HH in their final group game. Spain needed a draw if not a win to proceed to the knockout stages. Both teams were missing their star players. Brazil lost Pelé. HH ordered the still injured Di Stéfano to play, but he refused. HH was bullish about Spain's chances, arguing that Brazil without Pelé weren't that strong. When asked about Pelé's replacement, Amarildo, he responded with contempt: 'Amarildo? Who's Amarildo?'

Only two players – Puskás and Paco Gento – remained from Spain's team that played against Czechoslovakia. HH wanted more vim. He gave youth its head. The 35-year-old Puskás, the only player over 30 in the team, was an exception. The man was a freak. He scored a hat-trick in the 1962 European Cup final a few weeks before the World Cup finals started. After the tournament ended, he went on to be top scorer in La Liga for the following two seasons. Never write off a natural-born goalscorer.

The match was a thriller, the best one in the competition, according to Brian Glanville, the World Cup's august historian. Spain swarmed all over Brazil, playing their best football in the tournament in the first half. Adelardo, one of the tyros introduced into Spain's starting XI, scored from outside the box after 35 minutes. In the second half, Spain were denied an obvious penalty when Enrique Collar was fouled inside the box by Nilton Santos. The ref gave a free kick outside the area instead. Puskás floated the free kick into the mixer. A headed clearance was pounced on by Adelardo, who flashed a bicycle kick into the net. The ref inexplicably disallowed the goal, suggesting one of Brazil's defenders was pushed.

Then Garrincha turned the game on its head. His mazy dribbling left Spain's defenders punch-drunk. Adelardo threw his head back at the memory of Garrincha's chicanery, blowing air out of his mouth dramatically: 'Garrincha was out of this world. Garrincha won the match, and he won that World Cup for Brazil on his own.' Amarildo, dismissed by HH as a nobody before the game, scored two late goals for Brazil, with Garrincha providing the cross for the winner. Brazil, who had been on the verge of elimination, were suddenly through to the quarter-finals (and went on to defeat the Czechs in the final).

Czechoslovakia lost to Mexico in their final pool game, which meant a draw with Brazil would have been enough for Spain to advance. Football is a game of fine margins. Adelardo – who said he hasn't seen a Spain squad as talented in the World Cup finals since – was still aggrieved by the 2–1 defeat to Brazil. 'I believe the ref was bribed. How could he disallow my second goal? No, no, no. He knew if he allowed the goal the game was over – Spain would win. There was no foul. Why did he not give a penalty when Nilton Santos fouled Collar inside the box? The ref consulted with his linesman, but he gave a free kick outside the area. It was crazy.'

6.

HH resigned his post by telegram from Chile. He was vilified by the Spanish press for the team's early exit. Spain went on to win the 1964 European Championship, coached by José Villalonga, who remains the youngest manager to win the European Cup when, aged 36, he guided Real Madrid to their first victory in 1956. Angelo Moratti – fit again after his health scare – was back in the saddle at Inter as president. He summoned 19 of Inter's squad to help him decide HH's fate as coach. Most of the players voted to sack him. Moratti lined up a replacement, Edmondo Fabbri, but then he had a change of mind. He felt HH had been undone by suspect refereeing decisions in Spain's pivotal match against Brazil. Besides, he had a soft spot for him. Casting aside Fabbri – who was immediately appointed Italy's coach – he summoned HH back to Italy. The Spain squad left Chile a week after the defeat to Brazil. HH found his own way back to Europe – and unfinished business in Milan.

20. WHEN A BAD MAN BEHAVES WELL

1.

In 2012, the Spanish film director Pedro Almodóvar was asked to give one of his mentors, Gonzalo Suárez, a lifetime achievement award. At the ceremony, Almodóvar made a long, gushing speech. Gonzalo Suárez took to the stage. After a minute's applause and a bearhug from Almodóvar, he responded to Almodóvar's kind words with a roasting: 'It's a welcome surprise that Pedro Almodóvar has spoken so much about me, when he usually only talks about himself.' His dig brought the house down.

Gonzalo Suárez is a remarkable artist, an original. He spearheaded Barcelona's *gauche divine* movement in the 1960s, an underground scene – a young, beautiful bohemian set who looked across the Pyrenees for inspiration and who drank whisky and practised free love while the pavements of Madrid and Seville were clogged with priests and nuns. His novels are dazzling. He wrote one of them while living with his friend Sam Peckinpah in Los Angeles. He was the first notable Spanish film director to hit out for Hollywood, 'alternating between cinema and literature with insulting self-confidence,' as Javier Cercas, the Spanish writer, put it. He had an opera performed at the Venice Biennale. Almodóvar cast him in his film *¿Qué he hecho yo para merecer esto?* 'I tried to ruin the film,' said Suárez.

Enrique Vila-Matas claimed he might never have become a writer if he hadn't first read Gonzalo Suárez, who was writing journalism with a literary bent – later dubbed New Journalism – years before Tom Wolfe and Joan Didion. He wrote under the pen name Martín Girard, and was greatly influenced by the theatre of the absurd. He felt the mask allowed him to hide his shyness, and gave him licence to be daring, sardonic, aggressive. He threw questions like punches. His interviews are iconic, among them profiles of Salvador Dalí, James Cagney and Luis Buñuel.

Pelé once gave him a present of his football boots although in general Suárez found footballers tiring to interview. 'Footballers tend to be boring when it comes to answering the interviewer unless they are for sale or they're angry. With one exception. Alfredo Di Stéfano, although he always seemed angry, he never stopped being boring.' He was drawn to boxers and notorious characters. He once blagged his way into the Ritz hotel room of former Cuban dictator Fulgencio Batista to secure a world exclusive interview after the Cuban Revolution. Batista spent the last 14 years of his life on the run from Fidel Castro's hired assassins. In the hotel room, Batista was surrounded by 'gorillas', his bodyguards and a beautiful woman, who sat at a table. Gonzalo Suárez approached him and said: 'I already know you don't want to talk about politics. What do you have for breakfast?' 'Orange juice,' replied Batista. Then he started asking him about his mood.

Before he broke all this new ground, Gonzalo Suárez worked as a spy for his stepfather, HH, a man who also appreciated the absurdity of life.

2.

I met Gonzalo Suárez in a restaurant beside Madrid's Teatro Real. In old age, he looks a ringer for Richard Attenborough, with his round face and white beard; he has a similar impish sense of humour. He was born in 1934 in Oviedo. The city in Spain's north-west was on fire at the time he was a baby, as the Spanish Army was crushing a miner's revolution in the region. The quashing of the revolt – led by legionnaires wearing iron necklaces from which dangled the human ears of their victims – lives in infamy. It was a harbinger of things to come. Within a couple of years, civil war exploded across Spain. 'From the time I was young, I was bombed! I thought that was the normal world. I wasn't too wrong.'

His father was a French professor, writer and translator, who was assigned to Valencia during the Spanish Civil War. He remembers the family hid under their beds from bombs dropping overhead. He had a brutish schoolteacher, who was fond of welting four-year-old children with a stick. The school was a one-storey building beside a church. Whenever there was a bombing raid, the school kids were evacuated and lined up against a wall outside the school. One of his earliest memories is of bombs falling like fireworks on the horizon while he and his school friends peed absentmindedly against the wall.

'After the war and the bombings came the worst period. My father was a socialist. He was fingered, persecuted. We ended up in Madrid.' Only the intervention of Gonzalo Suárez's maternal grandfather, who was a Franco supporter, saved his father's life. His father was an inveterate note-taker (like HH). He kept notebooks itemising his children's development, their height, when they lost their baby teeth, and so on, as well as recording how fascism was losing support. He home-schooled his children until his son was aged 10 – anything to avoid having to sing the fascist anthem *Cara al Sol* and reciting catechism in Franco's schools. This influenced Gonzalo Suárez's irreverent way of thinking; he could never buy into religion.

The breakdown of his parents' marriage also profoundly affected Gonzalo Suárez. 'The war wasn't the problem; the problem was my parents' war.' He had no reference point. No one else around him had a broken family. Divorce was illegal in Franco's totalitarian Spain. It caused him to retreat into the world of books, reading adventure novels in a chair in their hallway. His mother, a beautiful, vivacious woman – unlike her academic husband in temperament – took a lover, which caused the separation. She dreamed of another life. Her husband was a loser in the war. The man she had the affair with was rich. He had a car. Then she fell in love with HH.

'I don't feel any bitterness towards Helenio about the cause of my parents' separation because he came into the picture after they split,' said Gonzalo Suárez. 'There was another guy before him. Helenio in psychoanalytical terms was the avenger for me – he was the man who took the woman from the guilty man who caused the separation of my parents.'

Gonzalo Suárez reckons HH – the two first met in 1950 while HH was coaching Atlético Madrid – caused a split in his personality. He was the man who rescued his mother, María Morilla Pérez (who later had two children with HH, Helenio Jr. and Rocío). HH was a man of action. A barbarian. He was important. He let a teenage Gonzalo Suárez sit in the dugout at matches. He let him travel in the team bus with Atlético's players. He led him to fall in love with football. Suárez still remembers HH's Atlético team, especially the forwards: Benbarek, Carlsson, Juncosa, Pérez-Payá, Escudero. It was thrilling to be in his slipstream. HH had a halo of fame, which was even more extraordinary because in Gonzalo Suárez's teenage mind celebrities – like Robert Louis Stevenson and Guy de Maupassant – were dead people. And his own father was an intellectual, sedate, a man who lived in his head. It's only with hindsight that Gonzalo Suárez has begun to admire his father more and more. (To paraphrase from a line of poetry by Michael Hartnett, a case of "I loved him from the day he died".)

'I've never known another person with so much magnetism as Helenio,' he told me. 'He had this intensity. It was infectious. This facility he had to enthuse his players: "We're going to be champions." Obviously, footballers then were more innocent. We all were more innocent – just look at the films people watched; it was frowned upon to have sex more than twice a week. Players were susceptible to being influenced by someone like Helenio, a character who was always very positive, saying things like "With 10 we'll play better than with 11". Part of it was fiction, of course,' he said, laughing, 'because if it was true, he'd have lined out with 10 players. But it lifted his players' morale. They loved him for it. You don't get this spirit of positivity amongst successful people in the arts world. On the contrary, artists are often masochists.

'Helenio had an aura. He was as famous as Di Stéfano at the time, or more so internationally. Nobody knew who Real Madrid's coach was, but everybody knew who Helenio was. He was a *caudillo*. He was such a complex man, impenetrable in some respects. It's difficult to unravel him. He had four passports: Argentinian, French, Spanish, Italian. He used them on a whim without altering his sense of self. Helenio was always Helenio. He had an extraordinary capacity to learn languages. He could get by in English, Italian, Spanish, French, but he had a very peculiar accent. He had such natural intelligence.

'It's a shame. Later, I had problems with him. A distance grew between us when he separated from my mother to be with Fiora Gandolfi, his next wife. She was a journalist. He didn't treat my mother well. Neither did he treat his daughter Rocío well. My mother had two children with him – Helenio Jr. and Rocío [who died in 2002]. He could have done more for Rocío. Because of all that there was a moment in my life when I didn't forgive him. We repaired our relationship when he was older.' As he was speaking, a fly hovered over our tapas. 'There could be a lot of flies about, but there's only one, so it could be the reincarnation of Helenio. There are worse things than a fly to be reincarnated as,' he said, smiling.

'Helenio was a tough man. He was hard on his players. He was hard on his family. He was consumed with achieving success, with his work in football, his ambition, his thirst for money. He had such a miserable childhood, haunted by hunger. Given his childhood, given he suffered so much poverty in Casablanca, it wasn't surprising that he was greedy. The child we have been haunts us all our lives and into old age. To be competitive, you must have blinkers on. You need to limit your vision. He associated the game of football with winning, not with enjoyment. He was passionate about football because it enabled him to get out of misery.'

Gonzalo Suárez said HH wanted to be like the darker characters Kirk Douglas played in American movies in the 1950s. He was a brute. 'Helenio wasn't a good man,' he stated. 'He was a bad man, but sometimes he behaved well, and when a bad man behaves well, it makes more of an impression. Whereas when a good man behaves badly – even if it's just the once – we demand that he asks for forgiveness.'

At this point he laughed. 'Anyway, I owe a lot to Helenio. He helped me at an important moment. I wanted to get into making films. He convinced the president of Inter, Angelo Moratti, to finance a film for me. What was more unbelievable was that he paid for my trip to Rome! I'll always be grateful to Helenio for doing that.'

I asked him about HH's parents. Gonzalo Suárez met HH's father, Paco, once in Seville, but it was HH's mother who was the dominant personality. HH danced to her tune. Gonzalo Suárez also verified details about the time HH nearly beat an Atlético fan to death for insulting his mother shortly after her funeral. 'Helenio's great passion in his life was for his mother. I never saw that Helenio had as much love for his children as he had for his mother.' When HH died, only four of his seven children attended the funeral. Inter's Giacinto Facchetti, the player he loved the most, gave the eulogy.

'His mother had extraordinary strength,' continued Gonzalo Suárez. 'She was very fat.' He recites the story – described earlier in this book – about the time she was on the verge of drowning and had to be pulled ashore at the port in Casablanca. 'The men on the dock demanded money to save her,' he said, laughing grimly. 'It's a regret that I never wrote a book about the second half of his life when Helenio proposed it. At the time, he was separated from my mother. Relations weren't the best between us. I have a certain tenderness for Helenio. At the bottom of it all, he was a child – and a big one, albeit a wicked child,' he concluded, with a laugh.

HH was an enigma. He was a charmer, yet he had no friends. He was never baptised, yet he was devoted to the Virgin Mary. He was the son of a dirt-poor immigrant father and a mother he adored. Fate dealt his father a bad hand; he was unable to cope in a harsh environment, a man unmoored. He lost prestige. He was one of life's losers. HH had to nudge him aside, usurping his position in his mother's affections. Something wild inside him drove HH forwards, a savage ambition. He would do anything to please his mother, to reward her for sacrificing so much, and to appease his guilt about the father who was cast aside. It made him become a ruthless careerist. Anyone who got in his way was trampled. Whatever it took to get across the river. Outlaw behaviour – cheating, disregard for other people's feelings – was a small price to pay. It had to be success, at all costs.

3.

Gonzalo Suárez wrote scouting reports for HH on rival teams in Serie A. It was a practice that he carried out during two full seasons for HH at Inter in the early 1960s, and for ad hoc games before and afterwards. No other team was doing the same. 'Curiously, Helenio had confidence in my football reports, which were absurd and sometimes very wrong, but he trusted my judgement,' he told me. His memory of that time is a daze: a succession of Italian football stadiums, hotels, airports. He delivered the reports to HH in Milan where HH quizzed him about his findings. He took part in training sessions with Inter's players. He became close friends with Giacinto Facchetti, Inter's legendary full-back. His fondest memories are of joining in to play in training matches at Inter's training campus, in the fog and the rain.

HH was obsessed with the idea that every goal was the result of a one-off mistake. There were only millimetres, specific circumstances, between scoring and missing and preventing goals. He believed himself to be a master strategist, capable of cheating God's roll of the dice. He gave his stepson specific instructions. He was interested in knowing strategic aspects, which television cameras didn't pick up, which journalists didn't report. He wanted to know what happened where the ball wasn't.

Gonzalo Suárez wasn't asked to scout players. HH already had files on rival players, enough to fill a library – details about their height, weight, diet, their health and lifestyles. HH wanted pragmatic data about what happened on the pitch. Where did players hit penalties? Who was slow? Who was left-legged? Who cuts inside or outside? Did a team's full-backs overlap or stay in position? Did a player rest his hands on his hips, suggesting he tired easily? He was told not to watch the ball but to look for where the empty spaces were created. In the land of creating space – the ability to launch attacks, to break down defences – was essential. The forward who knew where the ball was going to go in advance could do a lot of damage. It was exhausting work.

According to Gonzalo Suárez: 'Helenio revelled in the problem of Italian football. Effectively, you needed a brain, a player like Luis Suárez, in the middle of the pitch, to unlock defences. Also, you needed a guy who was strong at centre-forward, even if he was clumsy, to move defences around. He liked direct football: the ball played into space. Above all, players who played at speed. He admired footballers who were intelligent, who thought rapidly, who could anticipate where the ball was going to go, who could start transitions.

'It's a mistake to say Helenio was the creator of *catenaccio*. On the contrary, *catenaccio* was a problem for him. It was a shock to him when he arrived in Italy. At the start, his Inter team scored a lot of goals. He got the measure of the league, but then teams started to lock up. He concluded that to counteract the "door bolt" he must bring in his own door-bolt system. He moved a defender back to create more space up the pitch.

'The dilemma Helenio had was how to drag defences out of position, to create space. He was the first coach to put his wingers further back the pitch, which let his full-backs take advantage of this extra space by running into it. He prefigured total football. Sometimes, he got his centre-forward to tie up the opposition team's sweeper, to pull him out of the box. Always, he wanted to create space. The obsession with his spying reports was: "How can we find more space?" This was difficult to achieve in Italy.'

As well as spying for HH, Gonzalo Suárez did some grifting for him.

4.

Italian football clubs in the early 1960s were allowed only one foreign player on their squad; and one *fuori quota* (a foreigner who played in Italy for five seasons); and one *oriundo* – a player of Italian ancestry who was born abroad. Early one morning, HH phoned Gonzalo Suárez from Milan in a tizz. His stepson was lying in bed in Barcelona when the call came. HH had a problem he needed solving. He had this exciting young Portuguese player, who was born in Cape Verde. The kid didn't know who his father was. HH wanted to inscribe him as an *oriundo*. Gonzalo Suárez's task was to find an Italian 'father' who, upon payment, would agree to legally recognise the footballer. HH wanted to look for the fake father in Barcelona, which he knew had a sizable Italian immigrant community, so he could mislead the paparazzi. He trusted Gonzalo Suárez's discretion. There was a deadline for the mission: four days.

Gonzalo Suárez visited a neighbour of his. The neighbour was from Rome, but a fan of Inter. His father was also from Rome, and lived with him. As part of the brief, Gonzalo Suárez was warned by HH not to mention the club or the player, a restriction he found a bit unreasonable. The fee on offer was 50,000 pesetas – not a massive sum, he felt. The neighbour listened, stupefied, to his pitch. He was flattered at the thought of having a famous brother and a footballer for his preferred team as a sibling, but he was baffled about how he would persuade his father – and more so his mother. The pair approached the father, a man in his eighties. He was still in his pyjamas, sitting on his balcony, staring at the clouds. He listened to their offer and then started yelling: 'Never, ever! Not even if I were dead! I'm from Rome!'

Gonzalo Suárez retreated. He enlisted a friend to help with the search. They spread their net wide. Their proposal elicited different responses. Some people thought it was a joke. Some asked if it was for a TV show. Gonzalo Suárez knew Italians who would sell their soul, but it seemed that none would assume paternity. Then as the clock ticked down, a travelling circus arrived in Barcelona – I Fratelli Bonicelli. Bingo. The troupe comprised six kids, three adult brothers, two of their wives, a sister, a father and a mother. The father walked with a limp. His back was half broken from doing trapeze without a safety net.

Gonzalo Suárez approached the circus family and made his play. Everyone was in favour of the deal, said Gonzalo Suárez, including the six cats in the circus, except the old man. He feared travelling to Italy with a man he didn't know. 'What if they cut my balls off?' 'Don't be stupid,' blurted his wife. 'Does this guy have the face of a bullfighter?' The four women blamed the old man for his disability. He liked to spend his days stretched out in a rocking chair, smoking cigarettes, which he rolled neatly with one hand. On this one, he had to relent.

Gonzalo Suárez picked him up the next day. The circus man had spruced up: he reeked of aftershave, had gel in his hair, wore a suit. He smoked and talked all the way to Italy. HH and Inter's lawyer picked them up at the airport in Milan and planned to bring them straight to a notary. On their journey, the circus man, flattered by the welcome he received, started telling his hosts about his life. At a certain point, he brandished his ring finger to show them what was engraved on the ring. It was the date of his wedding, which had taken place about 20 years earlier.

The lawyer whispered something into HH's ear. The car pulled over. HH and the lawyer got out and started a heated discussion on the side of the street. They finished arguing and summoned Gonzalo Suárez from the car. He was told the circus man wouldn't do – the fact he was married after the date of birth of the player invalidated the operation. Gonzalo Suárez was back to square one. He had 24 hours to find a father. He compensated Bonicelli and sent him back to Barcelona that night.

Gonzalo Suárez stayed over in Milan, in the same hotel that Milan's players used when they were in *ritiro*. In the middle of the night, he got a knock on the door of his hotel room. There was an urgent phone call for him from Barcelona. He went down to reception to take the call. His accomplice from Barcelona was on the other end of the line. He had found another father.

The following day, Gonzalo Suárez returned to Barcelona and went straight to an apartment on Diagonal, one of the long avenues that cuts across the city. Inside the apartment, the only furniture was some chairs and crucifixes hanging on the walls. Sitting in the apartment, waiting, with his bag packed, was an elderly man. He wore a dark grey suit. He had a noble aspect. He came from an aristocratic family. He haggled over his fee. Gonzalo Suárez agreed to pay him double.

They set off immediately for Milan. On the plane, the aristocrat asked an air hostess for a glass of water and wolfed down some pills. Gonzalo Suárez asked if the pills were for travel sickness. He said, 'No.' He had suffered a heart attack 15 days previously. The doctor prescribed these pills and told him to take them anytime he felt pain. Gonzalo Suárez was stunned. His first father didn't make it to the notary; his second father was fit for a morgue. He could already picture himself carrying the deceased in his arms across the airport runway.

Again, HH and Inter's lawyer met Gonzalo Suárez at the airport. Gonzalo Suárez immediately pulled HH aside and filled him in on the old man's troubled heart. They set off for the notary's office, their car travelling through the streets of Milan at breakneck speed, hardly stopping at any traffic lights. After signing the papers and collecting his payment, the aristocrat stayed to meet his 'son', who was eating on a restaurant *terrazza* with Inter's footballers. The father asked the son to write to him, even a postcard. The son promised he would. He was an honourable kid. A month later, the aristocrat died of a heart attack. The player renounced the inheritance that fell to him, including the 100,000 pesetas for the 'adoption'.

La Grande Inter: (back row, l–r) Giuliano Sarti, Giacinto Facchetti, Aristide Guarneri, Carlo Tagnin, Tarcisio Burgnich, Armando Picchi. From the left kneeling Jair da Costa, Bruno Petroni, Luis Suárez, Sandro Mazzola, Mario Corso.

21. IL MAGO

1.

On 28 April 1963, Italy held a general election, but football fans were more preoccupied with events at a stadium in Turin. At midday, Juventus kicked off against Inter. The two giants of Italian football had been toe to toe for most of the season, having traded top spot in the league table since November. A costly 1–0 defeat at home by Juventus to Catania earlier in April helped Inter to open up a four-point lead with only four rounds of games to play. At this stage, Inter were trying to bridge a nine-year gap since their last *scudetto*. The pressure on both sides was huge.

HH's Inter led Serie A in spring for the previous two seasons, but faltered close to the finish line. A defeat would summon all the ghosts of Inter's late-season collapses. For HH, this was a day of reckoning. Sandro Mazzola opened the can for Inter with a goal midway through the first half, just as his teammate Franco Zaglio picked up a bad knee injury. It was obvious from the gravity of the injury that Zaglio would be useless for Inter, who were defending a one-goal lead, in the second half. HH knew he would have to give Mother Nature a helping hand.

'El Mago allowed [Dr] Quarenghi to take care of the treatment, but he also wanted to give him an amphetamine tablet or two,' claimed Manlio Cipolla, a doctor on the medical staff at Inter who was at loggerheads with HH over his systemic use of performance-enhancing drugs. 'How to escape the doping control? At the end of the game he brought on an ambulance, getting Zaglio to simulate that he was seriously injured and in need of hospitalisation. And for peace of mind, he had a well-known right-wing parliamentarian accompany Zaglio in the ambulance.'

The ruse worked. Zaglio was spirited out of the stadium at the full-time whistle unmolested by the doping authorities. Inter won 1–0, and strolled to the league title. A monkey was off HH's back, and he was back where he belonged – in the European Cup.

2.

Alongside Pablo Picasso and Joan Miró, the Barcelona artist Modest Cuixart is one of twentieth-century Spain's most highly regarded painters. At the Sao Paolo Biennial in 1959, at the age of 33, he electrified the art world by taking first prize, ahead of Francis Bacon. Over the following couple of years, he held exhibitions at London's Tate Gallery and the Guggenheim in New York. He was a doyen of the avant-garde, famous for his eroticism.

In 1963, Cuixart was presenting an exhibition in Barcelona entitled *Nens sense nom* – 'Children Without a Name'. It was a bleak exhibition, full of sinister, tragic images, of children with black heads and shattered dolls glued to fabric, symbolising the murder of children in war and, in particular, the pain and trauma of the Spanish Civil War. It was an important exhibition, but a hard sell. Abstract art is a minority pursuit, a niche concern. Cuixart and his art dealer were scratching their heads. 'How do you persuade a whole city to focus attention on a painter?'

They posed the question to Gonzalo Suárez. The writer thought for a second and then had a eureka moment. He slapped his forehead and exclaimed: 'It's easy! Do you want everybody talking about a painter? There can only be one solution: Helenio Herrera.' They were puzzled. Everyone had heard about HH, but what had a football coach to do with an art exhibition? Easy, explained Gonzalo Suárez. He was show business. Nobody touched him for notoriety. In 1963, if you wanted publicity, were eager to make a splash, he was your man.

Gonzalo Suárez picked up a phone and called Milan. He told HH the deal. He offered him money to come to Barcelona to accept a painting that was being gifted to him by Modest Cuixart, a renowned abstract painter, the winner of the Sao Paulo Biennial, 10 days before his exhibition was opening in the city. The sole condition was that HH must say he had bought the painting. It would help with promotion. HH listened carefully. The only hitch was that it was the week of Inter's coronation as winners of Serie A after almost a decade's pursuit, but HH could never turn down an earner. So he boarded a plane to Barcelona.

There was a twist. A week beforehand, the president of Barça had flown to Milan to find HH and offer a blank cheque to return as Barça's coach. The press jumped on the story. All of Barcelona believed that their messiah was set to return. How could his visit to the city possibly have anything to do with art? The timing for this PR stunt couldn't be better – and Gonzalo Suárez knew it. HH also knew that Gonzalo Suárez was being opportunistic, but he didn't give a damn. It was all part of the game.

The press camped at Barcelona's airport, giving HH a bigger reception than if it had been Queen Soraya, the sultry actress and recently divorced wife of the Shah of Iran, who was also due to land in Catalonia. The pandemonium didn't surprise HH. 'It's natural. Soraya didn't play football,' he said.

Journalists peppered him with questions at the airport, sceptical that he was an art enthusiast. 'But do you understand painting yourself?'

'Do you have to be a mechanic to buy a car?' he replied.

'Since when have you been interested in painting? What paintings do you have in your house?'

HH said he had paintings from two young artists in his home.

'What are their names?' they insisted, hoping to catch him out. For a second, HH thought of Picasso, who had been a young maestro, but he worried that it would be too exaggerated a response.

'Dupleix and Ronconi,' he said.

That shut them up. They made a note of the names. It's doubtful that they ever figured out Dupleix was one of Louis XV's ministers, notorious for his looting of India on behalf of the eighteenth-century French monarch, and that Ronconi was a forward with Cagliari in Italy's Serie B.

3.

HH rearmed in the summer of 1963. He brought in several new players, including veteran goalkeeper Giuliano Sarti and old-school centre-forward Aurelio Milani. HH was criticised for signing Milani, whom he lured out of retirement but he wanted a street fighter like Milani to tie up the opposition's centre-backs, a player who obeyed tactical orders, who would drag defenders out of position, disappearing so that others – like the Brazilian Jair and Sandro Mazzola – could appear. HH got rid of the Argentine midfielder-cum-forward Humberto Maschio, one of the legendary 'Angels with Dirty Faces'. He did so against the wishes of several directors. Maschio was too slow for HH's style of play and lasted only a season at the club. HH was tired of telling people he didn't need Maschio when his place in midfield was already occupied by Luisito Suárez.

HH also bet on the talented Sandro Mazzola, playing as his Number 10. Not everyone believed in the 20-year-old, a star player from the club's youth academy. He was the son of the immortal Valentino Mazzola. Sandro Mazzola, who inherited his father's ability to dribble at speed, was born in November 1942, a few weeks after the great Valentino joined Torino. Valentino had destroyed football in the 1940s: as captain of the *Grande Torino* team, he won five Serie A titles. He still holds the record for the fastest hat-trick in Italian football history: three goals in three minutes in a game against Venezia.

Off field, Valentino Mazzola's social life was the talk of the town. In 1946, he separated from his wife to be with his mistress, Giuseppina Cutrone. She was underage when their affair started, his 'white lady' and a witch in the eyes of the Italian public. Sandro lived in Turin with his father; his younger brother Ferruccio lived in Milan with their mother, who turned down an offer of a million lira to sign annulment papers. In April 1949, Valentino Mazzola went ahead and married his mistress in Vienna. His first wife found out about the wedding in a newspaper.

Two weeks later, Valentino was in Lisbon for a game against Benfica. Awaiting him on his return to Italy was a complaint for bigamy, filed by his first wife. Valentino was conscious of a dangerous precedent: Carlo Galeffi, a famous Italian baritone singer during the interwar years, remarried in Budapest and ended up in prison for three years. Valentino never made it home, however. He perished along with the rest of his *Grande Torino* teammates on the flight back to Italy. His premature death left a shadow hanging over his two sons, both of whom played for HH's Grande Inter team. (Decades later, Ferruccio Mazzola blew the whistle on the doping culture at the club during the 1960s.)

Sandro Mazzola had a gilded career. He scored important goals, including one on his debut for Italy against Brazil in 1963. He was part of Italy's European Championship-winning team in 1968, and a starter against Pelé's Brazil in the famous 1970 World Cup final in Mexico City. He commentated on Italian television for both of Italy's World Cup final victories in 1982 and 2006. He was the incarnation of Inter. Seventeen seasons an Interista. Captain. A one-club man. One of the few items of football memorabilia on display in his apartment in Monza, about 20km from the centre of Milan, is a Subbuteo figurine of himself with his distinctive pencil moustache decked out in Inter's black-and-blue strip.

4.

Before sitting down to interview Sandro Mazzola, I reminded him about my particular interest in HH. He immediately interjected and started shouting with a big smile: 'Il Mago! Il Mago!' HH, the Magician, had a profound influence on him. When I asked him to compare HH to some of his other coaches like, say, Edmondo Fabbri, his coach with Italy's national team, he scoffed: 'Fabbri pretended to be Il Mago. He tried to emulate him but that was impossible! Il Mago was a different coach to all the other coaches, totally different.'

HH's training sessions were a revelation. There was less focus on stamina, more on technical aspects than with other coaches who liked to flog players by getting them to run laps around the pitch. HH's sessions were shorter. Everything was done with the ball. Training drills were given numbers, which HH would shout out so the players had to execute them from memory. HH liked to train their brains before their legs. He was a doctor of the mind.

'Il Mago gave you exactly what you needed to improve your game,' said Mazzola. 'At first, we were sceptical of him, but then we realised his ability to get inside your head. He had this relentless desire to improve our performances. He never let up. He always said the right thing at the right time. He knew how to reassure and motivate players who might be worried about an upcoming game, and if he realised that someone was not fully focused, complacent, taking victory for granted, then he really got pissed off and would confront that player.

'He was unpredictable. He was funny, but it was difficult to know when he was joking or not – to separate his strict personality from his witty side. There were moments when he would crack a joke, maybe at your expense, but you were always wondering if he was mad with you or maybe not. You could never tell. It would wreck your head.'

Before every training session, HH liked to summon players for private counselling, one-on-one meetings that the players called 'confession time'. The team's masseur would come up to a player, and whisper in his ear: 'Il Mago wants to see you.' Players were terrified when they got called for an audience with HH in his 'office' – inside the team's dressing room, a private space, his own changing room, where he got togged out and took his shower. It was stacked high with boots, footballs and jerseys. Like football heaven. Players couldn't help but be impressed. HH's door remained shut until he was ready to receive them.

'I don't know why he made us wait outside his office, sweating,' said Mazzola. 'Your head would be dizzy wondering, *What is he going to say to me?* When you entered his office, you could barely breathe because of the anxiety. He'd put his finger on your forehead and tell you: "Now we've got the training session, and you must do this, this and that, because you'll have to replicate that in the game. OK? Have you understood?" I always answered, "Yes", but the truth was I often I didn't understand a thing, but I was too scared to say so.

'He hardly ever gave compliments. He'd rather tell you what you would have to do on the pitch to improve. If you had a very good game, he might say something nice, give you some praise, but it was never 100 per cent praise. There was always something to fix that he would point out. The first time I had one of these "office" meetings, he highlighted two or three things I did wrong on the pitch. I realised, *Hey, he's right about those things!* It prompted me to wonder: *We're a lot of players on the pitch, 11. How can he remember that level of detail? How can he recall what I did wrong as well as the other 10 players?* It was impressive – his photographic memory.

'I remember playing against a very strong English team. I scored the winner in the closing minutes. I wanted to shoot in a certain direction, but I miscued my shot and the ball accidentally ended up in the top corner. It was a lucky goal, sending the goalkeeper the wrong way. After the game Il Mago pulled me aside. He knew my shot was unintentional. He told me: "Good lad, but I must tell you something: your shot was misfired. This time you were lucky because the goalkeeper was a fool. You must do better next time!" When you left his office, everyone asked you to tell them what he had said, but you didn't know whether you were allowed to tell everyone else. You couldn't speak out of fear in case he found out you were blabbing. He could go mad.'

Life for Sandro Mazzola and his teammates during *ritiro* at Inter's sports campus, Appiano Gentile, was stifling. HH got his masseurs to check the players' rooms at night to make sure they weren't harbouring prostitutes, who roamed nearby, outside the sports campus grounds, waiting for tricks. What was more difficult to police was stopping players from breaking curfew at night-time – their rooms were on the ground floor, so it was easy for them to climb out of their windows and leave the campus to have sex with prostitutes.

HH kept weighing scales – a big one like those found in a butcher's – in his office. He was obsessed with players' weight. Every morning, he did a weigh-in with each player. He would yell: 'Weight control!' A queue would form outside his office. The younger players always went first. Then older players followed. Players would be climbing the walls. They would dawdle, trying to scupper the process. Some would hide in an attempt to make him lose time, so that he might start the training session without weighing them.

'For every extra 100 grams you were forced to pay a fine. It was withdrawn from your salary, which was a big problem because salaries were not like today,' continued Mazzola. 'Some players, typically the veterans, would climb out of their window during the night to go into his office so they could tweak the weighing scales. The problem with that dodge was that sometimes Il Mago would hide out in his own office in the dark. He'd stay there to see if someone tried to tweak the weighing scales. As soon as someone stepped inside the door, he'd let out a scream. Then he'd fine them.'

22. VIENNA

1.

The European Cup was every club's dream. It stole sleep from HH. The pursuit of it gave him chronic insomnia. Inter's obligation to fight on different fronts was gruelling, his trickiest challenge. There was never a chance to rest. The logistics required surgical precision. Serie A was always a dogfight. In Spain, as Barça coach, HH knew that Real Madrid were his great rival. In Italy, there were several other big clubs: Juventus, AC Milan, Roma and Fiorentina as well as resurgent clubs like Bologna. It made fighting for the league title tougher, bloodier. With one eye on the European Cup, it didn't help that the race for the 1964 *scudetto* would go down in history as an epic.

Some of Europe's greatest clubs were lined up against Inter in their first tilt at the European Cup, including tournament kings Real Madrid; Benfica, victorious twice in the early 1960s; reigning holders AC Milan; and the formidable West German team Borussia Dortmund. Inter drew Everton, the English champions, in the preliminary round. HH knew there wasn't a more difficult team to face in the competition.

In the autumn of 1963, HH went to the city of Liverpool to scout Everton, hunkering down in Goodison Park without being noticed. He enjoyed spy films, so he went in disguise, wearing sunglasses, a hat and with the lapels of his trench coat raised. It was impossible for him to walk around Italy undetected: everyone knew him and the advent of television elevated his notoriety. This was different to his experience in Spain, a country under the thumb of Franco. In Milan, he was mobbed on the streets every day. If he was sighted, fans surrounded him, shouting at others to come along, poking their fingers in his chest, taking photos, requesting autographs.

Parents called their sons after him. Some even called their daughters 'Helenia'. 'In Milan, he was called "Medici",' said Gonzalo Suárez. The country was divided between Herreristas and anti-Herreristas. HH revelled in the mutual abuse. He found it flattering. It emboldened him. The press stoked the rancour. The paparazzi feasted on rumours and gossip about his players' social lives, anything to cause scandal. Inter sold more newspapers than any other club. Inter couldn't lose without causing a riot. The declarations of the braggart HH, the triumphs of Inter, increased the media attention and Inter's rivalries with other clubs. Life in Milan became a frenzy for HH.

Watching Everton, in Beatlemania Liverpool, HH was struck by two things: firstly, the dilapidated nature of their old Victorian stadium, which was made almost entirely of wood. HH felt that it could have collapsed at any moment under the weight of the public. Secondly, he couldn't get over the noise. It was 'diabolical'. Everton had the noisiest fans in Europe. He couldn't hear himself think with the screaming and clattering of wooden rattle-clackers. Shortly afterwards, when his Inter team were about to run out on to Goodison Park and be met by a wall of sound, HH forewarned them, blasting into their ears: 'The noise doesn't score goals!'

The game finished 0–0. It was a performance by HH's men of 'granite perfection'. Everton did all the attacking but couldn't score. HH sacrificed Horst Szymaniak – his left winger fell back into midfield to pick up Everton's 'extra man'. Inter lined up, as was now traditional, with a *libero* (sweeper) – Armando Picchi hoovering up the ball behind Inter's back four. This was a revolutionary set-up for a British audience.

'Picchi never specifically marked anyone, yet he marked everyone,' explained the commentator, Kenneth Wolstenholme. 'He never ventured upfield. He never had a static position, yet he had all positions. If a player got behind the line of four backs, either by dribbling his way there or by creating space with a one-two passing movement with a colleague, he would be confronted by Picchi. Any player who ran through to pick up a long pass would be confronted by … Picchi. Any high lob or centre which was floated into the Inter goalmouth would be picked off by … Picchi.' Inter got flak for the defensive approach, for destroying football. HH defended his pragmatism. Football was evolving, he claimed. He was introducing a new aesthetic. This was a template Europe was going to become familiar with. Like it or lump it. In the return leg, Inter won 1–0 at San Siro to advance.

In the next round, Inter overcame Monaco, who had been 'double' winners in France the previous season. Monaco's star forward, who was kept scoreless over both legs, complained that if he ever had to be marked again by Inter's ruthless defender Tarcisio Burgnich he'd prefer to retire from the game. Inter was getting a name for itself as a master of the dark arts, a team that frustrated, that could grind out results. Inter swept past Partizan Belgrade in the quarter-final. Borussia Dortmund, who thrashed the mighty Benfica 5–0 in an earlier round match, awaited in the semi-final.

The semi-final was one of the finest hours of Luisito Suárez. He was Inter's crown jewel, its organiser. He maintained the team's rhythm. Whenever Inter were in trouble, HH always turned to him. Against Borussia Dortmund, Inter were on the rack. Suárez answered the distress call. The first leg was played in West Germany. Sandro Mazzola scored for Inter within a matter of minutes from kick-off. Then came the deluge. Roared on by patriotic singing from the terraces, Borussia Dortmund scored twice midway through the first half. HH thought the game was lost. Inter were overrun. It felt to HH that the West Germans weren't dribbling with the ball, but that they were trampling over his players.

The storm had to be weathered. Suárez stepped up. He gave a recital. Whenever the ball burned the feet of his teammates, they looked for him. Like all great players, time seemed to slow down when he was on the ball. He was fearless. Despite Borussia Dortmund's onslaught, he was eager to try things: feints, nutmegs, back-heels, no-look passes, long raking passes that landed softly. Until Suárez arrived in Serie A in 1961, the league's skilful, technical footballers tended to be slow. Suárez was different. His brain and his feet moved quickly. He knew where to send the ball before it got to him. He could put his foot on it when needed, spinning out of tackles, like that night in Dortmund. His *pausa*, as Spaniards say, took the wind out of the opponents' sails. Inter got an equaliser and escaped with a 2–2 draw. HH was ecstatic on the flight home. His men knew how to resist.

Luisito Suárez could look after himself, too. Back at San Siro in the return leg, he bared his teeth, kicking Borussia Dortmund's Dieter Kurrat in the stomach, which took the West German defender out of the game. Reduced to 10 men, Borussia Dortmund lost 2–0.

There was a postscript. Later that summer, a Yugoslav tourist met Branko Tešanić, the referee from the match at San Siro, on the Adriatic coast. The ref allegedly told the tourist that his holiday had been paid for by Inter. There was uproar in the West German press. UEFA never investigated the allegation, but the Yugoslavia Football Federation did, and suspended him. He never refereed another European Cup game.

2.

Real Madrid, who beat the holders AC Milan in the quarter-final, were nervy heading into the European Cup final. 'With Inter, no one can compete,' said Santiago Bernabéu, half-joking, half-serious. Since losing to Juventus in December 1963, Inter had enjoyed an unbeaten run of 24 games. But still, Real Madrid in a European Cup final was a daunting prospect. Inter, the favourites, were the coming force. The curtain was falling on Real Madrid's great team, who were playing in their seventh European Cup final in nine seasons. It was a last hurrah, but it wasn't beyond Alfredo Di Stéfano & Co to put in one final, glorious shift. They'd played so many finals, they knew how to win big games. It was in their DNA.

No one knew Real Madrid better than HH. They had a brittle defence, but a fearsome set of forwards. Paco Gento, who ran like a cut cat, was mesmerising on the wing. The young Amancio was electrifying the football world that season, which he finished on the Ballon d'Or podium. Di Stéfano scored in both legs of the semi-final. Puskás was the tournament's joint top scorer. HH must cut off his supply lines or else Puskás would break his heart. HH knew Real Madrid possessed magnificent skill, but this, paradoxically, was their weakness too. They were in love with their own sparkle, with individual touches and short passes, a lot of them unproductive. HH knew they weren't as energetic as his men. He vowed to run them ragged.

HH tasked Carlo Tagnin with neutralising Di Stéfano. Tagnin wasn't a talented footballer. He never played for Italy, but HH trusted him. He was a player who didn't shirk – and he owed his career to HH. Tagnin used to play for Bari. In May 1961, in the second last league game of the season, Bari needed to beat Lazio, who were already relegated, to avoid the drop. The game was at the Olympic Stadium in Rome. Tagnin played a season for Lazio in the late 1950s. He contacted his old teammate, Maurilio Prini, offering his Lazio team a bribe if they threw the match. Prini pretended to accept the offer, but then spilled the beans at the Italian Football Federation's inquest office.

Bari were busted for trying to fix the match. They were relegated and deducted 10 points for their following season in Serie B. Tagnin was slapped with a 30-month suspension. Close to hitting 30, he thought his career was over, but then came a lifeline. HH was sick of Franco Zaglio's repeated injuries and needed a replacement. He thought Tagnin could do the job. He approached Tagnin and told him he could resurrect his career, but he'd have to be patient. Then HH cranked Inter's legal machine into gear. The club's lawyer, Peppino Prisco, got the suspension reduced by a year and Tagnin was back in the game. As a result, he'd do anything for HH, whatever it took to help him win football matches.

Tagnin died in 2000 from a cancerous tumour in his bone. 'I remember doctors in the hospital asking if he took "weird" substances over the course of his career,' said his son Fabio in an interview after his death. Tagnin spent three seasons at Inter under HH. Ferruccio Mazzola, who was a whistleblower about the doping culture at Inter, remembers that Tagnin was one of the footballers who took the drugs on offer. He was old, already in his thirties, and needed a kick to compete. 'Carlo Tagnin,' he said, 'never refused pills because he wasn't a top player and he wanted to extend his career by racing around like a kid.'

Man-marking Di Stéfano in a European Cup final was the biggest job of Tagnin's football career. HH, the master sports psychologist, set to work on his mind. Every day for a week, he dragged Tagnin along the tree-lined avenues outside La Pinetina, Inter's training campus near Como, for walks and whispers in his ear. He persuaded him that he had the measure of Di Stéfano.

Why, Tagnin was the most tenacious footballer in the world, the perfect man to *mangriñánea* Di Stéfano, to take him out of the game! Tagnin was sold.

'Herrera convinced me that I was the strongest player in the world, stronger than Di Stéfano whom I had to mark,' said Tagnin. 'Seen from the outside, Herrera looked like a madman but, given his results, he was proved right. Sometimes, he went to absurd lengths. Like when my wife had come to see me before a game in *ritiro*. Seeing me, she tried to hug me, but Herrera forbade her: "No, *signora*. Your husband must stay focused."'

3.

On the night of the match in Vienna, Alfred Hitchcock took up his seat in the stadium behind Inter's president, Angelo Moratti. HH was convinced of his team's superiority. They were oiled like a machine. It's all he blabbed about to the press in the build-up to the game, but in the dark of the night he was haunted by one unknown factor. His team were novices, rookies. Apart from beaten finalists Luisito Suárez (1961) and goalkeeper Giuliano Sarti (1957), they were all playing in their first European Cup final. Would they freeze on the big day? HH didn't know, but he kept the doubt to himself.

In the tunnel, before the teams ran out on to the pitch, Sandro Mazzola couldn't take his eyes off Di Stéfano, this god who had come down to earth. As a teenager, Mazzola didn't have a television in his apartment. No one in his neighbourhood did. He went to a tavern to watch European Cup finals. It was the same film every year: Real Madrid emerged victorious. Mazzola was in love with Di Stéfano. Everyone said Di Stéfano played like his father Valentino. Mazzola loved Di Stéfano's regal bearing. He was elegant, skilful, always played with his head held high. When Mazzola saw him that night in the tunnel of the Prater Stadium, he was spellbound. For Mazzola, Di Stéfano was a TV star. He was shaken from his reverie by Armando Picchi, his captain, who hit him a smack: 'We're going out on to the pitch. Will you stay here looking at Alfredo all night?'

HH never believed for a second that his side would lose once the game began taking its course. Only for five minutes did he sense danger. Inter dominated. The incoherent attacks launched by Real Madrid were messy. HH knew their absurd, intricate passing movements in midfield were a risk to themselves. Real Madrid kept Inter at bay, but it was only a matter of time. Inter were experienced in breaking down 'locked' defences. Several of their players knew how to shoot from distance. Shortly before half time, Mazzola – who played the game of his dreams – scored from outside the box to put Inter ahead. Then, Inter sat back and invited Real Madrid towards their goal so they could unleash their favourite weapon – the counter-attack. They targeted the spaces left open by José Santamaría, Real Madrid's ageing centre-half.

Paco Gento hit the post early in the second half; Real Madrid missed the rebound when it seemed easier to score. Their final ended right at that moment. A few minutes later, Sarti caught a speculative long-range half-volley from Di Stéfano and launched a counter-attack which ended in a goal by Aurelio Milani, who struck from outside the area. Real Madrid were toast. They got a goal back, but Mazzola scored again, pouncing on an error by José Santamaría. Inter, 3–1 winners, were the champions of Europe. Out on the pitch after the game, Inter's players hoisted their president, Angelo Moratti, on to their shoulders in celebration. 'I saw in the eyes of Moratti a happiness that I have never seen again in a person,' said Luisito Suárez.

4.

Inter's enforcer Carlo Tagnin hardly gave Di Stéfano a sniff of the ball in Vienna. A week later, Real Madrid's coach left Di Stéfano out of the team for a Copa del Generalísimo replay against Atlético Madrid, which Real Madrid lost. Their season was over. Di Stéfano was turning 38. Santiago Bernabéu asked him to stay at the club, but not as a player. He offered him 'any' position he liked, but he was vague about the details. Di Stéfano wanted to continue playing. He met twice with Bernabéu to negotiate a contract renewal, including once at Bernabéu's house, but there was an impasse. Bernabéu offered him a fraction of what he earned on previous contracts. Di Stéfano got the hump and decided to join Espanyol. Bernabéu had called his fishing boat 'The Blond Arrow' in honour of Di Stéfano, the son he never had. After their falling out, he changed it to his wife's name. And he never offered Di Stéfano another job at Real Madrid. Football can be a cruel mistress.

23. 'THERE IS A SMALL ANNOYANCE'

1.

On the first day of March 1964, a few months before their European Cup triumph in Vienna, Inter crushed Sampdoria 5–1 in a Serie A game. The win enabled them to leapfrog AC Milan into second place in the table, two points behind league leaders Bologna, who themselves beat Milan 2–1 at San Siro. Bologna and the two Milan clubs were clear of the chasing pack in a three-horse race for the title.

Three days later, a bomb exploded: the Italian Football Federation announced that five Bologna players had been busted for doping. The negative doping tests were collected after a league match against Torino a month beforehand – in which Bologna won 4–1. Previously, the federation had doled out only small fines and bans for doping infractions, but under new stiffer regulations, the club was going to be hit with a draconian punishment, which would probably kill their title challenge. Sentencing was due to follow in a few weeks' time.

Bologna was one of the founding clubs of Serie A. The club was synonymous with Renato Dall'Ara, their president. Dall'Ara was Bologna, Bologna was Dall'Ara. He fought in the cavalry as a marshal in the First World War. He made his fortune in the knitwear industry. He married but never had any children and poured his soul into Bologna F.C. Becoming its president in 1934, he brought the club unimagined success: four Serie A titles between 1936 and 1941. But then came two decades without success.

In 1961, Dall'Ara appointed Fulvio Bernardini as head coach. It was a shrewd appointment. Bernardini was a former international midfielder known for his intellectual bent. His nickname was '*Il Dottore*'– The Doctor. He played with Roma in the 1930s. He had an interesting run-in with Benito Mussolini in 1935. He almost rammed a blue Lancia Astura car that wouldn't allow him to overtake, not knowing that *Il Duce* was in the car. He had his driving licence withdrawn for reckless driving. To retrieve it, he had to go to Mussolini's residence, Villa Torlonia, and be beaten in tennis by him. On arrival, he was welcomed icily: "Have you learned to drive?"

Bernardini was exceptional. He led Fiorentina to their first Serie A title in 1956. It was a staggering achievement, more so by the margin of victory: Fiorentina finished 12 points ahead of second-placed AC Milan. Once he got the job at Bologna, he promised Renato Dall'Ara he'd deliver a *scudetto* within three years. He looked as if he was about to keep his word when the doping ban was announced in the spring of 1964.

All hell broke loose in Bologna on the day the charges were made public. Foul play was suspected from one of the Milan clubs. Most of the fingers pointed at Inter. Bologna's fans were convinced this was a Mafia-style job, crooked men from the north doing one over on a provincial city. Bernardini captured the feelings of fans, alluding to a conspiracy hatched in the river valley that runs beneath Milan: 'It's unthinkable what they will invent to prevent us from winning the *scudetto*. Does it matter that the doctors in charge of the testing were born under the Po?' Roadblocks were set up between Milan and Bologna. Cars and motorbikes decked out with Bologna red-and-blue flags clogged Bologna's streets, hooting horns, crying havoc. Fans flooded into the city's centre to riot. Cars with Milan registrations were overturned and burned in Bologna's main square, Piazza Maggiore. It was as if the city had declared a state of siege.

Someone had to tell Renato Dall'Ara the bad news. The editor of Bologna's sports newspaper, *Corriere dello Sport Stadio*, as well as an old friend of Renato Dall'Ara, a businessman called Piero Goldoni, were tasked with the job. They called at his palatial villa in the hills overlooking Bologna in the morning. Dall'Ara was getting ready to have his breakfast. The grand old man had been bedridden a lot lately. He'd enough ailments to fill a hospital ward, including diabetes, heart attacks and a couple of ulcers, and he was at that moment recovering from bronchial pneumonia. The messengers knew they must tread carefully.

Dall'Ara's wife was delighted to see the visitors. She ushered them in, opening the door of her husband's bedroom with a flourish, gleefully announcing: 'Renato, look who's here! What a nice surprise.' Dall'Ara was propped up with two large pillows behind his back in an Impero bed, which was so high he was looking down on his two visitors. Both sat on two chairs and started making small talk about the weather: 'March is a crazy month. Down in Amalfi, the almond trees must be in bloom.' Then Goldoni braced himself and weighed in: 'By the way, there is a small annoyance.' When Dall'Ara heard the news, he burst into tears.

2.

Bologna's fans mobilised. Within a few days, three lawyers, who were Bologna supporters, filed a lawsuit against the Italian Football Federation with Bologna's public prosecutor. They questioned the way the doping tests had been carried out, claiming the vials had been compromised. A second analysis was requested.

Bologna F.C. were careful to distance themselves from the lawsuit, as the club risked expulsion from the league if seen to have instructed the three lawyers. The club went as far as issuing a statement that it fully supported the Italian Football Federation's authority.

This was an important intervention by the three lawyers, as the doping ban was no longer a federation issue. Now it was open to a judicial inquiry. Vittorio Carpinacci, a police chief in Bologna, went to the league's headquarters in Florence to seize all its documents and samples. A second set of vials collected on the day of the failed doping test had never been tested. He took both sets of vials to the University of Rome for analysis. On 8 March 1964, a besieged Bologna team beat Sampdoria 1-0 in a spiky encounter; two Bologna players were sent off for retaliation. A banner in the stadium hinted at the conspiracy afoot to derail Bologna's title challenge: *La Mafia non è solo in Sicilia* – The Mafia is not only in Sicily).

A week later, the Italian Football Federation tried to get ahead of the judicial investigation by issuing their judgement. Bologna's five 'doped' players had been acquitted, it explained, as they could have been drugged unwittingly. However, the club's coach Fulvio Bernardini and Bologna's team doctor, Igino Poggiali, were slapped with 18-month suspensions. Bologna were deducted three points. On hearing the sentence, Dall'Ara wept.

Two days later, Bernardini watched Bologna's game against Roma in the Olympic Stadium from the stands. Disguised in sunglasses and a chequered hat, he tried directing instructions to his dugout via a walkie-talkie, but it was seized by police. Bologna carved out a 1–0 win. A week later, Bologna hosted Inter in the league. The press, predicting an 'Easter of Blood', wrote about the febrile atmosphere in the city, which hadn't been as rancorous since the country's civil war in the 1940s. Extra police were on duty patrolling the game. Flags and banners were banned from the ground. Boos echoed around the stadium like claps of thunder when HH's name was announced on the public address system before kick-off. It did nothing to deter his men: Inter won 2–1.

On 4 May 1964, the Public Prosecutor's Office announced its preliminary findings. They declared that the first set of vials had been tampered with, laced with enough amphetamines to kill an ordinary human being. No amphetamines were found in the second vials. Their conclusions left the Italian Football Federation in a quandary. They immediately back peddled, acquitting Bologna and restoring their three deducted points. There was jubilation across the city.

With three rounds of league fixtures to play, Bologna and Inter were now tied on 50 points each at the top of the table – and that's the way the standings remained at the end of the season. This caused confusion. There was no precedent, and the federation had no rules about head-to-head results or goal average in the event of a tie. League officials and journalists convened at a hotel in Bologna to thrash out a solution. Some fevered imaginations toiled in the room.

The director of the Milan-based *La Gazzetta dello Sport* suggested giving the title to Inter and, as compensation, retrospectively awarding the 1927 *scudetto* to Bologna, who finished second that season to Torino. (The 1927 title had been taken from Torino because of match-fixing, but the Italian Football Federation's Bologna-born president left the title unassigned, fearing accusations of hometown bias.) Eventually, it was decided, for the first time in history, that the Serie A title would be settled by a play-off.

3.

The tiebreaker was set for Rome on 7 June 1964. Four days before the game, Renato Dall'Ara was invited to Milan for a meeting with his counterpart, Inter's president Angelo Moratti, together with the league's chief, with a view to finalising details for the play-off. Dall'Ara's specialist doctors – who forbade him from attending football matches because he'd endured two heart attacks earlier in the year – pleaded with him not to travel. Dall'Ara went against their wishes, travelling by car with his wife and his personal doctor. The meeting got ratty. Dall'Ara collapsed in the arms of Moratti – which was ironic, thought HH – and was rushed to hospital, where he died.

Bologna's players were in *ritiro* when they heard the news. 'They killed him!' roared Mirko Pavinato, the team's captain. He died 'like a soldier', wrote Vittorio Pozzo, Italy's two-time World Cup-winning manager. The Italian Football Federation were open to postponing the play-off, but Bologna's players decided to play in honour of their president. Dall'Ara was buried two days later at San Pietro, Bologna's Cathedral. Only two of Bologna's players, both injured, were able to attend, as their teammates had to play the match. On the morning of the game, Bernardini was so distracted he delivered his team talk wearing one trainer and one leather shoe.

The press in Milan were convinced HH would work his magic again, having won Inter its first European Cup 10 days earlier in Vienna. A columnist for *Corriere della Sera* claimed it was fitting that HH would be crowned in the capital city: 'It is right that this decisive match is played at the Olympic stadium … the only city qualified to place the crown on Helenio Herrera's head is the one surrounded by the busts of Charlemagne, Henry VII and Napoleon.'

HH was worried that talk of a coronation might be premature. Fatigue was his greatest enemy. He felt his men had spent themselves in winning the European Cup while also having to fight so doggedly in the title race. Once more into the breach? They'd need a pep for it – a shot of amphetamines. He knew Bologna would be at the same trick for sure. But how could he outflank the doping authorities? Émile Wanono, his quack French osteopath, assured HH that he could hoodwink the doping authorities by flavouring the speed with a herbal concoction. Inter's medical staff scoffed at the plan.

HH put forward a Plan B. He knew that the stadium in Rome, which had recently hosted the 1960 Olympics, was poorly protected by a moat no wider than a ditch. Overjoyed by victory, a battalion of fake Inter fans could invade the pitch at the final whistle and spirit their heroes away (from the clutches of the doping controls). Inter's medical staff, including doctors Manlio Cipolla, Angelo Quarenghi and Roberto Klinger, dashed to Angelo Moratti's Roman villa and woke the president to tell him about the plan. Moratti asked if by chance HH was mad and put a stop to the devilment.

HH was distraught. Nonetheless, he sent the same 11 Inter players out for the match who had triumphed in Vienna. Bologna's players wore black armbands in mourning for Dall'Ara. The neutral supporters in the stadium were cheering on Bologna and their coach Bernardini, a former Roma great as a player. The game kicked off late in the afternoon in stifling heat. It was a dour match. Inter could hardly muster a shot on goal and conceded two late goals, one an own goal, to lose 2–0. Bologna were league champions. They haven't won the title since.

4.

In 1966, the criminal case investigating the Bologna doping scandal came to a close in a courtroom in Florence. There was high farce to some elements of the case. The court established that the vials had arrived at the test centre in Florence unsealed. They were kept in an unlocked fridge, which was beside a glass cabinet containing, among other items, tubes of amphetamines. The building, which was undergoing maintenance at the time, was unguarded. Somehow, someone 'fraudulently introduced' amphetamines into the urine samples.

The criminal investigation could only establish what happened, not whodunnit. Rumours were rife. The press suspected several people, including a Florentine doctor who lodged a sizeable cheque from Milan at the time of the scandal and a member of Bologna's medical staff who threatened to sue Livorno's *Il Telegrafo* for 100 million lira until the newspaper retracted the allegation.

A couple of years later, one of Bologna's team doctors, Giampaolo Dalmastri, was on a flight to Budapest for the semi-final of the Fairs Cup. Giuseppe 'Gipo' Viani was sitting beside him on the plane. As a footballer, Gipo Viani had won a *scudetto* with Inter in 1930. It was in football management and administration, though, that he carved his reputation. His nickname was 'The Sherriff' because he looked like John Wayne.

At the time of the Bologna doping scandal, Gipo Viani had been a technical director at AC Milan – and a prime suspect. Italo Cucci, a journalist with Bologna's *Corriere dello Sport*, reckoned Viani hired a cycling team manager to tinker with the infamous vials. When he confronted Viani, he was evasive: 'It's better to talk about football.' Two years later, on the flight down to Budapest, Viani was feeling more talkative. 'Everyone blames Inter for the doping case,' he said, smiling boastfully, 'but do you know what? I happen to know Milan had something to do with it.'

5.

When the Bologna doping scandal blew up in the spring of 1964, *Der Spiegel*, a German news magazine famous for its investigative reporting, did some digging around. They had some skin in the game. Bologna's star player Helmut Haller was German, and a scorer in the 1966 World Cup final. He was named Serie A 'Footballer of the Year' in 1964, the first foreigner to win the accolade. An unnamed source from the Italian Football Federation told *Der Spiegel*: 'Everywhere in Italian football there is doping.' Clubs were beating the system with informers, sidestepping controls through advance warning. The most common way to get around checks was to slip "clean" urine from substitutes into testing vials. There was little or no control in drug-testing rooms. As late as the 1968/69 season, according to the whistleblower Carlo Petrini, his coach at Genoa, Aldo Campatelli, told his players: "As regards doping controls, there is no problem."

Haller, who had sandy-coloured hair and a smile that suggested life was just a ride, admitted to a confidant in his circle that Bologna's players were given injections at every game, but he didn't know what they were. There was no sympathy for HH, and the *scudetto* that slipped through his fingers, whether doping had had a hand in it or not. As one of his enemies remarked: 'He who robs a thief has a hundred years of pardon.'

24. 'MADE IT, MA! TOP OF THE WORLD!'

1.

HH ordered his players to mind themselves over the summer. The struggle for a huge prize awaited them in the autumn. His men trooped back for preseason training on 10 August 1964 with a sense of dread. They knew they would have to eat bitter for the next few weeks. They were a hardy bunch, though, and HH was pleased at their weigh-in. They had retained their fighting weight during the off-season, thanks to individual training regimes. It was a sign of their self-discipline and ambition. Now HH set to work against the clock, getting them fully fit for the two-legged Intercontinental Cup final in September.

The Intercontinental Cup was in its fifth edition. It pitted continent against continent: the European Cup winners v the Copa Libertadores champions, the Old World against the New. By the decade's end, Europe's teams would be fed up with the violence and intimidation they encountered, which reached a blood-soaked frenzy during the second leg of the 1969 final. At La Bombonera in Buenos Aires, Estudiantes fans threw boiling coffee at Milan's players as they ran on to the pitch. During the game, Milan's players were allegedly pricked with needles. Eduardo Manera, an Estudiantes defender, was thrown in jail for a month because of his thuggery during a match *La Gazzetta dello Sport* headlined 'NINETY MINUTES OF A MAN HUNT'.

Several European Cup-winning teams boycotted the tournament in the 1970s, including Ajax, Bayern Munich and Liverpool. In 1964, however, the trophy still had a great cachet. Pelé's irresistible Santos team won back-to-back titles in 1962 and 1963. HH would have preferred to face Santos. Instead, he got Independiente, an Argentine side stocked with footballers who played with a knife between their teeth. To prepare, he hand-picked Atlético Madrid for a warm-up game. Atlético didn't disappoint. Eager to defeat the European champions, they 'threw all their meat on the spit' for a feisty encounter. In fact, they led 2–0 but Inter fought back for a 2–2 draw. This was just the test of fire that HH was looking for, and further evidence of the attitude he'd fostered in his team: Never say die.

When HH arrived in Buenos Aires for the first leg against Independiente in early September 1964, the Argentine media went to war. HH was used to playing the villain. He was happy to take the darts in public so his players could prepare unmolested for big games; he'd written the playbook. But this was a whole other level. The press said that HH boasted Inter would win. That he demanded police protection, and that he would use the police protection to expel Argentine journalists from Inter's dressing room. It was all lies. The government had ordered the police to chaperone Inter. And of course he wanted to talk to his players in private.

Then things got dirty. A newspaper published a story that HH sexually assaulted a chambermaid in his team's hotel and that she reported the assault to the police. The investigation dead-ended, but rumours about the assault spread. The image of HH chasing a chambermaid around the corridors of a hotel made him the butt of jokes. In his mind, though, the funny thing was that the chambermaid was godawful ugly. The best way to quash the rumour, he thought, would have been to publish her photo.

2.

A moat separated the terraces from the pitch at Independiente's stadium. On the day of the match, a cordon of police surrounded the pitch. Armando Marques, a Brazilian who sent off Pelé in a game the year beforehand, was referee for the day. Before kick-off, he called the teams' captains and coaches into a huddle. 'Gentlemen, I'm willing to whistle everything, to send everyone off, even if it leaves only myself on the pitch. I've already said goodbye to my mother before coming here.' HH was impressed. Message received!

HH was delighted by his team's performance. His Inter team were fitter. Their precise defending left him in ecstasy. It was almost the perfect match, which recalled Inter's furious defending against Everton at Goodison Park a year beforehand in the European Cup. Even so, Inter lost. Their goalkeeper Giuliano Sarti blundered, dropping a ball he should have caught easily, which dribbled embarrassingly through his legs and over the line. Inter returned to San Siro for the second leg and won 2–0. The rules of the competition, which didn't account for goal difference, dictated that the teams meet again in a tiebreaker.

The play-off was set for the Santiago Bernabéu Stadium in Madrid three days later. It was under floodlights. There were no neutral fans in the stadium. The Madrid public, hurt after Real Madrid's defeat in the 1964 European Cup final, roared on Independiente. Inter had a friend, however, in the centre circle: the ref for the match was José María Ortiz de Mendíbil, a man who appears in the photo for several of Inter's victorious nights of international football.

The pitch was waterlogged from heavy rain. Inter were missing three players through injury – Tarcisio Burgnich, nicknamed 'The Rock'; Sandro Mazzola; and their Brazilian forward Jair da Costa. In the second half Joaquín Peiró got injured but played on. Inter were on the ropes. They traded punches. They suffered. This time, their goalkeeper Sarti was enchanted and made several good saves.

The game went to extra time. Tired legs kept trudging through the mud. With 110 minutes on the clock, Inter launched a counter-attack. Mario Corso received the ball deep in his own half, with his back to goal. He swivelled, broke free from a tackle, shimmied past another Independiente player and hurtled upfield, nudging the ball forwards with his famous left foot. The Israeli national team coach had christened him 'God's left foot' after a qualifier for the 1962 World Cup. It was said Corso used his right foot only to get on the tram.

Corso, with his socks pulled down around his ankles, bore down on Independiente's goal. He laid the ball off to Aurelio Milani on the right wing, who crossed to the far post. Joaquín Peiró gathered the ball and knocked it back towards the edge of the box, where Corso was waiting. With deft control, Corso trapped the ball with his chest, let it bounce once and then smashed the ball into the net. Game over. Inter weren't going to concede a goal now. After the game, Inter's president Angelo Moratti gifted Corso a Mercedes-Benz sports car for his decisive strike.

At the final whistle, HH strode on to the pitch like an emperor. He was dressed immaculately in a beige suit. As he soaked up the hosannahs, his only regret was that his mother wasn't there to share this moment of joy. Instead, it was his fixer Dezső Solti, a man with a blood-stained conscience from his time in Auschwitz, who walked beside him and gave him a hug. Memories of HH's childhood flooded his mind. He thought about how his family had fought for a place to live where scorpions didn't trespass. Who would have thought when he was an urchin roaming Casablanca's dirty alleyways that the king of Morocco would one day decorate him. If only his momma could see him now.

25. VOICES IN THE HEAD

1.

Ian St John – or 'The Saint', as people called him – was only 1.72 metres tall, but he always knew how to look after himself. He had a quick temper, a bad thing, but also good in that he feared no one. As a teenager, getting on the bus to Glasgow for a night out, he carried a knuckleduster in his pocket. This was the 1950s, during days of razor gangs and Teddy boys. He had it hard growing up. His father died aged 36, leaving behind six young kids for his mother to raise in a tenement building in Motherwell. She supplemented her widow's pension with work as a charwoman, cleaning and scrubbing floors. He mainly remembers the cold from his childhood: dressing for school under the bedcovers in the morning, wearing wellies for the outside toilet. His shoes had holes, so he inserted cardboard to keep the snow from soaking his socks. He noticed that the kids at school who had fathers tended not to have holes in their shoes.

Boxing was an escape. He loved hanging around the boxing club – with its rickety ring and punchbags – and the exhilarating feeling of stepping between the ropes when he knew he had his work done and he was ready to go to war. Clipping other fellas gave him confidence. It meant he could look after himself on the street and when it came to his other great pursuit – football. He developed a ferocious confidence in his own opinions, which he carried into his broadcasting career. He boxed officially for the first time aged 14 and started to win prizes, but the black eyes he picked up along the way left his mother distraught. She had enough to be worrying about. She pleaded with him to give up boxing and to focus on football. He knew he could excel at only one sport, so he bowed to her wishes and chose football – but he always hankered after the fight.

The Saint was a crafty, deep-lying centre-forward. He was still a teenager when he made his debut for Scotland at Hampden Park in a 3–2 win against West Germany. Two years later, in 1961, he was on the verge of signing for Newcastle United. Then Bill Shankly got in the way. He borrowed a Rolls-Royce from a director at Liverpool and drove up to Motherwell to persuade him to join his club instead. Shankly said he'd match the illegal £1000 signing-on fee Newcastle United were offering. The Saint couldn't resist his charm, or the fact that he was a Scot like himself. Shankly had an aura. The transfer fee agreed – £37,500 – was a club record for Liverpool, more than three times the ceiling agreed at board level, but Shankly pushed it through. Years later, he said landing The Saint – more than any other transfer – led to Liverpool's renaissance.

Shankly was a man like no other. He thrived on direct communication with his people. When he got his first coaching job at Carlisle United in 1949, he took to communicating with the fans over the stadium's loudspeakers before games: 'This is your manager speaking…' The fans loved it. They came to matches early just to hear him talk about team news and his hopes for the game. A decade later, when he fetched up at Liverpool, he resurrected a club in the doldrums. It was 'the biggest toilet in Liverpool', he admitted years later. It had no water to irrigate the pitch. Dead light bulbs hung around the bowels of the stadium unchanged. He set about painting the dressing rooms and toilets himself. He toiled day and night at the club, at the cost of his family life. Football kidnapped him. He was an absent figure for his children. He lived for Liverpool FC. He painted the front door and windows of his house bright red. (Years earlier, on their wedding day, he took his bride to watch Preston play a reserve match.)

There were no sides to Shankly. 'He was a good observer of people,' said The Saint. 'He hated people he couldn't trust – "cheats and liars", he'd mumble.' Shankly never administered fines. He felt if he had to fine a player, he was admitting they were lost. Instead, he kept players in line with his tongue. When assessing a footballer, he looked for character, men with a bit about them, who had an aggressive approach to life and football. He ostracised players who were injured, stopped talking to them. His magic power was his ability to motivate people. His confidence made his players confident. 'He wasn't 5ft 8in,' noted his assistant Joe Fagan, 'he was 6ft 4in.' He could transmit his enthusiasm like a charge of electricity through a dressing room – and across a working-class city like Liverpool. 'It's the greatest thing in the world – natural enthusiasm,' he said, hitting on the key to success in any walk of life. 'You're nothing without it. Nothing. If a manager is honest and he has this natural enthusiasm, while he can't go out on the field with the players, he can convey it to the players. You understand? He's with them and they're with him and they'll be successful.'

2.

The Saint formed a devastating partnership with Roger Hunt, a World Cup winner with England in 1966, up front for Shankly. The pair helped Liverpool gain promotion to the First Division in 1962. Within two years, Liverpool were league champions. In the summer of 1964, having won the title, Liverpool went on a six-week tour of North America. Shankly was in his element, retracing the steps of his idols. The Saint said Shankly lived in his own world of mobsters, gunslingers and old boxers. He even stood with a boxer's stance, ready always to fight. When the team arrived at Soldier Field in Chicago, Shankly felt he was standing on holy ground, the site of the famous Long Count Fight between Gene Tunney and Jack Dempsey in 1927. He collared the groundsman: 'Jesus Christ, you have to show me where the ring stood, and I don't want any guesses.'

Shankly was addicted to gangster movies. The characters played by James Cagney, George Raft and Humphrey Bogart were his kind of men. He spoke with their staccato delivery. He loved their virility, their fearlessness, which he urged his players to emulate. Sometimes the mobster voices in his head got the better of him. The Saint remembers Shankly turning on a reporter once at Anfield who dared criticise his team: 'Get out of here in your Elliot Ness overcoat!' Although the American pilgrimage fed Shankly's soul, it left his team exhausted. A slow start cost them the defence of their league crown. By Christmas, they were out of the title race. Their focus turned to two cups – the FA Cup and the European Cup, which they were playing in for the first time.

In the European Cup preliminary round, Liverpool beat an Icelandic team 11–1 on aggregate. Anderlecht were their opponents in the first round. Shankly went to Wembley to watch Belgium draw 2–2 with England a few weeks before the tie. Impressed by the Anderlecht players on display, he warned his men they'd have to be on their toes. He came up with a gimmick to intimidate the Belgians – he suggested Liverpool wear red shorts to go with their red jerseys. Red for danger, red for power. The Saint told him to go a step further and play with red socks too. Shankly liked his thinking. They'd glow on the pitch like a burning fire.

On the afternoon of the first leg, Liverpool hung out in a hotel in Southport. Shankly still hadn't picked his starting XI. He agonised over one place on the team – whether he should pick a teenager, Tommy Smith, in defence. He worried he was too inexperienced, having played only a handful of league games. Tommy Smith was born about a mile from Anfield, the stadium that gave him his nickname, 'Anfield Iron' – iron in the tackle, cast-iron self-belief. Before reaching the age of 17, he was badgering Shankly to give him his debut. When he went one day to Shankly's office insisting he should be in the first team, Shankly replied: 'Aye, son, you're right, but the problem is that they're not good enough for you yet.' Smith left the office baffled.

At the hotel in Southport, Shankly consulted with The Saint and Ron Yeats, his captain and another Scot, about whether to take a punt on Tommy Smith. They were surprised at his doubts. Smith got the nod. Liverpool swept Anderlecht aside 3–0 at Anfield. The Saint opened the scoring after 10 minutes. Liverpool were outplayed in the second leg but nicked a goal for a 1–0 victory. In the quarter-final, Liverpool drew 0–0 over two legs with Cologne. When they tied again 2–2 in a play-off, the referee tossed a coin to decide who would go through to the semi-final. When his coin landed on its side in the mud, he re-tossed it. Fortunately for Liverpool, they won the toss at the second time of asking. Waiting for them in the semi-final was HH's Grande Inter.

3.

Liverpool played Leeds United in the 1965 FA Cup final. The Saint scored Liverpool's winner, the most important goal of his career – a diving header in a cup final at Wembley with four minutes to go in extra time. The stuff of boyhood dreams. This was the first time Liverpool won the FA Cup. The team returned to Liverpool the following day for a parade. It was bedlam. 'We came back to all this razzmatazz,' said The Saint. 'It was amazing. I'd never seen crowds like it before. They were hanging from the rooftops. I don't think it's ever been bettered – the number of fans who turned out. The FA Cup was a special thing.'

Shankly didn't allow his players out to celebrate. The first leg of the European Cup semi-final against Inter was two days later at Anfield. On match day, the stadium gates opened at 3 p.m. Liverpool's fans streamed in. Kick-off wasn't due until 7.30 p.m. The Saint remembers it was eerily quiet when they drove into the stadium car park. Usually, fans would be milling about with their banners and red scarfs, but the Victorian terraced streets around the stadium were deserted. The gates were shut an hour before kick-off. The stadium, which was already full, was crackling inside.

The Saint was conscious that HH would be in Inter's dugout. HH had built a huge reputation in the game, having made Inter into an indomitable team, Europe's powerhouse, who were en route for another Serie A title in Italy that season. He had a mystique in football that carried across the seas. He was the great, cut-throat football tactician that everyone had to beat. Shankly knew this. He spoke about HH before the match, about pitting his wits against him. He wasn't too fussed, however, about the footballers in HH's team.

'We knew absolutely nothing about Inter. Nothing. We had them watched – our chief scout Geoff Twentyman went to Italy to see them play, but we didn't get a report back. Shanks wasn't bothered about hearing the report of his findings. He sent a guy halfway round the world to see them and then he says, "We're not interested in them. It's about how we play,"' said The Saint, laughing. 'That was it. As far as Inter were concerned, they could have a dozen European Cups behind them. It didn't matter. It was about us, about going out – after winning the FA Cup – and beating them at Anfield.'

I asked him if Shankly said anything about the threat of, say, Luisito Suárez or Sandro Mazzola. The Saint started laughing: 'No. Shanks wouldn't have known how to pronounce their names. He was funny that way… I remember we played against Ajax in the European Cup a couple of years later. Ajax had good players throughout their team, but Johan Cruyff was a great player. He could win the game for them on his own. Shanks was standing at a tactics board. He had white for their team, red for us, and numbers for each player. "Now, boys, Johann Strauss,"' he said. All the lads were laughing to themselves.'

Italian football teams on the European stage in the 1960s had a natural aura. The players walked with a strut. But not on this night. In the tunnel before kick-off, The Saint could see the surprise in the eyes of Inter's players. There was a flicker of doubt. They were clearly affected by the atmosphere coursing through the stadium. There was a venom in the chanting of the baying red mob, as they belted out: 'Ee-aye-addio, Mussolini's Dead!'

Shankly was never so animated before a game; words came spitting out of his mouth like machine-gun fire. He held his players back in the tunnel after Inter's players ran out on to the pitch. Then – always alive to some mind games – he sent Gerry Byrne and Gordon Milne out (both were missing the game through injury), to parade around the pitch with the FA Cup. 'Gerry was in a sling, the wounded soldier,' said The Saint. Shankly told them to walk around by the Anfield Road end first, and then to hit the Kop end. Perhaps the most famous terrace in football, the Kop was like an extension of Shankly. The people who stood there thought the same way as him. They paid his wages, and his players' wages, something that Shankly hammered home to his men. By the time Liverpool's starting XI took the field, the stadium was shaking. The Saint said he had never experienced an atmosphere like it before nor since in a game. It was transcendental. The energy in the air made him feel like he was playing 'outside my own skin'.

Within three minutes, Roger Hunt flashed in a goal to give Liverpool the lead. The game turned into a frenzy. A mistake by Ron Yeats led to an equaliser, scored by Sandro Mazzola. Ian Callaghan put Liverpool back in front with a clever goal from a free kick engineered on the training pitch. Chris Lawlor scored another goal for Liverpool, but it was erroneously disallowed for offside. Midway through the second half, Inter's goalkeeper Giuliano Sarti parried a shot by Roger Hunt. The Saint pounced to score from the rebound. 'And that could put Liverpool in the final,' crowed the ITV's commentator Hugh Johns. The game finished 3-1, although Liverpool could have scored seven on the night. HH admitted his team had been beaten before, but on this night, they were defeated. Liverpool's fans stunned them. Shankly was euphoric in the dressing room: 'It was men against boys, tonight. You showed that magician and his boys how to play.'

4.

The euphoria at Anfield turned to tears the following day. Liverpool's club secretary Jimmy McInnes was found dead under the Kop. 'He hung himself on the turnstiles,' said The Saint, dropping his head. 'He was a Scot. A kind man. He was a Liverpool player when the Second World War broke out. It was an awful thing. As club secretary, he handled any financial dealings, contracts and stuff. It definitely was at that time where there was a lot going on about European nights and travel. He had nothing to do before that, really, just getting ready for Saturday. All of a sudden, he had to arrange travel around Europe, hotel bookings, managing all these extra costs, lots of mail, phone calls. The whole thing was just so brand new for Jimmy. The pressure got to him … and he topped himself. It was down to pressure. It was so sad. So sad.'

Mersey Beat: Bill Shankly, Ian St John and Liverpool's squad boarding a plane on the hunt for European Cup glory.

26. MAN IN THE MIDDLE

1.

HH started beating the war drums before the second leg. He was eager to avenge what he described as 'the humiliation suffered in Britain', and his words whipped Inter fans into a fury. Eight days separated the two legs. On the weekend in between, Inter hit Fiorentina for six goals in a Serie A win at San Siro. During the game, an Inter supporters' club scattered nearly 50,000 leaflets from the roof of the famous stadium on to spectators below, marshalling them for the European Cup battle ahead. A second leaflet, among another 50,000 handed around the packed stadium, played the nationalist card: 'Dear Friends, we left Anfield Stadium to a chorus of insults and the shout "Go home Italians" sung to the tune of 'Santa Lucia'. The Liverpool supporters chose the song to deride us and make us feel we are just a race of cheap mandolin players.'

A group of Inter fans waited at Linate Airport to heckle Liverpool's players when they arrived in Milan, wielding hand-written placards, 'LIVERPOOL – WILD SAVAGES, DOPERS', and shouting threats: 'Go home now while you are still alive!' 'Wait till Wednesday – the night of revenge … Inter will murder you!' The Saint and his teammates couldn't understand what the Italian rabble were saying and laughed off the taunts. The word on the street in Milan was that Liverpool's players took amphetamines for the game at Anfield, which accounted for their electrifying performance. 'SHANKLY LAUGHS OFF DOPE SMEARS' reported the headlines from the travelling British press in Milan.

Shankly wasn't laughing, though, at the monastery bells that kept him and his team awake at the team's hotel on the shores of Lake Como. He ordered his assistant Bob Paisley to get them muffled, but Paisley was unable – even after pleading with a monk – to put a stop to centuries of Catholic tradition. The Saint remembers the commotion: 'The night before the match, we were in bed. The bell tower had a guy ringing a bell to keep us awake. It didn't help us, but did it put us off our game the next day? I don't know if it did. You've always got a reason, an excuse if you want to find one: "Oh, I never slept last night. They were ringing bells." If I heard any teammate saying that I'd have gone mad.'

2.

José María Ortiz de Mendíbil is a legendary figure in the annals of Spanish football. He was a referee from the Basque Country and the only Spaniard in history to referee a major international tournament final – the 1968 European Championship final at Rome's Olympic Stadium, in which Italy defeated Yugoslavia 2–0. After refereeing the 1969 European Cup final at the Santiago Bernabéu Stadium between Ajax and AC Milan, Spanish fans chaired him off the pitch. It was a source of pride to them that a Spanish man was in charge of the most important club game in the calendar. Once he retired from refereeing, he became a football pundit on Spanish television.

Ortiz de Mendíbil was tall, and he took great care with his appearance. His wife was an amateur golf champion. The couple enjoyed the pleasant things in life. When Ortiz de Mendíbil travelled by train in a sleeping car, he got train staff to park up his carriage on a siding at the train station until he woke up. Money was never an issue with him. If he didn't like a hotel, he'd pay up and check into another hotel. Linesmen in Spain – who typically were promising beginners selected from the same region as a top referee – crawled over themselves to work alongside him. It was a ticket to ride, recalled Ildefonso Urizar Azpitarte, one of his regular linesmen: 'What a difference! Between staying in Vizcaya [the Basque province where Ortiz de Mendíbil lived], refereeing a match in the third division in any old ground and being exposed to everything, travelling like a king, with him. And what you got to learn! About football, about life ... about everything!'

Ortiz de Mendíbil was a great friend to Inter. He refereed their 1964 Intercontinental Cup win in the rain against Independiente, and he was the man in black on the night of several other great continental conquests for Inter in the 1960s. Luis Suárez once remarked that Ortiz de Mendíbil had more winners' medals with Inter than himself.

Ortiz de Mendíbil was chosen to referee Liverpool's match at San Siro.

3.

San Siro was like an inferno on the night of the match. Inter's fans snuck in home-made smoke bombs, which turned the skies blue inside the stadium. One exploded close to Bob Paisley on the steps of the tunnel, covering his clothes in blue soot. 'They sure gave it the full Monty,' said The Saint, recalling the hostile atmosphere on the night, but his Liverpool team weren't intimidated. 'If you're going in with a team like we had, you're not frightened. They could throw all the smoke bombs they liked. When I was putting my boots on and I looked around the dressing room I knew I could trust everyone around me. We had a great team. Each man knew he had to do his bit. We played as a team and for each other.'

Inter's players were spoiling for a fight. 'Going to San Siro for that return leg, we were told obviously they would be up to all sorts of tricks and sure enough that's what they were like,' said The Saint. 'They were dirty, sneaky dirty – sneaky kicks and tugs and elbows. You can go in and hurt people with a legitimate tackle if you're physically strong and you get the timing right, if the other fella is off balance, but we're talking about the nasty stuff, the stuff that the referee doesn't see. Inter were great players, but they were pure nasty players as well. A few of them you'd like to meet on a dark night. Luis Suárez was a little bastard. He was their best player, but he could be dirty too.'

Ortiz de Mendíbil – flanked by his two linesmen – led both teams on to the pitch for kick-off, cradling the match ball in his right hand. Photographers walked backwards in front of him snapping their cameras furiously. Missiles rained down on to the pitch in front of Liverpool's goal during their warm-up. Ortiz de Mendíbil chatted with Inter's captain Armando Picchi at the centre circle while waiting for Liverpool's Ron Yeats to arrive for the coin toss. Within a few minutes of play, The Saint could see the way the wind was blowing. Inter kept winning free kick after free kick. Turning to Roger Hunt, he said they'd be lucky if 'this bloody referee gives us a throw-in'.

Eight minutes into the match, Inter's Mario Corso bore down on goal. He lost control of the ball and spilled to the ground from a tackle on the edge of the box. Ortiz de Mendíbil whistled a free kick for Inter. Liverpool's players protested in vain. Ortiz de Mendíbil placed the ball on the ground and then goose-stepped the regulation 10 paces, pointing where Liverpool's defenders had to construct their wall. When Ronnie Moran, one of Liverpool's defenders in the wall, was slow to take up his position 10 metres back, Ortiz de Mendíbil pushed him backwards in the chest. Corso took the free kick, curling the ball with his celestial left boot into the top corner of the net. Liverpool's players went into a fury, claiming the ref signalled the free kick was in-direct. Ortiz de Mendíbil waved them away.

Less than two minutes later, Inter broke down the left flank in attack. A long ball forward flew towards the side of Liverpool's box. Liverpool's keeper, Tommy Lawrence, came off his line to intercept it, plucking the ball from the feet of Inter's striker Joaquín Peiró, and sending him to the ground with a shoulder at the same time. Confident that Peiró was momentarily out of the game, Lawrence bounced the ball a few times as he got ready to launch a kick upfield. Peiró picked himself up off the ground, snuck around the side of Lawrence and dispossessed him with a deft flick and then stroked the ball into the net. '*Stupendo!*' greeted the Italian television commentator in excitement at Peiró's sleight of foot. Liverpool's players were incensed by Peiró's larceny, which, in Milan, earned him the affectionate nickname 'Thief'.

Inter continued the siege on Liverpool's goal. On the hour-mark, Giacinto Facchetti, one of the greatest wingbacks ever to grace the game, stole forward to get on the end of a beautiful passing move to score a third goal for Inter. The Saint had a goal disallowed. The game finished 3–0. Inter had pulled off an incredible comeback, going through to the final 4–3 on aggregate. It was too unbelievable for some of Liverpool's players to stomach. The worst feeling The Saint ever knew on a football pitch. He was clear that Liverpool were set up: 'The referee, a Spanish guy, was a bastard. He definitely had a few bob riding on the game.'

The minute the final whistle blew, Tommy Smith charged after Ortiz de Mendíbil. 'I remember Tommy at full time. I saw him booting the ref up the arse, screaming at him,' said The Saint with a guttural laugh. Shankly never fully got over the defeat. He couldn't shake off the memory of Ortiz de Mendíbil's refereeing. It fed his paranoia about cheating foreigners.

A couple of hours after the match, Liverpool's players wandered into Milan for something to eat. The Saint and Ronnie Moran – who went on to become part of Liverpool's legendary Boot Room coaching staff – found a table in the basement of a restaurant to decompress. A few fans were in tow, but the two footballers were no company, both lost in their own thoughts. When their party got up to leave, the restaurant tried to stiff them with an exorbitant bill. One of the Liverpool fans, a businessman, disputed the costs. It got heated. Angry waiters surrounded their table. The Saint and Ronnie Moran were in no mood for lip. Someone threw a punch. Then all hell broke loose. Muscle memory took over for The Saint. He was back on Motherwell's mean streets, bobbing, weaving, administering pain. At times, he felt he was fighting everyone. Next thing he remembers was going backwards up the stairs of the restaurant. This gave him a welcome few inches of height advantage, as he picked off Italians in his range with left and right hooks, before he and Ronnie Moran disappeared into the night.

4.

During the summer of 1964, HH had bought Joaquín Peiró. He immediately added Peiró to the team – at the expense of Aurelio Milani, who was more of a workhorse – up front. He was the final piece of a jigsaw. The team that lined up against Liverpool at San Siro – and that defeated Eusébio's Benfica 1–0 in the 1965 European Cup final and Independiente (again) over two legs in the Intercontinental Cup final later in the autumn – would become immortal. They were names that tripped off the tongue: Sarti, Burgnich, Facchetti, Bedin, Guarneri, Picchi, Jair, Mazzola, Peiró, Suárez, Corso. Their names were a nursery rhyme that could lull babies to sleep. They were like a perfect verse from Petrarch, noted one journalist:

> *septenario, septenario, dodecasílaba*
> *sarti burgnich facchetti*
> *bedin guarneri picchi*
> *jair mazzola peiró suárez corso*
> *baci da matalascanhas, huelva*

The notorious José María Ortiz de Mendíbil gets ready to toss the coin at the San Siro Stadium while team captains, Liverpool's Ron Yeats and Inter's Armando Picchi, shake hands.

27. A NINTH CIRCLE OF HELL

1.

During his final years, Josef Mengele suffered from intense abdominal pain. He had a habit of chewing the ends of his moustache, which caused a ball of hair to block his intestines. Mengele – the 'Angel of Death' – was one of the most wanted Nazi war criminals. He escaped from Auschwitz, scene of his ghastly war crimes, in January 1945, 10 days before Soviet forces seized the camp. He spent the rest of his life on the lam. After the war, he worked for a time as a farmhand in Bavaria, the German state where he grew up. In 1949, he fled along a ratline to Genoa in Italy before sailing for Argentina. His wife refused to travel with him.

Mengele floated around South America, mostly in Argentina and Brazil, on the run from Mossad agents. He eluded capture by using six aliases. In 1958, he married his widowed sister-in-law while on holiday in Uruguay. He died at a coastal resort close to São Paulo in Brazil in 1979, aged 67. He had a stroke while swimming in the sea and drowned. His body was hauled ashore. He was buried, but his corpse was exhumed in 1985 just to make sure it was Mengele who was dead. Arguably more than any other man, Mengele embodied the Nazi killing project.

2.

In May 1943, Mengele requested that he be transferred to Auschwitz. He arrived at the camp with an aura. He had spent most of the war on the Eastern Front with a Waffen SS unit, where he won an Iron Cross, and where he was wounded and declared medically unfit for combat. Going to Auschwitz was a career move. Mengele wanted a taste of the extermination camp because it would be the ideal theatre for his pseudo-medical experiments. He had qualified as a doctor before the war, but his passion was for genetics. Auschwitz would give him access to limitless inmates whom he could use for his research.

As an SS doctor, Mengele's job was to select prisoners for slave labour or those who were to be sent to the gas chamber. Most doctors at Auschwitz did no more than what was required of them, but Mengele worked in a fever, driven by a mix of scientific ambition and sadism. He looked at the faces and bodies of those prisoners who arrived on the platform at Auschwitz's train station for only a few seconds before pointing left or right with his finger or his walking cane, condemning them in their droves to death, whistling operatic tunes from Verdi, Wagner and Johann Strauss as he did his work.

No one could predict the criteria Mengele used in deciding who would be dispatched to the gas chambers. He acted on a whim, enjoying the pleasure of making inmates realise the power he had over their destiny. Some days, he announced he was selecting only those with, say, thick legs. In September 1944, on the day of Yom Kippur – the holiest day of the year for Jews – he mounted a bar between the posts of a football goal at the height of about a metre and a half. Those who didn't reach the height of the post – approximately a thousand children – were killed. He epitomised absolute evil – 'a doctor pledged to heal who kills instead'.

Despite its scale and conspicuousness, nothing about his barbarous behaviour seemed amiss to his peers. In August 1944, a camp physician carried out a performance evaluation on him, concluding Mengele was 'straight-forward, honest and absolutely reliable … in his demeanour he does not show any character weaknesses, tendencies or manias … his performance can be called outstanding … his character makes him a favourite with his comrades … while carrying out his duty as a physician in the most conscientious way.' It is difficult to know how many people died as a direct result of Mengele. *The New York Times* calculated a figure of 400,000 people.

Mengele was pathologically obsessed with order and hygiene. He dressed immaculately but also foppishly, his body scented with aftershave. His military costume included white gloves and black boots that glistened like shiny coal. He worked with a cheerful expression on his face. Prisoners were struck by his split personality – the difference between his calm, playful manner and the horror of his actions. He was kind to children. He gave them sweets. He enjoyed playing with them. He often took care of them medically before sending them to the gas chambers.

'He looked exceedingly well-groomed – in this sad environment, I noticed that immediately. His hair was very thick and dark. I remember his eyes; they were uncommonly bright. He really didn't look like a murderer,' said Dezső Solti, a Hungarian Jew interviewed by the US military at the end of the war, while held in Feldafing, a displaced persons camp in Germany.

Dezső Solti was a prisoner of Auschwitz. In the second act of his life, he had a career in football. Throughout the 1960s, Solti worked in the shadows for HH at Inter, bribing referees. Before serving HH, Solti served Mengele at Auschwitz as an assistant. Working for Mengele at Auschwitz conferred powers on Solti. He wielded uncommon influence in camp life. According to Solti's mother-in-law, who also survived the Holocaust, he paraded around Auschwitz like 'God Almighty'.

3.

To borrow a phrase, Solti is the kind of character who'd make a novelist's fingers itch. He was born on 17 September 1911 in Balmazújváros, a market town in eastern Hungary. His birth name was Dezső Steinberger. He changed his surname in 1948. As the son of a flour mill owner, he wasn't poor. He loved football but wasn't good at it, so he funded the local football team, which became a fulcrum of his life. There's a photo of him standing in a team photo from 1943, looking straight on and serious with his distinctive high forehead. He had a raised upper lip that gave the impression he was always on the verge of sneezing. His world was shattered on 25 May 1944, the day he was rounded up – with his extended family and several hundred other Jews from Balmazújváros – and shuttled to Auschwitz.

The Holocaust came late to Hungary, but with furious anger. By the time the Nazis began trawling their net around Budapest and its hinterlands – following their occupation of the country in March 1944 – their murder machine was terrifyingly efficient. Hungary accounts for the largest number of victims from a single country at Auschwitz. Eighty per cent of Hungarians, approximately 340,000 people, were found unfit for work and killed within hours of arrival at the camp gates. Solti's family was almost entirely wiped out. His father, his mother and his wife died in the Holocaust. A few relatives who survived the death camps emigrated to Australia in 1950. A niece, who was in hiding during the war, made it to the United States, but row after row of his relatives are listed in Yad Vashem's database of Shoah victims.

Solti took a winding train route through modern-day Ukraine and Slovakia before arriving in Poland at Auschwitz. Around a hundred prisoners were packed into each train wagon. A cargo of petrified, hungry, sick, exhausted humans. Patients from mental asylums were tossed on board alongside crying children and stunned old men and women. There was no room for stretching or going to the toilet. Everyone wanted to arrive, no matter where they were headed, as quickly as possible. The majority of those who were pushed on to the muddy train platform at Auschwitz didn't even enter the camp but were dispatched immediately to the gas chambers. Prisoners were often separated without a chance to say goodbye. Others didn't even notice what was happening, they were so confused.

Auschwitz was split into several camps over thousands of hectares. Solti, who was fit for work, was sent to the notorious Auschwitz–Birkenau, which was 2km from the central camp. Inmates ironically referred to the sub-camp as 'paradise' because being sent there meant almost certain death. It was built by Soviet POWs. Smart prisoners gave a manual profession on admission, which meant they could be of some use. It was dangerous to be listed as a shopkeeper, lawyer or teacher, which is why Solti identified himself as a mechanic and 'installer' when he was later moved to Dachau in November 1944.

Life in Auschwitz was a Darwinian swamp. Inmates did anything for a scrap of food. Without extra food, death was inescapable. Gold crowns were pulled out and exchanged for a piece of bread. The horrors of the camp, the daily beatings, broke down social bonds. Inmates were forced to look inside themselves for survival. They became 'cantankerous, mistrustful and in extreme cases even treacherous,' recalled one prisoner. 'Since the great majority of the inmates adopt these characteristics, even a placid person must assume an aggressive stance.' Often this meant stealing, using violence or betraying fellow prisoners, denouncing them to *kapos* in the hope of securing a bit of food.

The *kapos* were a secondary hierarchy for controlling the camp. They were assigned by SS officers to supervise prisoners, to carry out administrative tasks, to smooth the day-to-day running of the camp. Often, they were criminals or political prisoners. Below them, there was a network of collaborators, including night watchmen, interpreters and assistants' assistants. For doing the devil's work, *kapos* got privileges: better clothing, better food, alcohol and cigarettes. The pressure on them to prove their ruthlessness was unending. A *kapo* knew that when the camp's high command was no longer satisfied with him, and he was returned to other inmates, he'd be beaten to death the first night back in the barracks. Every Jew in Auschwitz faced moral dilemmas, but *kapos* lived permanently in a middle ground, caught between being victims and perpetrators. A ninth circle of hell. It hollowed out their souls, ate them up with guilt.

Disease was a constant companion. Solti's camp, Auschwitz–Birkenau, was built on marshland, so malaria was a grave threat. Many died within a few days of contracting dysentery. Those with diarrhoea had to pass faeces 10 or 20 times a day. Refusing inmates permission for the toilet was a favourite form of punishment. Holding back led to excruciating pain. Those who let shit run down their legs were called 'pigs' by the Nazi camp guards. Work accidents led to skin ailments, burns and fatal injuries. A broken rib wouldn't exempt a prisoner from slave labour, but it was guaranteed to accelerate his decline. Feet diseased by fungus were often a cause of death. Those who ended up in an infirmary were already three-quarters dead. Lying in hospital meant the risk of contracting scabies or typhus, which were rampant in hospital wards, or selection for the gas chambers.

At night, when Solti wasn't distracted by the sobbing and wailing around him, and he was left alone with his thoughts, his options presented themselves: death from work and exhaustion; death in hospital; death in the crematorium;

or suicide (although few people killed themselves at Auschwitz). This was Solti's greatest enemy – bad thoughts. If he dwelt too much on the hunger, the lice, his family's fate or the gas chamber, he'd collapse within days. A prisoner could last six months if his morale was good, but that life expectancy decreased to a month or two when morale was low. The broken of spirit shuffled about, with a fixed stare, no longer trying to fight, too weak even to spoon up soup spilt in the mud. There was an unwritten rule in camp: any prisoner who lasted more than six months was a crook because he lived at the expense of his companions. This was the Faustian pact Solti made.

4.

One day at Auschwitz, around the summer of 1944, Josef Mengele couldn't get his car started. By chance, Solti was on hand to help him out. Mengele, who was impressed by Solti's command of German, gave him a job as his assistant. This was Solti's ticket to survival. Reflecting on his role as an assistant of Mengele in Auschwitz, Solti's second wife was shocked but unsurprised at his opportunism: 'It's horrible and I don't want to believe it ... but he was the type of man who invented himself in all circumstances.'

It's difficult to verify the stories about Solti's behaviour at Auschwitz under Mengele. There are no documents on Solti (or specifically the prisoner Dezső Steinberger) in the official archives on Mengele at Auschwitz, although Solti is a witness in a 444-page report by the U.S. Department of Justice on Mengele. Solti was never charged after the war – when Israel did try collaborators. There are conflicting reports from Hungarian secret police files about Solti's time in Auschwitz as an informer and *kapo*, and second-hand accounts from Béla Szobolits, who made a documentary in the early 1990s that includes an interview with Solti. The problem with testimony by Solti is that nothing he said about his life – based on his record of lying and double-crossing – can be taken at face value. People claim that Solti was both a villain and a hero.

'Prisoners who lost the ability to work would be gassed,' said Szobolits. 'Mengele would line up all the workers and go along checking their buttocks. If he saw there was no flesh there, he would decide the prisoner was finished and send them to a separate line to go to the gas chambers. As Mengele continued down the line, [Solti] was able to save some prisoners by pushing them back into the main line.'

There is a first-hand account by Sándor Schwarcz, a survivor of Auschwitz (and a man who was once interviewed by Steven Spielberg) about a couple of incidents relating to Solti. The two men knew each other from before the war. Schwarcz arrived in Auschwitz in July 1944, shortly after Solti. Schwarcz got himself in a line-up for a camp football team by lying, claiming he played for

Bocskai, a Hungarian First Division team. His lie had only spilled out of his mouth when Schwarcz noticed Solti, who was acting as an interpreter, standing alongside a German officer picking the football team. 'I was dizzy from the recognition. I thought I was done for and that the paramilitary with the labour battalion was going to execute me. Steinberger (Solti) did not even blink even though he knew exactly who I was.'

Solti spent his life walking on both sides of the street. His refusal to rumble Schwarcz was noble, life-saving, but the Nazi regime had a lasting, corrupting effect on him. Whatever horrors Solti committed as a collaborator haunted him for the rest of his days. 'Auschwitz only worsened my position because I was weakened in everything,' he confessed. 'I was weak in character, in will, in everything. Auschwitz burned everything.'

Tamás Dénes, a Hungarian football historian and broadcaster, is reluctant to pass sentence: 'Solti is a controversial character, but generally people have sympathy for a man who survived Auschwitz. OK, Solti survived Auschwitz but on the other hand he was a sinister figure in the world of football. It's a Janus-faced situation. People such as Solti's mother-in-law denounced Solti for his behaviour in Auschwitz, but often these kinds of verdicts depend on personal connections: "If I hate you, I'm denouncing you as a collaborator; if I like you, OK, you were a hero." It's hard to know. It seems that Solti was a collaborator because of his connections. He had good business instincts. I can agree that he was not a Braveheart, but I don't like to judge these people because I was never in their situation.'

David Bolchover is a biographer of Béla Guttmann, the two-time European Cup-winning coach with Benfica in the early 1960s. Guttmann was an associate of Solti's, a fellow wartime Hungarian Jew, who dodged the death camps by hiding out for months in an attic near Budapest and later escaped a slave labour camp. Bolchover is struck by the speed with which Solti was able to assert himself at Auschwitz. 'He must have already been a very streetwise person, not only to survive, but also to assume a position at Auschwitz as a Jew where he had some influence. His reading of human nature must have been extremely developed.

'Solti was a fixer who made himself useful. Although his behaviour was morally questionable after the war, it is not clear that he did anything reprehensible in Auschwitz. There undoubtedly would have been some Jews who did bad things in order to stay alive, such as stealing food from other prisoners. But the vast majority of these people would have ended up dead too. Many of the *kapos* ended up in the gas chambers themselves. It is worth considering the story of Rudolf Kastner, a very controversial figure in Holocaust history. People still argue about whether he was a hero or a villain. Or the story of Hershl Sperling, who survived Treblinka, the camp which he said made Auschwitz seem like a holiday resort. He moved to Glasgow after the war, before committing suicide in 1989. Survivors had to go through another ordeal after the Holocaust, coping with the memories. Sperling did not survive the second test. He was eventually crushed by the memories. You could say that Solti was a dual survivor.'

Solti didn't live in a very fragrant world. In 1955, he was involved in a hit-and-run in Milan. Guttmann was driving Solti's car when he lost control and knocked down two students who were standing by their scooters, killing one of them, a 17-year-old boy. Guttmann and Solti abandoned their car and fled. Solti was arrested a week later in the Austrian Alps, hundreds of kilometres from Milan. Solti wasn't fazed by the Italian judicial system, conscious that he could pull some strings in the background. He took sole responsibility for the hit-and-run, accepting a payment from Guttmann in return.

Solti stood trial in 1957, by which time Guttmann was in South America, but the case collapsed when Solti sensationally retracted his confession. The case was retried in 1960 in Milan. Solti and Guttmann were charged with manslaughter. This time, they were both *in absentia*, apparently 'untraceable', which raises eyebrows because Solti was living in the city – and working for Inter – at the time. Solti was acquitted because of lack of evidence. Guttmann was sentenced to six months' imprisonment but pardoned on payment of damages to the aggrieved families.

'After the war, Holocaust survivors reacted in different ways,' said Bolchover. 'Some became religious. Some became atheists. Some must have lost their sense of right and wrong, thinking, *This is what happened to me. I'm out for myself now. I was imprisoned wrongly because I was a Jew, in a completely unjust way. I'm now going to look after myself.* That definitely came across to me when I was researching the story of the car crash. Guttmann and Solti killed a young boy and severely injured another girl. It seemed like they had little conscience about doing that. Maybe Guttmann looked back with some regret later, but they were determined to save their own skin. That was the survivor mentality: "Listen, we've been through a lot already. Life is tough. There's a lot of bastards out there. We've got to look after our own." There would certainly have been that mentality amongst some Holocaust survivors. Maybe Solti was like that already. Maybe it accentuated that element in his character. It's so difficult to work out.'

28. SZOBEL'S SHOW GIRLS

1.

In January 1951, Dezső Solti applied for assistance to the International Refugee Organization. He wanted to resettle in Uruguay where he had 'relatives'. He said he was tired of living under the yoke of Stalinism in Hungary. His application was a tissue of lies. He glossed over the Holocaust, claiming he worked in his father's mill in Balmazújváros from 1936 continuously until he was 'taken by Russians' to 'Zegelid concentration camp' in January 1945 because he was a 'capitalist'. His property was confiscated, and members of his family were taken by the Soviets at the same time as he was. He 'escaped' from Zegelid with 20 other prisoners in August 1945, which is quite something, as there is no gulag or place in the former Soviet Union's vast tracts of land called Zegelid.

So much of Solti's life is shrouded in mystery. After the war, he enrolled in an artist and dancing school in Budapest and trained as a magician. Posing as an entertainer was a scam to get a passport, which he secured from Hungary's Ministry of Interior in 1949. (It's believed he worked after the war as an informant for ÁVH, Hungary's secret police, which helped speed his passport application.) The passport put him back on the road again, enabling him to slip through the Iron Curtain unmolested. For the next few years, he traipsed around the nightclubs of Italy and other European cities with a troupe of 'dancers'. This was a front for trafficking prostitutes to the West. Solti's girls did residencies in La Porta d'Oro, the nightspot in Milan where Inter's Angelillo met and fell in love with Ilya López. They were called 'Szobel's Show Girls'.

Solti always liked to have a beautiful mistress on his arm. Usually, they were half his age. (At the end of his days, when he lived alone in an apartment in Milan, touching 80 years of age, he spoke a lot about women to anyone who lent him an ear.) Solti understood the language of women, remarked a Hungarian agent detailed to spy on him. Solti was courteous, he practised good manners. His smile was that of a rogue. He plied his Eastern bloc prostitutes with luxuries, leftovers from his labyrinthian smuggling operations. Two or three times a year, Solti loaded up his car and drove from Milan to Hungary with Italian delicacies – perfume, disposable nappies, cocoa powder and the like – which were unavailable behind the Iron Curtain. But these were only fripperies. It was by trading paintings and artefacts – like ancient Torah scrolls, for example – that he made serious money. He hid rare stamps in a secret compartment in his travel bag. At one point, Solti reckoned his private stamp collection kicked in at about $50,000 (more than half a million dollars in today's money).

The walls of his apartment in Milan were decorated like a Medici palace, according to a surveillance stocktake by secret police. His art collection included works by Picasso and old masters. There were 40 different valuable paintings hanging in his living room and bedroom. His office was full of paintings, while he also had hundreds of paintings rolled up in his attic. Solti ran an elaborate network to orchestrate his smuggling business. These included customs officials; airport security at Budapest's international airport; gallery owners; a fine art lecturer at Hungary's Institute of Cultural Relations; intermediaries who bought and sold paintings on behalf of private collectors. He also kept contacts to help get around bureaucratic roadblocks, such as a man at the Hungarian National Gallery who fixed him up with certificates so he could take paintings out of the country without hindrance.

2.

Solti immersed himself in the world of football. In the 1950s, you can find him pictured on the team coach of Hungary's Golden Team, sandwiched between Ferenc Puskás and Sándor Kocsis. According to Hungarian intelligence reports, Solti moved through the dressing room of Hungary's international team like a knife through butter. Their star forward, József Bozsik, prostrated himself whenever Solti was in his presence. Solti didn't fly under any particular flag. His services were always in demand by top clubs, and he worked for the highest bidder. According to his memoir, Solti worked during the late 1950s 'helping Real Madrid with their European Cup games'. In 1971, Solti fetched up in the Netherlands with a letter of introduction from Juventus, as a representative of the Italian club, in advance of a Fairs Cup game against FC Twente.

Solti had a Zelig-like ability to surface at so many key moments in post-war football history. When HH's Inter team flew back to Milan after their first European Cup win in 1964, they were met at the airport by delirious fans and banks of photographers. The team's captain, Armando Picchi, descended the steps of the plane cradling the European Cup. Behind him was HH. In front of Picchi, and first on to the runway's tarmac to receive the acclaim, was Solti. Five years later, when Inter's city rivals won the European Cup, Solti appears behind a shirtless Gianni Rivera, Milan's captain, as he holds aloft the trophy. In 1968, Solti represented Italy at the European Cup knockout stages draw among top football administrators from other countries.

Solti could access all areas. Before the 1964 European Cup final in Vienna, he invaded Real Madrid's dressing room to give Puskás a sledging. Holding the match ball in his hand, Solti dangled it in front of him: 'Take a good look at it, brother, because you're not going to touch it during the match!' In 1966, he skulked around behind the curtains at the World Cup finals in England with an international press pass for *Népsport,* a sports newspaper for which he never filed a report. During a first-leg European Cup quarter-final in Budapest between Vasas and Benfica in 1968, Solti went down to the Vasas dressing room at half time to give the home team some amphetamines, but they turned down his offer. Solti was disappointed: 'I had doping agents that would have helped, but they were afraid to use them.' Vasas lost the tie 3–0 on aggregate.

3.

In the 1960s, Solti travelled more regularly from his base in Milan back to Hungary. Typically, Sándor Barcs, an executive with UEFA and the Hungarian Football Federation, would pick him up at Budapest's international airport or Barcs would send a car to ferry Solti to his hotel. Solti's briefcase was stuffed with the business cards of Hungary's top five referees. The apartment of István Zsolt, one of those referees, was searched and his phone wiretapped by secret police, as part of a surveillance operation carried out on Solti. According to Hungarian secret police reports, 'Solti bribed Hungarian referees in advance who were assigned to the international matches of FC Internazionale.'

A bag drop by Solti at the Hungarian Football Federation, according to an agent spying on his movements, unfolded in recurring fashion like a scene from a John le Carré novel: Solti 'got out of the taxi, took out the suitcase, and then paid the fare, took quick steps at 16.20h towards house No. 47 on the People's Republic Road. At the gate entrance, there was already a man aged approx. 60 (we can't give a detailed description) waiting who took the suitcase from [Solti] and then went up to the offices of the Hungarian Football Federation on the 1st floor.'

It wasn't only referees and officials from football federations who were bribed, according to reports from Hungarian secret police and investigative reporting conducted by Brian Glanville in the 1970s for the *Sunday Times* newspaper. Solti kept anyone who was influential in the game sweet, including football chairmen and directors, former players, former coaches, journalists and agents. To win their favour, he lavished them with cash bribes, valuable gifts and jewellery (gold watches were a favourite), holidays in Italy, or the gratifications of a night with a prostitute.

4.

Hungary's intelligence agencies – from internal affairs to counter-espionage – spent decades monitoring Solti's movements. He appears in state archives under the pseudonym 'Manager'. The suspicious people who associated with him were given aliases like 'Bald', 'Umbrella', 'Fast', 'Beard', and the agents who spied on him took on names like 'Paul the Swallow'. State security organisations from other countries also kept tabs on him, including those from Czechoslovakia, Italy and Romania. 'The Austrian Football Federation doesn't look kindly on it when he shows up in Austria,' wrote one spy. 'Everyone studied' Solti, remarked another intelligence officer. Solti knew he was being spied on, but it didn't spook him; once, for example, he cheerfully quizzed a hotel maid in Budapest if his room had been searched yet.

Hungary's counter-espionage unit classified Solti as 'very dangerous', a 'primitive man', one 'soaked in money' who waltzed around Europe and South America's Cold War theatres, fraternising with bent politicians and businessmen, rabbis under surveillance, hoodlums and hookers. Was Solti a spy? If he swam in the murky waters of international espionage, of duplicity and double agents, which side did he work on? One of Solti's several wives – whom Solti married in 1969 and divorced a few months later – was interrogated by Hungarian secret police. Her statements suggest Solti worked for 'a hostile intelligence agency', most likely Israeli, and that Solti did assignments for 'Zionist circles of Western countries'. They concluded that Solti's work in football was a cover so he could move freely across borders and raise money. Intelligence agents reported in detail about his criminal activities, but it was the threat of treason to the Hungarian People's Republic that caused alarm.

Although the file was fat on Solti's lawless lifestyle, Hungary's counter-espionage unit didn't move on him until December 1968, when it put him on a list of people banned from entering the country, citing his corrupt behaviour in football. Solti was indignant. He fired off a letter to the National Central Office for the Control of Aliens, complaining: 'I can't be an enemy of the system, not only for the reason that I myself am a victim of the fascist regime, which I will forever remember by carrying bullets in my head and body right now. I am also a sworn enemy of the fascist regime because of the destruction of my family at their hands.' His case went right to the top. In September 1969, Solti's travel visa was reinstated on the say-so of András Benkei, Hungary's Minister of the Interior (the longest serving since the eighteenth century) and a notorious drunk. It seemed Solti was untouchable.

5.

In Italian society, there is the concept of the *furbo* character. A *furbo* is sly and street-smart. He's crafty enough to bend the world to his own advantage, knowing how and when to try it on, the shortcuts to take, whether they're legal or not. He does what's needed to get ahead, even at the expense of his fellow man. Every culture has their version of the *furbo*. In Ireland, they celebrate the *cute hoor*. In Argentina, they marvel at *el pícaro*, the rogue. Maybe it's a Catholic thing, places where people are quick to forgive a sinner, to laugh in the face of the uptight and the sanctimonious.

In the mind of the *furbo*, those who stick to the rulebook are fools, and easy prey for his schemes. They also have a name: the *fesso*. Writing in the 1920s, Giuseppe Prezzolini explained that you are a *fesso* in life 'if you pay the full-price rail ticket, don't get into the theatre free, don't have an uncle who is a *commendatore* or a friend of the wife who is influential in the judiciary or education; if you are neither a Freemason nor a Jesuit; tell the taxman your real income [or] keep your word even at the cost of losing thereby'. Prezzolini reckoned it wasn't intelligence that made a *fesso* different to a *furbo*, but that *fessi* have principles whereas *furbi* only have aims. Throughout his life – and certainly after Auschwitz – Solti wasn't bothered unduly by principles. He was only interested in his own goals.

Solti, the *furbo*, was a useful man to have around at Inter. He knew how to navigate in a fallen world. According to Hungarian intelligence files, Solti built up his close relationship with Inter's directors and players in the 1950s because he had a line on prostitutes. Solti never had an official title at Inter. The arrangement was best kept that way – at arm's length, so the club could keep their hands clean. Italo Allodi was Inter's sporting director during their glory years under HH. When asked in interview if Solti acted as a quasi 'Foreign Minister' for the club, Allodi responded with an evasive smile. Solti had cult status at the club and was warmly applauded by fans when he showed up at San Siro's VIP box in the early 1990s.

Solti turned his hand to different tasks. He worked as a travel agent – when, for example, Everton visited Italy for their first round European Cup tie against Inter in September 1963, Solti was Everton's liaison man, organising their travel arrangements and training facilities in Milan. He worked as an agent for Inter, brokering a deal to sign Ferenc Puskás in 1957, which ultimately fell through. Puskás – who was serving a worldwide FIFA ban at the time – ended up at Real Madrid a year later instead. When HH got itchy feet at Barça during the 1959/60 season, it was Solti he asked to fix him up with a Serie A club. Solti introduced him to Inter: HH met Angelo Moratti, Inter's president, at a motorway restaurant close to Milan (and the rest is history).

Solti maintained that Inter sent him to scout their European opponents – a far-fetched claim, according to Brian Glanville, who covered those years on the ground as a football journalist. Solti was fond of telling tall tales. He maintained he was in São Paulo once, scouting a striker for Inter. A good player, but he'd left his hair at home; a bald 34-year-old forward past his sell-by date. The trip wasn't in vain, however. A young, unknown kid called

Jair da Costa caught his eye. Solti swooped, claiming he bought the player for 60 million lira of his own money before selling him, at a hefty profit, to Inter. Couldn't be true – when Jair joined Inter in the summer of 1962, he was transferred from the Brazilian side Portuguesa, and he was already part of Brazil's World Cup-winning squad in Chile.

But Solti was undoubtedly an asset for Inter. Angelo Moratti had his back. In the mid-1960s, Solti was busted by Italian border police while travelling back into the country from Hungary with a dodgy passport. Moratti stepped in, cleaned up the mess and got Solti fixed up with an Argentine passport. Moratti needed Solti for club business. Solti was Inter's invisible hand, a man who could influence referees.

6.

After Easter weekend 1966, Inter stood six points clear of the chasing pack at the top of the league table in Italy. With six games to go, the retention of their *scudetto* title was in little doubt. They were a machine – only twice had they lost all season during Serie A's gruelling schedule. In Europe, the defence of their European Cup crown wasn't as clear-cut. Later that week, they faced Real Madrid, Europe's aristocrats, in the semi-final. Real Madrid had overhauled their team. Gone from their starting XI were Di Stéfano, Puskás and José Santamaría. Paco Gento remained from the old guard, surrounded by a cadre of young Spanish internationals like Zoco, Pirri and Amancio. The press in Madrid nicknamed the team the '*Yé-yés*', picking up on the 'yeah, yeah' chorus line in the song 'She Loves You' after a bunch of their players posed for the press with wigs, impersonating the Beatles. Pirri scored an early goal at the Bernabéu to give Real Madrid a 1–0 advantage in the first leg. It was a slim lead but Inter wanted to leave nothing to chance for the second leg. So, Solti was pressed into action.

György Vadas, a Hungarian referee, was appointed to ref the game. Puskás, who was on the bench for Real Madrid at this stage of his career, had a pop at him in the run-up to the game. He was quoted in a Spanish newspaper saying Vadas shouldn't referee the match, as he was a friend of Solti's from their days together in primary school in Hungary. This wasn't true – the pair weren't classmates – but Real Madrid's unease that something foul might be at play was made known. Once Vadas and his Hungarian linesmen touched down in Milan, Solti swooped, shadowing them from morning to night. The only time Solti wasn't around them was when they slept, making sure no one from Real Madrid tried to tap them up. On match day, Solti and Italo Allodi, Inter's sporting director, called at their hotel at 11 a.m. They brought with them greetings from Angelo Moratti and an invitation to visit him at his villa.

Allodi was also a *furbo*. He was born in 1928, the son of a railwayman. For decades, he was the great puppeteer of Italian football. He dominated the Italian transfer market for Inter in the 1960s, later for Juventus, and for Napoli during its Maradona era in the 1980s. He acted as Italy's general manager for the 1974 World Cup, a tournament that ended in disgrace when Italy were dumped out in the pool stages amid accusations they tried to bribe Poland, the winners of their group. Allodi enjoyed manipulating the course of events. He lived life according to a George Bernard Shaw maxim, wisdom he loved to quote: 'Only imbeciles justify the success of the best by attributing it to luck.' In 1986, Allodi was reduced to tears in a courtroom in Naples when accused of match fixing, but he steadied himself and made an aggressive defence when accused of bribing referees. 'Bullshit,' he said. 'If a gold watch or a mink coat were enough [to win football matches], we would all be world champions.' The tribunal, which was investigating an illegal betting ring, acquitted him. He was made of Teflon, and a posthumous inductee into Italian Football's Hall of Fame in 2017.

Allodi's influence in the game lived on after he passed away. Luciano Moggi was his protégé, admitting on the day of his death in 1999 that Allodi had 'created' him. Had seen something in him, an uncouth young man from rural Tuscany. Had made him a scout at Juventus – Moggi's big break in the game. Allodi also knocked some of the rough edges off him. Moggi used to eat like a wolf, and had a habit of using his tie to wipe his mouth. Allodi taught him about social graces – and how the football industry worked. In 2006, seven years after his mentor died, Moggi was revealed as the mastermind behind *Calciopoli*, the biggest scandal in the history of Italian football, which is saying something, a hurricane that cost Juventus relegation to Serie B and erasure of two league titles from its record books.

On that sunny April morning in 1966, hours before Inter played Real Madrid at San Siro in the European Cup semi-final, Allodi and Solti escorted the Hungarian referee György Vadas and his two linesmen to an audience with Angelo Moratti. The Hungarians gasped at the opulence on display at the villa of Inter's chairman. 'What a marvellous place it was! Name anything beautiful or wonderful, that place had it!' recalled Vadas years later. 'We lunched in a pleasant environment, and in an excellent mood… To start the lunch, Signor Moratti presented the three of us with a gold watch. Then, as the meal progressed, he told Solti that he should buy us this or that. We just ducked our heads in wonder … colour television sets – very rare in Hungary in those days – tape recorders, record players, electric razors, radios and other electrical devices. We three Hungarians looked at each other in amazement.'

They were only appetisers. For the main course, Solti isolated Vadas in his hotel room – the only time Vadas was alone during his trip to Milan – and dangled a cash bribe in front of him, totalling 'enough to buy five, maybe six Mercedes cars', to ensure Inter went through to the final. The bribe, which was to be paid in dollars, was scaled: starting with a payment for a straightforward win by Inter; doubling for a win by a penalty awarded at the end of normal time; quintupled for a win during extra time; and multiplied 10 times for a win by a penalty during extra time. Vadas refused to bend. He told his linesmen about the proposition and made up his mind to referee the game fairly.

When Amancio scored for Real Madrid after 20 minutes, it looked like Inter were finished. Solti was fit to explode. He cornered Vadas at half time, and bawled him out, cursing him for refusing Inter three 'justified' penalties. Vadas told him he must have been watching another game. Inter scored a late goal to tie the match, but it wasn't enough – Real Madrid went through to the final 2–1 on aggregate.

Solti was in an unforgiving mood after the final whistle. 'His behaviour was not that of a sportsman,' said Vadas, adding [Solti] 'shouted and screamed that my refereeing had been a swindle. Threatened to spare no effort to have me struck off the FIFA list of referees. That was a threat he was able to make good. The screwing had been done well before I arrived home. At five o'clock in the morning after the game, Solti phoned the general secretary of the Hungarian Federation, György Honti, to tell him that, in Solti's words, I had cheated them out of the game.'

Vadas reckoned Inter's exit from the European Cup left Solti $30,000 out of pocket in bonuses from Inter. Vadas reported Solti's attempted bribery, but no action was taken by football's regulators. The career of Vadas as a top-flight referee was finished. Another *fesso* crushed under a wagon wheel. He was blacklisted – withdrawn from upcoming UEFA matches he was scheduled to referee. Gone were any dreams of running on to the turf at Wembley for that summer's World Cup finals in England. Solti liked to follow through on his vendettas. (He was eventually rumbled. In 1974, UEFA suspended him indefinitely from the game due to match-fixing allegations, although he was never tried in court.)

In May 1966, Real Madrid's *yé-yé* side won the European Cup final at Brussels' Heysel Stadium, defeating Partizan Belgrade 2–1. HH knew it was a golden opportunity missed. He was left to lick his wounds, and to scheme and fight again, until he got Inter back into the final the following season against an unheralded club from Britain.

29. THE PITS

1.

Jock Stein started his working life a thousand feet underground. His parents didn't want him grafting in coal mines, but like the rest of the fit young men in his village outside Glasgow, and his father and grandfather before him, he couldn't resist the pull of the pits. They were the only place to make a decent wage in Scotland during the 1930s. This was a time of soup kitchens and economic depression. Two of his sisters died in childhood.

After leaving school, Stein spent 13 years as a coal miner. The work was brutal. Cramped conditions. Lying on his side, in wet mud, hacking with a shovel. His back lacerated from sliding on rocky floors so he could get at coal seams. Sweat stinging the cuts. Ice-cold water dripped on him from overhead. Rats scurried at his feet, brazen ones sitting on his lap, to get at food crumbs while he ate. The sound of booming gelignite bellowed in his ears. It affected his nerves. A drop of water falling on a stone nearby could scare the wits out of him. Darkness deep underground can't be described. It has to be experienced. When his lamp went out, there were no shapes around, nor silhouettes. He couldn't see anything; there was nothing but the inside of his head.

Hardly a month passed without a workmate dying on the job. Stein knew that if a fatal accident didn't kill him, lung disease lurked around the corner. This was a horrendous station, yet it was the making of him. He never met finer men than those he toiled with down the pits. He carried miners' codes of behaviour with him through his adult life and into the world of football – their socialist spirit, the camaraderie, the trust established with the man crawling beside you.

'They didn't just get their own work done and go away,' he told Hugh McIlvanney, the football writer who built up a friendship with him until Stein's death in 1985. 'They all stayed around until every man had finished what he had to do, and everything was cleared up. Of course, in the bad and dangerous times that was even more true. It was a place where phoneys and cheats couldn't survive for long.'

2.

Football was Stein's passport to a living above ground. He played semi-pro while working in the pits. By the time he got his first full-time contract with a non-league side, down in Wales with Llanelli Town, he was 27 years old. He was a defender. He wasn't a classy player. He just stopped others from playing

– with his left foot and his right knee, as he liked to say. He joined Celtic in December 1951 – midseason (the same season Gil Scott-Heron's father played for the Hoops). On the cusp of his thirties, Stein was signed as a centre-half for the reserve team, someone to mentor younger players coming through. Then a plague of injuries to the first team's defence provided him with an opening, which he grasped. By the following season, he was captain. In 1954, he led Celtic to its first league and Scottish Cup double in 40 years.

The unexpected, glory-filled chapter with Celtic at the end of his playing career wasn't universally applauded within his circle. Stein was a Protestant playing for a Catholic club in one of the most sectarian cities in the world. He had grown up as a Blue Nose, supporting Rangers, and the rumour among Celtic's fans was that he had a tattoo of King Billy on his chest. Glasgow was a powder keg in his youth. Protestants and Catholics were at each other's throats. The violence on the streets was vicious, with riots involving thousands on both sides, young men belting each other in scenes that prefigured the worst era of football hooliganism half a century later. Stein was an outlier. He met his wife, a Catholic, in a chip shop. She was 15; he was 19. Once they started dating, he walked her home along back streets to avoid getting attacked. After joining Celtic, his own people looked at him as a turncoat. His best childhood friend never spoke to him again. When Stein left his parents' house to play a match against Rangers, his mother wished him luck and said she hoped he won the match. His father never did. He couldn't bring himself to do so, and never went to see his son play in an Old Firm game.

Stein was born to be a football manager. He was like a tornado at Dunfermline and Hibs, a disruptive presence who brought success to both clubs. Celtic, who were struggling in the league, appointed him as head coach in March 1965. The city shook, as Stein became the club's first Protestant manager. Several aspects came to define his time in football management. Beating Rangers came top of the list. It consumed him. It was personal with him, the be all and end all, a chance to wreak revenge on the bigots who turned their back on him.

Stein's philosophy of the game was built on attacking football. Watching Real Madrid's rapturous 7–3 win in the 1960 European Cup final at Hampden Park was a moment of enlightenment. There were more than 127,000 people with him at the match. Normally people are anxious to get a bus home after a big match, but it seemed nobody wanted to leave the stadium. Goals kept flowing in. The experience moulded Stein. He noticed how Real Madrid's backs swept forward, thirsting to get involved in the game. Only their centre-half, José Santamaría, was fixed in position. He was a stopper. Whenever he was in trouble, Santamaría hoofed it. He never took risks. Every other white shirt stroked the ball. They wanted to entertain. This was the licence Stein gave to his footballers.

Once on the pitch, Celtic's players had free rein to express themselves; off it, Stein had complete dominion over them. Stein had a natural aura. Players knew when he was in the room. They could feel his presence before seeing him. When he spoke, they stood up on their toes. Stein knew when to make them laugh and when to make them cower. They were fearful of his moods. He was unpredictable, volatile by nature. They never knew when a thunderstorm would roll in. He jumped into the players' bath one time, fully clothed, to finish an argument with Billy McNeill, the team's captain. Some of it was for effect. He'd fly into a rage to get a reaction, an actor on stage. He'd wink sometimes to Seán Fallon, his assistant coach, before launching into a bollocking.

A favourite trick was to kick open the dressing room door, summoning the players' attention. Then he would go to town on them. It was a chilling sight, tearing through each player one by one. No one escaped a dressing-down. He was a bear of a man. Towering over his players, he would bawl into their faces, spittle flying. He had no time for pampering. He kept his training ground austere like a Shaolin monks' temple. Only first team players were allowed to wear jerseys under their training tops, which were as scratchy as the cloth on a potato sack. It was easy to know a reserve team player trying to break through to the first team because he carried a rash on his chest.

An injury to his right ankle put an end to Stein's playing career. And left him with a limp for the rest of his life, which also lent a ghoulish aspect to his role as martinet. Jimmy Johnstone, the team's star player, once threw mud at Stein in the dugout after being substituted. 'Jock pursued him,' said Hugh McIlvanney, stifling a laugh. 'The story that went the rounds was that Johnstone ran right out of Celtic Park and down through the East End of Glasgow to escape Stein. That never happened. Johnstone told me afterwards that Stein chased him, his limp producing a sinister irregularity as he was pursuing Wee Jimmy to give him a doing! Johnstone got as far as a toilet, and he locked the door. Stein was banging on the door while Johnstone pleaded: "Will you not hit me? Will you not hit me?"'

3.

Jim Craig got on the Celtic train at the right station. The full-back signed for the club in January 1965, a couple of months before Stein's appointment as manager. He made his debut the following season, which ended with a Celtic title win, breaching a 12-year gap. (Stein's Celtic went on to win nine championships in a row.) Born in 1942, Craig grew up within walking distance of Rangers' stadium. Nearly every terraced house in the neighbourhood was Blue Nosed. Manchester United's famous manager Alex Ferguson – who played against Craig at schoolboy level and later in Old Firm matches – went to school around the corner from his home. Craig had been dating his future wife, Elizabeth, a few months when she remarked that he could be quite aggressive.

'I told her, "I'll tell you why I can get aggressive sometimes",' said Craig. 'I went to school in Govan. It was about a quarter of a mile from Ibrox Park. They gave me a green blazer to wear when I was at school; and when I became a prefect, they gave me a gold braid to wear around the edge of the blazer. It was like I had a bloody target on my back saying "Catholic". What I quickly learned was that if somebody was aggressive, I was equally aggressive back, and in 90 per cent of cases they backed down because they weren't interested in going any further than a bit of verbal.'

Craig was a late bloomer by professional football standards. He captained the Scotland schoolboys' team in 1961 but parked his aspirations of becoming a pro footballer to study dentistry at Glasgow University. He was 22 years old when he made his Celtic debut. He practised as a dentist until he was 74, squeezing in a top-flight career as a footballer in his twenties. Stein was happy for him to double-job – better than having him frittering away his spare time in pubs and betting shops. It set Craig apart from his peers on Celtic's team, but he was quick to lay down a marker.

'I was the incomer from Govan,' recalled Craig. 'I was also doing dentistry, something entirely different from other players. There was just the very slightest suspicion. I remember we were playing five-a-side one day. I passed the ball to Jimmy Johnstone, and he was tackled at the same time, and he looked at me and said, "What kind of fucking pass is that?" I shot back: "If you'd killed it the first time, you'd have been alright. Alright Jimmy?" That was me accepted because I answered him back.' His teammates gave him the nickname 'Cairney', which came from the surname of the lead actor in *This Man Craig*, a popular Scottish TV drama series in the 1960s.

Years after he quit the game, Craig enjoyed visiting Stein in his office at the Scottish Football Association (SFA). Craig's dental practice was close by. Stein was Scotland's football manager at the time, guiding them to World Cup finals in 1982 and '86. The pair had long, rambling chats about football and the wonder of life. Craig was struck by Stein's natural intelligence. It was something that registered with Hugh McIlvanney too. Stein had a profound influence on his players. Sometimes they thought he'd seen the game before it was played. He told them what was liable to happen, what their opposite number was likely to do, and how they could outwit the opposition. As well as tactical intelligence, Stein was an incredible motivator. Nothing got his juices going like an Old Firm game.

'I remember we were preparing for a match against Rangers,' said Craig. 'We played them in the Scottish Cup final in '69 and it turned into a punch-up shop. It was brutal. We kicked them off the park before we played any football. We won

4–0. We were brought up before the SFA for misconduct. About four months later, we played them again at Parkhead in the League Cup. Just before the game, the chairman Bob Kelly came in. He was knighted earlier that year. Jock said, "Hold on a second, lads. The chairman would like a word. In you come, Sir Robert." In he came and delivered his speech: "Well, I'd just like to say the last time you played this team there were some terrible scenes on the park and the image of football was very badly spoiled, so make sure you win tonight, but make sure you also keep the image of football in your mind when you're playing." Jock ushered him towards the door: "OK, Sir Robert, thank you very much. Can I open the door for you?" Then he turned to us and said: "You can fucking forget all about that for a start…"'

4.

In March 1967, Celtic lost 1–0 away in the first leg of their European Cup quarter-final against Vojvodina, a team from Yugoslavia. Celtic were overrun, and lucky to lose by only one goal. 'It was our toughest game en route to the final,' remembered Craig. 'They were a really good side. Tam Gemmell was short with a back pass, which is how they got their winning goal. A guy stepped in and struck it away. One of the papers wrote: "At the banquet after the game, Jim Craig walked across and seemed to have pity on Tommy Gemmell, and he sat down and offered condolences." I sat down and said to him: "You made a fucking balls of that." Which is how you speak as one footballer to another. Sympathy me eye. He said, "I did fuck up alright, Cairney, but don't worry I'll make it up to you." I said, "I know you will, son."'

HH had his eye on Celtic. He landed in Glasgow in early May 1967, a couple of weeks before his Inter team faced them in the European Cup final. He wanted to see them first hand, and chose an Old Firm game at Ibrox for reconnaissance. Celtic needed a point from the match to clinch the league title, but Ibrox wasn't a kind stadium to them – they'd suffered seven defeats there in their previous eight visits in the league; the other game was a draw. Rangers were a fearsome team. Later that month, they lost – but only in extra time – to Franz Beckenbauer's Bayern Munich in the European Cup Winners' Cup final.

HH flew to Scotland in comfort, aboard Angelo Moratti's private plane. HH already knew about Jock Stein. In November 1963, several months before HH's Inter team won their first European Cup, Stein was selected – along with another promising Scottish coach, Kilmarnock's Willie Waddell – for a trip to Italy to observe HH on the training ground. The excursion to HH's mountain retreat was bankrolled by the *Daily Record*, a Scottish newspaper. Stein coached Dunfermline at the time. HH couldn't help but notice Stein from the sidelines. He said Stein was like 'a big ant', buzzing around the place, full of enthusiasm.

Stein was struck by technical aspects during the tutorial: the variety of HH's training methods; HH's obsession with strength, conditioning and deep-breathing exercises; and the way HH could suddenly launch a counter-attack movement from deep, sometimes with eight players all surging forward at the same moment. When Stein returned to Scotland, he tinkered briefly with playing a 'sweeper' in his line-up, a *catenaccio* principle learned from HH. But what stayed in Stein's mind most was the total control HH exerted over his players, and the copious files he kept on each of them. 'I'm an absolute dictator here!' admitted HH.

The pitch at Ibrox on the day of the Old Firm game in May 1967 was like a gluepot. Glasgow was soaked in rain, which caused electrical failures across the city. The Underground broke down. Traffic lights were out for several hours. Photographers swarmed around HH, the world's greatest football coach and the embodiment of Mediterranean glamour, as he strode up Edmiston Drive to the stadium's entrance. Sean Connery was also in attendance, a month before the premiere of his fifth outing as James Bond, *You Only Live Twice*.

Despite the muddy conditions, the game was a classic. Rangers went ahead a few minutes before half time. A minute later, following a Celtic shot that hit the post, Jimmy Johnstone nicked in to equalise from the rebound. 'Jinky' Johnstone was a marvel, all 1.6 metres of him. At pedestrian crossings, years after he retired from the game, Glaswegian kids were told by their parents: 'Wait for the Jimmy Johnstone – wait for the little green man.' He had a magnetic personality. In 2000, the Hollywood actor Robert Duvall spent several months in Scotland shooting *A Shot at Glory*, a mawkish football film in which Johnstone worked as an advisor. Duvall couldn't help falling under Jinky's spell. 'Jimmy Johnstone from Celtic,' said Duvall. 'What a character: the voices, the rhythms, the speech patterns ... and he'd sing to me like Neil Diamond. He'd drink and come on to women. I named a dog after him.'

Johnstone's hellraising put years on Stein, who deployed a spy network in Glasgow to tip him off about which pub Johnstone might be drinking in. Sometimes Stein would phone the bar using a fake voice and ask to be put through to Johnstone. When Johnstone picked up the phone, Stein would bawl him out of it. Each tolerated the stress he caused the other. Johnstone was Stein's greatest piece of managerial work. In 1965, Johnstone was 20 years old, but after a promising start, his career had stalled. Stein yanked him from Celtic's reserves and squeezed 10 years of majesty from him. When Stein let him leave the club in 1975, Johnstone's career nosedived again.

Johnstone scored the greatest goal of his career in the second half of that mud-splattered Old Firm match. With about a quarter of an hour left to play, he received the ball from a throw-in inside Ranger's half, out on the right flank.

Four Rangers defenders blocked his route to goal. He took them on a merry dance, floating across the pitch's mucky surface before curling a shot from outside the box into the top corner. It was like he hit the shot while gliding on air. Rangers equalised, tying the game 2–2, but the draw was enough to secure the title for Celtic.

Celtic had just won back-to-back league titles, and they'd completed a domestic quadruple – but in European terms, they were half-unknown. Celtic had no pedigree abroad. The European Cup was the preserve of continental giants like La Grande Inter, who knocked out the holders, Real Madrid, in the quarter-final. Celtic were a curiosity, the first British team to reach the final. They had no international stars in their team, which was cobbled together from the streets of Glasgow and its hinterland.

Glasgow was a grim-looking city in the 1960s, riddled with tenements. It had more of a reputation for gangs and drunkenness and sectarianism than it did for world-class football teams. Inter were on course to win three consecutive *scudetti*, a feat unmatched since the great Torino side of the 1940s. They were red-hot favourites to win their third European Cup in four years. Previewing the final, *World Soccer* magazine predicted they would strangle Celtic: 'Soccer is said to be unpredictable but Inter, with their ruthless, relentless tactical system, have reduced uncertainty to a complete insignificance. When Inter win the final…'

The international press may not have rated Celtic, but Jim Craig reckoned what he saw in Glasgow on that rain-sodden May afternoon would have troubled HH. 'Any manager would have been impressed that day. It was a really tough game. It was a difficult surface, a soaking wet day, but the game was played at a tremendously high pace, and our ball control was good. So, if you're watching that, you'd think this Celtic team can play a wee bit.' HH bolted out of the stadium at full-time.

Stein had wanted to do his own bit of recce. Inter were playing Juventus the following day in a Serie A match at San Siro, and HH had promised to fly him back to Milan on Moratti's private plane. HH broke that promise at the last second. He claimed there was no longer room on board.

Stein was cute enough to keep a previously booked airline ticket, involving a transfer in Rome. He arrived in Milan the following morning, to be greeted by HH with a warm embrace and apology for the mix-up with the seat on the private plane. HH now told him that arrangements had been made for a car to take Stein to the stadium for the match, and that a ticket would be left aside for his attention. Again, Stein was disappointed. The chauffeur never surfaced, the match ticket fell through. Stein managed to get a press ticket from some British journalists. He told them not to make any noise about the incident. It would only embolden HH. 'My time will come,' he muttered.

30. COOKED

1.

On New Year's Day 1966, Inter were scheduled to play Juventus in a league game. HH locked up his players in *ritiro*, for the usual prematch retreat, at *Pinetina*, their training complex on the outskirts of Milan. They were banned from leaving their rooms the night before a match. New Year's Eve was cancelled for Inter's overachieving footballers. That didn't stop them. On the afternoon of New Year's Eve, the players commandeered a bottle of spirits and a *panettone*, a traditional Italian Christmas cake. They hid their stash and left a window open so they could congregate later in the TV room to ring in the New Year.

As the clock ticked down to midnight, the TV channel the players were watching connected with the celebrations at Casinò di Campione, Europe's oldest and largest casino, in Campione d'Italia, a picturesque town on the banks of Lake Lugano. The players were stunned when the television cameras showed HH and his wife on the dance floor in the middle of the celebrations, living it large, when they thought he was in bed a few corridors away. Livid, they broke into a drinks' fridge and emptied it of booze. Before going to bed, they left their empties outside his bedroom door. When he returned at dawn and found the empty bottles, he smashed them in a rage. It was a rare misstep by HH, a crack in the edifice, his authority undermined.

Life for Inter's players under HH became a grind. He made them train everywhere – in churchyards, in garages when it snowed. The players spent more time sleeping with their roommates than they did with their wives. It felt like all they did was train, eat, sleep. With little to distract them in *ritiro*, they had nothing to do or think about except the next game, the next opponent – he put pictures of rival attacking players on the bedside lockers of his defenders. He wanted them to dream about their opponents.

HH's senior officers – including Armando Picchi, Giacinto Facchetti, Aristide Guarneri, Mario Corso, Luis Suárez and Sandro Mazzola – had been on a war footing with him for six, seven years. It was a long time marching to his beat. Mazzola confronted him one day. He said he was on the verge of cracking up, couldn't take it any more, needed a break. HH listened to the *cri de coeur*. Play a good game on Sunday, he told him, and you'll get a vacation. After the game, HH waited for Mazzola at the door of the dressing room with a greeting: 'What vacation?! Holidays for someone who scores three goals. You must be crazy!'

Since their breakthrough Serie A title in 1963, Inter had been awash in silverware, but the relentless pursuit of success, the whip-cracking, took its toll. After losing the 1966 European Cup semi-final to Real Madrid, Gianni Brera wrote that Inter lost because their players had the glassy-looking eyes of cyclists cooked at the foot of Col du Tourmalet, the mountain in the Pyrenees that provides a gruesome climb during the Tour de France. HH fumed at the criticism. According to Inter's captain, Armando Picchi, HH doubled their training load the following season to prove that Brera was nothing but a drunk.

2.

For the European Cup final, HH found a hotel half an hour from Lisbon. He booked the entire hotel for his travelling party. No expense spared. No distractions. It was a huge hotel, which looked out on to the Atlantic Ocean. From the minute the team's bus drove in the hotel gates – until the match three days later – Inter's players hardly saw a sinner. Not even club directors were allowed to stay. They spent their time rattling around the deserted hotel like Jack Nicholson's family in *The Shining*. HH tried to fill their brains with 'video' sessions on Celtic and dossiers on each of their players. At night, his Inter players stared at the ceiling, or wandered the hotel's corridors, unable to sleep. The strain was unbearable.

'There was nobody there except for the players and coaches,' said Tarcisio Burgnich, the man who marked Pelé in the 1970 World Cup final. 'By that stage, we had reached our breaking point. None of us could sleep. I was lucky if I got three hours a night. All we did was obsess over the match and Celtic's players. Giacinto Facchetti and I would stay up and listen to our skipper, Armando Picchi, vomiting from the tension in the next room.'

Four Inter players puked during their prematch team talk on the day of the final at Jamor Stadium, but they got off to a dream start. Seven minutes into the game, Inter's striker, Renato Cappellini, tumbled over Jim Craig's leg in the box. The referee whistled, pointing to the penalty spot. It was a soft penalty to concede; Cappellini had used his street smarts. Jock Stein, who was conspicuously wearing black sunglasses at the start of the game, was furious. He turned and started swearing at HH further up the touchline, suspecting this was how it was – Italian football teams bribe refs. Sandro Mazzola – playing in the same stadium where his father played his last match before dying in the Superga air disaster – slotted the penalty. Neutrals watching on television let out a heavy sigh. One-nil to HH's Inter, a scoreline from a hundred matches.

Jim Craig's father was disconsolate. 'My father hadn't wanted to go to Lisbon because he thought that Inter would win – they would be too strong for us.

He didn't want to go all that way to see us getting beaten. I had a ticket for him and a seat on a plane for him. I kept saying, "Are you coming?" He kept responding: "They'll be too strong." It was only on the Sunday before the game that I persuaded him to come. So, he flew out the day before the game. When I gave away the penalty, he was sitting up in the stands behind the goal with my Uncle Phillip and he turned to him, and he said: "I've come all this bloody way to see that."'

But from that moment on, it was one-way traffic. Inter sat back, conceding the ball to Celtic, who drove forward, peppering shots at Inter's goal. Giuliano Sarti, Inter's goalkeeper, was inspired and kept Celtic at bay. Jock Stein's nerves were fraying with every shot Sarti parried, causing him to repeatedly grind his fist into his palm. The score remained 1–0 at half time. Kenneth Wolstenholme's co-commentator on BBC, Archie Macpherson, was despondent: 'A heart-breaking game, not only for Celtic supporters but for all those who cherish attacking football. Inter are the very negation of this. Celtic aren't just obviously taking on Inter. They are trying to end the ice age of defensive European football. They must sustain their aggression in the second half.'

Rather than heading down the tunnel with his players at the break as he normally did, Stein made a beeline for Kurt Tschenscher, the German referee. Tschenscher would referee Pelé's last game for Brazil in 1971. Afterwards, Pelé gave him his jersey. Stein was in a less generous mood. He got right in his grill and unloaded: 'You're a Nazi bastard! A penalty kick? You were conned! Where are you gonnae get your villa?' The ref looked stunned. Stein kept spitting vitriol at him until they neared the tunnel. Then Stein turned his ire on HH. The pair traded insults, almost coming to blows.

Stein composed himself before entering his team's dressing room. He sought out Jim Craig. 'At half time in the dressing room, Jock was quite calm,' recalled Craig. 'He came to me and said, "Forget about it. You're doing fine." After the game, he said, with a slight smile, "You were careless, Cairney, you were careless."

Craig got his chance to make amends. Midway through the second half, he picked up a pass on the edge of Inter's box. He ran at his opposing number and shimmied slightly before laying off a no-look pass to Tommy Gemmell who was charging forward. Gemmell hit the ball first time, smashing it into the net. The teams were level – and Gemmell had kept his promise, making amends for his blunder in the quarter-final in Yugoslavia. Celtic now kept raining shots down on Inter's goal. They couldn't overcome Sarti, but it seemed only a matter of time. Inter's players were on the ropes. They knew they were doomed, according to their defender Tarcisio Burgnich: 'I remember [Armando] Picchi turned to Sarti and said: "Giuliano, let it go, just let it go. It's pointless. Sooner or later, they'll get the winner." I never imagined my captain would tell our keeper to throw in the towel, but that only shows how destroyed we were.'

With five minutes to play, Bobby Murdoch lashed a shot from outside the box, which whizzed towards Stevie Chalmers, Celtic's centre-forward. Chalmers was a lucky man. As a teenager, he had contracted tuberculous meningitis, a killer disease in the 1950s. He was given three weeks to live, but his doctor experimented with a new drug and saved his life. Now, as the ball flew towards him, he swivelled and got a touch on it. The ball skated past Sarti into the bottom corner of the net, sending Celtic's fans off to the moon. The match finished 2–1. Celtic were champions of Europe.

After the game, HH pointed the finger at Dr Angelo Quarenghi for Inter's listless performance; he blamed his club doctor for mixing up the potions, according to Gianni Brera. Across Europe, however, there was rejoicing at Inter's defeat. Those with a romantic heart said HH was a coward, an enemy of football. Celtic had delivered a deadly blow to the negative football of *catenaccio*, marginal victories and HH's refusal to play entertaining football.

'Inter got well and truly banjoed that night,' said Hugh McIlvanney. 'Celtic annihilated them. They played them off the park. Inter were never at the races. There was a lot of happiness in football when Celtic did them in. In the dressing room after the match, there was an elderly Portuguese official who came up to Jock Stein and said: "With this attacking football, you've won a victory for the true meaning of the game."

'In Italy, too – given the regional rivalries – there was a lot of *schadenfreude* around. It was quite palpable how much resentment there was at Herrera's emphasis on defence. *Catenaccio* became a dirty word. There's nothing wrong with pragmatism, but some of us would prefer the spirit of other managers who go out to slaughter the opposition. I don't warm to people who think the first thing is to put a stranglehold on you, and then we'll see how long you keep breathing.'

3.

After his Waterloo, HH retreated to Milan. He had unfinished domestic business. With four games to play, it looked as if Inter's league title was again in the bag, with a four-point cushion over Juventus. The Turin side – who hadn't won a *scudetto* since 1961 – cut that deficit to two points when they beat Inter 1–0 the weekend Jock Stein flew to Italy on his spying mission. Their persistence was bugging HH. Early in the season, he had said Juventus had a better chance of winning the national lottery than Serie A.

Juventus were managed by HH's clone, a Paraguayan ex-footballer named Heriberto Herrera. The press – who loved stirring bad blood between the pair –

gave him the nickname 'HH2'. He even looked like HH, with the same thick, wavy soot-black hair and prominent nose. He also shared several managerial traits. He was intolerant of egos; he prized the group over individuals. He kicked Omar Sívori, a Ballon d'Or winner, out of the club. He was an ascetic who didn't drink alcohol or coffee, only water and *mate* tea. He believed footballers should share his joyless view of the world and demanded they be in bed by 10 p.m. each night, going as far as to take the light bulbs out of players' rooms so they wouldn't stay up late. Like HH, he was niggardly when it came to conceding goals, and maniacal about the fighting weight of his players.

And, just like HH, Heriberto Herrera was a firebreather. He loved using the stick to motivate players. 'From [Heriberto] Herrera, I learned seriousness,' said Claudio Ranieri, a protégé. His drillmaster streak came from his time serving as a sergeant in the military back in Paraguay. He thought nothing of punching and insulting his players to get a reaction out of them. Shortly after Giovanni Sacco, a midfielder in his Juventus squad, was involved in a fatal car accident, he yelled at him in training: 'You're only good at killing old people!'

With a game to play, HH2's Juventus reduced Inter's lead at the top to a point. When Juventus beat Lazio 2–1, Inter had to win their postponed game to claim the title or draw and face a play-off. Their opponents were Mantova, a mid-table team with a squad value a hundred times less than Inter's. The match was played in their tiny stadium in Mantua. Only three days had passed since Inter's defeat in Lisbon. HH rushed back Luisito Suárez, who had missed the European Cup final through injury, into the starting XI, but the move failed to kick-start the team. Inter played like the walking dead. Early in the second half, Beniamino Di Giacomo, a cast-off from Inter, came back to haunt HH. He hit a harmless shot, which Giuliano Sarti, so imperious in Lisbon a few days earlier, fumbled. The ball dribbled over the line, and Sarti headbutted his goalpost in anger. The goal was all that separated the teams at the final whistle. Mantova, with nothing to play for, had won – and Juventus were crowned champions. The press reported that their victorious coach, Heriberto Herrera, deserved to inherit the title HH.

4.

Things continued unravelling. Ten days later, Inter were dumped out of the Coppa Italia semi-final by Padova, a Second Division team. There were recriminations. During the summer, HH began a clear-out. A rebuild was necessary. He got rid of several lieutenants, including his team captain, Armando Picchi; Aristide Guarneri, a veteran of three European Cup finals; and the Brazilian striker, Jair. But none of the recruits who came in the door made their mark. Inter finished fifth in the title race the following season, mustering only 33 points from 30 games. The cycle of La Grande Inter was at an end. Angelo Moratti, HH's patron, left the club in May 1968, by which time HH had checked out mentally. His kingdom lay in ruins, but there were other lands to conquer where his stock was still high. He set off for Rome, where Caesar sat, lured by the fattest contract in the history of football.

Celtic's 'Lisbon Lions' led by manager Jock Stein parading the European Cup trophy during a victory parade at Glasgow's Celtic Park, following their historic 2–1 win over Inter in the 1967 final.

All roads lead to Rome: HH was appointed AS Roma manager in the summer of 1968, tasked with winning the *scudetto*, which the club hadn't won since 1942.

IV

ROMA
(1968-70)

31. THE RED LADY

1.

Rome was swinging in the late 1960s. Jobs and disposable income were plentiful. Dreamers and chancers flocked to the city. It was less uptight than, say, Milan, the nation's industrial powerhouse, and was a place where fantasies could flourish, in real life and on screen. After the success of Federico Fellini's *La Dolce Vita*, which was a cultural phenomenon at the start of the decade, Rome's gigantic film studio, Cinecittà, was still attracting the world's most glamourous actors from overseas as the '60s drew to a close, including Warren Beatty and Yul Brynner, Brigitte Bardot and Jane Fonda. Chet Baker, the 'Prince of Cool', and other musicians (including Liberace) followed in their slipstream. They hung out in restaurants and nightspots along Via Veneto, mingling with powerful men like the Aga Khan, all of them looking for a good time. The Eternal City was where people fell in love.

Fiora Gandolfi was drawn to the city to study languages at the University of Rome. She was raised in a well-to-do and cultured Treviso household, not far from the canals of Venice. Her mother was from aristocratic stock. Gandolfi studied in French schools. Her parents distrusted conventional teaching methods. She grew up influenced by the Montessori method, a philosophy that gave free reign to her imagination and natural instincts. Her working and creative life has been spent floating between disciplines, from journalism and writing to painting and photography, from conceptual art to costume design.

She had no idea who HH was when her newspaper editor at *La Stampa* told her in 1969 to do a celebrity story from the world of football. Her beat was interviewing famous artists like David Hockney and Francis Bacon. She only dabbled in sport. She was the first female reporter sent to cover the Giro d'Italia in 1964, but football wasn't her bag, so she asked a colleague from *Corriere dello Sport*, Giorgio Tosatti, one of the great masters of Italian football journalism, for advice. He recommended she try AS Roma's new coach, HH, a man whose fame transcended sport. So, she pointed her little Fiat 500 car towards the hills outside Rome. HH was holed up at Grottaferrata with his Roma players, trying to put some manners on them after taking charge the previous summer.

HH sat her down at a table in an ugly bar beside a football pitch. It was cold outside. From her research, she expected to meet a boorish figure, a monster, but she was struck by his elegance, the fragrant oil in his hair. He didn't have false teeth, as someone had told her. His teeth were crooked, but magnificent, like the teeth of a canine. He had a brilliant smile. He was courteous towards her – which perhaps wasn't surprising. Fiora Gandolfi was gorgeous. She had long red hair, sallow skin and beautiful cheekbones. She was 26 years younger than him and recently separated from her husband. When HH began speaking in French, she was disarmed, intrigued by this mysterious man. She couldn't tell where he was from. She could see that he came from poverty – his conversation was coarse, direct – but he wasn't provincial. He didn't drink. He didn't smoke. He swam against the tide. He was different from other men. Her ex-husband was an intellectual, a writer, a communist, and she had found him boring. She loved HH's sarcasm. He made her laugh. He was thrilling, unconventional, a showman waging war on the world.

They began dating. The paparazzi sniffed a scent on the trail. Sensing an affair was afoot, they gave her the nickname 'The Red Lady', HH's scarlet woman. The pair fell in love, which ruptured HH's 20-year relationship with his second partner, María Morilla Pérez, the mother of the famous film director Gonzalo Suárez Morilla from a previous marriage, who gave birth to two of HH's children. HH and Gandolfi married in secret in Paris in 1972. Gandolfi gave birth to their son, Helios, HH's seventh child, two months later. (He was born by caesarean section, which was scheduled for a Monday afternoon so it wouldn't interfere with HH's football matters on Sunday.) In 1976, HH and Gandolfi came upon a sick two-year-old girl on a bench in Plaza del Pino, in Barcelona's Gothic Quarter, the daughter of a fan of HH. They brought the girl back to Italy for a life-saving operation. Later, they adopted her, giving her the name Luna. (*Helios* after the sun, *Luna* the moon.)

The family settled in Naples. HH's conviction, his unwavering self-belief, gave Gandolfi strength in everything she did in life. He helped bring out the best in her. He was the love of her life. They were two mavericks, who did and said and thought however they pleased. They stayed together until HH's death and since then, she has been the keeper of his flame. She manages a website celebrating his career. She has helped curate exhibitions about him and published books about his football triumphs and unorthodox coaching methods. She believes a man like HH is only born once a century – that he was a visionary, a sorcerer. Shortly before he died, conscious that she would write about him, and with his eyes fixed sternly on posterity, HH concluded: 'I did so much for football that coaches should make a monument … for what I have allowed them to become. They were slaves until I arrived, and I gave them dignity.'

2.

Towards the end of my research for this book, I travelled to Italy for some final interviews. I spent a few weeks in advance lining up interviewees. I emailed

Fiora Gandolfi. She was the lady with the keys to the kingdom. Nobody knew HH better. She shared his bed. She loved him, this unfathomable man. She understood his genius. She knew his flaws and many of his secrets, she forgave him his sins. In my email pitch, I gave some brief professional details and explained I was writing a book on HH, mentioning people I'd interviewed whom she would know. I said I would love to interview her in Venice on a day that suited her. I added that I didn't speak Italian, only English and Spanish, knowing she spoke Spanish. She replied that evening with a one-line response in Spanish, all in lowercase: 'i speak perfect spanish fiora'. Her response was encouraging, but nothing was left confirmed.

I emailed her again several times, but the trail went cold. I flew into Italy and scurried around the country in a cheap rental car doing interviews. After a few days, I arrived back in Milan from Pisa. I had a little over 48 hours left in Italy, and was juggling a few more interview prospects in Milan, Rome, over the border in Switzerland. I tried Fiora Gandolfi one more time. She responded, giving me her phone number. Bingo! She included some written directions, but they were confusing. I phoned her straightaway, and told her excitedly I could be in Venice the next day to do the interview. In my haste, I neglected to fully explain who I was. She chided me for my poor decorum, but we arranged to meet the following afternoon.

Venice is a watery maze, a warren of narrow lanes, foot bridges and canals. The easiest thing to do there is to get lost. I followed her directions to a colourful old *patisserie* with a marble-tiled floor, called Ponte delle Paste. I was instructed to ask behind the counter for where Fiora lived. They would know. I got there an hour early and, sure enough, the lady behind the counter knew Fiora and explained that there was a buzzer for her building outside the door of the *patisserie* to the right, along a narrow footpath only a couple of feet wide, which hugged the canal. There was her name, 'Fiora Gandolfi Herrera', on the buzzer.

An hour later, I buzzed her apartment, but there was no answer. I tried again every few minutes while gondoliers ferried dreamy tourists alongside me, but there was no response. I started to get anxious. I'd been down this road before. As a journalist, I was used to doorstepping people for news stories and getting the door closed in my face. I'm familiar with getting the run-around. I once travelled twice from Barcelona to Madrid for a radio documentary interview with a Spanish aristocrat, who had committed to do an interview, but it fell through, both times. Days of my life squandered for nothing. Now it looked like Fiora Gandolfi had gone missing.

Finally, a neighbour from her building emerged, walking slowly with his old golden retriever dog. He let me into the building, which is spectacular. It dates to 1406, and is a few paces from the Rialto Bridge, the oldest of the bridges that spans Venice's Grand Canal. The building had no elevator. To reach her *palazzo*, I – and the poor old wheezing golden retriever dog that lived in the building – had to zig-zag up wide steps made from centuries-old flagstones. I knocked on her door a few times until she appeared, wearing a hairband made from a bouquet of artificial flowers, looking like she didn't have a care in the world.

3.

When I met Fiora Gandolfi she was 87 years old, the same age as HH when he died. She was born in 1936, the year the Spanish Civil War started. 'The year of *catapum*, as they say in Spain – the big bang!' she said with relish. She still lives in the same medieval *palazzo* she shared with HH. We spent hours traipsing around it chatting, drinking tea and absinthe. (In his retirement, HH drank a finger or two of absinthe to give himself a pep in the evenings.) 'Look at what you like,' she instructed me. 'Go on – open the wardrobe. It's interesting to see inside other people's houses. More than words, looking at where a person lives tells you more about them.' I politely fingered some of HH's ties.

It was impossible to tell how many rooms were inside the *palazzo*. It's like a labyrinth. When I asked her, she scolded me: 'Don't be so English.' It has small rooms, big rooms and long rooms. Spiral staircases, rooms connected by a ladder. Chandeliers. Pianos. Doors that creak, doors that you squeeze through to pass into the next room.

The *palazzo* isn't carpeted. Every floor inch is covered in colourful rugs. Couches and armchairs are draped in throws. The place is drenched in bright colours – oranges, pinks, purples, yellows. The walls are decorated with sketches and paintings and zany Venetian face masks. There are thousands of books on the shelves. Phone numbers are scrawled in marker on lampshades and two white armchairs. The legs of an upside-down Daliesque mannequin shoot skywards from one armchair. She maintains that most of the artefacts in the *palazzo* have been retrieved from the rubbish.

The *palazzo* is dark because it is short of access to natural light. Its windows are small, narrow. Some are stained glass. It has a frozen-in-time aspect that brings to mind Miss Havisham's mansion, but there is nothing cold or bleak about the dwelling. It would be impossible – Gandolfi is such a radiant woman, impish, irreverent and friendly. Like a pixie. Anxious not to overstay my welcome, I declined the offer to stay for dinner at the end of our interview. She asked me if I needed to go to the toilet before leaving. When I said it was unnecessary, she scratched her head: 'What are you going to do? Pee in the canal?'

4.

Fiora Gandolfi has been a rebel all her life. When she was a teenager, she played truant from school. Her friend had a motorcycle, a Mondial 125. The two girls used to take off down the highway and pass the day on the beach, sunbathing nude, reading. 'Afterwards,' she said, 'I would have a shower; otherwise, my mother would sniff something was up: "What smells of salt?" It was rare in the early 1950s to see a woman on a motorbike.' She always had boyfriends, but it was HH who stole her heart. She said that control was the bedrock of his success in football.

'Helenio was very severe with his footballers. He controlled everything – their diet, their social lives. He patrolled their dormitories. He was like the Gestapo. He was very controlling, but also, he was smart. Sometimes players needed a release. Occasionally, he would let them break out from "concentration". At Milan, his Inter players escaped through a window. They would hop the wall. They'd find a place to eat rabbit and potatoes and have a glass of wine. He knew about it but would turn a blind eye sometimes. Footballers aren't like they are today. They were capable of anything in his time. Helenio was like a German. He was very Prussian. Discipline was the basis of everything.'

When the England striker Gerry Hitchens was sold by HH in 1962, he said leaving Inter was like coming out of the army. 'If Helenio said he'd do something, he'd do it,' she added. 'He was very organised, precise, and a perfectionist.' Gandolfi maintains HH established the template for the cult of personality that surrounds the modern football coach. Think Alex Ferguson – the siege mentality, the rage burning inside him, the ability to instil fear in a dressing room, yet he, like HH, had the charisma to motivate different personality types. Think Pep Guardiola – the obsessiveness, always on top of his players, the slavery to tactics, his need for control. He embodies so many of HH's traits, especially the obsession with control – on the pitch and off it. Guardiola, for example, in his first management job in charge of Barça's reserve team, used to phone his players after midnight on their home phonelines. If they'd broken their curfew, they were hit with a heavy fine.

Think José Mourinho; his techniques are straight from the HH playbook. Take, for example, Mourinho's mind games with rival teams and managers. Or his mantras. HH used to write motivational slogans on the walls at Inter's training ground, phrases such as "Class + athletic preparation + intelligence = *scudetto*". Mourinho, writing to his Chelsea players, four decades later, used almost an identical template and exhortation: "Motivation + Ambition + Team Spirit = SUCCESS."

Mourinho's outlandish public persona is a ringer for the celebrity profile HH cultivated. HH understood instinctively how the media works – that publicity was a game within a game. He figured it out for himself. He was a natural pitchman. The press was a platform to be manipulated – to help sell tickets, to distract attention or to provoke a reaction. Anything to get noticed. It was all show business. It helped that he enjoyed causing a ruckus, and his face lent itself easily to caricature, whether newspaper cartoonists dressed him up like a Roman emperor in a toga or refashioned his thick black hair into a matador's hat.

HH was a born hustler. If there was a wall in front of him, he could go around it, or over it, or through it. He had great emotional intelligence. His understanding of how people think was key to his success. No one could coax a tune out of a footballer like HH, making them believe they could achieve anything, building up their self-confidence. Always in their ear. Encouraging them before games, providing constructive criticism afterwards. Getting them to embrace sacrifice. He was an optimist. He was convinced human beings realised only 30 per cent of their potential. It became his life's mission to get the best out of himself. It made him obsessive about self-improvement. It explained the manic way he drove his players. 'The reason he was always so desperate to win wasn't about coming first,' she said. 'It wasn't about beating another coach or another team. That wasn't important to him. It was about doing the best possible, achieving the maximum. Winning a match or a trophy was a symbolic thing.'

HH kept his mind and body agile, refusing to use his arm as a lever to rise from an armchair; he preferred to give his leg muscles a workout instead. He did mental exercises daily like, say, multiplying 354 by 621. He counted money in French. 'He loved money. He never spent money in a stupid manner,' said Gandolfi, as she asked me to take a note out of my wallet. 'If you said: "Helenio, can you give me a thousand lira?", he'd say: "Here, take it,"' she said, acting out a comic scene where we both pulled at the banknote in her fist like in a tug-of-war.

A love of speed was a defining characteristic. 'He did everything quickly,' she said. 'He ate quickly. He ran upstairs. He took showers in a second. *Rapidísimo*. He always wanted to do more things. He didn't like slow people.' He reckoned walking slowly tired him out. That a lazy person must work twice as hard. HH brought his obsession with speed into football. It marked his teams out. He wanted his players to 'run like madmen'. They had to do everything fast, thinking and playing. HH hated players dribbling with the ball. He knew the ball travelled faster without a player behind it, and that speed was the essential ingredient of counter-attacking football.

Despite his reputation for trash-talking, he cherished silence. He loved hiding in churches for thinking and taking notes. When he had a big decision to make, he liked to walk outside alone, 'looking for the sky, water, earth, the air,' said Gandolfi, 'because he was the fire.' HH filled his thoughts with Eastern philosophies and relaxation techniques, meditating in the morning, restricting himself to a spartan diet. He never let dread overtake him.

Whenever his enemies were lined up against him after a misstep, HH banished the doubts inside his mind. He would dwell on death, which had come for his three brothers when they were small boys. Beside the mystery of death and nothingness, any misadventures in life were put in perspective. It was an outlook that set his mind free. 'I am alive,' he liked to repeat to himself whenever there was bad news. Those precious words: 'I am alive.' The tide goes in and out. Fortune changes. And when cornered, he was ruthless with his adversaries. 'With the good be good, with the bad be three times bad, with the cunning be three and a half times cunning' was a favourite mantra.

Gandolfi admits that HH had an unhealthy obsession with football, an almost carnal relationship with the sport. Sometimes she would speak to him while he was watching a football match on television and never get a response. The game consumed him. His notebooks on the intricacies of the game, the frantic scratchings of a research scientist, are scattered all over their *palazzo*. One time, HH bumped into a former player he coached at Sevilla in the 1950s. HH couldn't recognise him from his face, which had aged, but when he made him walk, he immediately recalled his name.

Yet HH kept no friends in the world of football. None ever visited their *palazzo*. He was a football monk, concluded Gandolfi, and he forced his players to live the same ascetic way. It was, after all, HH who made popular the practice of the prematch retreat, *il ritiro*. Apart from football training, playing cards was practically their only chance at distraction. HH was inspired by the texts of Ignatius of Loyola, a mystic who once spent several months praying in a cave in Catalonia. HH wanted his footballers' minds to be emptied of thoughts – in a state of absolute concentration, away from temptation – before important games.

5.

Before his spiritual conversion to a religious life, Ignatius of Loyola was a womaniser. HH, too, was lecherous. He devoured women. Gandolfi knew HH attempted to seduce every beautiful woman he met. He tried to be discreet, but sometimes his adultery caught up with him. Once in a perfume store in downtown Milan, a shop assistant fussed about her, telling Gandolfi she had the perfume in stock her husband always bought when he came visiting from Venice. Gandolfi played dumb. She lied. 'Ah, I love this brand. Many thanks,' she said. She never received a gift of perfume from him.

'I found a woman in my bed here in this apartment,' she told me. 'She was there lying on the bed, in my white linen sheets. I gave her a dress and said,

"Get out of here. Bye-bye."' Men are like this. I knew that. My father had a lot of lovers too. I never had any lovers during my marriage, but it's normal to have a lover. I'm not a jealous person. I was very much in love with Helenio."

HH couldn't stop thinking about sex. His philandering was a distinctive feature of his personality right until the end. His eyes never rested, darting about for a woman who might arouse him. In his final days, he escaped from hospital in Madrid and was strong enough to return to Venice, where he was readmitted to hospital. He rallied. It seemed he might be recovering, but Gandolfi could sense he was restless. He didn't feel calm. Maybe he had a premonition of death.

'But what is it that makes you feel bad?' she asked him. 'What makes you feel uneasy?'

'Their asses are too fat,' he grunted, in Spanish, so other patients in the ward wouldn't understand what had him so agitated. All the nurses on duty had large, sagging backsides; it frustrated the wolf in him. There was no way for his wife to reassure him. Years after he died, Gandolfi, his widow, used to find orchids – the flower symbolic of love in Greek mythology – scattered by a mistress at his tombstone.

What fuelled HH's ravenous sex drive, his frenetic love life? Was it about sex or power, about conquests without a feeling for the consequences? Was HH in the grip of a pathological condition like sex addiction? An aspect of being a sex addict is about control, about using other people so you don't feel controlled and used yourself: you fuck women, and you fuck them away, so they don't hurt you. HH was obsessed with control – with controlling himself (his diet and so on) and he liked to control others.

Or perhaps we should be careful of judging HH by today's standards. The world was a different place in the mid-twentieth century. Easier for a *machista* like HH. Certainly, it seems HH was oblivious to the impact his philandering had on Gandolfi and the mothers of his children. He broke all his vows. A wife like Gandolfi, a bohemian in spirit, was willing to tolerate his infidelity, able to forgive his trespasses.

A remarkable feature of HH's philandering was that he seemed above the law, avoiding scandal like, say, the cyclist Fausto Coppi. He left behind him a trail of destruction, of broken hearts, in fiercely Catholic countries – Franco's Spain, and Italy, where he moved to live in 1960. That said, there is often a lot of hypocrisy in Catholic countries when it comes to morality: some people get punished for their sins; others (usually the rich and powerful) are judged differently. HH flaunted conventions. He was an anarchist like his father. He operated in a moral vacuum and didn't give a damn about what people thought. He was rare. Most people have some kind of social radar, but HH cared only about himself. He was pathologically selfish, driven to satisfy his own desires.

He also had the advantage of being a man. It wasn't until 1968 – the year before he hooked up with Gandolfi – that the notion that adultery was worse when committed by women than by men was struck down in Italy; divorce became legal there only in 1970. This allowed him to divorce his first wife, Lucienne Léonard – whom he married before the Second World War – so he could marry a heavily pregnant Gandolfi. Meanwhile, when the divorce papers came through, María Morilla Pérez – his partner of 20 years – had to pack her bags and leave Rome with two of his children. HH had feathered a new nest for himself.

HH was full of contradictions. He was cold-hearted yet a charmer of women. As a football coach, he demanded total loyalty from his players, all or nothing at all. Yet he was serially unfaithful in marriage and in his relationships. He lived by double standards. Perhaps it's no surprise he never trusted his players when they were holed up in *ritiro*, or staying in hotels on foreign trips for European Cup games, their doors left open so he could spy on them. He couldn't trust anyone. How could he when he couldn't trust himself?

HH retained an impulse for violence throughout his life. Aged 77, he was charged with assaulting a car park attendant in Venice. I asked Gandolfi if she thought HH was a violent man. 'Not with me, but the natural instinct of a man is to be violent. He was violent if he saw something wrong. He never hit his children, but in the world of football, yes, he could be violent because it had so much corruption. So many people who said one thing and then did another. He found out that one of his players at Roma was selling matches to lose. To lose a match? Can you imagine? It was inconceivable for Helenio. To manipulate to win? Yes. But to lose? No, no. When he found out, it was like a dagger to the heart. It's disgusting – the level of corruption in football.'

At one stage, I asked Gandolfi what was the most surprising thing about HH. She lay backwards on the flat of her back on a chaise longue and thought for a second. Then she began to answer: 'That he could lie really well. He knew how to lie. You wouldn't see it in his face. I can remember a scene. We have an apartment in Plaza Mayor in Madrid. One day, he opened a letter from somebody. It was from a lover. Right to my face, he lied. He said he didn't know who the letter was from, that it must have been somebody who wrote the wrong address on the envelope. He was a liar when it came to mistresses. He had skills to escape from situations.'

32. 'HOW CAN AN ATHLETE DIE LIKE THAT?'

1.

Fabio Capello's father was a schoolteacher. He was dealt a rotten hand during the Second World War. In 1940, Benito Mussolini decided Italy should enter the war on the side of Hitler. Swept along in the Nazis' slipstream, Italy scored a few early soft military victories, but big, humiliating defeats followed swiftly. When Mussolini's fascist regime fell in the summer of 1943, Italy U-turned and joined the Allies.

Capello's father – who fought as an officer on the Russian steppes, in the war's most brutal theatre – was left hanging out to dry. Along with about a million Italian soldiers who refused to continue fighting for Hitler, he was thrown into a prison camp in Germany, where he was savaged as a turncoat. He nearly starved to death. After the war, he made it back to Pieris, his hometown on the Adriatic coast, in late summer 1945. Most of his neighbours didn't recognise him. His body was ravaged, reduced to a little over 45kg in weight.

His son, Fabio, was born less than a year later. Father and son bonded hunting animals in the hills and woodlands around Pieris and at the local football club. Capello Sr turned his hand to every chore at the club, from coaching to lining the pitch early in the mornings with lime. Capello Jr excelled at football. He was a midfielder, exacting by temperament, with a precocious ability to understand the rhythm of a game.

In the summer of 1962, Capello's father signed a contract for him to join the youth academy at Spal, a nearby club that barely trod water in Serie A. A day or two later, Gipo Viani, Milan's legendary sporting director, knocked on their door. Viani, who twice coached Milan to Serie A titles in the 1950s, was the man who knew where the bodies were buried in the 1964 Bologna doping scandal. Viani wanted Capello to sign for Milan and told Capello's father that the signing-on papers for his son weren't filed yet. It would be easy to get out of the deal. All he had to do was say he had been drunk when he signed his son's contract and that he had since changed his mind. How could he turn down the chance for his son to play with the reigning league champions? Capello's father refused to go back on his word. Principle was important in the Capello household.

Capello broke into the Spal first team two years later – and made waves. HH, who was coaching Inter at the time, tried to sign him, but Spal's president blocked the transfer. In 1967, Capello was transferred to Roma for a hefty fee. HH arrived at the club the following season. The two gelled immediately. Capello became his lieutenant on the pitch – and never forgot HH because of the faith he showed in him. Capello's knees plagued him throughout his career, but HH never withdrew his backing. Indeed, he instilled in Capello unbreakable self-belief, the idea that he should never fear an opponent.

'I liked Helenio a lot. I always have,' said Capello. 'He changed football in Italy in his era. His teams played with greater speed, with original ideas. He did things differently to any of the other coaches I worked with. He was 10 years ahead of them in his thinking. He was more forward-thinking, an innovator. He got players to interchange positions. He was great at getting the team moving without the ball.

'His training sessions were very demanding. Everything was done at pace. He had lots of energy. He always held to his belief, his mantra "As we train, so we play" – if you maintain high standards, things will go well. It stuck with me. With other coaches, training was more relaxed. It was done at a slower pace. Helenio's obsession was that everything must be done at speed. Other coaches focused more on physical work, less on technical aspects. He was the first coach I worked with who did everything with the ball. He didn't care about endurance training. Every drill, always with the ball.'

HH wasn't Capello's friend, however. 'Helenio only worked. He lived for football. He was a perfectionist. He was excellent at preparing for matches. On the morning of a game, he pulled players aside and spoke with them individually, highlighting things to be mindful of – what an opposition player might do. He could convince players. He would grab a player by the chest: "You are the strongest!"'

In training, if HH saw anyone standing around, or moving slowly, he'd lambast them. Capello said HH was flexible when it came to tactics. He gave players freedom on the pitch. He listened to Capello and Joaquín Peiró. They could suggest tactical adjustments, which he accepted. He trusted them. Peiró had soldiered with HH on several fronts – with Spain in the 1962 World Cup; as one of HH's La Grande Inter team; and with Roma, Peiró's last club as a player. HH drove Peiró to despair, but Peiró couldn't resist his coach when he turned on the charm. Once, for example, Peiró lost his place in the starting XI.

'He didn't let me play,' said Peiró. 'I hated him. We didn't talk to each other. He didn't speak to me. But when it happened that he needed me because the guy who had taken my place was injured, or for some other reason, he was diabolical. He transformed. From Monday to Saturday, he would take me aside as if we were bound by an affectionate relationship. He would tell me that I was the best. And I fell for it. I believed him. I went on to the pitch very motivated, galvanised.'

Capello had a long, impressive playing career. After leaving Roma, he won *scudetti* with Juventus and Milan. His favourite memory playing for Italy's national team came in 1973. He scored Italy's only goal in its first victory over England at Wembley. Princess Anne got married on the same day. Capello was irritated by a British tabloid newspaper that wrote on its front page that '20,000 Italian waiters came to watch the game'. It was a slight. He dedicated his winning goal to those waiters.

After retiring in 1980, Capello went into coaching. Few coaches can match his CV. He won league titles with every club he managed – Milan, Real Madrid, Roma, Juventus (although his two titles with Juventus were revoked because of the *Calciopoli* scandal). Athens was the scene of his greatest triumph, the city where Milan crushed Johan Cruyff's Barcelona 'Dream Team' 4–0 in the 1994 Champions League final. When it came to coaching, HH was Capello's North Star. He was HH's greatest pupil. He put into practice lessons learned at the feet of HH. He brought HH's basic structure for how a team should be set up into coaching himself: midfield and defence must form a solid block, freedom for the forwards. 'Helenio always fought for his players, to protect the team,' said Capello.

'Seventy per cent of the things I did in coaching, I learned from Helenio. I took his ideas completely on board in my work as a coach. Helenio was different to coaches like, say, Nils Liedholm, who coached me at Milan. Helenio was far more visionary about football. He had ideas from the future. I can see things that people do now that he did a long time ago. He showed me things I hadn't seen before. He influenced so many people. He took our game as a nation to another level.'

HH taught Capello that football matches were won with the brain, not the feet. Capello took into management HH's guiding principle – that a coach must control his players. He must dominate them. Total respect. Like HH, Capello was a stickler for punctuality and diet. Ice cream was off the menu. Capello also liked order. It drove him crazy if he saw flip-flops on the floor of a dressing room. He believed in hard work and discipline. He liked, in his own words, 'to put a razor blade up against players' arses'. Footballers followed his orders. They learned to do what they were told and not to ask why. The spirit of HH never left him.

'My strongest memory of Helenio was when I went to Juventus in 1970. The coach at Juve, Armando Picchi, who was incidentally captain of his Grande Inter team, didn't have the same systems as Helenio. I had problems reconciling myself to Picchi's methods. I remember when I left Roma, I never again had the same feeling of being as good as I was with Helenio. I was OK, but never like when I played under him. When I joined Juve, it was like taking a step backwards.'

2.

HH suffered a heart attack in February 1969, halfway through his first season in charge at Roma. The stress was getting to him. He found it difficult to weave his magic in Rome. After the hype in the summer that trailed his appointment, he struggled to move the dial at Roma. The fans adored him – they loved his arrogance – but the team's performances were patchy. By Christmas 1968, the club was in the wrong half of the table, the same as previous seasons before his arrival. They languished in ninth position in a 16-team division. All that remained to fight for was the Coppa Italia. It seemed the only shining light at Roma was Giuliano Taccola, their exciting young striker.

Everybody loved Taccola for his humility, even fans of Lazio, the rival team in Rome. Taccola had grown up in Uliveto Terme, a town of a thousand people in Tuscany. As a 14-year-old, he moved up the coastline to Genoa's football academy. Football was his ticket out of poverty. He was reserved and timid, but if there was a loose ball in the box it was his. He was a prolific goalscorer, and fast – he could run 100 metres in 11 seconds. He joined Roma from Genoa in the summer of 1967. He scored in his Serie A debut for Roma against Inter at San Siro. HH watched the goal from Inter's dugout. The following season, he scored after 30 seconds in HH's league debut as Roma coach. By Christmas 1968, he had scored seven goals in 12 league games for a mediocre team. He was a hot property. The press reported that Fiorentina, who finished the season as league champions, were going to pay 200 million lira for him the following summer, more than twice the fee Roma had paid.

Taccola suffered from intermittent fevers in the autumn of '68. Despite taking antibiotics, he couldn't shake off flu-like symptoms. Taccola was hoping to rest up and spend Christmas with his wife and their two young kids, but HH wouldn't hear of it. He had organised a winter training trip to Spain for his team, so Taccola reluctantly went. He trained hard, scoring in both games against Sevilla and Málaga.

Taccola's impressive performances failed to cheer him up. The flight home from Spain did nothing to alter his sense of gloom. As the plane struggled to land in Rome, rocking from side to side, one of its wings nearly touched the ground. The rocky landing left Taccola shaken to the core. He was gripped by morbid thoughts. He was afraid of dying, of never seeing his family again. The continuous fevers were playing havoc. Bad, delirious thoughts flooded his mind. He was thinking he needed to transfer everything he owned into his wife's name. He was afraid he had caught some terrible disease.

The medics in Rome reckoned tonsillitis was the problem. His tonsils were taken out on 5 February 1969. HH came to visit him in hospital while he was recovering. The press took photos of a smiling HH at the bedside, with Taccola's eldest child sitting on his lap and Taccola's wife standing on the opposite side of the bed. HH wanted his player back playing again. Taccola was discharged six days after his operation. His specialist, Professor Filipo, warned him to take a month's complete rest, and to avoid windy and damp conditions. He had lost a lot of blood during the operation. Six days later, Taccola went for a check-up. His doctor said the post-op recovery was going well, but he was concerned about his physical condition: Taccola had lost 4kg. He organised blood tests.

HH thought the doctor was talking nonsense. He told Taccola he didn't need more blood tests, just fresh air back in his lungs. The following day, a week after discharge from hospital, Taccola resumed training at Flaminio, Roma's training ground. His wife was furious: 'Giuliano didn't go to Flaminio that day to train but to request [blood] tests – tests that were denied to him. Then he was thrown on to the pitch against his will to train, which he didn't want to do.'

The fevers were still plaguing him. Antibiotics and aspirin weren't bringing relief, and as soon as Taccola put a foot on a football pitch his temperature went up. The following week, Taccola fainted during a mid-week De Martino tournament match. A few days later, on 2 March 1969, HH threw Taccola in to play against Sampdoria in a league game. During the match, Sampdoria's Francesco Morini, an international defender with Italy, turned to the Roma bench, and, pointing at the haggard-looking Taccola, said: 'He can't play in these conditions.'

Professor Massimo Visalli, a club doctor at Roma, was increasingly worried about the player's well-being. A couple of times Taccola left Roma's training retreat at Grottaferrata to go home because he was running a high temperature. Professor Visalli voiced his concerns to club president Alvaro Marchini. The pair agreed Taccola should be sent to a retreat in Terminillo to get some rest and fresh air in the mountains, but HH rubbished the plan. On 5 March 1969, Taccola trained in the rain. He ran a temperature of 38°C that day. Four days later, Professor Visalli challenged HH, criticising him for not following his medical advice. HH blanked him. Professor Visalli complained about his obstinate behaviour. The doctor was fed up with being overruled by HH, who regularly made players train when he recommended rest, and who forbade players from taking antibiotics three days before a match because it 'weakened' them.

3.

On Thursday night, 13 March, Taccola felt exhausted. The next day he was due to travel to the island of Sardinia with Roma's squad for a league match against Cagliari. According to his wife, he didn't want to go. Earlier in the week, Taccola went for an appointment with a specialist to vouch that he wasn't fit for the trip to Sardinia, but he yielded to pressure from HH to travel. HH wanted him with the squad even if he wasn't playing. The matches were coming thick and fast. Worst case, HH needed him ready for the Coppa Italia match a few days later against Brescia.

In Sardinia on Saturday morning, Taccola trained with the team. At 6 p.m., he phoned his wife. He told her he had gone to the cinema with his teammates and felt a bit tired. That night he slept poorly. The team were staying in the prestigious Hotel Mediterraneo, which looks out on to the Gulf of Cagliari. Taccola roomed with Franco Cordova. The two were close friends and shared a room on trips and in *ritiro*. They were an unlikely pair. Taccola was introverted; Cordova was a chest out kind of bloke, all leather jackets and long, flowing sandy hair. A midfielder by trade, he became captain of Roma in the 1970s, but a 14-month suspension, as part of a match-fixing investigation, left a stain on his career.

On match day, the morning of 16 March 1969, Cordova and Taccola were woken at 9 a.m. by Roberto Minaccioni, the team's masseur. Minaccioni told them to get up because HH wanted them to go and train. Taccola told Cordova he didn't want to get up. He felt tired. They looked out the windows and saw trees dancing in the wind. Cordova convinced Taccola to get dressed and go down for training. Taccola could hardly stand up. 'He was pale, emaciated,' said Cordova. 'He didn't even have the strength to go to the bathroom to shave. I tried to rouse him, even teasing him a bit. I told him that he was unpresentable – that he looked like a bum.'

Taccola struggled through a short training session on the beach amid icy winds coming in off the sea. He failed the fitness test. HH finally accepted he wasn't fit to play and let him sit out the match. When the squad gathered for a light, early lunch – cooked ham; a fillet of roast beef with mashed potatoes; stewed fruit; and half a glass of red wine – teammates recalled that Taccola looked pale. He asked Dr Visalli, Roma's doctor, for an aspirin because he felt a bit feverish. Professor Visalli advised him to stay in the hotel, but Taccola went to watch the match, although he confided in a teammate, Sergio Santarini, a gnawing sense of dread: 'I'm very worried. I'm afraid I have some virus.'

Sitting in the stands beside Cordova, who was suspended for the game, and two other teammates, Taccola shivered his way through the match. At full-time, following a 0–0 draw, he went down to the dressing room. Chatting and joking with two teammates, sipping on an orange soda, he suddenly felt dizzy. He said to Professor Visalli, who was tending to two injured players: 'Excuse me, Doctor. I don't feel well. My head is spinning.'

'Lie down, Giuliano. Let's see you immediately. Do you still have a fever?'

'I don't know. I can't stand up.'

Professor Visalli sent Roberto Minaccioni, the team masseur, to the Cagliari dressing room to get a bottle of penicillin. Taccola got a shot and lay down on a massage table waiting to recover. In the dressing room, Roma's players were milling about, largely oblivious to the unfolding tragedy, grabbing showers and joking. Laughter filled the air. Only those gathered around Taccola on the massage table got increasingly worried. For a minute, Taccola seemed to revive himself. He tried to sit up but fell back again with spasms of coughing as if he was going to vomit. He started to turn blue with cyanosis, and made a chilling plea: 'Help me, I'm suffocating!'

Professor Visalli and Minaccioni were panicking. They could feel Taccola slipping away. They measured his pulse rate. His heart was beating rapidly, desperately trying to compensate for the drop in his blood pressure. Professor Visalli consulted with Cagliari's team doctor, Augusto Frongia, and decided to give him Coramine (a respiratory stimulant) and a mix of other medicines.

Nothing worked. Taccola remained motionless, his breathing becoming more laboured. Professor Visalli knew that Taccola was in the throes of a serious crisis but felt helpless. He couldn't make sense of what was going on. Was Taccola having a heart attack? Was it an anaphylactic shock? Players, half-naked, began to gravitate towards the commotion. It was a nightmare.

'Guys, get back, get back! There's nothing to see here. Let us work!'

Confusion reigned. Players entered and left the dressing room, in some cases without even realising the seriousness of Taccola's condition. Some stood in front of journalists' microphones for ritual post-match declarations outside the dressing room door. Cordova, who was collared by a journalist for an interview, could hear screaming inside the dressing room, and couldn't understand the reason; the match had been a dull 0–0 draw.

Meanwhile, Taccola seemed to have passed out. Professor Visalli and Minaccioni grew increasingly hysterical. In their efforts at cardiopulmonary resuscitation (CPR), they punched Taccola's sternum. An ambulance was called. Frantically they tried mouth-to-mouth resuscitation. By now, there was pandemonium in the dressing room. A Roma player, Francesco Carpenetti, remembered seeing Taccola lying on the massage table without his shoes on. His feet had turned pale and yellow through loss of circulation. His eyelids were upturned. An ambulance arrived outside.

Professor Visalli was still trying mouth-to-mouth resuscitation. Minaccioni pushed on Taccola's stomach, which caused waves of hiccups, as if he was trying to vomit. The team's goalkeeper, Alberto Ginulfi, stepped in and tried to revive Taccola.

HH walked over and untied Taccola's shirt and tie. He looked around, amazed.

Ginulfi, exhausted, finally stopped his efforts at mouth-to-mouth resuscitation. Forlorn and with tears in his eyes, he slumped down on a stool.

Roma's dressing room was now packed with people. Roma and Cagliari players mixed together. They looked lost. Some younger players began to cry. 'They're kids and you have to be careful what you say to them. Please don't say anything,' HH said to Cagliari's team doctor, Dr Augusto Frongia. The doctor took HH's concern in good faith, thinking he was worried about their feelings, but HH was already thinking three moves ahead. The kids in the dressing room would have a football match to play in a few days' time. He didn't want their heads messed up.

Ambulance personnel entered the dressing room. They loaded Taccola on to a stretcher and connected him to a defibrillator. The ambulance rushed to the San Giovanni di Dio hospital, weaving through swathes of football fans milling around the stadium. Taccola was confirmed dead on arrival. He had died inside the dressing room. His body was covered with a sheet and taken to the hospital morgue, awaiting an autopsy and a manslaughter investigation.

Capello remembers the pandemonium in the dressing room that afternoon as life drained from his teammate. Most of all he recalls how suddenly things went awry: 'Giuliano died within 15 minutes in the dressing room. It all happened very quickly. It was dreadful, devastating, an awful shock. The doctor who was with us tried to revive him. I remember he administered an injection, an infusion of some medicine, but he lost him totally. There was nothing he could do. Nothing, nothing, nothing. He died so suddenly.'

He added: 'What does one think at a time like this? That your friend is gone. That we're here. Where are we? Where is he? You never know when your number will be up. When are you not going to be here? It was very painful. So sad. You can never think that a friend of yours, an athlete can die like that. Never. How is that possible? How is it that the doctor tried to do everything and nothing worked?'

4.

When Roma's club president Alvaro Marchini heard about Taccola's collapse in Cagliari, he phoned the stadium to speak to HH. His coach confirmed that Taccola was in a coma, then started blabbering about the upcoming match in a few days' time. The team would need to replace the young player.

Marchini was taken aback by HH's indifference, by the cold heart that beat within him.

Roma's players were in shock. They didn't know what was going on when they left the stadium, or how serious the situation was when Taccola was taken away in an ambulance. They boarded their coach quickly, which took them to the airport. At the airport, a phone call came from Cagliari's sporting director. HH went to answer it. When he came back, he gathered the players in a corner. He gave them three words: 'He is dead.' Then he reminded them they must get back to Rome. On Wednesday, they had Brescia in the cup. Life goes on. They must win it for Taccola.

Cordova, who was rooming with Taccola for the weekend, couldn't believe the words that came out of HH's mouth. He told HH to go to hell or he'd strangle him, adding that he wouldn't leave the island. A scuffle broke out between the two men. A couple of other Roma players piled in on top of HH. Other players intervened to break up the scrap. In the end, three players refused to board the plane: Cordova, Paolo Sirena and Vito D'Amato. They wanted to accompany Taccola's body back to Rome for his funeral.

In the days that followed, the press insinuated that HH had flogged a racehorse to death. *La Stampa*, one of Italy's oldest newspapers, ran with a headline 'FOOTBALLERS ARE LIKE ROBOTS' the morning after Taccola died. The paper's Cagliari correspondent, Giuseppe Fiori, wondered how much responsibility lay with HH – and how much with Taccola, who was clearly unfit. HH's old captain at Inter, Armando Picchi, and Milan's star player Gianni Rivera, who were both spokesmen for the new players' union, also complained about the dangers that resulted when footballers were turned into 'robots'.

The 22-year-old Fabio Capello weighed in, criticising the lack of medical and emergency equipment available in the stadium: 'He was in the dressing room for an hour before the ambulance arrived! An hour! And we were asking everyone possible to send us an ambulance. There was no oxygen tank. Nothing. Is it possible we should be required to play important matches in these conditions? We're not beasts but human beings!'

The media quoted players and Roma's president Marchini, who pointed the finger at HH, denouncing his authoritarian style, his contempt for doctors and his doggedness in getting Taccola playing and training even if it was clear he was unwell. Rumours abounded. An untrue story filtered back to Taccola's widow – which she regurgitated in interviews – that when her husband died in the dressing room, Roma's staff were so shocked and embarrassed they shut the dressing room door for a huddle, to get their story straight, before calling an ambulance.

5.

People in Roma's orbit wondered why HH was so insensitive. It was mentioned that four years earlier, in the spring of 1965, HH didn't shed a tear at the funeral of Danièle, his 22-year-old daughter, although mourners can be grief-stricken but not necessarily show it. HH preferred to lean on his 'life goes on' motto. At the time, he was flying high with Inter – who were tied at the top of the table with city rivals Milan in the race for the *scudetto*. His mind was preoccupied with thoughts of a looming European Cup semi-final against Liverpool. Football was a more important matter than life or death.

HH's daughter Danièle died from sniffing paint fumes. It was a tragic death, which left unanswered questions hanging in the air. To bury a child in the ground goes against nature. For a parent, it's the cause of unspeakable, lingering pain. Why was HH so impassive at her graveside? Maybe he feared losing control. He had encountered so much tragedy already, most of it early in his life. HH had been brought up in the slums of Casablanca where life was cheap. His three older brothers were in the grave, having died so young in childhood that he never got to know them. His mother and father were gone. His only sister died before she reached middle age.

It seems an extraordinary coincidence that HH suffered a heart attack a month before Taccola died. HH had had a brush with his own mortality. He stared death in the face, which gives a man a renewed sense of what it's all about. Life is short. Try and be compassionate when you can to your fellow man. But it seems it didn't give HH any sense of perspective, beyond a flippant comment he made to his new mistress, Fiora Gandolfi, two months after his heart attack, in April 1969: 'How lucky I am! Think what would have happened if I hadn't had the heart attack in Milan, where there are good doctors, but in a mountain village.'

HH was only interested in dwelling on his own good fortune. He was trapped in a cycle. All that mattered was fulfilling his furious ambition. Did he feel any guilt that a young footballer in his care had lost his life, leaving behind a 23-year-old widow and two small children?

6.

On the Sunday evening, Roma's squad arrived late at Fiumicino, Rome's international airport, and were temporarily transferred to Fregene, a coastal town nearby, waiting to leave for Brescia in northern Italy where their cup match was scheduled for Wednesday. Alberto Ginulfi, the team's goalkeeper, slipped away and telephoned the club's president Alvaro Marchini. He asked him to speak to HH, to convince him to allow the grieving players home, at least for a while before leaving for Brescia. Marchini also heard a plea from Dino

Viola, the team's match-day delegate, begging him to have a word with HH, to release the players home. A blunt telephone conversation ensued between Marchini and HH.

'Go home? Why, are we not playing any more? Is the football season finished?'
'Do as I say! It's an order!'

The players slept in their own beds that night. The following morning, bleary-eyed and bereft, they trained at Tre Fontane, Roma's training ground. Two days later, the team lost 1–0 to Brescia. Taccola was buried the following day.

The memory of Giuliano Taccola lives on. AS Roma fans hold aloft a banner remembering him during a Serie A match between AS Roma and US Sassuolo at Rome's Stadio Olimpico, 17 March 2024.

33. TUSCANY

1.

Elio Barsocchi was Giuliano Taccola's best friend in Rome. As kids growing up, they played football together in Uliveto Terme, their hometown in Tuscany. Barsocchi was a decent footballer. He was a central defender, but he gave up the game to focus on a business career. His job with Olivetti took him to Rome around the time Taccola joined Roma. They did everything together. On Sundays, when Barsocchi was at the Olympic Stadium watching Taccola play for Roma, their wives took their kids to the park. There were only a few months' difference in age between Barsocchi's four-year-old son and Taccola's son. Both boys had blond hair and Beatles haircuts. People often mistook them for brothers.

The day I visited Uliveto Terme, a spa town a few miles from Pisa, I stumbled upon Barsocchi sitting outside the town's main bar. It was mid-morning. He was with seven other men sitting in a perfectly formed circle, like a council of elders. One of them had gone to school with Taccola. Another played football with him as a kid. Inside the bar was a huge black-and-white framed photo on the wall of Taccola soaring in the air, high above a few Juventus defenders. At the back of the bar is the town's football pitch where Taccola played as a boy.

At Taccola's funeral inside the basilica of San Paolo fuori le Mura in Rome, Barsocchi sat close to the coffin. He told me half of Rome and all of Tuscany were at the funeral. Microphones relayed the mass for mourners congregated outside. He remembered there were more people crying than those who weren't. Taccola's children were taken inside the church briefly and then ushered outside again. The thing that sticks in Barsocchi's mind from the funeral was the bedlam outside the church. As Taccola's kids and his son were put inside his car, there was a frenzy when people realised who they were. Men and women, in a state of delirium, started shaking the car, denting its side panels. They were desperate to touch Taccola's kids to console them. To escape the mayhem, Barsocchi drove the kids back to Uliveto Terme to stay with their grandmother.

Barsocchi remembers meeting HH when he was Roma's coach. He said HH spoke in a sing-song manner and dressed in 'the English style' – a jacket and tie and pants with perfect creases. 'I'll be honest, I didn't like Herrera,' he said. 'He had a superiority complex. He didn't show people respect. He treated his players like soldiers, like they were parts in a machine. He was always right. What he said must be done. He was a dictator. He was forever on the players' backs. Giuliano was a very, very patient guy. He always stayed calm. He knew all of Herrera's defects, but he did what he was told. He never complained.'

I asked him if he knew why Taccola died so tragically. 'There are so many rumours about his death,' he said. 'Did he take something too strong? Was he forced to play when he shouldn't? Who was to blame? Herrera? The doctor? "The fault dies young," as we say in Italy. Nobody knows. There is an *omertà* in football.'

2.

Taccola's nephew, Marcelo Candidi, runs a small café that doubles up as a tobacconist and sweet shop in Uliveto Terme. It has a framed colour photo of Taccola in his Roma jersey on the wall. Marcelo Candidi is a season ticket holder with Roma. As a kid, during the football season, he would squeeze into a car at weekends with his father and a few other townsmen to travel to Rome or around Italy to watch Taccola play. Journeys could take up to 10 hours. Sometimes, they left the day before the game. Seeing Taccola in the flesh, scoring a goal, was an indescribable feeling for him as a 10-year-old boy. Taccola's father never travelled for matches. He stayed in the local bar in Uliveto Terme, listening to the radio. If Taccola scored, a round of aniseed-flavoured liqueurs was passed around the bar in celebration. Taccola often visited Uliveto Terme on Mondays after a game. People waited around the bar to talk to him – a conquering hero returned home.

On the day Taccola died, Marcelo Candidi was in Uliveto Terme. He hadn't travelled to the match because it was played on the island of Sardinia. That same afternoon, he'd gone to the cinema instead. When he came out around 8 p.m., a boy came up to him and said: 'Your uncle just died.' A neighbour took him home. He remembers Taccola's body coming back from Rome to Uliveto Terme. Roma's players and HH joined the procession for the burial. Taccola's mausoleum is looked after, kept neat, with fresh flowers and plants keeping vigil. Framed photos of Taccola adorn its altar, one of him standing proudly beside his white sports car. Beside the altar is a bronze sculpture of the Capitoline Wolf, the she-wolf that nursed the twins Romulus and Remus when they were abandoned in the wild by an irate king.

Every year until 1985, four or five buses of Roma fans made a pilgrimage to Uliveto Terme to pay their respects to a fallen hero. Taccola's mother served them coffee. She passed away in 2019. On the night before Taccola died, he phoned his mother. He told her he had had a fever the night before and hadn't slept much, but that everything would be OK. Taccola's mother wasn't unduly worried. Apart from his tonsillectomy operation the previous month, she believed he was a fit young athlete. It was later that the doubts started to invade her mind.

'Herrera forced my uncle back into playing too soon after his tonsillectomy operation,' said Candidi. 'He forced him to take pills. Herrera blackmailed him into playing. He was docked wages if he didn't play [i.e. in lost bonuses].' HH changed the bonus structure at Roma. Bonuses previously were divided up between the squad. HH brought in a system where bonuses were awarded only to footballers who played. This annoyed Roma's players, but HH wanted them to be more cut-throat, to be desperate to play and win. According to Franco Cordova, he used it as a stick to beat Taccola, knowing that Taccola needed cash to build apartments in Uliveto Terme. 'Taccola made big investments at the time. He needed money. Herrera knew it well. "No play, no pay," he told him.'

Candidi added: 'Herrera knew Taccola had a lot of expenses because he was building four apartments here in Uliveto Terme; one was supposed to be for his mother. She believed Herrera was a murderer, but it's a complicated situation.'

Candidi made a comparison with the star Juventus forward Roberto Bettega, who missed nearly a year playing football in 1972 because of tuberculosis. He was cared for diligently by Juventus. After recovering from TB, he went on to win six more Serie A titles, the last one in 1982. 'My uncle should have stopped playing like Roberto Bettega. He was the victim of a football system.'

3.

As a teenager, Taccola had joined Genoa's youth academy. After spending a few years out on loan, he broke into Genoa's first team during the 1966/67 season. Genoa's head coach was Giorgio Ghezzi, a legendary goalkeeper who was Italy's goalkeeper at the 1954 World Cup. He played the bulk of his career with Inter, but also played several seasons for Milan, winning a European Cup with them in 1963. His only season as a manager was with Genoa, which coincided with Taccola's season in the first team before transferring to Roma. Ghezzi was too hot-headed to be a good manager. Like many goalkeepers he had a mad streak in him. His nickname was 'Kamikaze' because of a disregard for his personal safety in the heat of a match.

When Ghezzi instituted a doping programme at Genoa in the summer of 1966, he told his players not to be afraid of his experiments. He assured his players that his 'injections of tonic' would improve their performances. He had taken these injections himself as a player for many years at Inter. He led by example, preparing a reddish liquid one day in front of them, injecting himself and then asking them to observe the impact. Genoa's players were warned not to talk to anyone about the club's doping programme, not even to family members, for any reason.

Carlo Petrini was a teammate of Taccola's at Genoa that season. In a confessional memoir, Petrini describes being haunted by a scene in Genoa's dressing room on the day of a league match in 1967. He remembers seeing 'Giuliano Taccola, our right wing, lying on a massage table in the large room of the infirmary … writhing in pain, as pale as a corpse. None of us thought about the injections which became so routine that for us it was like having a massage or a shower. Taccola would die two years later, at the age of 25, and no one knows why.'

As explored earlier, in the 1960s, doping was endemic in Italian football, as in professional cycling. Ferruccio Mazzola, the whistleblower brother of Sandro Mazzola, recalled playing for Lazio against Roma in a Rome derby match in 1969. HH was in Roma's dugout. Before the game, Mazzola took some amphetamines, which had been procured in Scotland. They were red pills that made him move at the speed of a train. Lazio's players nicknamed them 'Barons' after the Red Baron, the famous German fighter pilot from the First World War.

According to Giacomo Losi, Roma's captain, at their first training camp, HH summoned his new players to give them pills that HH's osteopath, Émile Wanono, prepared for them in Paris. Losi recalled: 'I've never had a reason or proof to say they were pills with performance-enhancing substances, but instinctively I didn't trust [Herrera]. When the coach offered them to me, I openly refused them. Not only that, but as team captain I made sure that others rejected them too. The year Herrera arrived we went on retreat to Grottaferrata, to a hotel owned by [Roma's president Alvaro] Marchini, which had a garden with a large fountain in the centre. At the foot of that fountain, the players stopped taking them and then, following my instructions, they threw them away. At a certain point, however, Herrera noticed this and began delivering the pills directly in the dressing room, standing in front of players to see if they had taken them. Some players swallowed them; some flushed them down the toilet.'

4.

All the world lives around little Uliveto Terme. Taccola's daughter, Giuliana – who is named after her dad and was six years old when he died – works in a supermarket in an adjoining village. 'I don't have closure,' she said about her father's death more than half a century ago. 'They wouldn't let me stay mourning beside his coffin. I haven't been able to finish my grieving.' Her memories of him are only in snatches, like when she was taken to watch him train. Her mother and Taccola's widow, Marzia Nannipieri, lives close by, at the foot of a beautiful medieval monastery.

Taccola and Marzia Nannipieri met at a picnic when she was 13 years old; he was two years older. He was smitten. When they began dating – on a trip to the cinema, say, or going for a walk along the meandering road in front of where Nannipieri still lives – their mothers chaperoned them, sitting behind them at the cinema, strolling behind them on the road, which was the custom in Catholic Italy in the 1950s. They became engaged when Nannipieri was 15 years old and married when she was 17. When they moved to Rome, Nannipieri led a quiet life at home, raising their two small children. Taccola liked to keep his family sheltered from the spotlight. He didn't want his wife mixing with the actors and artists who roamed Rome's nightspots. One of his personal treats was to visit his tailor on Via Veneto. He loved tailor-made suits.

When I met Nannipieri at her apartment, she apologised because it wasn't grand. 'It's not the apartment of a famous footballer,' she said. She had just come home from work. 'I was working when I was 13 years old and I'm working now, at the age of 78.' We chatted in the sitting room, which was like a shrine to her dead husband with framed photos of him everywhere. It's clear a clock stopped for her on 16 March 1969, the day her husband died. She writes and distributes an article about him every year on the anniversary of his death. She said her husband shouldn't have played again for the rest of the season after his tonsillectomy operation in February 1969. 'If I operate on him, the season is over,' the surgeon told her. Instead, Taccola was rushed back to train after being discharged from hospital. She often wonders about all the 'shit' they gave him to make him play.

'Herrera didn't ask the doctors if Giuliano was fit to play, he asked Giuliano.' She recalled that eight days before he died, Taccola had fainted twice while at the training camp at Grottaferrata. 'Giuliano called me at midnight. He said he was getting a taxi home. When he got home, he had a fever of 39°C. His hands were trembling. He was told when he left the training camp that he would lose his match bonuses. A doctor and nurse arrived the next morning at 8 a.m. They said they had to give him an injection. Giuliano said: "I'll give an injection to the person who sent you." He refused to go with them. He stayed in bed. He rejected the injection. He couldn't take it any more.'

On the following Wednesday – four days before Roma's match in Cagliari – his fever abated, and he went back to training. The next day, he asked the club to do some blood tests, but he was told he didn't need any more. He tried to phone his surgeon, Professor Filipo, who did his tonsillectomy operation, but the doctor was abroad in Spain. The next day, Friday, Taccola convened at the club for the trip to Cagliari against his better judgement. 'If I don't go, they will pick me up by force,' he told his wife.

Taccola's death was reported in the media before she was told what had happened. According to Nannipieri, Roma's president, Alvaro Marchini, consoled her by saying: 'It's better that your husband has died. He wouldn't have recognised you.' She went to the island of Sardinia until Taccola's corpse was taken back to Rome. She didn't eat for two days. On the day of the funeral, a doctor sedated her. The last thing she remembers was fainting after the funeral mass. HH never went to offer his condolences.

'I remember Herrera went to visit Giuliano in hospital when he was recovering from his tonsillectomy operation,' she told me. 'Giuliano was surprised by how friendly he was towards me. "How did you get him to talk to you? He doesn't talk with any of the players," he said to me.' And she added: 'Herrera was a very closed person. Even when Herrera's daughter died a few years before Giuliano, he stood under the rain, not moving, not talking, until he said: "Let's go. Tomorrow, we have a football match."'

34. INQUEST

1.

The jockeying for position – men diving for cover, getting their stories straight, smearing colleagues, hiding files – started immediately after Giuliano Taccola's death. Taccola had a dicky heart; the dogs on the street knew it. In his youth, he suffered from brucellosis or 'Malta fever' as it was then known in Italy. He was a tall and robust teenage boy, with an athletic physique, so he easily overcame the viral affliction, but it likely left a mark on his heart, exposing him to subsequent health problems.

Brucellosis can cause endocarditis, a life-threatening inflammation of the inner lining of the heart's chambers. 'Endocarditis' is a medical word that looms large in Taccola's tragic story. It was known in Italian football circles from at least 1964 – five years before he died – that Taccola had heart disease. The coaching staff and medics at Genoa, Taccola's first club, were aware of problems. Dr Fino Fini, Italy's national team doctor when it won Euro 1968 and the 1982 World Cup, knew. So too did people inside the walls at Roma.

In December 1966, during his breakthrough season with Genoa's first team, Taccola was sent to the medical department at Coverciano, the Italian Football Federation's nerve centre, for examination. What Dr Fini found was alarming. Taccola's heart revealed 'clearly pathological' anomalies. In a written report, Dr Fini informed both Taccola and Genoa about his concerns. A copy of the file was kept in Coverciano's archives until it was confiscated, at a later date. It had all been noted there, in black and white: 'the recovery times of the player are slowing down … he should not undergo excessive workloads … under exertion the heart showed problems.'

Dr Fini also briefed Genoa's coach, 'Kamikaze' Ghezzi, about his disturbing findings. At the end of Taccola's visit, Dr Fini recommended a check-up in two months' time. Taccola never made the appointment. When police showed up at Genoa immediately after Taccola's death, in order to seize any relevant documents for their investigation, they left empty-handed. They were told that club policy was to destroy all medical files of players who had been sold.

In the summer of 1967, Roma were on the cusp of signing Taccola. They were concerned, though, by an apparently 'innocent' breath detected in the 24-year-old striker. An innocent breath is a harmless sound created by normal, turbulent blood flow through the heart, but in Taccola's case it warranted further investigation. Roma's club doctor, Catello De Martino, visited Dr Fini in July 1967 for his assessment. Dr Fini told him that Taccola represented an 'interesting' case from a 'clinical and electrocardiogram' point of view – basically that he had a heart murmur.

Roma were still keen to get their man. They saw great potential. To dispel their doubts, Roma sent Taccola to Dr Giuseppe Di Giorgio for a second medical opinion in August 1967. Or so it was claimed. We can't be certain about what happened at that medical, and the discussions afterwards, but what we do know is that Roma's president Franco Evangelisti – despite being aware of the whispers flagging the heart problems – went ahead and signed the player.

It wasn't just medics who knew about Taccola's heart problems. When 'Kamikaze' Ghezzi was fired as Genoa coach in 1967, he was replaced by Paolo Tabanelli, a man who spent over 20 seasons coaching mid-ranking Italian clubs. Tabanelli lasted only a few months at Genoa, and got a gig in Atalanta the following season. His season in charge coincided with Elvio Salvori, a defender who spent the following season as a teammate of Taccola's at Roma – and who learned about his heart problems from Tabanelli.

Franco Evangelisti, Roma president at the time Taccola was signed in 1967, wasn't disappointed by his bet in the short term. It was a good business move. Within a year, his asset more than doubled in value, as Fiorentina began laying the ground to sign Taccola from Roma at the end of the 1968/69 season. Roma had paid 90 million lira for him, and were about to flip him for 200 million lira. A tidy profit. If concerns raised in Dr Fino Fini's detailed medical report from December 1966 had been noted by the directors at Genoa and Roma, it might have meant a premature end to Taccola's playing career at 23 years of age … and a lot of money in transfer fees and cuts for the middlemen involved would have been left on the table.

2.

Police raided Roma's offices on 23 March 1969, a week after Taccola's death – and didn't find any medical report from Professor Di Giorgio about Taccola. The one that had apparently green-lit Taccola's transfer from Genoa to Roma in 1967 had disappeared. Police interrogated Dr Di Giorgio, but he was unable to provide any useful files about Taccola's medical history. Mysteriously, his medical report turned up in his personal papers a year later, but at that stage the investigating magistrates didn't take it into account in their deliberations. Once told there didn't seem to be any files on Taccola from his Genoa period, they had moved on, focusing their investigation on his spell at Roma in the months leading up to his death, together with evidence they were able to gather during that short window. It was a gross omission.

The inquest into Taccola's death began in 1970. There were two men in the dock: HH and Professor Massimo Visalli, Roma's club doctor. Both were under investigation for involuntary manslaughter – that is, that their actions indirectly caused the death of Taccola. The doctor was charged with 'incompetence', basically medical negligence; and HH with 'imprudence', i.e. forcing Taccola to play when he was sick. Between the two of them, given the evidence, HH appeared to be the more guilty party.

Taccola's autopsy revealed he had bacterial endocarditis. Technically, this is what killed him. It's a bacterium that settles in the heart. Specifically, it infects the inner lining of the heart chambers and valves, which explains the fevers he had been experiencing. The bacterium can be contracted in various ways. He could have got it at, say, a dentist's, or after his tonsillectomy operation in February 1969 – though he was suffering from strange fevers before the tonsillectomy operation, so that possibility seems to be ruled out. Or the bacterium could have been picked up from an infected needle, which is often a source of endocarditis. Several ex-footballers in the 1950s and '60s contracted hepatitis from dirty needles. Some died when those with chronic hepatitis developed liver cirrhosis or cancer.

Bacterial endocarditis is a rare infection, and is still lethal today if not treated with antibiotics, which explains why Professor Visalli was in a frenzy trying to get his hands on antibiotics during the minutes leading up to Taccola's death. The tragedy for Taccola is that endocarditis is a treatable disease, provided it's recognised in time. As explained earlier, it seems his regular doctors made the mistake of thinking his fevers were due to chronic tonsillitis. But tonsilitis just diverted attention, fatally. His tonsils were whipped out, and he lost a lot of blood during surgery. Weakened, he was hit with pneumonia – a double whammy. The infectious attack on his airways rapidly spread to his bronchi and lungs even as the fevers continued to assault him. Unless he rested and obtained a proper diagnosis, he became a dead man walking.

Taccola's environment confounded his situation. His health problems spiralled out of control against a background of chaos at Roma, a club with three different presidents during that fateful 1968/69 season. The club was an organisational shambles, characterised by unprofessional medical practices and poor decisions. Its doctors conflicted with each other, which showed up in the inquest documents. They often confused players. There were gaps in responsibility, and HH took advantage. Whether HH was getting good medical advice or not about Taccola is a moot point, however. HH was a sceptic who spent his life sneering at Western medicine.

HH got his healing advice from the universe. During his childhood in Casablanca, he became entranced with mystics, natural healers and magical rites. It's where the aura of 'The Magician' took hold. HH reckoned rubbing precious stones or camels' toes on a bone fracture was as likely to heal it as anything else. He was a do-it-yourself man, training himself in massage and physiotherapy. He also believed in the power of the mind. In 1970, for example, HH crashed his Mercedes car in a motorway accident. When his sidekick, the osteopath Émile Wanono, saw him in a body cast he advised him to see a French doctor friend. The doctor insisted that the plaster of Paris practised in Western medicine was a waste of time. HH removed the cast, to his relief, and, according to Fiora Gandolfi, without negative consequences.

After Taccola's discharge from hospital following his tonsils operation, HH pushed him back into training with indecent haste. He wanted him back on the pitch, scoring goals, at all costs. He was adamant there was nothing wrong with Taccola – who was just another malingering footballer, work-shy, play-acting to avoid training. He resisted giving Taccola antibiotics for his fevers because, as a rule, HH thought they sapped a player's energy. And on the player's last day alive, summoned him from his bed to run on a beach, with the wind rolling in off the sea.

3.

HH's role in Taccola's demise looked bad, very bad. So he chose attack as the best form of defence. He sniped at Professor Visalli, the other individual investigated for the manslaughter of Taccola. During criminal proceedings, the public prosecutor, Enrico Altieri, quizzed HH about the pressure he exerted to keep Taccola training and playing while he was clearly unwell. HH denied pushing the player against his will. He rubbished the idea that he never listened to doctors. On the contrary, he insisted he had always respected the opinion of club doctors, that he had never prevented their presence on the pitch during training. He claimed his accusers were trying to tarnish his reputation.

HH couldn't help admitting, however, that he preferred his footballers to take only vitamins in the days running up to a match, and that he frowned on the use of antibiotics at that critical juncture. He had wanted to keep their bodies free of antibacterial agents before they went into combat. He took advantage of his time in the stand to malign Professor Visalli, considering him to be inexperienced in sports medicine, leaving it unsaid that Il Mago was better equipped to tend to the medical and psychological needs of his players.

In the frantic final hour before Taccola's death, a loose chain of events immediately emerged. Taccola fainted in the dressing room in Cagliari. Professor Visalli reacted by administering a shot of penicillin – in effect, antibiotics. Taccola started suffocating. Did he die from an allergic reaction? (Even though he had taken penicillin-based medicines since at least the autumn of 1968;

a person can, however, have reactions to drugs previously taken without issue.) In the first few hours after Taccola's death, various witnesses made statements that it was the penicillin injection that was fateful. HH had been the first person to make this claim. He said he was convinced it was the reason for Taccola's heart attack. HH and Professor Visalli were sworn enemies. It cost HH nothing to put the club doctor in the firing line, shifting blame.

Under pressure from the press and criminal investigators, Professor Visalli declared that Taccola had become an 'unrecoverable patient' and that this was well known. He later backtracked. He claimed he had never said the phrase 'unrecoverably ill' and that he had discovered only a few days before Taccola's death – from his predecessor at Roma, Professor De Martino – that the footballer was suffering from a slight heart murmur. He said he had been disappointed that Taccola was made to train on the Saturday and Sunday morning of the match in Cagliari, especially as the weather had been cold and blustery. He never clarified in court if it was Taccola who refused his invitation to stay in the hotel and rest on the morning of the match. Or if Taccola's arm was twisted.

4.

In January 1971, the expert report into Taccola's death was leaked. The public prosecutor Enrico Altieri failed to get a conviction. The verdict was that Taccola had died because of several factors: an underlying heart disease; pneumonia, which had kicked in 15 days before he died; there had been medical negligence; and because he had been pushed too hard. Could he have been saved? Yes, but it was difficult to locate blame for his death. Taccola, the judge concluded, died from bad luck. His death was a tragedy. He was felled by a perfect storm of malign circumstances and a sneaky illness. Because he was a strapping young athlete, he had resisted its attacks, almost in denial and determined not to lose his place in the team. Although it wasn't explicitly stated by the judge, or anyone in Taccola's orbit, the suggestion was left hanging that Taccola had been complicit in his own death.

Taccola's widow, Marzia Nannipieri, was bereft. She was left twisting in the wind. The case was dismissed, but the investigating report wasn't officially published. The circus tent was dismantled. Altieri moved from Cagliari to Pisa and on to other professional challenges. Taccola's widow waited for the official report to be published so she could appeal against it as an 'injured party', but it never emerged. She was left in limbo, trapped in a never-ending Kafkaesque legal nightmare. In 1979, she reported the missing document to the police.

In the 1990s, after a decade more of silence, a judge, Francesco Saverio Borrelli, picked up the baton. He sent the case to a public prosecutor's office in Cagliari. There was a second inquest. In 1995, Taccola's widow won her day in court. She denounced Roma and the Italian Football Federation in a civil case in Rome, but the trial dead-ended. For decades, she had stormed the gates at Roma. Occasionally she was granted an audience with whoever was club president. One president, exasperated, told her to stop pestering the club, that Roma couldn't do anything more for her husband; he was dead.

This has all taken a horrendous toll on her. She has spent her life carrying a cross, unable to recover from Taccola's premature death. She has never rebuilt a life, never stopped struggling with what happened on that Sunday in Cagliari in March 1969, replaying events over and over in her mind. A woman consumed with bitterness, frustration and sleepless nights, tossing and turning. Empty promises have left a sour taste in her mouth. Giulio Onesti, president of the Italian National Olympic Committee from 1946 until 1978, offered her work as a secretary. The job never materialised. In front of a photo of her dead husband, Senator Dino Viola, president of Roma throughout the 1980s, promised that a branch of Banca di Roma would open in Pisa and she would be its first employee. Another broken promise.

Life has been a perpetual struggle. She turned her hand to whatever she could to try and put food on the table for herself and her two children: inventing a job as an artisan, making leather bags; working as a cleaning lady. Her family never stayed living under the same roof for long. Her mother took them in for a spell. They rented apartments. They suffered evictions, and the shame that comes with it. Pitiful whispers trailed in her ears, echoing that she was 'the poor wife of Taccola'. Her son Gianluca's dreams of becoming a professional footballer came to nothing. At one stage, without a roof over their heads, she and her daughter ended up living temporarily in their car.

At the time of writing, more than half a century after Taccola's death, she is still campaigning for justice.

5.

In 1998, after being approached by several widows of ex-footballers, Raffaele Guariniello, a supreme court magistrate, opened an investigation into doping in Italian football. He looked at the medical records of 24,000 footballers between 1960 and 1996, which included 400 deaths, 70 of which were mysterious, among them Taccola's, the first 'white death' in Italian football. Guariniello investigated the unusually high incidence amongst ex-footballers of illnesses such as cancer and amyotrophic lateral sclerosis, or Lou Gehrig's disease. So-called after an American baseball player who was a victim, Lou Gehrig's disease, which is the most common subtype of motor neurone disease, attacks the nervous system and spinal cord. It's a rare disease. Guariniello expected to find one Lou Gehrig's disease case in his study. Instead, he discovered 45, with

13 footballers already dead from the illness. He also found that liver and colon tumours were twice as high as the national average.

Sandro Mazzola was one of the ex-footballers who testified in the investigation. Many of Mazzola's Grande Inter teammates didn't fare well after leaving the game. His captain, Armando Picchi, died from cancer at 36. Gerry Hitchens died from a heart attack aged 48. Carlo Tagnin died in 2000 from bone cancer. Mauro Bicicli died the following year from liver cancer. Ferdinando Miniussi died the same year from cirrhosis of the liver. Giacinto Facchetti died in 2006 after suffering over a long period from pancreatic cancer. Marcello Giusti – the Inter youth academy player HH had cruelly left to run down a motorway high on amphetamines after missing the team bus's departure following a game at Como in 1962 – died in his early fifties from a brain tumour.

Guariniello ended his study in 2007, having failed to draw any convincing conclusions. He was disillusioned by the *omertà* in football. 'It's easier to find a confessing mafioso than a confessing football professional,' he said. Was Guariniello on a fool's errand? It's next to impossible to demonstrate a correlation between doping and subsequent death when there's a gap between a player retiring and dying in middle age. So much time passes. The body is a mysterious vessel. So many variables can account for premature death. But the statistics Guariniello uncovered in his investigation, and the untimely deaths of so many footballers from his sample, give reason to pause. Some of the coincidences are uncanny.

Taccola's widow said that Roma gave her husband injections to eliminate fatigue and fever. Franco Cordova, Taccola's teammate at Roma, corroborates her claim, adding: 'When poor Giuliano had a fever, [HH] made him take certain injections, which got him back on the pitch.' Cagliari's team doctor Augusto Frongia watched Taccola's life slip away in Cagliari's dressing room. He argues that doping was not the decisive factor in Taccola's death – that it wasn't the wrong cures that killed Taccola, but rather the cures that he wasn't given. We'll never know for sure. What is certain is that Taccola's death was not inevitable, but he should have been retired from football, and that complete light has never been shed on what happened to him. It remains one of football's mysterious cold cases.

6.

HH was off the hook. In the leaked 1971 report into Taccola's death, HH was criticised for interfering and refusing to heed the advice of Roma's doctors, and for forcing Taccola to train in the days before the away match in Cagliari.

In his defence, it cited mitigating factors – that he was misled by Taccola, who sometimes appeared physically fine and by Taccola's own statements that he was fit to train and play. It concluded that HH was guilty of 'elements of culpable conduct due to negligence or imprudence', but that his actions weren't responsible for a 'causal role in the death', arguing that HH's part in Taccola's death would be indisputable only if Taccola had died during a training session or in a match.

HH dodged a bullet, but something broke within him. After Taccola's death, he regrouped and led Roma to a Coppa Italia victory in June 1969. It was a notable feat, but Taccola's manslaughter case hung over him. He had left the building by the time of the inquiry's leaked report. He never fully believed in the project at Roma. He was dismayed by what he perceived as a lack of professionalism in some players. Moreover, he had a toxic relationship with the president, Alvaro Marchini. The club was second-rate in HH's eyes. He dreamed of returning to Inter or Barça. He told the press – in a quip heard around the world – that Roma won their only *scudetto* back in 1942 because Mussolini had been coach. He was sacked shortly afterwards.

For several years, HH suffered from shakes in his hands. His stint managing Roma left his nerves tattered. Gandolfi puts it down to his suspicion that Roma players were taking bribes to lose matches. He returned – unsuccessfully – to the Inter bench for a season in the mid-1970s, and to Barça for a second spell, winning his final trophy, the Copa del Rey, in 1981.

Years after HH retired from coaching, a Catalan football journalist called on spec to visit him at his *palazzo* in Venice. HH ushered him inside the door and asked him to wait in the hallway for five minutes. He disappeared, only to reappear wearing a Barça tie he hadn't been wearing when he opened the door. He had wanted to send a message back to Catalonia. He was ready to serve again. The magic might have been gone, but his spirit was still willing.

EPILOGUE

HH had admirers right until the end. In November 1997, when he was in hospital, on the verge of dying, he took out a letter he had received and asked Fiora Gandolfi to read it, as he wasn't wearing his glasses and the room was dimly lit. It was an hour before midnight. He pulled the letter – a sheet of foolscap folded in four – from under his mattress with two fingers.

'But you're crazy to keep documents under your backside, they could get wrinkled!' she said.

'Just read it!' he blurted.

It was a letter from a lover of his, with very poor handwriting. She had written in haste.

'Look how this one writes to a sick person!' he grumbled.

In the letter, she told HH that she always fell in love with the wrong man. It was the last love letter HH received. A few hours later, he was moved into isolation, in an intensive care unit. There he died, alone.

HH's ashes are on the island of San Michele, in the Venice lagoon. The island served as a prison before becoming the city's cemetery in the nineteenth century. It's covered in cypress trees and is alive with the sound of birdsong. His ashes are kept in an urn inside a replica European Cup, which is mounted against a cemetery wall. It's draped with club scarves, including one from Inter. Beside it there's a copy of *Tacalabala*, a book by Fiora Gandolfi about HH's football philosophy and techniques. Fake flowers are scattered on the ground underneath.

Close by lie the remains of Ezra Pound, Igor Stravinsky and a Staffordshire man whose family gleefully announced on his tombstone that he 'Left us in peace, Febry 2, 1910'. HH was born that same year – 1910, although it was a secret he took to the grave. When he arrived in Spain to coach in the late 1940s, HH maintained he had been born in April 1916. (It was a lie. He kept his age secret for the rest of his life, although there was speculation in one of his obituaries that he was older than 81.) Fiora Gandolfi discovered his true date of birth when she found his passport after his death. He was born on 10 April 1910. She modified his tombstone with a black marker, changing the year 1916 to 1910.

As a footballer, HH was an also-ran. As a coach, he was somebody. He did some reinvention in between. The twentieth century was a good time to start over, especially emerging from the rubble of the Second World War. It was an age before digital footprints. HH had a blank slate. The story he could tell about himself was up for grabs. Did he come from Buenos Aires or Casablanca or God knows where?

His widow thought it appropriate that he doctored his date of birth, adding a tail to the zero to make it a six: 'After all, every myth has a mysterious origin like Romulus and Remus.'

Here lie the remains: HH's ashes are kept inside a replica European Cup on the island cemetery of San Michele in Venice.

HH showing off the European Cup to fans at Milan's Linate Airport in May 1964, the day after Inter defeated Real Madrid 3–1 on a famous night in Vienna.

CAREER AND HONOURS

PLAYING CAREER

1928–1931: Roches Noires
1931/32: Racing Athlétic Club de Casablanca
1932/33: CASG Paris
1933–1935: Stade Français
1935–1937: FCO Charleville
    1936, FINALIST: Coupe de France
1937–1939: Excelsior Roubaix
1940–1942: Red Star Olympique
    1942, WINNER: Coupe de France
1942/43: Stade Français
1943/44: EF Paris-Capitale
1944/45: Puteaux

MANAGERIAL CAREER

1944/45: Puteaux
1945–1948: Stade Français
1946–1948: France
1948/49: Real Valladolid
1949–1953: Atlético Madrid
    1950, WINNER: La Liga
    1951, WINNER: La Liga
    1951, WINNER: Copa Eva Duarte
1953: Málaga
1953: Deportivo La Coruña
1953–1957: Sevilla
    1955, FINALIST: Copa del Generalísimo
    1957, RUNNER-UP*: La Liga
1957/58: Os Belenenses

1958–1960: Barça
 1958, WINNER: Inter-Cities Fairs Cup
 1959, WINNER: La Liga
 1959, WINNER: Copa del Generalísimo
 1960, WINNER: La Liga
 1960, SEMI-FINALIST: European Cup
 1960, WINNER**: Inter-Cities Fairs Cup

1959–1960: Spain

1960–1968: Inter
 1963, WINNER: Serie A
 1964, FINALIST, play-off final: Serie A
 1964, WINNER: European Cup
 1964, WINNER: Intercontinental Cup
 1965, WINNER: Serie A
 1965, WINNER: European Cup
 1965, WINNER: Coppa Italia
 1965, WINNER: Intercontinental Cup
 1966, WINNER: Serie A
 1966, SEMI-FINALIST: European Cup
 1967, FINALIST: European Cup

1962: Spain

1966–1967: Italy

1968–1970: Roma
 1969, WINNER: Coppa Italia
 1970, SEMI-FINALIST, lost on a coin toss: European Cup Winners' Cup

1971–1973: Roma
 1972, WINNER: Anglo-Italian Cup

1973/1974: Inter

1976, 1979: Rimini

1980/1981: Barça
 1981, WINNER: Copa del Rey

2015: Italian Football Hall of Fame

* As runner-up, Sevilla qualified for the European Cup.
** HH was sacked a couple of days before Barça played the second leg of the 1960 Inter-Cities Fairs Cup final, in which Barça defeated Birmingham City 4–1 on aggregate.

HH relaxing on the Venetian Lagoon in 1986, retired from coaching but still working as a football pundit on Italian television.

ACKNOWLEDGEMENTS

The first person I must thank is Michelle, my beautiful wife and the love of my life. Writing books is a selfish pursuit. For six years, she bore my obsession with fortitude and helped with advice and translations. It's great being married to a bookworm who shares the same sense of humour. *Gracias, mi amor.*

Someone else at the top of the pile is my wonderful agent, Melanie Michael-Greer, who believed in the manuscript from the off. She's a joy to work with – clever, super professional and half-Irish to boot!

It's a blessing getting to work with Matt Lowing, my editor at Bloomsbury. He's calm, like the guys in a Western, and has a brilliant literary mind. He got all the big decisions (and small ones) right about the book's direction. I've also been fortunate to work with a fantastic copy editor, Caroline Curtis, who brought great rigour and tabled valuable questions. Thanks to my brilliant proofreader, Lucy Doncaster, her eagle eye saved innumerable blushes.

I can't thank my two first readers enough for whipping the early manuscript into shape – Eoin Kirwan, always the smartest guy in the room, whether it's sport, literature, culture, you name it; and Paul Howard, who is obviously a brilliant writer and one-time killer sports journalist, but also the funniest raconteur around.

I adore the book cover! Hope you do too. Huge thanks to James Watson's creative genius in designing it. Thanks also to marketing guru, Xanthe Rendall, and Katherine Macpherson and the publicity team, for getting the word out there about HH.

I badgered so many people into helping with aspects of the manuscript. They include my brother Finbar, a doctor, who patiently explained some of the finer medical details in the book, and made corrections where necessary. The best gift in life is having a brother to travel along the trail with you. *Un abrazo grande, hermano.*

Thanks to the great Jimmy Burns, my dear friend and mentor in all things Spanish and football-related; Jacqueline Hurtley, Emeritus Professor at the University of Barcelona, for forensically poring over the manuscript and correcting factual, cultural and writing errors; and to Nancy Belfiore for spotting the Italian mistakes!

Thanks to the excellent football journalist Alessandro Bai, who helped as my interpreter in Italy, and to the amazing Chiara Celli, who opened so many doors in Uliveto Terme and explained so much about life Tuscany.

Many thanks to the brilliant Lee Greenberg; to Tim Desmond, from the RTÉ *Documentary on One* team, a master when it comes to the art of storytelling; to Phil Gordon, the Scottish football oracle, and for hosting a memorable evening in Glasgow with his wife, Louise, and himself; and to Matt Watson-Broughton, the Mighty Magyar!

I'm inordinately grateful to Robert J. Friedman for schooling me in Holocaust-related matters, for sourcing and sharing so much extraordinary archival material and for answering

Acknowledgements

so many queries about Dezső Solti's wartime and post-wartime experiences. Thanks also to Wanda Malicka at the Auschwitz-Birkenau State Museum for helping clarify items about Dezső Solti and the horrors that befell his relatives.

I've got to thank Mark Rutherford, my first newspaper editor, all those years ago in San Francisco. I'll never forgot how he punched an early story, an interview with a boxer Seamus McDonagh, into shape. Took out all the flab, a lesson I'll never forget, making me fall in love with short sentences. He's The Wheel.

So many people kindly helped with research or contacts or arcane questions. I know I'm forgetting people, please forgive me, but some of them include the peerless Alfredo Relaño; Manuel Tomás Belenguer, who hosted me in Barça's archives at the Centre de Documentació i Estudis; Nick Lloyd and his wonderful Spanish Civil War walking tour; Gemma Comerma; Carles Viñas; David Salinas; Frederic Porta; Pere Escobar; Ramon Besa; Vicente del Bosque; Javier Daucik Kubala; Andy Mitten; Ragnhild Lund Ansnes; Mark Lawrenson; Alan Kennedy; Tom 'Va-Va-Voom' Williams; Dr David Kilpatrick; Michael McLoughlin; and to Vicki Bailey for Macclesfield-related research!

The joy in writing a non-fiction book are the interviews. Nothing tops good conversation. I was lucky to have some memorable encounters. Sadly, so many of the people I spoke with on the phone or met for interviews have passed on, including Justo Tejada, Denis Law, Ian St John, Hugh McIlvanney, Brian Glanville, Rodri, Luis Suárez Miramontes and Ferran Olivella. May they rest in peace.

I'll never forget the afternoon, for example, I spent scrambling under briars and branches in woods at the edge of a golf course in the Wirral with The Saint and his dogs, listening to his hilarious stories. Undoubtedly one of the great football men.

I owe a huge debt of gratitude to my magnificent audio partners for steering me through the audiobook process – to Ashleigh James for her coordination skills and sound advice; to DJ Antic, aka Dominic Furlonge, for technical wizardry and making available his music studio in Barcelona; and Paul Fegan, my producer in Dublin. Thanks to my pronunciation tutors: Michelle, Nancy, Charlotte Irrgang, Vladislava Pavlova, Monica Nahas, Franck Ferrerira and Tim van Brussel.

A shout-out, too, to Patrick O'Connor, my cousin and *consigliere*; to the mighty Sean O'Neill; Des O'Driscoll, the best newspaper editor in the business and a Cork City *ultra*; Gaffer, Nobby and the Buzzmen for teaching me cunning – football is, after all, a cut-throat business; and to the lads at the Avenue – Mannix, Mallers, Greg and Jimo.

Word up also to Liam, our football-mad son, a *Culé*, who knows more about football than his dad. It's magic having a wingman like him. And hi to his cousin and hero in life, Tom (a Man City fan, bad) and my godson Deckie Molony (a Liverpool fan, good).

Lastly, to our daughter Chloe, the most wonderful girl in the world, for whom this book is dedicated. Basketball is her sport, but she's always open-minded when her kid brother tries to engage her in discussions about football: 'Like, Chloe, who would you prefer to marry? Pelé, Maradona or Messi?'

NOTES

Chapter 1: A Disease of the Bones

'the music of serpents': Helenio Herrera, *Yo: Memorias De Helenio Herrera* (Editorial Planeta, 1962), 25. There is a David Copperfield feel to the early chapters of Herrera's memoirs, as the protagonist reflects with a wistful eye on his psychological and moral growth against a background of murderous poverty. It could have been subtitled 'The Personal History, Adventures, Experience and Observation of Helenio Herrera the Younger of Casablanca (Which He Never Meant to Publish on Any Account)'.

'real universities': M.M. Owen, 'Albert Camus, his love for football and the most famous misquote in philosophy', *The Blizzard: The Football Quarterly* (Issue 32), March 2019.

Chapter 2: Good Men Who Lost Their Way

'acted illegally throughout his career': Juan José Paradinas, 'La UEFA veta a Guijarro como intermediario', *El País*, 28 June 1978.

'I remember … player himself': José Ignacio Corcuera, 'Luis Guijarro: claroscuros de la intermediación futbolística', *CIHEFE* magazine, 1 May 2017.

'Withdraw? Don't talk nonsense … could play like that' and 'Thirty eight degrees? Brilliant … play even better': Helenio Herrera, *Yo: Memorias De Helenio Herrera* (Editorial Planeta, 1962), 100–102.

Chapter 3: Scent of Cut Flowers

'that he believed himself to be intelligent': Alfredo Relaño, 'Pérez-Payá, al Madrid con coche atlético', *El País*, 1 August 2022.

'problems which … time solved': Paul Preston, *Franco: A Biography* (Fontana Press, 1995), 648.

'It was not a civil war … cancer that corroded us': Enrique Moradiellos, *Franco: Anatomy of a Dictator* (I.B. Tauris, 2018), 149.

ritiro: The practice of an eve-of-match get-together (*retreat* in English; *retiro* in Spanish) is most famously associated with HH during his time as Inter coach in the 1960s, so the Italian spelling of the word is used in this book.

'Magnificent, muchachos … score more than three goals': Helenio Herrera, *Yo: Memorias De Helenio Herrera* (Editorial Planeta, 1962), 121–122.

Chapter 4: Thou Shalt Not Kill

'the wounded … were abandoning them': Teresa Pàmies, *Quan érem Capitans: Memòries d'aquella Guerra* (Dopesa, 1974), 149–50.

'At the side … during the night': Paul Preston, *The Spanish Holocaust: Inquisition and Extermination in Twentieth Century Spain* (Harper Press, 2012), 466. Teodor Garriga recounted his experiences of what was known as the *Retirada* (Withdrawal) on Catalunya Ràdio in 2006.

Preston's *The Spanish Holocaust* is a harrowing read. Preston felt justified in using the term *Holocaust* in his book title because of the scale and the cold-blooded nature of Franco's investment in terror. Long after the civil war finished, Franco continued to eliminate 'those who do not think as we do'. Not to mention his systemic torture of prisoners, abuse of women and children and the horrors of slave labour and forced exile. Thousands of exiles were left languishing in French concentration camps or were handed over to the Nazis during the Second World War, as Marshal Philippe Pétain detested Spanish Republicans; unknown numbers died from disease and hunger.

'One is happier living austerely': Paul Preston, *Franco: A Biography* (Fontana Press, 1995), 642.

'deplorable' and 'on and off the pitch': Barça's board meeting notes, 26 March 1958. FC Barcelona, Centre de Documentació i Estudis.

'It was a source of joy for citizens': *Barça Magazine*, 11 October 1957.

'I was in Barcelona … in Spain': Helenio Herrera, *Yo: Memorias De Helenio Herrera* (Editorial Planeta, 1962), 139.

Chapter 5: Crazy About Money

'Picasso is a communist, me not so much': Vanessa Graell, 'Picasso es un genio, yo también', *El Mundo*, 20 March 2015.

'Gentlemen … single penny': Pere Escobar i Pichi Alonso, *Helenio Herrera* (Barcanova, 1998), 45.

'With a forward like this … dressing room floor.': Lluís Lainz, *De Puertas Adentro: Los 113 Años del FC Barcelona Contados en 113 Historias* (Corner, 2012), 113.

'He was a man … tank': Helenio Herrera, *Yo: Memorias De Helenio Herrera* (Editorial Planeta, 1962), 146.

'Goodbye to the battering ram': *El Mundo Deportivo*, 1 October 1984, 10.

Chapter 6: People Should Talk About You Even If It Is Good

'Come on … bonus!': Joan Rovira I Andreu, *Converses amb l'avi Barça* (Edecasa, 2011), 45.

'Enjoying a vermut in Ciudad Condal': David Salinas, 'Ganaremos sin bajar del autocar', *Diario Sport*, 16 March 2019.

'You see what a fucking mess … very good lads … this guy is a magician': Pere Escobar i Pichi Alonso, *Helenio Herrera* (Barcanova, 1998), 47–48.

'A man can lose … give it your all': ibid. 50.

Chapter 7: The Face You Saw Everywhere

catalanismo: Spelled in Spanish for consistency, although it is known as *catalanisme* in Catalan; similarly with *franquismo*/*franquisme*, etc.

Notes

'the unarmed army of Catalonia': Joaquín Manso, 'Barça: ejército simbólico y corrupto', *El Mundo*, 18 February 2023.

'Losing league titles … by God and the Generalísimo': Antonio Munne, *Cuando Nunca Perdíamos* (Alfaguara, 2011), 13.

'Dear God … it takes to die': Enrique Moradiellos, *Franco: Anatomy of a Dictator* (I.B. Tauris, 2018), 93.

'All Catalans are pieces of shit': Jaume Sobrequés i Callicó, *Història del FC Barcelona: El Barça, un club, una ciudad, un país*. Vol III (Editorial Labor, 1993), 53.

Chapter 8: Their Tongues Were 'Dirty'

'the necessary murder': Colm Tóibín, *Homage to Barcelona* (Simon & Schuster, 1990), 150.

'The church must disappear … filthy pimping' and 'Priests Die Praying': Paul Preston, *The Spanish Holocaust: Inquisition and Extermination in Twentieth Century Spain* (Harper Press, 2012), 222–224.

'but they are factories for baby Moors': Paul Preston, *Franco: A Biography* (Fontana Press, 1995), 32.

'without scruple or hesitation those who do not think as we do': Paul Preston, *The Spanish Holocaust: Inquisition and Extermination in Twentieth Century Spain* (Harper Press, 2012), xiii.

'Catalan problem … morally and politically sick': ibid. 466.

'war tax': Antony Beevor, *The Spanish Civil War* (Cassell, 1982), 367.

'One day, I decided to turn the page … told to me by somebody who was there': 'Barcelona: ciutadans en temps de guerra', Barcelona Televisió, available at https://beteve.cat/esports/ramallets-guerra-civil-barcelona-bt/.

stepson: The mother of Gonzalo Suárez Morilla was HH's partner for two decades. They had two children together. Technically, Gonzalo Suárez Morilla wasn't HH's stepson, as his mother never married HH. She was already married when they met and divorce was illegal in Franco's Spain.

Chapter 9: Sodom and Gomorrah

'Silence in the room / Kubala's coming … with a hot babe': Antonio Munne, *Cuando Nunca Perdíamos* (Alfaguara, 2011), 192.

'There are six things on earth … the shit of Espanyol': Manuel Vázquez Montalban, 'Kubala, entre Gamper y Cruyff', *El País*. 18 May 2002.

'a hole in his lungs the size of a silver coin': Ramón Besa, 'Atleta y señor', *El País*, 18 May 2002.

'unfit for sports': Miguel Ángel Lara, *Marca*, 9 June 2014.

'You had to move the dial wheel … Franco censored': Antonio Munne, *Cuando Nunca Perdíamos* (Alfaguara, 2011), 191.

Chapter 10: A Cancer in the Team

'Fans whistled me whenever … for the other team': Gil Carrasco, *Luisito: Luis Suárez, el Balón de Oro que el Barça no supo apreciar* (Edicions Saldonar, 2015), 80.

Chapter 11: Barça of the Hungarians

'it was like someone closing the door of a Rolls-Royce': Richard Williams, quoting Geoffrey Green of the *Times*, 'Jimmy Greaves was a genius, the purest finisher England has produced', *Guardian*, 19 September 2021.

'the first time England were beaten on home soil by a foreign enemy since 1066': Technically speaking, the Republic of Ireland was the first foreign team to defeat England on home soil when it won a friendly international 2–0 at Goodison Park in 1949.

'slippers' and 'We should be alright here … the proper kit': Ferenc Puskás (ed. by Rogan Taylor and Klara Jamrich), *Puskás on Puskás: The Life and Times of a Footballing Legend* (Robson Books, 1998).

'Sanyi! Sanyi! … miss from there??': David Bailey, *Magical Magyars* (Pitch Publishing, 2019).

'the support that the rope gives to a hanged man': Stefan Pelev, 'In terms of foreign policy was Khrushchev a reformer?' Lund University research paper, March 2016.

Chapter 12: Speed

'like rockets': Scott Murray, 'Monkey Glands,' *The Blizzard: The Football Quarterly* (Issue 27), December 2017.

'Before you played … you felt you could go again': *Busby, Stein & Shankly: The Football Men* (BBC, 1997).

'Brilliant … clear twice as many balls!': As told to the author by Gonzalo Suárez.

'To triumph in football … without any effort': Pere Escobar i Pichi Alonso, *Helenio Herrera* (Barcanova, 1998), 7.

'The cards are on the table … There is no other option': *Barça* magazine, 14 April 1960.

Chapter 13: Don Santiago

'Long live death!' and 'who had done so much for the country' and 'I heard, Excellency … How did it go?' and 'I just went for the air' and 'fixed': Julián García Candau, *Madrid-Barça: Historia de un desamor* (El País/Aguilar, 1996), 130–132.

'Sluts! What are you doing here … unworthy! Sluts!' and 'If you've any shame left … Don't embarrass me anymore!': Alfredo Relaño, *366 Historias del Fútbol Mundial Que Deberías Saber* (Martínez Roca, 2010), 672–673.

'Those who say … despite the Catalans' and 'When we went through … a town has no future': Alfredo Relaño, *Nacidos Para Incordiarse: Un Siglo de Agravios Entre El Madrid y El Barça* (Ediciones Martínez Roca, 2012), 217–220.

Chapter 14: 'He Could Have Played with a Tuxedo On'

'Tomorrow, training at half past 10! On the dot!': Helenio Herrera, *Yo: Memorias De Helenio Herrera* (Editorial Planeta, 1962), 184–186.

'I like a clean, united dressing room and, if possible, a happy one': Pere Escobar i Pichi Alonso, *Helenio Herrera* (Barcanova, 1998), 70.

'could have played with a tuxedo on': Gil Carrasco, *Luisito: Luis Suárez, el Balón de Oro que el Barça no supo apreciar* (Edicions Saldonar, 2015), 16.

'Is there any reason why … no goal this time': Wolves v Barcelona, European Cup semi-final, British Pathé newsreel, 1960, available at https://www.youtube.com/watch?v=n8w68PO3e9Q.

'In my memory ... of the post-war years' and 'You in England ... no method, no technique': Brian Glanville, *Champions of Europe: The history, romance and intrigue of the European Cup* (Guinness Publishing, 1991), 26–27.

'he would shoot his poison arrows': Eduardo Galeano, *Soccer in Sun and Shadow* (Verso, 1998), 105.

'We know for sure ... Di Stéfano does not like him': Ian Hawkey, *Di Stéfano* (Ebury Publishing, 2016), 213.

Chapter 15: A Murder of Crows

'Maradona was Maradona sometimes ... every day': Ezequiel Fernández Moores, 'Messi, más de cuatro mil días siendo Maradona', *La Nación*, 25 December 2019.

'a violinist ... the entire orchestra': José Antonio Ávila López, 'Helenio Herrera, único', *La Vanguardia*, 13 November 2022.

'We'll beat them there [Camp Nou] and we'll win the final': Agustín Martín, 'Primer Madrid-Barça en Europa: Cuando el rey siguió en el trono', *Diario AS*, 27 April 2020.

'Don't this lot ever tire ... The ones who are losing': Ian Hawkey, *Di Stéfano* (Ebury Publishing, 2016), 218.

'It's Herrera! It's Herrera! ... Who's to blame? Puskás': Helenio Herrera, *Yo: Memorias De Helenio Herrera* (Editorial Planeta, 1962), 196–197.

'Go collect your bribe!' ... You're already hired by them!': Alfredo Relaño, *366 Historias del Fútbol Mundial Que Deberías Saber* (Martínez Roca, 2010), 266.

'Helenio Herrera attacked by the public. Police force had to intervene': Helenio Herrera, *Yo: Memorias De Helenio Herrera* (Editorial Planeta, 1962), 198.

'the malicious lies circulated' and 'growing obsession with [money] before sporting interests' and 'his transition to other sporting entities' and 'HH era': Barça's board meeting notes, 29 April 1960. FC Barcelona, Centre de Documentació i Estudis.

'soul of Kocsis': Javier Marías, *Salvajes Y Sentimentales: Letras de fútbol* (Alfaguara, 2010).

Chapter 16: The Sweet Life

'Italians lose wars ... as if they were wars': John Hooper, *The Italians* (Penguin Books, 2015), 204.

'Bread was no longer ... was purchased': John Foot, *The Archipelago: Italy Since 1945* (Bloomsbury, 2018), 89.

'could only deliver tenderness': Gabriele Salvatores, Michele Astori, Massimo Fiocchi, dirs., *1960* (Italy: Offside, RAI Cinema, 2010).

'mods': Shawn Levy writes eloquently about how Italy became the world's epicentre of style in *Dolce Vita Confidential: Fellini, Pucci, Paparazzi and the Swinging High Life of 1950s Rome* (Weidenfeld & Nicolson, 2017).

'There are times ... spanked and sent home to bed': Eddie Firmani, *Football with the Millionaires* (The Sportsmans Book Club, 1960), 60.

'The Human Machine Gun ... The Pastry Eater': *Dolce Vita Confidential: Fellini, Pucci, Paparazzi and the Swinging High Life of 1950s Rome* (Weidenfeld & Nicolson, 2017), 227–233.

Chapter 17: Angel With a Dirty Face

'I'm not a charlatan ... the worse for them': Maria Teresa Lattanzi, 'La Grande Inter di Herrera e Moratti', Storie di Calcio website, 18 August 2018.

'In Milan, there was La Madonnina ... then came Angelillo': John Foot, *Calcio: A History of Italian Football* (Fourth Estate, 2006), 400.

'practically all the time': Julian Barnes, 'The Hardest Test: Drugs and the Tour de France', *The New Yorker*, 13 August 2000.

'Without pillows?': William Fotheringham, *Fallen Angel: The Passion of Fausto Coppi* (Yellow Jersey, 2009).

'By supporting Fausto ... our stupid and listless country': Gianni Brera, *Coppi e il diavolo* (Rizzoli, 1981), 146.

'The beautiful Giulia ... an ace of diamonds': John Foot, *The Archipelago: Italy Since 1945* (Bloomsbury, 2018), 123.

'They say the crisis ... your fault, Miss López' and 'malicious reporting': 'Intervista al giocatore Angelillo dopo il suo ritiro', Archivio Luce Cinecittà, 7 February 1963, available at https://www.youtube.com/watch?v=ko8VBZj50Bs.

'the greatest centre-forward in the world' and 'breastfed': Gianni Brera, 'L'angelo Innamorato', *la Repubblica*, 7 September 2019.

'took note ... by the economic boom': John Foot, *The Archipelago: Italy Since 1945* (Bloomsbury, 2018), 158.

'office' and 'words that cut': James Horncastle, 'The Man who Made Calcio', *The Blizzard: The Football Quarterly* (Issue Two), September 2011.

'drunken sclerotic' and 'a genius': John Foot, *Calcio: A History of Italian Football* (Fourth Estate, 2006), 210, 513.

'Angelillo's decline ... taken with non-sporting passions': Gianni Brera, *Herrera* (Longanesi, 1966), 76.

'Herrera the hurricane' and 'fraud' and 'bluff': Helenio Herrera, *Yo: Memorias De Helenio Herrera* (Editorial Planeta, 1962), 210.

'far away from temptation': John Foot, *Calcio: A History of Italian Football* (Fourth Estate, 2006), 399.

'We all pray for him': Helenio Herrera, *¡Suspense ...!* (Ediciones Ferré, 1965), 155.

'Why would I go to the funeral ... what could I say?': Curino Luca, 'Ricordi di Grande Inter', *La Gazzetta dello Sport*, 11 November 1997.

Chapter 18: Great White Nights

'I like discipline. It's true ... we all have to sacrifice to get success': Helenio Herrera, *Yo: Memorias De Helenio Herrera* (Editorial Planeta, 1962), 230.

'I feel strong, serene ... and I am good-looking': *Tacabala: Esercizi di magia di Helenio Herrera* (Fiora Gandolfi Herrera, 2002), 35.

'I'm married to a ball': Xavier G. Luque, 'La confusa vida del mago Helenio Herrera,' *La Vanguardia*, 14 November 2022.

'Am I happy?' ... also more money. Of course': Helenio Herrera, *Yo: Memorias De Helenio Herrera* (Editorial Planeta, 1962), 228.

'Don't worry about your fitness ... I understood immediately' and 'box of tricks' and 'vitamins': Ferruccio Mazzola, *Il Terzo Incomodo: Le pesanti verità di Ferruccio Mazzola* (Bradipolibri, 2004), 60–66.

'Pensa alla partito! Pensa alla partito!': Brian Glanville, *Champions of Europe: The history, romance and intrigue of the European Cup* (Guinness Publishing, 1991), 62.

'jimmyfollie': John Foot, *Calcio: A History of Italian Football* (Fourth Estate, 2006), 408.

'It's ridiculous … never knowingly taken any pep drugs' and 'I think the medical experts … the after-effects of sugar': Simon Goodyear, *The Gerry Hitchens Story: From Mine to Milan* (DB Publishing, 2010), 88–89.

'a small hospital': Rob Hughes, 'Juventus doping conviction casts aura of doubt on sport', *The New York Times*, 27 November 2004.

'Herrera didn't let himself be played … before the game': Ferruccio Mazzola, *Il Terzo Incomodo: Le pesanti verità di Ferruccio Mazzola* (Bradipolibri, 2004), 55.

'Il Mago encouraged us … to use sugar': ibid., 63.

'They were like bombs … to get into the big leagues': ibid., 58.

'He can catch up with us at the toll bridge': ibid., 56.

'There was a thousand ways to get away with it' and 'Things changed in the international cups … to take a risk': Ferruccio Mazzola, *Il Terzo Incomodo: Le pesanti verità di Ferruccio Mazzola* (Bradipolibri, 2004), 60–62.

'Before the game … in the anti-doping room': Fabrizio Calzia and Massimiliano Castellani, *Palla Avvelenata: Morti Misteriose, Doping e Sospetti nel Calcio Italiano* (Turin: Bradipolibri, 2003), 135–136.

'It's naïve to think [Inter] … Italy, Europe and the world': Ferruccio Mazzola, *Il Terzo Incomodo: Le pesanti verità di Ferruccio Mazzola* (Bradipolibri, 2004), 56.

'If I wanted to hurt Inter … especially in the cups': Alessandro Gilioli, 'Quelle pillole che ci dava Herrera', *L'Espresso*, 16 May 2005.

'pick-ups': Danilo Sarugia, *Grande Inter, Figlia di Dio: La leggendaria squadra di Moratti è Herrera* (Storie E Miti, 1996).

'tried to make amphetamine … cherry-flavoured herbal tea': Manlio Cipolla, *Calcio verità* (Fortunalibri, 1976).

'All the "vitamins" they made us take … those two seasons at Inter': Ferruccio Mazzola, *Il Terzo Incomodo: Le pesanti verità di Ferruccio Mazzola* (Bradipolibri, 2004), 60.

Chapter 19: Team of a Million Stars

'You have done wrong … be less naïve': Xavier G. Luque, 'Esperando a Di Stéfano', *La Vanguardia*, 31 May 2018.

'If you wanted to find … your aim has been sensational' and 'It is a total disregard for us … with the national team' and 'The appointment of Herrera … a contempt for Spanish coaches': José Hernández Armenteros, 'España 1962, Helenio Herrera y la H3C', *Cuadernos de Fútbol (Primera parte)*, 4 April 2014.

'I understand now … a coach is justified': Helenio Herrera, *Yo: Memorias De Helenio Herrera* (Editorial Planeta, 1962), 172.

'malnutrition, illiteracy, alcoholism and poverty' and 'as rare as faithful husbands': Conor Heffernan, 'The Battle of Santiago at World Cup 1962', *These Football Times*, 18 October 2014.

'Yes, Italians and all the other footballers in the world take stimulants … a lot of players take jabs': José Hernández Armenteros, 'España 1962, Helenio Herrera y la H3C (Segunda parte)', *Cuadernos de Fútbol*, 4 April 2014.

'less a World Cup and more a World War': Simon Burnton, 'World Cup stunning moments: The Battle of Santiago', *Guardian*, 22 March 2018.

'Good evening … Just see what you think': David Coleman's BBC broadcast introducing Chile v Italy in the 1962 World Cup, available at https://www.youtube.com/watch?v=nDLvgv3_Iy4.

'clinically mad … driven so by chemicals?': John Foot, *Calcio: A History of Italian Football* (Fourth Estate, 2006), 453.

'Amarildo? Who's Amarildo?': Nicolás de Marco, 'En Chile 1962, a Brasil le sobra sin Pelé', Goal.com website, 16 November 2022.

Chapter 20: When a Bad Man Behaves Well

'It's a welcome surprise … talks only about himself': Fotogramas de Plata 2012 award ceremony, available at https://www.youtube.com/watch?v=rIRpYRJtjn8.

'alternating between cinema … with insulting self-confidence': Javier Cercas, 'Gonzalo Suárez: doble contra sencillo', *El País*, 22 November 2000.

'Oedipal material': In his book, *Our Age of Unreason: A Study of the Irrational Forces in Social Life* (Lippincott, 1942), the psychoanalyst Dr Franz Alexander sketched out a life trajectory for an ambitious immigrant like HH – a victim of social and cultural circumstances – which was eerily accurate, years before anyone had heard about HH, one of the greatest coaches in football history.

Chapter 21: Il Mago

'El Mago allowed Quarenghi … Zaglio in the ambulance': Manlio Cipolla, *Calcio verità* (Fortunalibri, 1976), 32.

'It's easy! … one solution. Helenio Herrera' and 'It's natural. Soraya didn't play football … Dupleix and Ronconi': Helenio Herrera, *¡Suspense …!* (Ediciones Ferré, 1965), 144–145.

Chapter 22: Vienna

'Picchi never specifically marked anyone … would be picked off by … Picchi': *A Game of Two Halves*, ed. by Stephen F. Kelly (Mandarin, 1993), 308.

'With Inter, no one can compete': Helenio Herrera, *¡Suspense …!* (Ediciones Ferré, 1965), 150.

'I remember doctors in the hospital … over the course of his career': Ferruccio Mazzola, *Il Terzo Incomodo: Le pesanti verità di Ferruccio Mazzola* (Bradipolibri, 2004), 69.

'never refused pills … racing around like a kid': Alessandro Gilioli, 'Storia del Doping nel Calcio: Inter pioniera-squadra che uccide', *L'Espresso*, 16 May 2005.

'He convinced me … "No, signora. Your husband must stay focused"': Curino Luca, 'Ricordi di Grande Inter', *La Gazzetta dello Sport*, 11 November 1997.

'I saw in the eyes of Moratti … again in a person': Gil Carrasco, *Luisito: Luis Suárez, el Balón de Oro que el Barça no supo apreciar* (Ediciones Saldonar, 2015), 136.

Chapter 23: 'There Is a Small Annoyance'

'You have no idea … born under the Po?': Giuseppe Pastore, 'Il misterioso caso del settimo scudetto del Bologna', *l'Ultimo Uomo*, 16 January 2018.

'Renato, look who's here…' and 'March is a crazy month…' and 'there is a small annoyance': Giuseppe Pastore, 'The mysterious case of Bologna's seventh championship', *L'Ultimo Uomo*, 16 January 2018.

'They killed him!': Storie di Calcio, 'Bologna 1963/64: Meravigliosa creatura', available at https://storiedicalcio.altervista.org/blog/bologna_63_64.html

'like a soldier': Vittorio Pozzo, 'Il cuore non ha retto alla passione sportiva,' *La Stampa*, 4 June 1964.

'It is right that … busts of Charlemagne, Henry VII and Napoleon': Indro Montanelli, 'I protagonisti', *Corriere della Sera*, 7 June 1964.

'fraudulently introduced': Dan Carney, 'The Final Fling', *The Blizzard: The Football Quarterly* (Issue 36), March 2020.

'It's better to talk about football' and 'Everyone blames Inter for the doping case … know Milan has something to do with it': Giuseppe Pastore, 'The mysterious case of Bologna's seventh championship', *L'Ultimo Uomo*, 16 January 2018.

'Everywhere in Italian football there is doping': 'Zur Halbzeit Gift', *Der Spiegel*, 17 March 1964.

Chapter 24: 'Made it, Ma! Top of the World!'

'Gentlemen, I'm willing … to my mother before coming here': Helenio Herrera, *¡Suspense …!* (Ediciones Ferré, 1965), 165.

Chapter 25: Voices in the Head

'This is your manager speaking…': *Busby, Stein & Shankly: The Football Men* (BBC, 1997).

'the biggest toilet in Liverpool': Leo Moynihan, *The Three Kings* (Quercus, 2020), 140.

'It's the greatest thing in the world … and they'll be successful': Telegraph staff, 'Bill Shankly 50th anniversary: famous sayings of legendary Liverpool manager', *Daily Telegraph*, 1 December 2009.

'Aye, son, you're right … they're not good enough for you yet': Ian St John, *The Saint: My Autobiography* (Hodder & Stoughton, 2005), 172.

'It was men against boys … how to play': ibid. 162.

Chapter 26: Man in the Middle

'the humiliation suffered in Britain': Dave Horridge, *Daily Mirror*, 10 May 1965.

'Dear Friends, we left Anfield Stadium … a race of cheap mandolin players': Leslie Poole, *Daily Express*, 9 May 1965.

'What a difference! Between staying in Vizcaya … about everything!': Alfredo Relaño, 'Salió a hombros, "ganó" la Eurocopa e inauguró la moviola', *El País*, 11 July 2016.

Chapter 27: A Ninth Circle of Hell

'a doctor pledged to heal who kills instead': Robert Jay Lifton, 'What Made This Man? Mengele', *The New York Times*, 21 July 1985.

'straight-forward, honest and absolutely reliable … in the most conscientious way': Office of Special Investigations Criminal Division, *In the Matter of Josef Mengele: A Report to the Attorney General of the United States* (U.S. Department of Justice, 1992), 36–37.

'He looked exceedingly well-groomed … He really didn't look like a murderer': Vera B. Profit, *The Devil Next Door: Toward a Literary and Psychological Definition of Human Evil* (Rodopi, 2014).

'God Almighty': Csaba Vörös, 'Amikor Solti Dezső pénzért leülte Guttmann Béla börtönbüntetését', Hungarian *FourFourTwo*, April 2018.

'cantankerous, mistrustful … must assume an aggressive stance': Jack Fairweather, *The Volunteer: One Man, an underground Army, and the Secret Mission to Destroy Auschwitz* (WH Allen, 2019), 59.

'It's horrible … man who invented himself in all circumstances': Csaba Vörös, 'Amikor Solti Dezső pénzért leülte Guttmann Béla börtönbüntetését,' Hungarian *FourFourTwo*, April 2018.

'Prisoners who lost the ability to work … by pushing them back into the main line': Jonathan Wilson, *The Names Heard Long Ago: How the Golden Age of Hungarian Football Shaped the Modern Game* (Blink 2019), 227.

'I was dizzy from the recognition … exactly who I was': Péter Csillag, 'Recollections of Sándor Schwarcz, prisoner no. 17854 of Auschwitz', *Nemzeti Sport*, 6 August 2021.

'Auschwitz only worsened my position … Auschwitz burned everything': Béla Szobolits, dir., *Futballdezső* (Budapest: Hétfői Műhely Stúdió Alapítvány, 1991).

'untraceable': David Bolchover, *The Greatest Comeback: From Genocide to Football Glory* (Biteback Publishing, 2017), 156.

Chapter 28: Szobel's Show Girls

'relatives' and 'taken by Russians' and 'Zegelid concentration camp' and 'capitalist' and 'escaped': For a copy of Dezső Solti's Application for IRO Assistance, 25 January 1951, see Arolsen Archives: International Center on Nazi Execution in Germany.

'helping Real Madrid with their European Cup games': A phrase used by Dezső Solti in his memoir to describe his work with Real Madrid, which is quoted in Brian Glanville's book *Champions of Europe: The history, romance and intrigue of the European Cup* (Guinness Publishing, 1991), 91.

'Take a good look at it, brother … during the match!': András Gáll, 'A háttérhatalom az Inter és a Juve mögött: Solti Dezső', Hungarian *FourFourTwo*, 2012.

'I had doping agents … but they were afraid to use them' and 'Solti bribed Hungarian referees … matches of FC Internazionale' and 'got out of the taxi … Hungarian Football Federation on the 1st floor' and 'The Austrian Football Federation … shows up in Austria' and 'Everyone studied' and 'very dangerous' and 'primitive man' and 'soaked in money' and 'a hostile intelligence agency' and 'Zionist circles of Western countries' and 'I can't be an enemy … family at their hands': Csaba Vörös, 'Amikor Solti Dezső pénzért leülte Guttmann Béla börtönbüntetését', Hungarian *FourFourTwo*, April 2018.

'if you pay the full-price rail ticket … of losing thereby': John Hooper, *The Italians* (Penguin Books, 2015), 33.

'Bullshit … we would all be world champions': Gli Inizi, 'Allodi Italo: l'uomo dei trionfi e dell'oblio', Storie di Calcio website, 12 November 2015.

'What a marvellous place … looked at each other in amazement' and 'enough to buy five, maybe six Mercedes cars' and 'justified' and 'His behaviour was not that of a sportsman … cheated them out of the game': Quotes from György Vadas about how Dezső Solti attempted to bribe him in Milan in April 1966 are taken from Brian Glanville's book *Champions of Europe: The history, romance and intrigue of the European Cup* (Guinness Publishing, 1991). Glanville took his account from Péter Borenich's book *Only the Ball has a Skin* (Magánkiadás, 1983).

Chapter 29: The Pits

'They didn't just get their own work done … phoneys and cheats couldn't survive for long': Hugh McIlvanney, 'Hero worshipped by his people,' *Observer*, 15 September 1985.

'a big ant' and 'I'm an absolute dictator here!': Archie Macpherson, *Jock Stein: The Definitive Biography* (Highdown Books, 2004), 85.

'Jimmy Johnstone … I named a dog after him': Kevin McCarra, *Celtic: A Biography in Nine Lives* (Faber and Faber, 2012), 123.

'Soccer is said to be unpredictable but … when Inter win the final…': Stephen Sullivan, *Sean Fallon: Celtic's Iron Man* (BackPage Press, 2013), 235.

'My time will come': Archie Macpherson, *Jock Stein: The Definitive Biography* (Highdown Books, 2004), 147.

Chapter 30: Cooked

'What vacation?! … You must be crazy!': 'Un personaggio pesante', *La Repubblica*, 16 November 1997.

'There was nobody there … vomiting from the tension in the next room': Kevin McCarra, *Celtic: A Biography in Nine Lives* (Faber and Faber, 2012), 134.

'You're a Nazi bastard! … Where are you gonnae get your villa?': Archie Macpherson, *Jock Stein: The Definitive Biography* (Highdown Books, 2004), 151.

'I remember [Armando] Picchi turned to Sarti … how destroyed we were': Stephen Sullivan, *Sean Fallon: Celtic's Iron Man* (BackPage Press, 2013), 238.

'From Herrera, I learned seriousness': 'Movimiento', Il Nobile Calcio website, 5 March 2021.

'You're only good at killing old people!': Cesare Lanza, 'C'erano una volta: Heriberto Herrera', *La Verità*, 12 March 2018.

Chapter 31: The Red Lady

'I did so much for football that coaches … I gave them dignity': José David López, 'Helenio Herrera: El primer técnico mediático', *Panenka*, 27 February 2019.

Chapter 32: 'How Can an Athlete Die Like That?'

'He didn't let me play … onto the pitch very motivated, galvanised': Cesare Lanza, 'C'erano una volta/Helenio Herrera', *La Verità*, 20 November 2017.

'to put a razor-blade up against players' arses': Gabriele Marcotti, *Capello: Portrait of a Winner* (Bantam Books, 2008), 215.

'Giuliano didn't go to Flaminio … But he didn't want to': Roberto Morassut, *Giuliano Taccola: La Punta Spezzata* (Modena: Palombi Editori, 2016), 182.

'He can't play in these conditions': Roberto Morassut, *Giuliano Taccola: La Punta Spezzata* (Modena: Palombi Editori, 2016), 36.

'He was pale, emaciated … he looked like a bum' and 'I'm very worried … some virus' and 'Lie down … Do you still have a fever?' and 'Excuse me, Doctor … stand up' and 'Help me, I'm suffocating!' and 'Guys, get back … Let us work!' and 'They're kids … Please don't say anything': Roberto Morassut, *Giuliano Taccola: La Punta Spezzata* (Modena: Palombi Editori, 2016), 39–44.

'FOOTBALLERS ARE LIKE ROBOTS': Giuseppe Fiori, 'Giocatori come robots', *La Stampa*, 17 March 1969.

'robots' and 'He was in the dressing room … not beasts but human beings!': 'Siamo considerati dei robots, dichiarano Rivera e Picchi', *Paese Sera*, 17 March 1969.

'How lucky I am! … but in a mountain village': *Tacabala: Esercizi di magia di Helenio Herrera* (Fiora Gandolfi Herrera, 2002), 36.

'Go home? … It's an order!': Alvaro Marchini, *Io Presidente: Autobiografia di un parapalle*. (Rome: Trevi Editore, Rome, 1976), 57.

Chapter 33: Tuscany

'Taccola had made big investments … 'No play, no pay,' he used to tell him': Ferruccio Mazzola, *Il Terzo Incomodo: Le pesanti verità di Ferruccio Mazzola* (Bradipolibri, 2004), 145.

'injections of tonic' and 'Giuliano Taccola, our right wing … and no one knows why': Fabrizio Calzia and Massimiliano Castellani, *Palla Avvelenata: Morti Misterioso, Doping e Sospetti nel Calcio Italiano* (Turin: Bradipolibri, 2003), 135.

'Barons': Ferruccio Mazzola, *Il Terzo Incomodo: Le pesanti verità di Ferruccio Mazzola* (Bradipolibri, 2004), 148.

'I've never had a reason or proof … flushed them down the toilet': Roberto Morassut, *Giuliano Taccola: La Punta Spezzata* (Modena: Palombi Editori, 2016), 160.

Chapter 34: Inquest

'clearly pathological': Roberto Morassut, *Giuliano Taccola: La Punta Spezzata* (Modena: Palombi Editori, 2016), 197.

'the recovery times of the player are slowing down' and 'he should not undergo excessive workloads' and 'under exertion the heart showed problems': Roberto Molinari, 'Libri Giallorossi: Vita e morte di Giuliano Taccola in un libro: "Si poteva salvare" (di Roberto Morassut)', www.TuttoASRoma.it website, 17 October 2016.

'interesting' and 'clinical and electrocardiogram': Roberto Morassut, *Giuliano Taccola: La Punta Spezzata* (Modena: Palombi Editori, 2016), 198.

'It's easier to find … a confessing football professional': Daniel Drepper, 'How prevalent are drugs in soccer?' CORRECTIV website, 10 December 2012.

'When poor Giuliano had a fever … got him back on the pitch': Fabio Belli, 'Giuliano Taccola: una morte senza spiegazioni', Storie Fuorigioco website, 1 April 2019.

'elements of culpable conduct due to negligence or imprudence' and 'causal role in the death': Roberto Morassut, *Giuliano Taccola: La Punta Spezzata* (Modena: Palombi Editori, 2016), 208.

SELECT BIBLIOGRAPHY

Alexander, Franz. *Our Age of Unreason: A Study of the Irrational Forces in Social Life* (Lippincott, 1942)

Bailey, David. *Magical Magyars* (Pitch Publishing, 2019)

Beevor, Antony. *The Spanish Civil War* (Cassell, 1982)

Bolchover, David. *The Greatest Comeback: From Genocide to Football Glory* (Biteback Publishing, 2017)

Borenich, Péter. *Only the Ball has a Skin* (Magánkiadás, 1983)

Brera, Gianni. *Coppi e il diavolo* (Rizzoli, 1981)

Brera, Gianni. *Herrera* (Longanesi, 1966)

Burns, Jimmy. *Barça: The People's Passion* (Bloomsbury, 1999)

Burns, Jimmy. *La Roja: A Journey Through Spanish Football* (Simon & Schuster, 2012)

Burns, Jimmy. *Spain: A Literary Companion* (John Murray, 1994)

Calzia, Fabrizio and Castellani, Massimiliano. *Palla avvelenata: Morti misteriose, doping e sospetti nel calcio italiano* (Turin: Bradipolibri, 2003)

Carrasco, Gil. *Luisito: Luis Suárez, el Balón de Oro que el Barça no supo apreciar* (Edicions Saldonar, 2015)

Carreño, Fernando. *Guante blanco, manga ancha: la historia negra del Real Madrid* (Ediciones Meran, S.L., 2013)

Castillo, Juan José. *Kubala: el fútbol es mi vida: biografía de un mito* (El Mundo Deportivo, 1993)

Cipolla, Manlio. *Calcio verità* (Fortunalibri, 1976)

Closa i Garcia, Antoni. *Croniques del Barça: 1899–1992* (Gasca & Asociades, 1992)

Dunphy, Eamon. *A Strange Kind of Glory: Sir Matt Busby & Manchester United* (Aurum Press, 1991)

Escobar, Pere i Alonso, Pichi. *Helenio Herrera* (Barcanova, 1998)

Fairweather, Jack. *The Volunteer: One Man, an Underground Army, and the Secret Mission to Destroy Auschwitz* (WH Allen, 2019)

Finestres, Jordi. *El Barça en guerra: 1936–1939* (Angle Editorial, 2006)

Firmani, Eddie. *Football with the Millionaires* (The Sportsmans Book Club, 1960)

Fitzpatrick, Richard. *El Clásico: Barcelona v Real Madrid, Football's Greatest Rivalry* (Bloomsbury, 2012)

Foot, John. *Calcio: A History of Italian Football* (Fourth Estate, 2006)

Foot, John. *The Archipelago: Italy Since 1945* (Bloomsbury, 2018)

Fotheringham, William. *Fallen Angel: The Passion of Fausto Coppi* (Yellow Jersey, 2009)

Friedman, Alan. *Agnelli and the Network of Italian Power* (WH Allen, 1988)

Galeano, Eduardo. *Soccer in Sun and Shadow* (Verso, 1998)

Gandolfi, Fiora. *Maghi si diventa* (Fiora Gandolfi, 2012)

Gandolfi Herrera, Fiora. *Tacalabala: esercizi di magia di Helenio Herrera* (Fiora Gandolfi Herrera, 2002)

García Candau, Julián. *Madrid-Barça: historia de un desamor* (El País/Aguilar, 1996)

Glanville, Brian. *Champions of Europe: The History, Romance and Intrigue of the European Cup* (Guinness Publishing, 1991)

Glanville, Brian. *Football Memories* (Virgin, 1999)

Glanville, Brian. *The Story of the World Cup* (Faber and Faber, 2010)

Goodyear, Simon. *The Gerry Hitchens Story: From Mine to Milan* (DB Publishing, 2009/2013)

Hawkey, Ian. *Di Stéfano* (Ebury Publishing, 2016)

Herrera, Helenio. *Yo: Memorias de Helenio Herrera* (Editorial Planeta, 1962)

Herrera, Helenio. *¡Suspense …!* (Ediciones Ferré, 1965)

Hooper, John. *The Italians* (Penguin Books, 2015)

Hughes, Robert. *Barcelona* (Harvill, 1992)

Kelly, Stephen F. (ed.). *A Game of Two Halves* (Mandarin, 1993)

Kuper, Simon. *Football Against the Enemy* (Orion, 1994)

Lainz, Lluís. *De puertas adentro: los 113 años del FC Barcelona contados en 113 historias* (Corner, 2012)

Law, Denis. *Denis Law: An Autobiography* (Queen Anne Press, 1979)

Select Bibliography

Leamer, Laurence. *Capote's Women: A True Story of Love, Betrayal, and a Swan Song for an Era* (G.P. Putnam's Sons, 2021)

Levy, Shawn. *Dolce Vita Confidential: Fellini, Pucci, Paparazzi and the Swinging High Life of 1950s Rome* (Weidenfeld & Nicolson, 2017)

Lowe, Sid. *Fear and Loathing in La Liga: Barcelona vs. Real Madrid* (Yellow Jersey Press, 2013)

Macpherson, Archie. *Jock Stein: The Definitive Biography* (Highdown Books, 2004)

McCarra, Kevin. *Celtic: A Biography in Nine Lives* (Faber and Faber, 2012)

Marchini, Alvaro. *Io Presidente: Autobiografia di un parapalle* (Rome: Trevi Editore, Rome, 1976)

Marcotti, Gabriele. *Capello: Portrait of a Winner* (Bantam Books, 2008)

Marías, Javier. *Salvajes y sentimentales: letras de fútbol* (Alfaguara, 2010)

Mazzola, Ferruccio. *Il terzo incomodo: Le pesanti verità di Ferruccio Mazzola* (Bradipolibri, 2004)

Melcon, Ramón and Smith, Stratton. *The Real Madrid Book of Football* (Souvenir Press, 1961)

Moradiellos, Enrique. *Franco: Anatomy of a Dictator* (I.B. Tauris, 2018)

Morassut, Roberto. *Giuliano Taccola: la punta spezzata* (Modena: Palombi Editori, 2016)

Moynihan, Leo. *The Three Kings* (Quercus, 2020)

Munne, Antonio. *Cuando nunca perdíamos* (Alfaguara, 2011)

Office of Special Investigations Criminal Division. *In the Matter of Josef Mengele: A Report to the Attorney General of the United States* (U.S. Department of Justice, 1992)

Pàmies, Teresa. *Quan érem capitans: memòries d'aquella guerra* (Dopesa, 1974)

Parks, Tim. *Italian Ways: On and Off the Rails From Milan to Palermo* (Vintage, 2014)

Preston, Paul. *Franco: A Biography* (Fontana Press, 1995)

Preston, Paul. *The Spanish Holocaust: Inquisition and Extermination in Twentieth Century Spain* (Harper Press, 2012)

Preston, Paul (ed.). *We Saw Spain Die: Foreign Correspondents in the Spanish Civil War* (Constable, 2008)

Profit, Vera B. *The Devil Next Door: Toward a Literary and Psychological Definition of Human Evil* (Rodopi, 2014)

Relaño, Alfredo. *366 historias del fútbol mundial que deberías saber* (Martínez Roca, 2010)

Relaño, Alfredo. *Nacidos para incordiarse: un siglo de agravios entre el Madrid y el Barça* (Ediciones Martínez Roca, 2012)

Reyero, Francisco. *Sinatra: nunca volveré a ese maldito país* (Fundación José Manuel Lara, 2015)

Rovira I Andreu, Joan. *Converses amb l'avi Barça* (Edecasa, 2011)

Rovira I Andreu, Joan. *El que et falta saber del Barça* (Sport, 2005)

Santacana i Torres, Carles. *El Barça i el franquisme: crònica d'uns anys decisius per a Catalunya, 1968–1978* (Mina, 2005)

Sarugia, Danilo. *Grande Inter, figlia di dio: la leggendaria squadra di Moratti è Herrera* (Storie E Miti, 1996)

Sobrequés i Callicó, Jaume. *Història del FC Barcelona: el Barça, un club, una ciudad, un país. Vol III* (Editorial Labor, 1993)

Schulberg, Budd. *What Makes Sammy Run* (Vintage, 1993)

Spector, Dr. Shmuel and Wigoder, Dr. Geoffrey (ed.). *The Encyclopaedia of Jewish Life Before and During the Holocaust* (NYU Press, 2001)

St John, Ian. *The Saint: My Autobiography* (Hodder & Stoughton, 2005)

Sullivan, Stephen. *Sean Fallon: Celtic's Iron Man* (BackPage Press, 2013)

Suárez, Gonzalo. *Los once y uno* (Plaza & Janés Editores, S.A., 1997)

Suárez, Gonzalo. *La suela de mis zapatos: pasos y andanzas de Martin Girard* (Seix Barral, 2006)

Sykes, Herbie. *Juve!: 100 Years of an Italian Football Dynasty* (Yellow Jersey Press, 2020)

Taylor, Rogan and Jamrich, Klara (ed.). *Puskás on Puskás: The Life and Times of a Footballing Legend* (Robson Books, 1998)

Tóibín, Colm. *Homage to Barcelona* (Simon & Schuster, 1990)

Townson, Nigel (ed.). *Spain Transformed: The Late Franco Dictatorship, 1959–77* (Palgrave Macmillan, 2007)

Treglown, Jeremy. *Franco's Crypt: Spanish Culture and Memory Since 1936* (Chatto & Windus, 2013)

Tremlett, Giles. *España: A Brief History of Spain* (Head of Zeus, 2022)

Vázquez Montalbán, Manuel. *Fútbol: una religión en busca de un dios* (Debate, 2005)

Viñas, Carles. *Barcelona Blaugrana: Una història de la ciutat a través del Barça* (Angle Editorial, 2012)

Wilson, Jonathan. *Angels With Dirty Faces: The Footballing History of Argentina* (Orion, 2016)

Wilson, Jonathan. *Inverting the Pyramid: A History of Football Tactics* (Orion, 2014)

Wilson, Jonathan. *The Names Heard Long Ago: How the Golden Age of Hungarian Football Shaped the Modern Game* (Blink, 2019)

MAGAZINES

Barça
CIHEFE
Cuadernos de Fútbol
Der Spiegel
Hungarian *FourFourTwo*
Panenka
The Blizzard: The Football Quarterly
The New Yorker
These Football Times

FILMS AND DOCUMENTARIES

1960, Offside, RAI Cinema, 2010
Agnelli, HBO, 2017
Auschwitz: The Forgotten Evidence, Flashback Television Ltd, 2004
British Pathé News
Busby, Stein & Shankly: The Football Men, BBC, 1997

Freedom's Fury, Wolo Entertainment/Cinergi Pictures Entertainment, 2006
Glasgow 1967: The Lisbon Lions, IMG Productions, 2017
Goal!: 1966 FIFA World Cup Official Film, Frigo, 1966
Once in a Lifetime: The Extraordinary Story of the New York Cosmos, Passion Pictures et al., 2006
Viva Brazil: 1962 FIFA World Cup Official Film, Sport Film Munich, 1962

NEWSPAPERS

Corriere della Sera
The Daily Express
The Daily Mirror
The Daily Telegraph
Diario AS
Sport
El Mundo
El Mundo Deportivo
El País
Guardian
L'Espresso
La Gazzetta dello Sport
La Nación
La Repubblica
La Stampa
La Vanguardia
La Verità
Marca
Nemzeti Sport
The New York Times
The Observer
Paese Sera
The Times

WEBSITES

Arolsen Archives
Center for Jewish History
European Holocaust Research Infrastructure
Il Nobile Calcio
l'Ultimo Uomo
Museum of Jewish Heritage
Rec.Sport.Soccer Statistics Foundation; www.rsssf.org
Storie di Calcio
Storie Fuorigioco
United States Holocaust Memorial Museum
Yad Vashem Museum

HH with Fiora Gandolfi, his last wife, who believed a man like HH is only born once in a century.

HH poses with the Intercontinental Cup and the European Cup, which Inter won in both 1964 and 1965.